eat out in pubs

The 2011 edition of our guide contains details of over 500 pubs. As ever, the crucial factor for selection in the guide is the quality of the food served, and though the style of cooking and the menus may vary from one pub to the next, our independent inspectors ensure that each and every pub listed reaches the required standards.

Cooking in British pubs continues to reach new heights, and there is an enormous amount of choice now available to diners. Some pubs proudly take the organic route with the support of small local suppliers, while others focus more on regional specialities and long-established local recipes. Some serve creative, contemporary cooking with more of an international flavour, but equally, there are plenty offering traditional British favourites too.

If you're having trouble choosing where to go, the descriptive texts give an insight into the individual character of each pub, highlighting what we found to be most memorable and charming, and the accompanying pictures reveal a little bit more of their personality.

Some of these pubs serve their food by the fireplace in the bar; others may have a more formal dining room, but whatever their style, they all have one thing in common: carefully prepared, flavoursome food made from fresh, quality ingredients.

Readers of the Michelin Eating out in Pubs guide write thousands of letters and emails to us every year, praising or criticising current entries or recommending new entries. Please keep these coming and help us to make the next edition even better.

contents

SCOTLAND
Northern Ireland
North East
Yorkshire & The Humbe
Isle of Man
IRELAND
North West
Republic of Ireland
Ea
ENGLAND
WALES
West Midlands
Sout
South West
Isle of Wight
Channel Islands

ENGLAND

IRELAND

How to use this Guide

How to find a pub

There are 3 ways to search for a pub in this guide:
- use the regional maps that precede each section of the guide
- use the alphabetical list of pubs at the end of the guide or
- use the alphabetical list of place names also at the end of the guide

Town / Village name

One of our favourite selections

Country or region and county names

Coloured pages border

- East Midlands
- East of England
- London
- North East
- North West
- South East
- South West
- West Midlands
- Yorkshire & The Humber
- Scotland
- Wales
- Northern Ireland
- Republic of Ireland

England • South East • Oxfordshire

Toot Baldon

The Mole has made quite a name for itself in the area and deservedly so. Beautiful landscaped gardens and a pleasant terrace front the building, while inside attractive beamed ceilings and exposed brick walls create a warm and welcoming atmosphere. The menu is equally appealing, catering for all tastes and appetites; you might find sautéed squid with linguine and chorizo, followed by twice-cooked belly of pork with gratin dauphinoise. Sourcing is a serious business and it's a case of 'first come, first served' if you want the full choice. The Tuesday grill and Wednesday fish night menus are decided the day before, so if there's something you've set your heart on, it's worth calling to reserve your dish. Service remains smooth under pressure.

Closing times
Open daily

Prices
Meals: a la carte £ 23/30

Typical Dishes
Smoked haddock with poached egg & cauliflower
Venison steak with truffle potato
Chocolate praline mousse & blackcurr… sorbet

6 mi southeast of Oxford, between B 480 and A 4074. Parking.

316

Name, address, telephone, e-mail and website of the establishment

15

Entry number

Each pub or inn has its own entry number.

This number appears on the regional map at the start of each section to show the location of the establishment.

Pubs with bedrooms

For easy reference, those pubs that offer accommodation are highlighted in blue on the maps

Built by local benefactor Lord Wantage, the picture perfect village of Ardington is, in fact, a Victorian model village. Set in the Vale of the White Horse, the village's centrepiece is the attractive 18C part-timbered Boar's Head, which once paid for the village's lighting through its profits. The pub is now better known as a provider of good food and has built itself quite a reputation in recent years. The central room displays cosy wood floors and a warming fire but the bright, sunny colours and fresh flower displays help to create an airy, informal style. Wide-ranging menus offer something for everyone, from a 'Rapide' lunch to a gourmet dinner selection – and even a seven course tasting menu. Bedrooms are modern, stylish and spacious.

Closing times
Open daily

Prices
Meals: £ 18 (lunch) and a la carte £ 25/38
3 rooms: £ 80/140

Typical Dishes
Salmon tartar with asparagus vinaigrette
Roast saddle of rabbit & wild mushroom cannelloni
Hot praline soufflé & nougat glacé

2 mi east of Wantage by A 417. Next to the church. Parking.

317

Symbols

- Meals served in the garden or on the terrace
- A particularly interesting wine list
- No dogs allowed
- VISA Visa accepted
- AE American Express accepted
- Diners Club accepted
- MasterCard accepted

Closing times Prices rooms

Approximate range of prices for a three-course meal, plus information on booking and annual closures.

Some inns offering accommodation may close mid-afternoon and only allow guests to check in during evening hours. If in doubt, phone ahead.

Room prices range from the lowest-priced single to the most expensive double or twin.

Breakfast is usually included in the price.

Prices are given in £ sterling, except for the Republic of Ireland where €uro are quoted.

How to get there

Directions and driving distances from nearby towns, an indication of parking facilities and any other information that might help you get your bearings. Nearest Underground / train station indicated for London entries.

The blackboard

An example of a typical starter, main course and dessert, chosen by the chef.

Whilst there's no guarantee that these dishes will be available, they should provide you with an idea of the style of the cuisine.

The Hinds Head

High St, Bray, SL6 2AB

Tel: (01628) 626 151

e-mail: *info@hindsheadbray.co.uk* – **website** : *www.hindsheadhotel.co.uk*

see page 236 for more details

True, we're a bit more careful with our money these days but that doesn't mean that we've stopped eating out. In fact, going out for a meal seems to be one of the few things that we haven't been willing to sacrifice.

Throughout the year, our team of impartial inspectors have been travelling the length and breadth of Britain and Ireland to find the 500+ pubs that are included in this year's guide. But there can be only one pub that's awarded the title 'Pub of the Year'; somewhere that has successfully achieved the balance between a relaxed atmosphere, good service and great food.

The Location

As the only place outside London to boast two 3 star restaurants, Bray-on-Thames knows a thing or two when it comes to good food. The Waterside Inn put the area on the map, but today many people associate it with The Fat Duck and Heston Blumenthal's culinary pyrotechnics. More and more people, however, are beginning to link it to Heston's pub too, which, although in close proximity to its alma mater, couldn't be more different in terms of its food.

The Pub

First and foremost, this is a proper English pub: the bar attracts plenty of drinkers and the selection of ales is given just as much thought as the wine list. The building dates back to Tudor times and over the years has seen some notable guests (including Errol Flynn and Walt Disney); it even played host to Prince Philip's stag night celebrations. The rich oak furnishings, heavy beams, flag floors and log fires provide a charming, almost medieval ambience. Booking ahead for the dining room is essential but it's the bar (which doesn't take reservations) that provides the more atmospheric setting.

The Chef

Born in London but raised in Buckinghamshire, Heston is a self-taught chef who has taken cooking to new levels. He opened his own 'research and development' kitchen in 2004 and is often labelled as a 'molecular gastronomist' due to his experiments into different cooking techniques and the 'eating' experience. He is well-known for using low temperature, ultra-slow cooking and water baths – and was the creator of the now ubiquitous triple-cooked chip. The Channel 4 TV series Heston's Feasts highlighted his passion and creativeness, as well as his penchant for unique and innovative techniques.

The Food

Heston's pub menu, however, is a world away from this more radical style of cooking. His vision was to uncover long-forgotten recipes and recreate down-to-earth dishes but using up-to-date techniques. He spent time behind the scenes with food historians from the Tudor Kitchens at Hampton Court Palace and even more time perfecting his recipes. The results are seen in rich, filling dishes that are big on flavour and satisfyingly gimmick-free. You'll find comforting British classics such as lamb shank or shepherd's pie; historical desserts like Sussex Pond or Quaking Pudding; and a lighter bar menu featuring the likes of Scotch quail's egg.

Inspectors' favourites

All the pubs in this guide have been selected for the quality of their cooking. However, we feel that several of them deserve additional consideration as they boast at least one extra quality which makes them particularly special.

It may be the delightful setting, the charm and character of the pub, the general atmosphere, the pleasant service, the overall value for money or the exceptional cooking.

To distinguish these pubs, we point them out with our "Inspectors' favourites" Bibendum stamp.

We are sure you will enjoy these pubs as much as we have.

ENGLAND

EAST MIDLANDS

EAST OF ENGLAND

LONDON

NORTH EAST

NORTH WEST

Beer in the U.K. and Ireland

It's easy to think of beer as just bitter or lager. But that doesn't tell half the story. Between the two there's a whole range of styles and tastes, including pale ales, beers flavoured with spices, fruits and herbs, and wheat beers. It's all down to the skill of the brewer who'll juggle art, craft and a modicum of science to create the perfect pint.

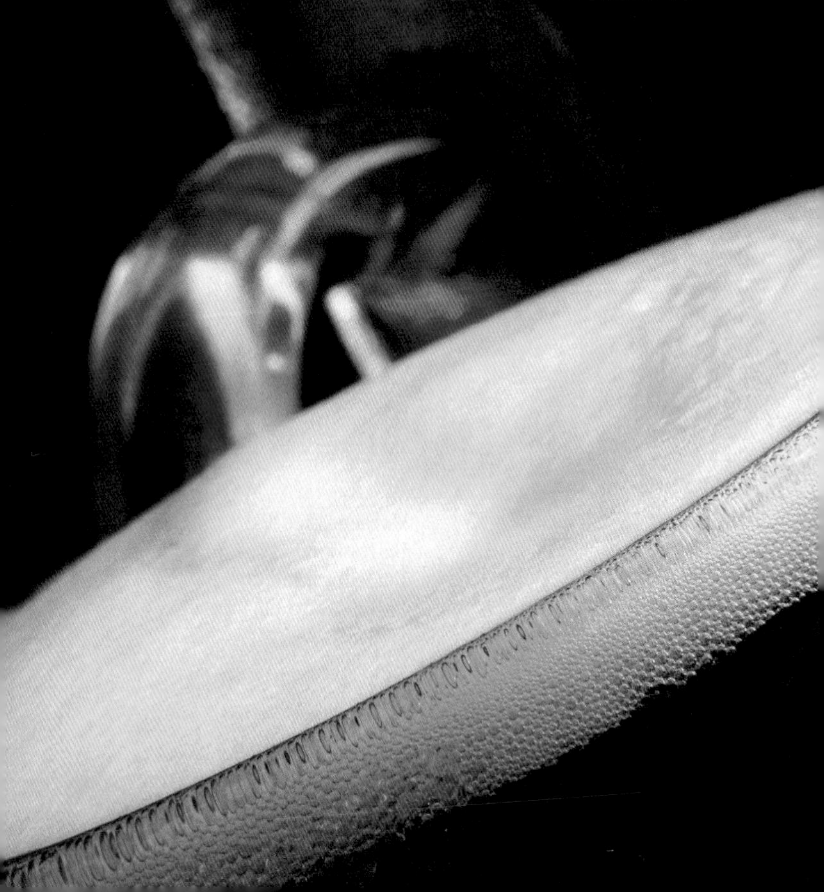

Grist and wort may sound like medieval hangover cures, but they're actually crucial to the brewing process. Malted barley is crushed into grist, a coarse powder which is mashed with hot water in a large vessel called a mash tun. Depending on what sort of recipe's required, the brewer will add different cereals at this stage, such as darker malt for stout. The malt's natural sugars dissolve and the result is wort: a sweet brown liquid, which is boiled with hops in large coppers. Then comes the most important process of all: fermentation, when the hopped wort is cooled and run into fermentation vessels. The final addition is yeast, which converts the natural sugars into alcohol, carbon dioxide and a host of subtle flavours.

Finally, a beer has to be conditioned before it leaves the brewery, and in the case of cask conditioned real ales, the beer goes directly into the cask, barrel or bottle. The yeast is still active in there, fermenting the beer for a second time, often in a pub cellar. All the time there's a delicate process going on as the beer is vulnerable to attack from micro-biological organisms. But as long as the publican cares about his beer, you should get a tasty, full-flavoured pint.

Beer's as natural a product as you can get. This is what's in your pint:

Barley
It's the main ingredient in beer and rich in starch. Malted before brewing to begin the release of sugars.

Hops
Contain resins and essential oils, and used at varying times to give beer its distinctive flavour. Early on they add bitterness, later on they provide a spicy or citrus zest.

Yeast
Converts the sugars from the barley into alcohol and carbon dioxide during fermentation. It produces compounds that affect the flavour of the beer.

Water
Burton and Tadcaster have excellent local water, and that's why they became great ale brewing centres. Meanwhile, the water of London and Dublin is just right for the production of stouts and porters.

Real quality

The modern taste for real ale took off over thirty years ago when it looked like the lager industry was in the process of killing off traditional "warm ale". There are several styles, but the most popular in England and Wales is bitter, which boasts a seemingly inexhaustible variety of appearance, scent and flavour. You can have your bitter gold or copper of colour, hoppy or malty of aroma, dry or sweet of flavour (sweet flavoured bitter? This is where the term "bitter" is at its loosest). Sometimes it has a creamy head; sometimes no head at all. Typically, go to a Yorkshire pub for the former, a London pub for the latter.

Mild developed its popularity in Wales and the north west of England in Victorian times. Often dark, it's a weaker alternative to bitter, with a sweetish taste based on its hop characteristics.

In Scotland, the near equivalent of bitter is heavy, and the most popular draught ales are known as 80 shilling (export) or 70 shilling (special). And, yes, they have a heavy quality to them, though 60 shilling ale – or Light – is akin to English mild.

Full-bodied and rich, stouts (and their rarer porter relatives) are almost a meal in themselves. They're famously black in colour with hints of chocolate and caramel, but it's the highly roasted yeast flavour that leaves the strong after taste.

The world No.1 in tires with 16.3% of the market

A business presence in over 170 countries

A manufacturing footprint at the heart of markets

In 2009 **72** industrial sites in **19** countries produced:

- **150** million tires
- **10** million maps and guides

Highly international teams

Over **109 200** employees* from all cultures on all continents including **6 000** people employed in R&D centers in Europe, the US and Asia.

*102 692 full-time equivalent staff

The Michelin Group at a glance

Michelin competes

At the end of 2009

- **Le Mans 24-hour race**
  12 consecutive years of victories
- **Endurance 2009**
  - 6 victories on 6 stages in Le Mans Series
  - 12 victories on 12 stages in American Le Mans Series
- **Paris-Dakar**
  Since the beginning of the event, the Michelin group has won in all categories
- **Moto endurance**
  2009 World Champion
- **Trial**
  Every World Champion title since 1981 (except 1992)

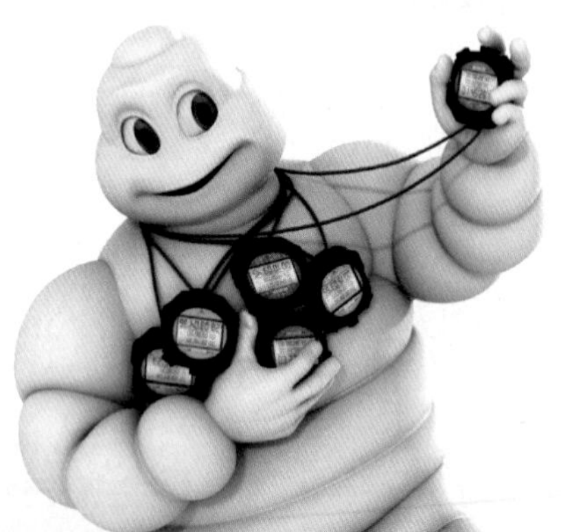

Michelin, established close to its customers

○ **68 plants in 19 countries**

- Algeria
- Brazil
- Canada
- China
- Colombia
- France
- Germany
- Hungary
- Italy
- Japan
- Mexico
- Poland
- Romania
- Russia
- Serbia
- Spain
- Thailand
- UK
- USA

● **A Technology Center spread over 3 continents**

- Asia
- Europe
- North America

● **Natural rubber plantations**

- Brazil

Our mission

To make a sustainable contribution to progress in the mobility of goods and people by enhancing freedom of movement, safety, efficiency and pleasure when on the move.

Michelin committed to environmental-friendliness

Michelin, world leader in low rolling resistance tires, actively reduces fuel consumption and vehicle gas emission.

For its products, Michelin develops state-of-the-art technologies in order to:
- Reduce fuel consumption, while improving overall tire performance.
- Increase life cycle to reduce the number of tires to be processed at the end of their useful lives;
- Use raw materials which have a low impact on the environment.

Furthermore, at the end of 2008, 99.5% of tire production in volume was carried out in ISO 14001* certified plants.

Michelin is committed to implementing recycling channels for end-of-life tires.

*environmental certification

Passenger Car
Light Truck

Truck

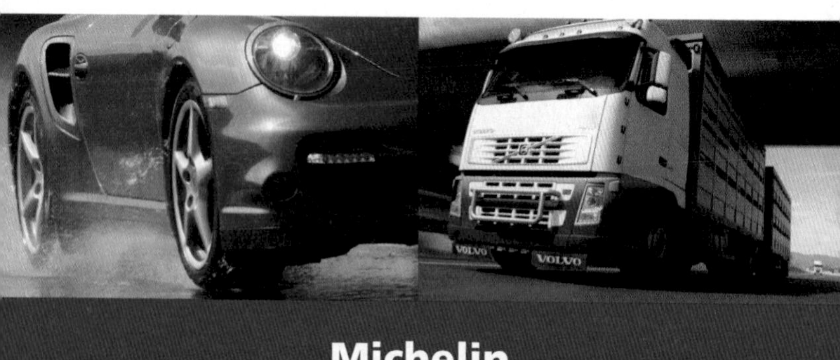

Michelin
a key mobility enabler

Earthmover

Agricultural

Two-wheel

Distribution

Partnered with vehicle manufacturers, in tune with users, active in competition and in all the distribution channels, Michelinis continually innovating to promote mobility today and to invent that of tomorrow.

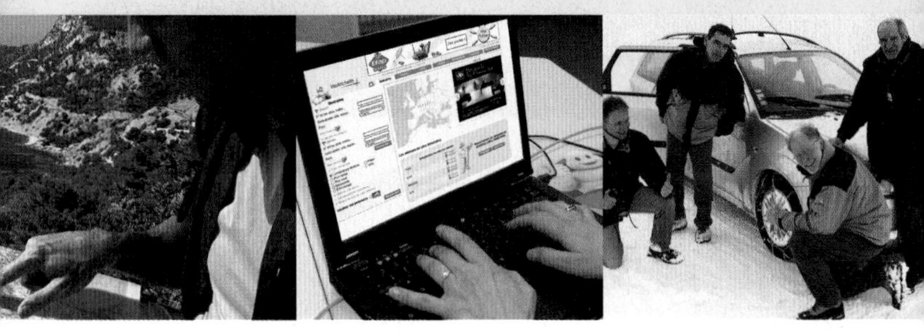

Maps and Guides

ViaMichelin, travel assistance services

Michelin Lifestyle, for your travel accessories

MICHELIN
plays on balanced performance

- **Long tire life**
- **Fuel savings**
- **Safety on the road**

... MICHELIN tires provide you with the best performance, without making a single sacrifice.

The MICHELIN tire pure technology

1 Tread
A thick layer of rubber provides contact with the ground. It has to channel water away and last as long as possible.

2 Crown plies
This double or triple reinforced belt has both vertical flexibility and high lateral rigidity. It provides the steering capacity.

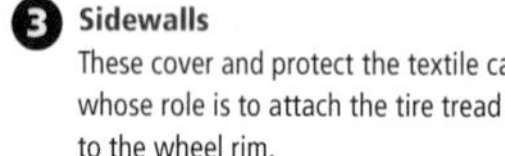

3 Sidewalls
These cover and protect the textile casing whose role is to attach the tire tread to the wheel rim.

4 Bead area for attachment to the rim
Its internal bead wire clamps the tire firmly against the wheel rim.

5 Inner liner
This makes the tire almost totally impermeable and maintains the correct inflation pressure.

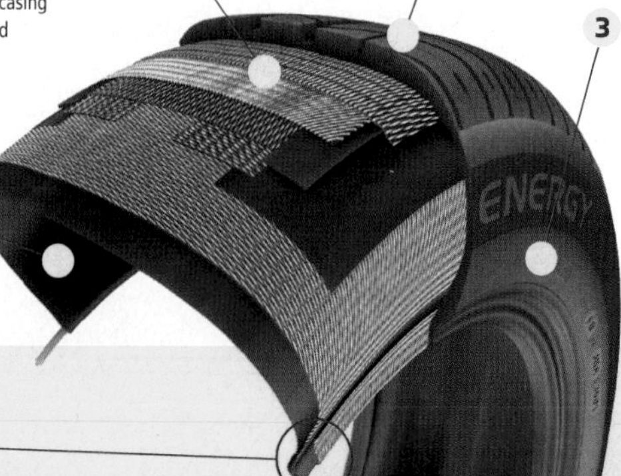

A vision of England sweeps across a range of historic buildings, monuments and rolling landscapes. This image, taking in wild natural borders extending from the rugged splendour of Cornwall's cliffs to pounding Northumbrian shores, seeks parity with a newer picture of Albion: redefined cities and towns whose industrial past is being reshaped by a shiny, steel-and-glass, interactive reality. The country's geographical bones and bumps are a reassuring constant: the windswept moors of the south west and the craggy peaks of the Pennines, the summery orchards of the Kentish Weald, the "flat earth" constancy of East Anglian skies and the mirrored calm of Cumbria's lakes. The pubs of England have made good use of the land's natural bounty over the past decade; streamlined establishments have stripped out the soggy carpets and soggier menus and replaced them with crisp décor and fresh, inventive cooking. England's multi-ethnic culture has borne fruit in the kitchens of your local…

61
41

An area that combines the grace of a bygone age with the speed of the 21C. To the east (Chatsworth House, Haddon Hall and Burghley House) is where Pride and Prejudice came to life, while Silverstone to the south hosts the Grand Prix. Market towns are dotted all around: Spalding's cultivation of tulips rivals that of Holland, Oakham boasts its stunning Castle and Great Hall, and the legendary "Boston Stump" oversees the bustle of a 450 year-old market. The brooding beauty of the Peak District makes it the second most visited National Park in the world. Izaak Walton popularised the river Dove's trout-filled waters in "The Compleat Angler" and its surrounding hills are a rambler's dream, as are the wildlife habitats of the National Forest and the wind-swept acres of the pancake-flat fens. Above it all looms Lincoln Cathedral's ancient spire, while in the pubs, local ale – typically brewed in Bakewell, Dovedale or Rutland – slips down a treat alongside the ubiquitous Melton Mowbray pie.

Yorkshire & the Humber
North West
EAST
West Midlands
South East
Huddersfield
Oldham
Holmfirth
Barnsley
Doncaster
Wigan
Leigh
MANCHESTER
Ashton-under-Lyne
Conisbrough
Glossop
Stocksbridge
Peak District
Rotherham
Altrincham
Hyde
Stockport
SHEFFIELD
Bawtry
High Peak
Maltby
Knutsford
Castleton
Whaley Bridge
Chapel-en-le-Frith
National
Dronfield
Worksop
Northwich
Macclesfield
Buxton
Staveley
Baslow
Chesterfield
Middlewich
Congleton
Bakewell
Park
Chatsworth House
Tuxford
Sandbach
Little Moreton Hall
Clay Cross
Hardwick
Crewe
Kidsgrove
Leek
Matlock
Mansfield
DERBY
Alfreton
Sutton-in-Ashfield
Newcastle-under-Lyme
Ashbourne
Ripley
Southwell
Audlem
STOKE-ON-TRENT
Belper
Heanor
Hucknall
Market Drayton
Stone
Ilkeston
NOTTINGHAM
Uttoxeter
Derby
Bingham
West Bridgford
Eccleshall
Sudbury
Long Eaton
Stafford
Abbots Bromley
Burton-upon-Trent
Rempstone
Newport
Rugeley
Shepshed
STAFFORD
Swadlincote
Loughborough
Cannock
Ashby de la Zouch
Gailey
Brownhills
Lichfield
Coalville
LEICESTER
Tamworth
Walsall
WOLVERHAMPTON
Sutton Coldfield
Atherstone
Hinckley
Oadby
Dudley
Nuneaton
BIRMINGHAM
Stourbridge
Bedworth
Market Harborough
Lutterworth
Kidderminster
Halesowen
Solihull
Bewdley
COVENTRY
Husbands Bosworth
Rugby
Stourport
Bromsgrove
Kenilworth
Rothwell
Redditch
WARWICK
NORTHAM
Henley
Royal Leamington Spa
Wellingborough
Droitwich
Worcester
Warwick
Alcester
Southam
Daventry
WORCESTER
Stratford-upon-Avon
Great Malvern
Evesham
Ettington
Pershore
Upton
Chipping Campden
Shipston-on-Stour
Towcester
Banbury
Wolverton
Broadway
Moreton
Brackley
Tewkesbury
Winchcombe
Milton Keynes
Stow-on-the-Wold
Chipping Norton
Buckingham
Bletchley
Gloucester
Cheltenham
OXFORD
Derwent

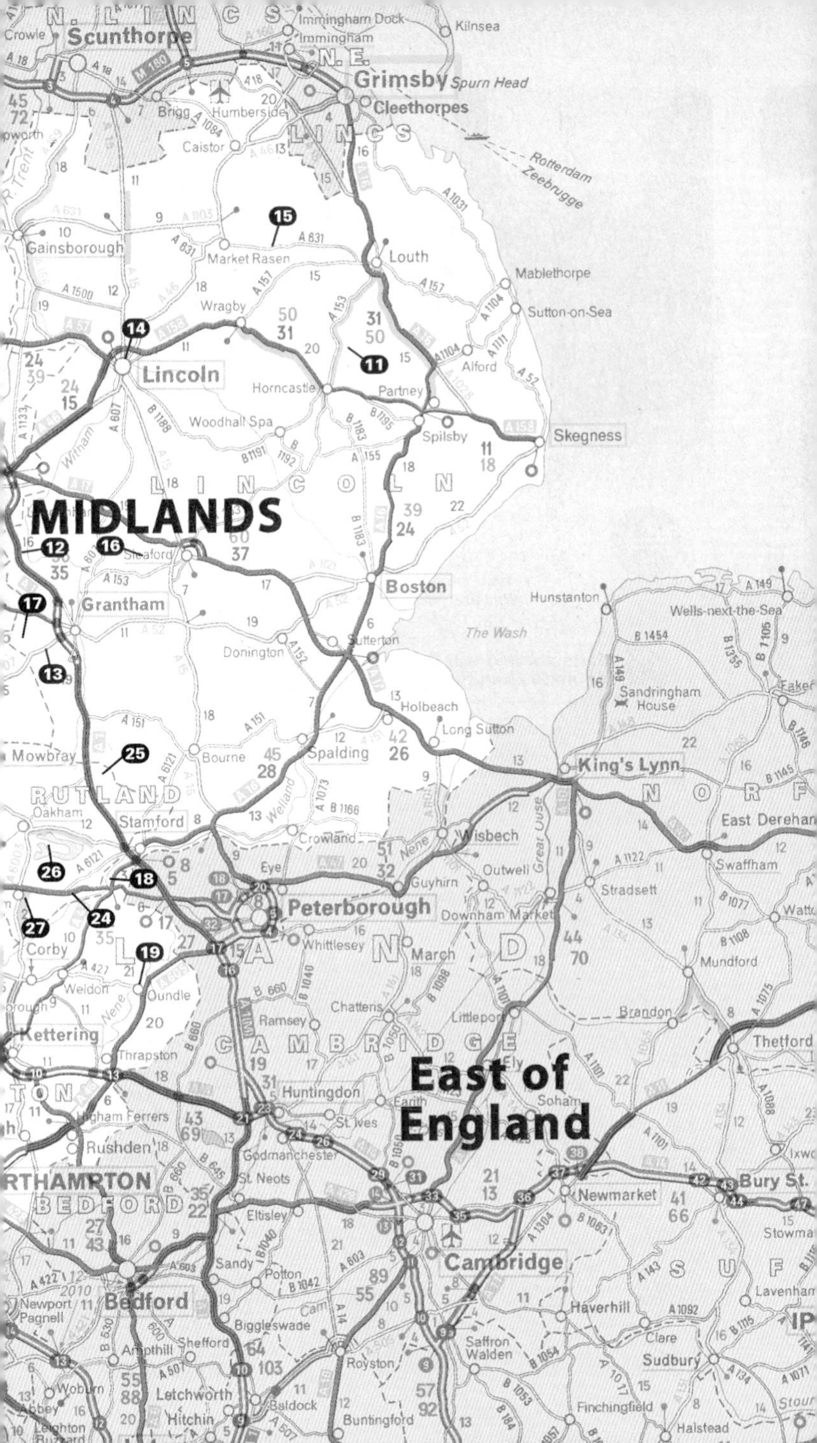

MIDLANDS
East of England
Scunthorpe
Grimsby
Cleethorpes
Immingham Dock
Immingham
Kilnsea
Spurn Head
Crowle
Brigg
Humberside
Caistor
Rotterdam
Zeebrugge
Gainsborough
Market Rasen
Louth
Mablethorpe
Sutton-on-Sea
Wragby
Lincoln
Alford
Horncastle
Partney
Woodhall Spa
Spilsby
Skegness
Sleaford
Grantham
Boston
Hunstanton
Wells-next-the-Sea
The Wash
Sutterton
Donington
Holbeach
Long Sutton
Sandringham House
Mowbray
Bourne
Spalding
King's Lynn
RUTLAND
Oakham
Stamford
Crowland
Wisbech
East Dereham
Eye
Outwell
Swaffham
Guyhirn
Stradsett
Peterborough
Downham Market
Whittlesey
March
Corby
Weldon
Oundle
Mundford
Chatteris
Ramsey
Littleport
Brandon
Thetford
Kettering
Thrapston
Ely
Huntingdon
Earith
Soham
Higham Ferrers
St. Ives
Rushden
Godmanchester
St. Neots
Newmarket
Bury St.
Eltisley
Cambridge
Stowmarket
Sandy
Potton
Bedford
Newport Pagnell
Biggleswade
Haverhill
Lavenham
Clare
Ampthill
Shefford
Saffron Walden
Royston
Sudbury
Woburn Abbey
Letchworth
Baldock
Finchingfield
Leighton Buzzard
Hitchin
Buntingford
Halstead
LINCS
N.E. LINCS
LINCOLN
CAMBRIDGE
NORFOLK
BEDFORD
NORTHAMPTON

1 **The Devonshire Arms**

Devonshire Sq,
Beeley, DE4 2NR
Tel.: (01629)733259 – Fax: (01629)733259
e-mail: enquiries@devonshirebeeley.co.uk
Website: www.devonshirebeeley.co.uk

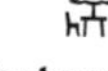  

Chatsworth Gold, Thornbridge Jaipur, Black Sheep and regularly changing guest ales

Part of the Chatsworth Estate, this old stone inn can be found just minutes down the road from the main house, in a small hamlet also owned by the eponymous Duke and Duchess. There are two clear parts to the place: a homely bar with exposed stone, oak beams and open fires, and a modern extension with a glass-fronted wine cave and lovely village views. If you're making a flying visit then the 'Afternoon Feast' offers scones, teacakes and waffles; if you have longer, dinner could include butternut squash panna cotta or crumbed pavé of codling, followed by a list of Devonshire classics and daily market dishes. Produce is from the Estate and surrounding villages. Bedrooms in the main house boast low beams; those next door are larger and brighter.

Closing times
Open daily

Prices
Meals: a la carte £ 20/36

8 rooms: £ 99/175

Typical Dishes
Clay pot baked Derbyshire lamb
Smoked chicken breast & saffron risotto
Chocolate & praline parfait

5 mi southeast of Bakewell by A 6 and B 6012. Parking.

2 The Druid Inn

Main St,
Birchover, DE4 2BL
Tel.: (01629)650302
e-mail: thedruidinn@hotmail.co.uk
Website: www.thedruidinn.co.uk

Druid Ale and regularly changing guest ales

Set in the middle of nowhere, this stone inn is a pleasant surprise for the hungry hikers who stumble across it. There are many legends surrounding local druid activity, including a story that the druids would gather naked at the nearby Nine Ladies stone circle to celebrate the summer solstice. The only druid you're likely to spot nowadays, however, is a pint of the local ale. The interior is quite unusual: there's a cosy bar, a two-tabled windowless 'wine cave' and a contemporary split-level dining room. In summer they get a lot visitors, especially from the nearby campsite, while in winter, the locals frequent the place. Cooking is kept simple and in a largely classical vein; expect liver and bacon, battered fish, steaks and plenty of pies.

Closing times
Closed Sunday dinner

Prices
Meals: £ 13 (weekdays) and a la carte £ 20/30

Typical Dishes
Soft-shell crab, chilli mayonnaise
Rump of lamb & red cabbage
Classic miniature desserts to share

7.5 mi northwest of Matlock by A 6 and 5.5 mi from Bakewell. Parking.

Bradwell

3 **Samuel Fox**

Stretfield Rd,
Bradwell, S33 9JT
Tel.: (01433)621562 – Fax: (01433)623770
e-mail: thesamuelfox@hotmail.co.uk
Website: www.samuelfox.co.uk

 **Black Sheep**

This smart, stone-built pub stands out like a beacon in the Derbyshire village of Bradwell, its neutral colour schemes and rattan-style furniture giving it the fresh, light feel of an upmarket French bistro. It's run by a young couple and while he beavers away in the kitchen, she provides efficient, cheery service out the front. The set price lunch menu offers dishes such as corned beef hash with a fried egg, while the evening à la carte menu displays more ambitious dishes such as breast and leg of guinea fowl stuffed with wild mushrooms. Cooking is simple, reasonably priced and full of flavour, with game featuring strongly in winter and fish in summer. Four comfortable, modern bedrooms come with the added bonus of sherry and chocolates.

Closing times
Open daily

Prices
Meals: £ 15 and a la carte £ 19/29

4 rooms: £ 75/115

Typical Dishes
Home-smoked salmon
Braised shoulder of lamb
Gin & lime posset

 *12 mi northeast of Buxton by A 6 and B 6049. Parking.*

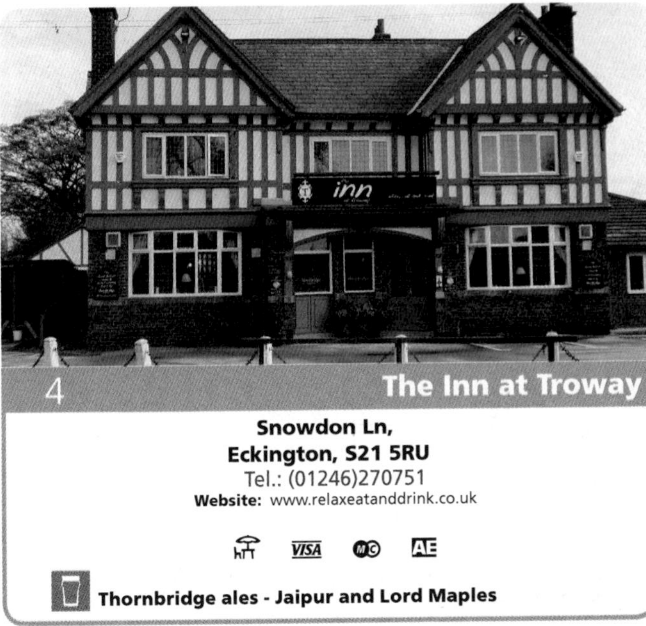

4 **The Inn at Troway**

Snowdon Ln,
Eckington, S21 5RU
Tel.: (01246)270751
Website: www.relaxeatanddrink.co.uk

VISA MC AE

Thornbridge ales - Jaipur and Lord Maples

This early Victorian pub is set in a picturesque location and offers delightful views out over the rolling countryside; make the most of these by grabbing a seat either on the terrace or in the rear dining room. This is an area popular with walkers and the food is satisfyingly hearty; perfect for refuelling after a brisk morning hike. Among the earthy options available on the wide-ranging menu might be seven-hour braised brisket of beef, fisherman's pie or a good value mature steak; be sure to try the onion rings. For those who've given the walking a miss, lighter options listed on the blackboard include tapas-like plates like black pudding or local sausages. There's a fine selection of regional ales and staff bend over backwards to help.

Closing times
Closed 25 December
booking advisable

Prices
Meals: £ 12 and a la carte £ 15/25

Typical Dishes
Bubble & squeak pasty
Fish pie & Y-Fenni cheese mash
Sticky toffee pudding

7.5 mi southeast of Sheffield by A61 and B 6056 Eckington Rd. Parking.

5 **The Chequers Inn**

Hope Valley,
S32 3ZJ
Tel.: (01433)630231 – Fax: (01433)631072
e-mail: info@chequers-froggatt.com
Website: www.chequers-froggatt.com

   VISA MC AE

Bakewell Best Bitter, Black Sheep and Charles Wells Bombardier

This 16C inn is built right into the stone boulders of Froggat Edge and even has a direct path from its garden up to the peak. As traditional inside as out, it's a comfortingly no-nonsense sort of place, boasting a cosy fire, gleaming brass, a large bar and a quieter, cosier room across the hall. The majority of diners are walkers, but the jolly team welcome one and all as if they were locals. Cooking is unfussy, wholesome and tasty, featuring traditional dishes that always include fish and chips, bangers and mash, and a pie. More imaginative specials appear on the blackboard alongside the starters and desserts – the latter of which usually includes a local Bakewell pudding. Weary travellers will find bedrooms comfy; the one to the rear is best.

Closing times
Closed 25 December

Prices
Meals: a la carte £ 18/29

5 rooms: £ 75/100

Typical Dishes
Scallops with pea & pancetta purée
Duck breast with ginger & coriander mash
Caramelised banana panna cotta

Situated on the edge of the village. Parking.

6 **The Queen's Head**

2 Long St,
Belton, LE12 9TP
Tel.: (01530)222359
e-mail: enquiries@thequeenshead.org
Website: www.thequeenshead.org

VISA

Queen's Special, Marston's Pedigree, Beaver Bitter

Nicely located in the village centre, this pub is divided into two distinct parts. To the right, it boasts a cream and chocolate coloured bar-lounge furnished in sleek, pale wood; to the left, a more formal, minimalist two-roomed restaurant. Menus offer plenty of choice, with a daily set selection, an à la carte and a list of 'Classics' – the latter best sampled on Tuesdays, when 7 dishes are offered at £7 each. You'll always find a few things available in two sizes and yet more diversity appears on Sundays, when they offer brunch. For special occasions there's a private dining room with covered deck, while for the weary, modern bedrooms offer good facilities. The only thing that can sometimes be lacking here is the enthusiasm of the staff.

Closing times
Closed 25-26 December and Sunday dinner

Prices
Meals: £ 16/23
6 rooms: £ 70/100

6 mi west of Loughborough by A 6 on B 5234; on the Diseworth/Breedon rd. Parking.

Breedon on the Hill

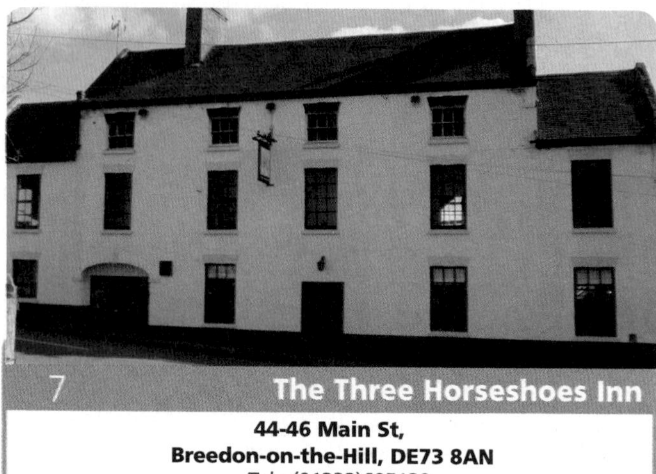

7 **The Three Horseshoes Inn**

44-46 Main St,
Breedon-on-the-Hill, DE73 8AN
Tel.: (01332)695129
e-mail: ian@thehorseshoes.com
Website: www.thehorseshoes.com

 **Marston Pedigree**

This large, whitewashed building may not look much like a pub but open the door and you can rest assured that you're in the right place. It's more dining pub than your typical village local but it's still characterful; full of books, artefacts and paintings. Numerous interlinking rooms allow you to create a different experience each time you come: choose maybe an antique table beside the exposed brick fireplace, an intimate corner in one of the smaller rooms, or in summer, a pleasant alfresco spot. A friendly, efficient team point out the blackboards that are scattered about the place, displaying classical, seasonal dishes which prove robust and flavoursome. If 3 courses are too much, don't worry – take something home from the shop for later.

Closing times
Closed Sunday dinner

Prices
Meals: a la carte £ 22/33

Typical Dishes
Oak-roasted salmon & egg with dill dressing
Fillet of beef with peppercorn sauce
Chocolate whisky trifle

 *4 mi southwest of Castle Donington by Breedon rd off A 453. Parking.*

8 **The Joiners**

Church Walk,
Bruntingthorpe, LE17 5QH
Tel.: (0116)2478258
e-mail: stephenjoiners@btconnect.com
Website: www.thejoinersarms.co.uk

VISA

Greene King, Timothy Taylor

You can't help but feel that the locals had a part to play in the naming of this pub, which started life as the Joiners Arms and has since been renamed The Joiners. Set in a small rural village, this neat whitewashed building dates back to the 17C and boasts characterful wood floors and low beams. Run by an enthusiastic husband and wife team, it's more of a dining pub than a place for a casual drink; although the group of regulars crowded round the pine fitted bar would probably tell you otherwise. Menus display a mix of refined pub classics and more brasserie-style dishes, all cooked and presented in a straightforward yet effective manner. There's a good value set lunch, a fairly-priced à la carte and a wide selection of wines by the glass.

Closing times
Closed Sunday dinner and Monday
booking essential

Prices
Meals: £ 14 (lunch) and a la carte £ 22/28

Between Leicester and Husbands Bosworth off A 5199.

England • East Midlands • Leicestershire

Stathern

9 Red Lion Inn

2 Red Lion St,
Stathern, LE14 4HS
Tel.: (01949)860868 – Fax: (01949)861579
e-mail: info@theredlioninn.co.uk
Website: www.theredlioninn.co.uk

VISA MC

Red Lion Ale, Fuller's London Pride, Brewsters Marquis Bitter

Set in the village centre, this spacious whitewashed pub, with its rustic bar and characterful dining rooms, is very much part of the community. Whilst it maintains a healthy drinking trade, it's the food here that's the main attraction. As you walk past the allotment, a blackboard informs you of the latest produce to be planted and picked – and it's this seasonal variation that guides the menus. The à la carte arrives with a map of suppliers' locations on the back and it's reassuring that they don't stray far from the doorstep; you'll find sausages from the village butcher, game from the Belvoir estates and cheese from nearby dairies. Cooking is straightforward and unfussy, resulting in refined pub classics with the odd local or global twist.

Closing times
Closed Sunday dinner
booking essential

Prices
Meals: £ 19 (lunch)
and a la carte £ 22/32

Typical Dishes
Smoked salmon with dill pancakes
Braised blade of beef
Crème brûlée & shortbread biscuit

8 mi north of Melton Mowbray by A 607. Parking.

10 **The Bakers Arms**

Main St,
Thorpe Langton, LE16 7TS
Tel.: (01858)545201 – Fax: (01858)545924
e-mail: office@thebakersarms.co.uk
Website: www.thebakersarms.co.uk

 **Langton Brewery Baker's Dozen**

If you're looking for character, this thatched, yellow-washed pub in the small village of Thorpe Langton has plenty. It's deceptively large inside but the low beamed ceilings, scrubbed tables and array of rustic dressers ensure that it's cosy and welcoming. The food here is constantly evolving, depending on the latest produce that's available, and the large blackboard menu changes not only daily but between – and even during – services. You'll find plenty of pub classics and reliable combinations: your lamb will come with pea mash and your lemon sole with parsley butter; while desserts take you back to your childhood and might include vanilla ice cream with chocolate sauce or sticky toffee pudding. Thursdays feature a list of seafood specials.

Closing times
Closed Tuesday-Friday lunch, Sunday dinner and Monday
booking essential

Prices
Meals: a la carte £ 22/28

Typical Dishes
Pear & haggis with crème fraîche
Rack of local lamb
Spiced plums & hazelnut shortbread

 *3.75 mi north of Market Harborough by A 4304 via Great Bowden. Parking.*

Belchford

11 **The Blue Bell Inn**

1 Main Rd,
Belchford, LN9 6LQ
Tel.: (01507)533602
e-mail: sue.jacksonh53@ntlworld.com

   MC

Black Sheep and local guest ales

Situated in a tiny village in the heart of the Lincolnshire Wolds, this whitewashed pub is a popular destination for those walking the Viking Way. You can't miss the big blue bell that hangs outside, however, when you delve deeper into it nobody really knows why it's there, since the pub was originally named after the bluebell flower. It's very much a traditional kind of place, boasting a cosy bar with exposed wooden beams, a typical black wood counter and old-style armchairs – as well as a linen-laid dining room – and despite being run by a young couple, still has an friendly, old-fashioned air. Dishes are listed on numerous blackboards above the fire in the bar and include sandwiches, old pub favourites and some more ambitious creations.

Closing times
Closed 2 weeks mid January, Sunday dinner and Monday

Prices
Meals: a la carte £ 17/28

Typical Dishes
Pea, ham & mint soup
Rump steak with mushrooms & chips
Bakewell tart

4 mi north of Horncastle by A 153 and righthand turn east. Parking.

12 Wheatsheaf Inn

Main St,
Dry Doddington, NG23 5HU
Tel.: (01400)281458
e-mail: wheatsheafdrydoddington@hotmail.co.uk
Website: www.wheatsheaf-pub.co.uk

  VISA

Timothy Taylor Landlord, Tom Woods' Best Bitter, Greene King Abbot Ale and Batemans XB

Set next to a characterful 17C church and overlooking a pretty village green, this smartly kept pub positively beckons you through the door. Once inside, you'll discover a cosy bar with a wood burning stove, settles scattered with cushions, and plenty of wood panelling, as well as a laid-back restaurant with upholstered chairs and painted stone walls; while to the rear, a small courtyard makes the perfect suntrap. The light bites lunch menu keeps things simple, offering unfussy dishes that keep the locals happy (such as beef, ale and mushroom pie), while the à la carte presents some more ambitious offerings like braised blade of beef – supplemented by daily blackboard specials in the evening. The local steaks and twice-baked chips are a hit.

Closing times
Closed Monday and lunch Tuesday

Prices
Meals: £ 14 (lunch) and a la carte £ 21/30

Typical Dishes
Diver-caught scallops
Slow-roast pork belly
Vanilla panna cotta & poached rhubarb

 *11 mi northwest of Grantham by B 1174 and A 1. Parking.*

Harlaxton

13 **The Gregory**

The Drift,
Harlaxton, NG32 1AD
Tel.: (01476)577076
e-mail: info@thegregory.co.uk
Website: www.thegregory.co.uk

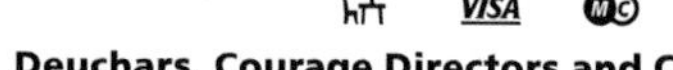
Deuchars, Courage Directors and Charles Wells Bombardier

The Gregory has been serving the local community since the 19C, when workers from the eponymous family's estate made it their favourite haunt. When later relocated to its present spot, it was responsible for supplying the village with its coal. These days, the pub has a very modern feel, with a spacious dining room – for which you will need to book – and a smaller lounge. The menu offers a selection of pub classics, including plenty of steaks and homemade pies, alongside dishes such as risotto and fillet of sea bass. Sandwiches supplement at lunchtime, with old-fashioned puddings for afters. Thursday is steak night, whilst early evening Monday-Saturday means 'Super6ixes': six dishes, each available for the princely sum of six pounds.

Closing times
Closed dinner 25-26 December and 1 January

Prices
Meals: a la carte £ 20/35

Typical Dishes
Tempura king prawns
Chargrilled rib-eye of pork & fondant potato
Sticky toffee pudding

 *2 mi southwest of Grantham by A 607. Parking.*

14 **Wig & Mitre**

30-32 Steep Hill,
Lincoln, LN2 1LU
Tel.: (01522)535190 – Fax: (01522)532402
e-mail: email@wigandmitre.com
Website: www.wigandmitre.com

VISA MC AE D

 **Young's Golden Gold, Warsteiner, Black Sheep, Batemans XB**

Nestled among period shops on a steep hill, this well-established, part-14C pub is something of a Lincoln institution; standing midway between the castle (used as a court) – hence the 'Wig' – and the cathedral – hence the 'Mitre'. There's a cosy bar downstairs, and two period dining rooms and a light, airy beamed restaurant above. The menu changes quarterly, displaying largely classical dishes with the odd Mediterranean or Asian influence. There's a good value set selection weekdays and for those who enjoy a hearty homemade breakfast, they open at 9am. With wine books and maps dotted about the place, over 50 wines by the glass and a recommendation for every dish, it comes as no surprise to find that they own the next door wine shop too.

Closing times
Open daily

Prices
Meals: £ 15/20
and a la carte £ 21/29

Typical Dishes
Coarse paté & homemade pickle
Rump of lamb & lemon-crushed new potatoes
Apple crème brûlée

 *Close to the Cathedral. Lincoln Castle car parks adjacent.*

Ludford

15 **The Black Horse Inn**

Magna Mile,
Ludford, LN8 6AJ
Tel.: (01507)313645
e-mail: reedannam@aol.com

Tom Wood' s Best, Cathedral Golden Imp and Poacher's Shy Talk

Having moved from Lancashire to Lincolnshire to chase their dream of buying a pub and going it alone, Paul and Anna are in it for the long-haul. They may not have huge amounts of money but they do have passion and you have to admire their determination. The building itself might be a little worn but it has a warm, well-loved feel, with homely décor, simple furnishings and welcoming open fires. The horse racing prints are a reference to nearby Market Rasen, while the model planes are a tribute to the Lancaster Bomber veterans, who meet here for their reunions. The menu is concise, featuring good old-fashioned classics that always include some sort of steak. Plenty of pies and stews are on offer in winter, alongside ever-popular game dishes.

Closing times
Closed Sunday dinner and Monday

Prices
Meals: a la carte £ 17/31

Typical Dishes
Smoked Lincolnshire Poacher cheese & leek soufflé
Cassoulet
Bakewell tart

 *6 mi east of Market Rasen by A 631. Parking.*

16 The Bustard Inn

44 Main St,
South Rauceby, NG34 8QG
Tel.: (01529)488250
e-mail: info@thebustardinn.co.uk
Website: www.thebustardinn.co.uk

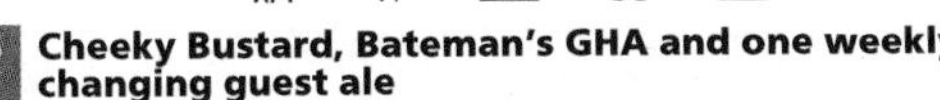
Cheeky Bustard, Bateman's GHA and one weekly changing guest ale

From the outside it resembles a schoolhouse, but The Bustard Inn is hardly bookish. Its flag-floored bar is simple and uncluttered while its more spacious restaurant, with its cream-tiled floor and exposed brick, has a touch of the Mediterranean about it. Traditional pub favourites like sausage and mash and fish and chips are listed on the blackboard bar menu, while the restaurant's à la carte steps things up a gear with an array of modern-style dishes, ranging from pork and black pudding terrine or roast chump of lamb to glazed breast of Gressingham duck or pan-fried sea bream. Slay your thirst with a pint of specially brewed 'Cheeky Bustard' beer and enjoy reassuringly old-fashioned desserts like apple crumble or sticky toffee pudding.

Closing times
Closed 1 January, Sunday dinner and Monday

Prices
Meals: a la carte £ 24/40

4 mi west of Sleaford by A 17 and minor road south. Parking.

Woolsthorpe by Belvoir

17 **The Chequers**

Main St,
Woolsthorpe-by-Belvoir, NG32 1LU
Tel.: (01476)870701
e-mail: justinnabar@yahoo.co.uk
Website: www.chequersinn.net

VISA AE

Everards Tiger and Woodforde's Wherry - weekly changing ales

If you like a side of history with your lunch then this quaint little village owned by the Belvoir Estate is the place to come. A pub has stood on this spot since 1692 – the first being run by the same family for 213 years – and it's just as much a community meeting place as ever. Locals nurse pints by the roaring fires, fixtures for the adjacent cricket pitch hang by the door and you can even sit beside the remains of the old village bread oven. Lunch is fairly simple, offering the likes of homemade burgers, pies and local sausages, while dinner adds things such as game or rib of beef for two; there's also a good value daily set menu and 7 dishes for £7 between 6 and 7pm. Crisply furnished, modern bedrooms are located in the old stables.

Closing times
Closed dinner
25-26 December
and 1 January lunch

Prices
Meals: £ 17 and a la carte
£ 21/33

4 rooms: £ 50/70

7.5 mi west of Grantham by A 607. Parking.

18 The Collyweston Slater

87-89 Main Rd,
Collyweston, PE9 3PQ
Tel.: (01780)444288
e-mail: info@collywestonslater.co.uk
Website: www.collywestonslater.co.uk

 **No real ales offered**

Some pubs like to keep things traditional, with comforting classics like ploughman's and pies, while others fancy themselves as fine dining establishments, offering luxurious ingredients like truffles and foie gras. Here you can have both. Sit on tub chairs by the wood burner for a salad or a sandwich, or venture into the more formal dining room for such delights as cured salmon with ginger jelly and crème fraîche sorbet or tonka bean crème brûlée with bee pollen and cola sherbet. Dishes are bursting with flavour, the service is friendly and there are homemade preserves for sale on the bar. Originally a coaching inn, the pub also has several bedrooms. They're clean, comfortable and modern in style; Ortega and Bacchus are the largest.

Closing times
Open daily

Prices
Meals: a la carte £ 22/34
5 rooms: £ 75/120

Typical Dishes
Smoked salmon terrine with cucumber sorbet
Roast wild bass with mussel risotto
Lemon tart with raspberry sorbet

 *3 mi southwest of Stamford by A 43. Parking.*

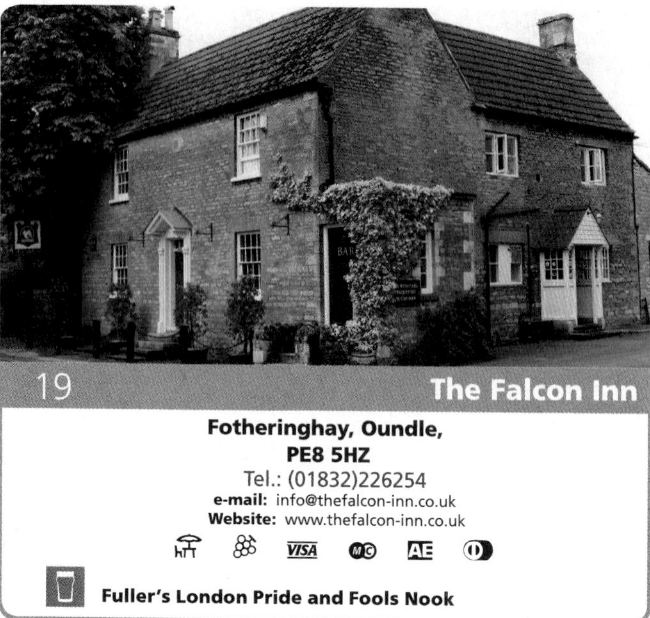

19 **The Falcon Inn**

Fotheringhay, Oundle,
PE8 5HZ
Tel.: (01832)226254
e-mail: info@thefalcon-inn.co.uk
Website: www.thefalcon-inn.co.uk

VISA MC AE

Fuller's London Pride and Fools Nook

In the pretty village of Fotheringhay – the birthplace of Richard III and the deathplace of Mary Queen of Scots – under the shadow of a large church, sits the attractive, ivy-clad Falcon Inn. It boasts a neat garden and a small paved terrace, a pleasant private dining annexe and a beamed bar with an unusual display of 15C bell clappers. You'll find the regulars playing darts and drinking real ales in the small tap bar, and the diners in the conservatory restaurant with its wicker chairs, formally laid tables and garden outlook. Good-sized menus include unusual combinations and some interesting modern takes on traditional dishes; you might find purple sprouting broccoli in your stilton soup or red pepper and dandelion dressing on your crab.

Closing times
Open daily

Prices
Meals: £ 16 and a la carte £ 28/35

Typical Dishes
Rabbit rillette
Chargrilled fillet steak & fondant potato
Sticky toffee pudding

3.45 mi north of Oundle by A 427 off A 605. Parking.

20 Caunton Beck

Main St,
Caunton, NG23 6AB
Tel.: (01636)636793 – Fax: (01636)636828
e-mail: email@cauntonbeck.com
Website: www.wigandmitre.com

 **Marston's Pedigree, Batemans GHA, Black Sheep**

With tan coloured bricks and a wrought iron pergola this doesn't look much like your typical village pub; step inside, however, and locals supping cask ales will soon reassure you. When the weather's right, make for the large front terrace hung with colourful flower baskets. When it's not so good, head for the bar, with its scrubbed pine furniture and daily papers, or the traditional restaurant with its polished period tables and wheel-back chairs. Changing four times a year, the menu offers gutsy, manly cooking with the odd global influence. Daily specials include plenty of fish and there's a good value 3 course menu during the week. If breakfast is your thing, they open at 8am with the likes of smoked salmon, scrambled eggs and champagne.

Closing times
Open daily

Prices
Meals: £ 15 and a la carte £ 23/28

Typical Dishes
Smoked haddock & spring leek soufflé
Local rump of beef with game chips
White chocolate & spiced cranberry cheesecake

7 mi northwest of Newark by A 616, 6 mi past the sugar beet factory. Parking.

Colston Bassett

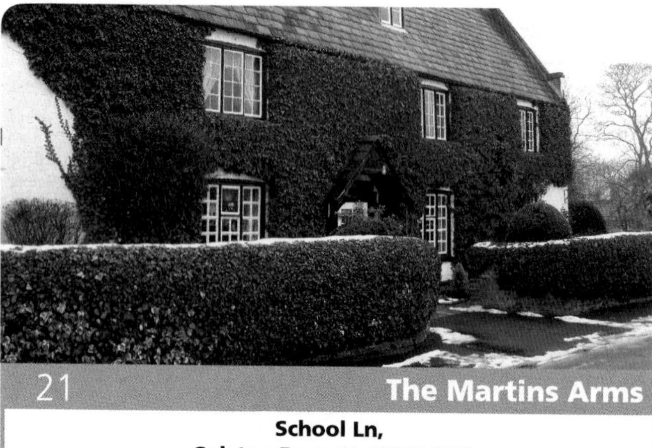

21 **The Martins Arms**

School Ln,
Colston Bassett, NG12 3FD
Tel.: (01949)81361 – Fax: (01949)81039
e-mail: martins_arms@hotmail.com
Website: www.themartinsarms.co.uk

VISA

Black Sheep, Bass, Greene King IPA, Pedigree, Timothy Taylor Landlord, Harvest Pale and Wherry

Blazing log fires cast a welcoming glow in the cosy bar of this creeper-clad pub; full of feminine touches like fresh flowers, comfy cushions, tea lights and gleaming copperware. Originally a farmhouse on the Martin family estate, it contains several articles salvaged from the original manor house, including the carved Jacobean fireplace and the old library shelves, now used to hold drinks in the bar. Said bar is the place for an impromptu lunch, while the period furnished dining rooms, adorned with hunting pictures, are more suited to a formal dinner – but be sure to book in advance. The menu has a strong masculine base with some Italian influences and the odd global flavour; portions are hearty and there's plenty of game in season.

Closing times
Closed dinner 25 December and Sunday dinner

Prices
Meals: a la carte £ 21/32

Typical Dishes
Serrano ham, asparagus & smoked hollandaise
Coconut-poached halibut with mushrooms
Rhubarb 'Tiramisu'

East of Cotgrave off A 46. Parking.

22 Waggon and Horses

The Turnpike,
Mansfield Rd., Halam, NG22 8AE
Tel.: (01636)813109 – Fax: (01636)816228
e-mail: info@thewaggonathalam.co.uk
Website: www.thewaggonathalam.co.uk

Thwaites Lancaster Bomber and Wainwrights

Lancashire has its hotpot, Yorkshire has its pudding and now Nottinghamshire has its pie, thanks to a 'wizzard' idea from Waggon and Horses' chef Roy Wood. His home county may have laid claim to lace and the legend of Robin Hood, but was lacking its own regional dish – until Roy stepped up to the plate. If you find this beef, leek and mustard pie with its potato, stilton and crumb topping rather moreish; fear not, for the recipe is thoughtfully provided. The blackboard menu features plenty of fresh fish and local meats – and a side order of vegetables comes free with every main course. Modern flower displays add a splash of colour to the unfussy interior – and the cheery serving team, headed up by Roy's wife, Laura, complete the picture.

Closing times
Closed Sunday dinner and Monday

Prices
Meals: £ 15 (weekdays) and a la carte £ 20/38

1.75 mi west of Southwell, opposite the school. Parking.

23 The Reindeer Inn

Main St,
Hoveringham, NG14 7JR
Tel.: (01159)663629
Website: www.thereindeerinn.com

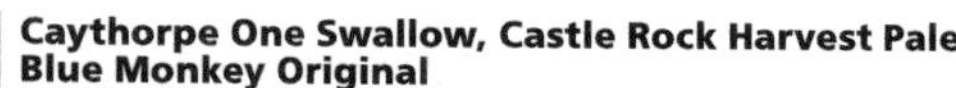

Caythorpe One Swallow, Castle Rock Harvest Pale, Blue Monkey Original

Behind The Reindeer's modest exterior lies a characterful country inn, with low ceilings, wood beams and a snug bar replete with locals. It's a pleasant place to dine at any time of the year; in winter one appreciates the blazing log fire and the cosy, relaxed atmosphere, while in summer, the cricket pitch behind the pub becomes the focal point, with drinks delivered through a hatch when a game is in full swing. Reasonably priced menus offer an eclectic mix; alongside recognisable dishes like rib of beef and pan-fried calves liver, you will also find more unusual offerings like pork cheeks braised in cider or vegetable tagine. Regular themed evenings like fish and lobster night go down a storm – and they even provide a take-away service.

Closing times
Closed 2 weeks mid May, Monday and lunch Tuesday

Prices
Meals: £ 7 (lunch) and a la carte £ 19/34

Typical Dishes
Oriental rare tuna, Thai basil sorbet & crispy greens
Rib of Nottinghamshire beef
Hot chocolate soufflé

5 mi south of Southwell by A 612. Parking.

24 **Exeter Arms**

28 Main St,
Barrowden, LE15 8EQ
Tel.: (01572)747247 – Fax: (01572)747247
e-mail: enquiries@exeterarms.co.uk
Website: www.exeterarmsrutland.co.uk

 **Barrowden ales: Pilot, Bevin, Beech, Hopgear and Black Adder**

If you like your real ales then this is the place for you, as behind the pub, in the old barn, you'll find its very own micro-brewery. Set in a sleepy village, this traditional sandstone building is just what a pub should be. Its front terrace boasts pleasant village green views and the simple, yellow walled interior displays framed pictures and photos, which tell the story of the pub and the area's past. The same menu is served throughout, so you can stay in the open-fired bar or move to the more formal dining room with its exposed stone walls. Cooking is traditional and straightforward, offering well-priced classical combinations that are delivered by the friendly, efficient owner. Cottage-style bedrooms offer pond and countryside views.

Closing times
Closed Sunday dinner and Monday lunch

Prices
Meals: a la carte £ 19/25
3 rooms: £ 45/79

 *11 mi southeast of Oakham by A 6003 and A 47. Parking.*

25 The Olive Branch & Beech House

Main St,
Clipsham, LE15 7SH
Tel.: (01780)410355 – Fax: (01780)410000
e-mail: info@theolivebranchpub.com
Website: www.theolivebranchpub.com

VISA

Local ales

You want the character and rusticity of a proper country inn but carefully crafted, highly accomplished food: enter The Olive Branch. It has the heart and soul of a real community pub – so you'll find farmers nursing pints beside the bar – but it also boasts a menu of well-prepared, classically based dishes and a friendly, informative serving team; not forgetting a truly charming garden and BBQ area. Cooking is flavoursome, robust and relies on fresh, local ingredients; and although descriptions may sound ordinary, the reality is anything but. Rather than chasing TV's bright lights, the chef gives cookery demonstrations in the old barn. Bedrooms provide a stylish contrast and include a host of extras. The homemade breakfasts are delightful.

Closing times
Open daily
booking essential

Prices
Meals: £ 21/28
and a la carte £ 25/45

6 rooms: £ 95/190

Typical Dishes
Tapas board
Chargrilled pork chop, pease pudding & apple fondant
Blackcurrant treacle tart

9.5 mi northwest of Stamford by B 1081 off A 1. Parking.

26

Finch's Arms

Oakham Rd,
Hambleton, LE15 8TL
Tel.: (01572)756575
e-mail: finchsarms@talk21.com
Website: www.finchsarms.co.uk

VISA AE

Black Sheep, Abbot Ale and Phipps

With its light sandstone walls and dark slate roof, this attractive 17C building is the very essence of a traditional country pub in outward appearance: inside, however, it offers a whole lot more. True, you'll find the regulars drinking real ales in a rustic bar among beams and flagstones but, the rest of the rooms take on a surprisingly Mediterranean feel, displaying round, stone topped tables and rattan chairs. Continue through yet further and to the rear of the pub you'll find its biggest draw: a large paved terrace, boasting beautiful views across Rutland Water. You can eat in any of the rooms – choosing from both classic and modern British dishes – but the terrace is definitely the place to be. Bedrooms are smart and exceedingly stylish.

Closing times
Open daily

Prices
Meals: £ 15/19
and a la carte £ 25/35

6 rooms: £ 75/95

3 mi east of Oakham by A 606. Parking.

27 **Old White Hart**

51 Main St,
Lyddington, LE15 9LR
Tel.: (01572)821703 – Fax: (01572)821978
e-mail: mail@oldwhitehart.co.uk
Website: www.oldwhitehart.co.uk

VISA

Greene King - Abbot and IPA, Timothy Taylor Landlord

Set in the pleasant village of Lyddington, this 17C former coaching inn ticks all the right boxes. It boasts a neat garden, a smart canopy-covered terrace and several cosy open-fired rooms crammed full of old pictures and objets d'art. In keeping with the place, the monthly changing menu offers a selection of traditional pub dishes, cooked and served in a simple, unfussy manner. You might find roast loin of lamb, toad in the hole or pan-fried calves liver, followed by maybe lemon meringue pie or crumble of the day. If you fancy a bit of light competition, book yourself in for one of the petanque evenings, where you get plenty of game play before dinner. Bedrooms are modern and stylish – one has a spiral staircase leading to a private jacuzzi.

Closing times
Closed Sunday dinner in winter

Prices
Meals: £ 14 and a la carte £ 18/28

10 rooms: £ 70/95

Typical Dishes
Goose liver parfait with homemade walnut & date bread
Roast rack of lamb
Chocolate marquise

1.5 mi south of Uppingham off A 6003; by the village green. Parking.

Wide lowland landscapes and huge skies, timber-framed houses, a frowning North Sea canvas: these are the abiding images of England's east. This region has its roots embedded in the earth and its taste buds whetted by local seafood. Some of the most renowned ales are brewed in Norfolk and Suffolk. East Anglia sees crumbling cliffs, superb mudflats and saltmarshes or enchanting medieval wool towns such as Lavenham. Areas of Outstanding Natural Beauty abound, in the Chilterns of Bedfordshire and Hertfordshire, and in Dedham Vale, life-long inspiration of Constable. Religious buildings are everywhere, from Ely Cathedral, "the Ship of the Fens", to the fine structure of Long Melford church. The ghosts of great men haunt Cambridge: Newton, Darwin, Pepys and Byron studied here, doubtless deep in thought as they tramped the wide-open spaces of Midsummer Common or Parker's Piece. Look out for Cromer crab, samphire, grilled herring, Suffolk pork casserole and the hearty Bedfordshire Clanger.

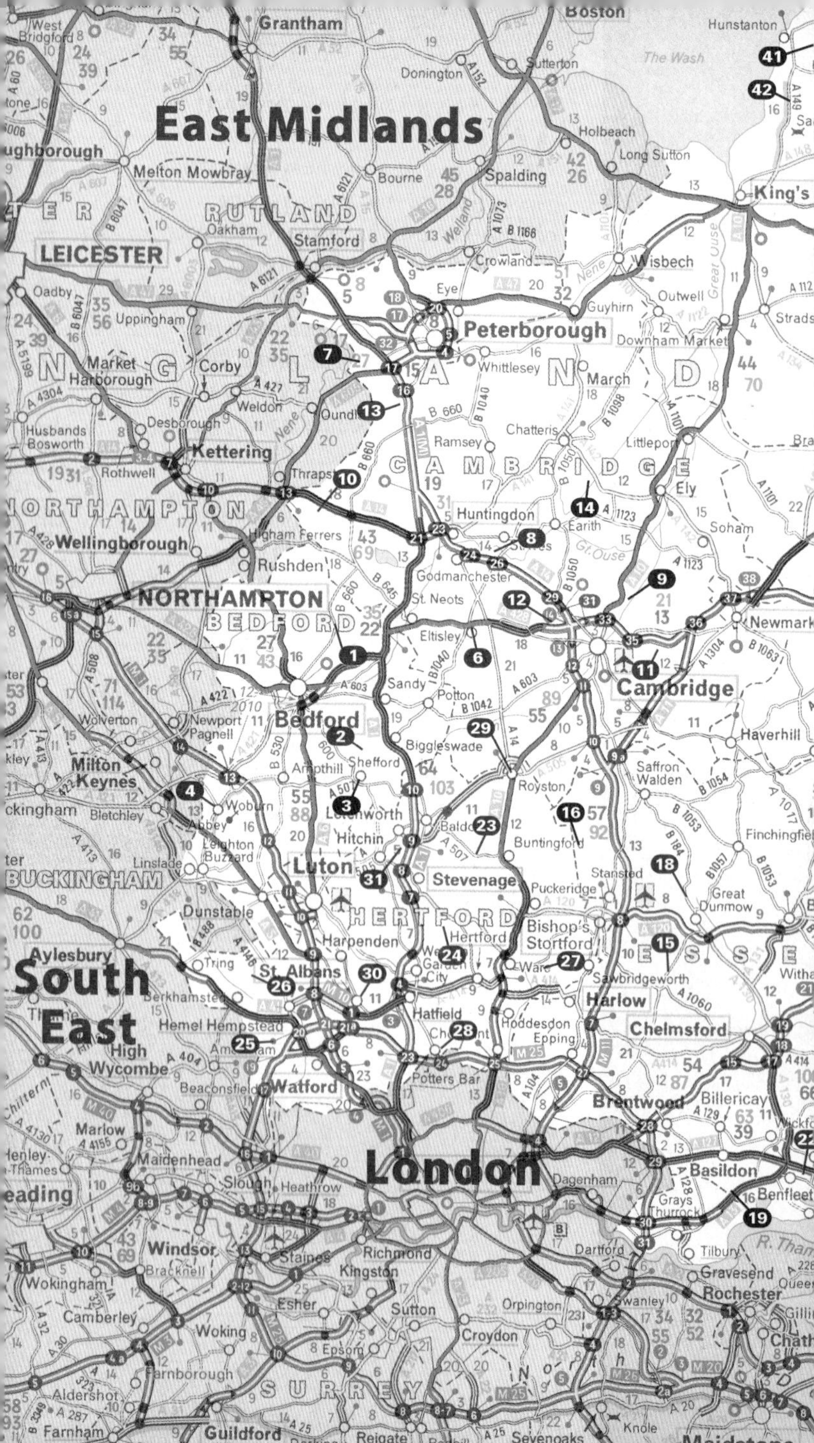

East Midlands
South East
London
Grantham
Boston
Hunstanton
The Wash
Melton Mowbray
Spalding
Peterborough
LEICESTER
RUTLAND
Stamford
Kettering
Wellingborough
NORTHAMPTON
BEDFORD
Bedford
Huntingdon
Cambridge
Ely
Wisbech
King's Lynn
Milton Keynes
Luton
Stevenage
St. Albans
Hertford
Harlow
Chelmsford
Watford
Aylesbury
High Wycombe
Slough
Reading
Windsor
Guildford
Croydon
Basildon
Brentwood
Dartford
Gravesend
Rochester
Sevenoaks
BUCKINGHAM
HERTFORD
CAMBRIDGE
SURREY

Sheringham
Cromer
Wells-next-the-Sea
Blakeney
Holt
Mundesley
Fakenham
North Walsham
Guist
Aylsham
Low Street
NORFOLK
East Dereham
Swaffham
Bure
Acle
Great Yarmouth
NORWICH
Wymondham
Watton
Gorleston-on-Sea
Yare
Mundford
Attleborough
Lowestoft
Bungay
Beccles
Thetford
Harleston
Waveney
EAST OF ENGLAND
Halesworth
Southwold
Ixworth
Dennington
Yoxford
Bury St. Edmunds
Saxmundham
Leiston
Stowmarket
Aldeburgh
SUFFOLK
Lavenham
Woodbridge
IPSWICH
Hadleigh
Stour
Halstead
Felixstowe
Harwich
Esbjerg
Hoek van Holland
Cuxhaven
The Naze
Colchester
Walton-on-the-Naze
Frinton-on-Sea
Brightlingsea
Clacton-on-Sea
W. Mersea
Maldon
Bradwell-on-Sea
Burnham-on-Crouch
Foulness Point
Southend-on-Sea
Grain
Sheerness
Isle of Sheppey
Leysdown-on-Sea
Birchington
Margate
Herne Bay
North Foreland
Whitstable
Broadstairs
Sittingbourne
Ramsgate
South East
Sandwich

1 **The Plough at Bolnhurst**

Kimbolton Rd,
Bolnhurst, MK44 2EX
Tel.: (01234)376274
e-mail: theplough@bolnhurst.com
Website: www.bolnhurst.com

Inspectors' favourites

 **Potton Brewery Local Village Bike, Buntingford Highwayman IPA and Adnam's Best**

This smart Tudor pub is a hit with locals and visitors alike, who frequent the place come rain or shine. The garden, with its trickling stream and boules pitch, is the place to be in summer, while on colder days there's the choice of bar or restaurant – both with cosy low beams and warm fires – the latter a little smarter, with modern wallpaper and upholstered chairs. The same seasonal menu is served throughout, with many dishes displaying strong Mediterranean influences. You might find roast chorizo or sweet Spanish pickles, followed by 28-day aged Aberdeenshire steaks – including côte de boeuf for two – and other dishes containing maybe Sicilian olive oil or black olive purée; all finished off with nursery puddings and Neal's Yard cheeses.

Closing times
Closed 2 weeks January, Sunday dinner and Monday

Prices
Meals: £ 18 (weekday lunch) and a la carte £ 24/38

Typical Dishes
Black pudding, cheese hash
Croxton Park pork belly
Sticky toffee pudding

7 mi north of Bedford by B660, on south side of village. Parking.

2 Hare & Hounds

The Village,
Old Warden, SG18 9HQ
Tel.: (01767)627225
e-mail: thehareandhounds@hotmail.co.uk
Website: www.hareandhoundsoldwarden.co.uk

Inspectors' favourites

 **Youngs Bitter, Eagle IPA**

With its ornate feature bargeboards and attractive manicured shrubs, this pub could easily appear on the front of any chocolate box. A charming building set in an idyllic village, it boasts four cosy rooms with brightly burning fires, bucket chairs and squashy banquettes, as well as a friendly team. If you're looking to eat, there's the choice of blackboard bar 'snacks' – although you could hardly call them so, as you might find fish and chips or pie of the day – or a monthly changing à la carte that offers robust, flavoursome dishes such as sea bass, pheasant or venison. Bread and pasta are made on the premises; meat is from local farms; fish is from sustainable stocks; and they have an allotment planted with various herbs, salad and berries.

Closing times
Closed Sunday dinner and Monday except bank holidays

Prices
Meals: a la carte £ 22/28

 *3.5 mi west of Biggleswade by A6001 off B658. Parking and at Village hall.*

3 **The Black Horse**

Ireland,
Shefford, SG17 5QL
Tel.: (01462)811398 – Fax: (01462)817238
e-mail: blackhorseireland@myway.com
Website: www.blackhorseireland.com

Fuller's London Pride, Adnam's Best Bitter and Black Sheep

Don't be deceived by the picture perfect chocolate box exterior; if you're looking for a quaint country inn you're in the wrong place. It may look traditional from the outside, but inside it's as ultra-modern as you can get. Contemporary light fittings are set amongst marble-style flooring and a granite-topped counter, and there's a walled courtyard complete with mirrors and fairy lights. The friendly staff serve an equally eclectic mix of generously portioned dishes. Lunch could include anything from suet crust pie to potted crab, while dinner might offer pork brawn followed by oxtail pudding or sweet potato tagine; finished off with good old-fashioned puddings. Accessed via a meandering garden path, bedrooms are comfy and delightfully cosy.

Closing times
Closed 25-26 December, 1 January and Sunday dinner

Prices
Meals: a la carte £ 23/29

2 rooms: £ 55

Typical Dishes

Potted Brixham crab

Pan-fried roulade of Cornish lamb

Mango & passion fruit soufflé

1.45 mi northwest of Shefford by B 658 and Ireland rd. Parking.

4

The Birch

20 Newport Rd.,
Woburn, MK17 9HX
Tel.: (01525)290295 – Fax: (01525)290899
e-mail: info@birchwoburn.com
Website: www.birchwoburn.com

 **Fuller's London Pride, Adnams**

Appearances can be deceiving and none more so than at The Birch. An attractive cream-washed building with pleasant porch, smart topiary shrubs and hanging baskets, it couldn't provide more of a contrast inside, where cavernous rooms are filled with bright colours, bold pictures and contemporary furnishings. A large conservatory and small enclosed terrace only add to its appeal – so if you don't arrive early you could find yourself battling for a parking space. The charming young team are well versed in the daily specials but there's always a selection of more familiar favourites such as pork belly or medallions of lamb too. If you like to watch your meal being prepared then opt for the fish or steak, which is cooked to order on the griddle.

Closing times
Closed 25-26 December, 1 January and Sunday dinner
booking essential

Prices
Meals: a la carte £ 18/39

0.5 mi north of Woburn on A5130. Parking.

Eltisley

6

The Eltisley

2 The Green,
Eltisley, PE19 6TG
Tel.: (01480)880308
e-mail: theeltisley@btconnect.com
Website: www.theeltisley.co.uk

Youngs, Wells and one regularly changing guest beer

You might imagine that this chic, stylish gastro-pub is a strictly dining affair, but the contemporary bar is equally as welcoming to drinkers as diners; the latter, who can sit and watch their meal being prepared from the windows in the snug. For a more formal occasion head through to the restaurant, where grey walls meet wood and tile flooring, and bold designs are offset by swanky chandeliers. Large parties should ask for the 'Wurlitzer', a stylish high-backed semi-circular banquette, while for summer dining the terrace is ideal. Cooking is simple, unfussy and relies on quality local ingredients: meat is from nearby farms and vegetables, from their allotment. Everything from the bread and pasta to the desserts and ice cream is homemade.

Closing times
Closed Sunday dinner and Monday except July-September

Prices
Meals: a la carte £ 23/33

Typical Dishes
Chicken & grape pressing
Croxton Park organic sausages & mustard mash
Chocolate, orange & honeycomb torte

 *12 mi west by A 1303 from Cambridge and A 428. Parking.*

7 **The Crown Inn**

8 Duck St,
Elton, PE8 6RQ
Tel.: (01832)280232
e-mail: inncrown@googlemail.com
Website: www.thecrowninn.org

   AE

Oakham JHB, Greene King IPA, Golden Crown Bitter, Barnwell Bitter, Black Sheep and Tydd Steam Barn Ale

With its 17C honey-stone walls, charming thatched roof and lovely location in a delightful country parish, The Crown Inn really is a good old-fashioned pub. To start, sup a cask ale beside the characterful inglenook fireplace in the bar, then head through to the cosy dining room, large octagonal conservatory or out onto the spacious decked terrace. The same seasonally changing menu is served throughout, featuring old British favourites such as steak and ale pie or Lancashire hotpot, and often several dishes of a more Mediterranean persuasion. To finish, try the swan-shaped profiterole which swims on chocolate sauce. Individually designed bedrooms come in a mix of classic and modern styles; some have four-posters, sleigh beds or roll-top baths.

Closing times
Closed 1-7 January, Sunday dinner and Monday lunch

Prices
Meals: £ 15 (lunch) and a la carte £ 15/30

5 rooms: £ 60/120

6 mi southwest of Peterborough by A1139, A605 and minor road north. Parking and on village green opposite.

Hemingford Grey

8 The Cock

47 High St,
Hemingford Grey, PE28 9BJ
Tel.: (01480)463609
e-mail: cock@cambscuisine.com
Website: www.cambscuisine.com

Wolf Golden Jackal, Nethergate IPA, Pot Belly Beijing Black and Tyddsteam Barnale

As you approach this 17C country pub you'll come across two doors: one marked 'Pub', leading to a split-level bar and the other marked 'Restaurant', leading to a spacious L-shaped dining room. Run by an experienced team, it has a homely feel, with warm fabrics, comfy seating and attractively papered walls throughout. In winter, the best spot is beside the fire and in summer, the most pleasant is by the French windows. Cooking rests firmly on the tried-and-tested side of things, with classic pub staples such as lamb shank and belly pork; good value set lunches; and a list of daily changing fish specials. A tempting sausage board also offers an appealing mix and match selection of several varieties of homemade sausage, mashed potato and sauces.

Closing times
Open daily

Prices
Meals: £ 16 (lunch Monday-Saturday) and a la carte £ 22/31

Typical Dishes
Duck parcel with sweet & sour cucumber
Chump of lamb & pearl barley bake
Coriander & hazelnut cheesecake

5 mi southeast of Huntingdon by A 1198 off A 14. Parking.

9 Crown and Punchbowl

High St,
Horningsea, CB25 9JG
Tel.: (01223)860643
e-mail: info@thecrownandpunchbowl.co.uk
Website: www.thecrownandpunchbowl.co.uk

VISA MC AE

Hobson's Choice

This is more of a dining than a drinking establishment, as despite the fact that it's a pub, there's no real bar area. In relation to the fairly formal service, the place itself is surprisingly homely, with its wooden beams, simple furniture and pleasant conservatory, terrace and gardens. To start, you'll be brought a board of olives and ciabatta, and to finish, homemade fudge. In between, you'll find a real mix of dishes: some British, some European; some old classics, some with a more ambitious edge – such as confit leg of pheasant with chestnut mash. There's also a tasty mix and match sausage menu and a daily fish board, which could include halibut with beetroot and bouillabaisse sauce. Bedrooms are simple, tidy and handy for the airport.

Closing times
Closed 26-30 December, Sunday dinner and bank holiday Monday dinner

Prices
Meals: £ 19/40

5 rooms: £ 74/95

4 mi northeast of Cambridge by A1303 and B1047 on Horningsea rd. Parking.

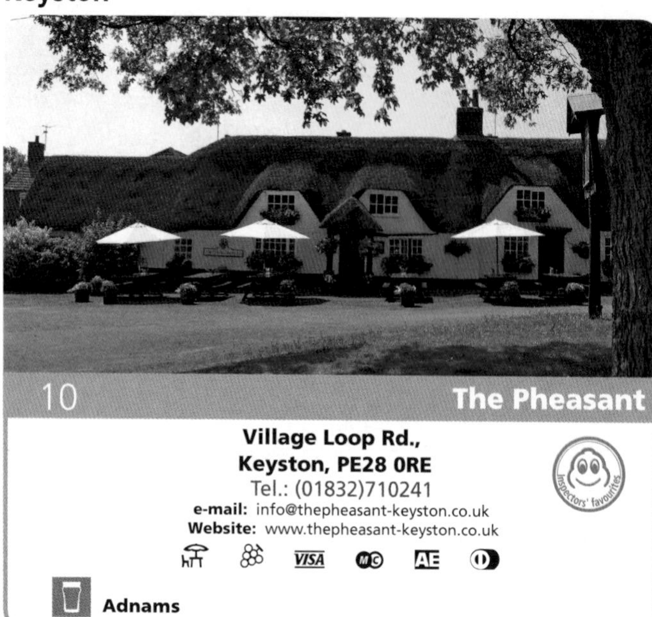

10 The Pheasant

Village Loop Rd.,
Keyston, PE28 0RE
Tel.: (01832)710241
e-mail: info@thepheasant-keyston.co.uk
Website: www.thepheasant-keyston.co.uk

VISA AE

Inspectors' favourites

Adnams

Since the former managers took over, this charming thatched pub has gone from strength to strength, despite becoming less 'village local' and more 'destination dining pub'. Set in a sleepy little hamlet and framed by colourful flowers, it offers the choice of classic or contemporary dining rooms. Flip over the daily changing menu and you'll find an explanation of what's in season, who supplied it and a glossary of terms. Flip it back and you'll find tasty homemade bread and hors d'oeuvres, followed by maybe a classic coq au vin or more international Thai black bream salad. One of the chefs spent time at London's St John restaurant, so you'll also find kidneys, ribs, tongues and hearts; the trimmings going into the popular pheasant burger.

Closing times
Closed Sunday dinner
booking essential

Prices
Meals: £ 20 (lunch)
and a la carte £ 28/32

Typical Dishes
Dorset crab & blood orange salad
Veal chop with sautéed new potatoes
Chocolate three-ways

Signposted off junction 15 of A 14. Parking.

11 The Hole in the Wall

2 High St,
Little Wilbraham, CB21 5JY
Tel.: (01223)812282
e-mail: jenniferleeton@btconnect.com
Website: www.the-holeinthewall.com

VISA MC

Woodforde's Wherry, Milton Brewery's Tiki and Old Cannon's Rusty Gun

It may be off the beaten track but that doesn't mean this pub has lost touch with the culinary world; far from it, in fact – and others would do well to follow in its footsteps. Many people look on this as an 'occasion' type of place but you're more than welcome to pop in just for a snack or a bowl of soup. The same menu is served throughout, offering traditional English cooking in flavoursome dishes, with local produce used wherever possible – and if you don't have time to visit the other 'hole in the wall', don't worry, the lunchtime à la carte provides particularly good value. The 15C part of the building boasts characterful low beamed ceilings, so mind your head or make for the more recently built, sympathetically designed extension.

Closing times
Closed 2 weeks in January, 2 weeks in September, 25 December, 26 December dinner, Sunday dinner and Monday

Prices
Meals: a la carte £ 21/34

Typical Dishes
Twice-baked broccoli & goat's cheese soufflé
Pork cutlet with haggis & potato cake
Rhubarb & Bramley apple crumble

5 mi east of Cambridge by A 1303 and minor road south. Parking.

Madingley

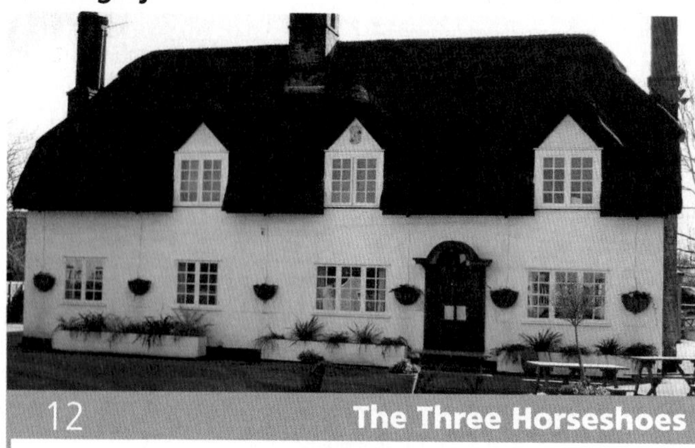

12 The Three Horseshoes

High St,
Madingley, CB23 8AB
Tel.: (01954)210221 – Fax: (01954)212043
e-mail: 3hs@btconnect.com
Website: www.threehorseshoesmadingley.co.uk

VISA AE

Adnams Southwold Bitter, Everards Tiger and City of Cambridge

Set in a pretty village – famous for its stunning Hall – this pub, with its whitewashed walls and attractive thatched roof, fits right in. To the front, scrubbed wooden furniture is set beside a welcoming fireplace and small bar; to the rear, a more formal linen-laid conservatory with Lloyd Loom chairs looks out over the garden. The bar menu offers pork scratchings, olives and a concise three course selection, while the daily changing Italian à la carte – part written in Italian – features straightforward combinations and uncluttered, tasty dishes; maybe linguine di cozze or agnello arrosto. The bustling bar has a great atmosphere, not dissimilar to a trattoria, so if you're looking for a romantic table for two, make for the conservatory.

Closing times
Open daily
booking advisable

Prices
Meals: a la carte £ 23/40

Typical Dishes
Soft polenta with sausage sauce, tomato & parmesan
Chargrilled Loch Duart salmon with peas & lentils
Lemon tart & raspberry sorbet

4.5 mi west of Cambridge by A 1303. Parking.

13 Village Bar (at Bell Inn)

Great North Rd,
Stilton, PE7 3RA
Tel.: (01733)241066 – Fax: (01733)245173
e-mail: reception@thebellstilton.co.uk
Website: www.thebellstilton.co.uk

Greene King IPA, Fuller's London Pride, Oakham Ales' Bishop Farewell and Digfield's Fools Nook

It's hard to believe that this sleepy market town is just minutes off the A1, or that this 17C inn – famous as the birthplace of Stilton cheese – is set on what was once the most popular coaching route from York to London. Look closely however, and you can still see the distances to the major cities inscribed on what was the original archway from the road to the stables. Step inside and you have the choice of a characterful bar or more modern bistro setting. Classically based dishes are a step above your usual pub fare, so you might find wild boar and cranberry terrine, followed by grey mullet on tomato risotto or Label Anglais chicken with parsnip potato pancakes. Cosy, traditionally styled bedrooms can be found in the adjoining inn.

Closing times
Closed 25 December

Prices
Meals: £ 17/30
and a la carte £ 19/29

4 mi south of Peterborough by A 15; in centre of village. Parking.

Sutton Gault

14 **The Anchor Inn**

Sutton Gault,
CB6 2BD
Tel.: (01353)778537 – Fax: (01353)776180
e-mail: anchorinn@popmail.bta.com
Website: www.anchor-inn-restaurant.co.uk

  VISA  AE

Weekly rotating guest ales including Hobsons Choice, Pegasus, Dionysus

It may seem like a strange name for a pub that's nowhere near the coast – but it does have some watery connections. Built in 1650, this building was originally used to house the workers who created the Hundred Foot Wash in order to alleviate flooding in the fens. If you fancy a river view, head for the wood panelled rooms to the front of the bar, where you'll discover a pleasant outlook and a tempting menu, which might include smoked eel, pork loin in Parma ham, tea-infused duck or the house speciality of grilled dates wrapped in bacon. There are always some fish specials chalked on the board and occasionally dishes such as oxen or zebra from the nearby Denham Estate. Neat, pine furnished bedrooms include two suites; one boasts river views.

Closing times
Closed dinner 25-26 December and 1 January

Prices
Meals: £ 16 (lunch) and a la carte £ 20/30

4 rooms: £ 60/130

Off B 1381; from Sutton village follow signs to Sutton Gault; pub is beside the New Bedford River. Parking.

15 **Axe & Compasses**

Dunmow Rd,
Aythorpe Roding, CM6 1PP
Tel.: (01279)876648 – Fax: (01279)876254
e-mail: axeandcompasses@msn.com
Website: www.theaxeandcompasses.co.uk

  VISA

 **Nethergate, Suffolk County, Sharp's Doom Bar and several guest ales**

Comforting childhood dishes like faggots and peas, corned beef hash and treacle tart, and hearty pub favourites like steak and ale pie and toad in the hole form the nucleus of this pub's varied menus. Since the owners are Essex born and bred, their tasty and attractively presented food is fruit of the fertile local landscape; from the Leigh-on-Sea cockles to the rack of lamb and the rib of beef. The owners wanted the Axe & Compasses to be a proper British pub and the building's characterful cottage style – complete with part-thatched roof and white picket fence – certainly lends itself to the job. Inside the décor follows suit, with exposed brick, plaster and wooden beams – plus a display of saucy seaside postcards in the gents.

Closing times
Closed 26 December

Prices
Meals: a la carte £ 22/25

Typical Dishes
Cromer crab on toast
Steak & kidney pudding
Black cherry & chocolate sundae

 *6 mi south of Great Dunmow by B 184 and minor road east. Parking.*

Clavering

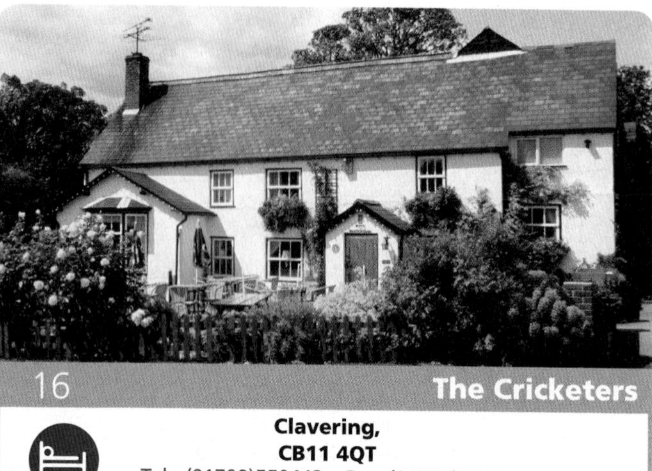

16

The Cricketers

Clavering,
CB11 4QT
Tel.: (01799)550442 – Fax: (01799)550882
e-mail: info@thecricketers.co.uk
Website: www.thecricketers.co.uk

VISA MC AE

Adnams Bitter and Broadside, Woodforde and Nethergate

Set in a charming village, this attractive whitewashed pub exudes old-world charm aplenty. Rustic brick walls and ancient wood beams are complemented by contemporary furnishings and stylish fittings, and there's a welcoming feel about the place. Cosy up beside the fire in the bar or head to the restaurant for a touch more formality. One menu is served throughout – priced per dish in the bar and per course in the restaurant – and cooking is precise, flavoursome and simply presented; with the odd Italian touch thrown in. Local produce is key, so you'll find plenty of regional meats, fresh fish and veg from son Jamie Oliver's garden. Bedrooms are split between the courtyard and pavilion: the former, simple and modern; the latter, more traditional.

Closing times
Closed 25-26 December

Prices
Meals: £ 30 (dinner)
and a la carte £ 25/30

14 rooms: £ 65/110

Typical Dishes
Bruschetta of buffalo mozzarella & tomato
Fillet of gurnard fish & asparagus
Baked coffee cheesecake

6 mi southwest of Saffron Walden on B 1038. Parking.

17 **The Sun Inn**

High St,
Dedham, CO7 6DF
Tel.: (01206)323351
e-mail: office@thesuninndedham.com
Website: www.thesuninndedham.com

VISA MC AE

Adnams Broadside, Brewers Gold, Earl Soham and Cliff Quay Bitter

Set in an idyllic village in the heart of Constable Country, this brightly painted pub offers guests a slice of sun even when the skies are cloudy and grey. Log fires create a cosy feel, there's a superb burr elm bar counter, a two-tiered dining room and a pleasant garden and terrace. At lunchtime, the bar board tempts with a selection of doorstop sandwiches, terrines and tarts. The à la carte lists its simple, tasty dishes in Italian, followed by their English translation – if you don't mind sharing, try the antipasti; options like lamb stew or pan-fried ox liver mean you can keep your meal all to yourself. Five contemporary bedrooms provide a restful night's slumber; Elsa, with its four-poster, is named after the resident ghost.

Closing times
Closed 25-26 December

Prices
Meals: £ 14 and a la carte £ 18/30

5 rooms: £ 70/150

7 mi northeast of Colchester by A 137 and minor road; in the centre of the village opposite the church. Parking.

Great Easton

18 The Green Man

Mile End Green,
Great Easton, CM6 2DN
Tel.: (01371)852285 – Fax: (01371)852261
e-mail: info@thegreenmanrestaurant.com
Website: www.thegreenmanrestaurant.com

 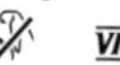  VISA

 **Greene King IPA**

This low slung, cottage style pub is as immaculate inside as it is out, with a contemporary, minimalist look. The original roof and wall beams have been retained, as has the large inglenook fireplace; there's a formal linen-clad restaurant, a neat garden and sun-splashed terrace. Although there are dishes like fish and chips or sausage and mash alongside sandwiches on the lunch menu, the kitchen has loftier ambitions in the evenings, with some interesting styles and flavours; maybe scallops with pea and mint gnocchi to start and slow roasted belly pork set on roasted fennel and chilli as a main course. Desserts are of the classic variety; perhaps plum and apple crumble or chocolate tart. Attentive, assured service completes the experience.

Closing times
Closed two weeks in January, Sunday dinner and Monday

Prices
Meals: a la carte £ 26/36

Typical Dishes
Pan-fried scallops & black pudding
Halibut with tomato & cockle broth
Lemon cheesecake & berry compote

 *2.5 mi north of Great Dunmow by A 184. Parking.*

19 The Bell

High Rd,
Horndon-on-the-Hill, SS17 8LD
Tel.: (01375)642463 – Fax: (01375)361611
e-mail: info@bell-inn.co.uk
Website: www.bell-inn.co.uk

VISA MC AE

Greene King IPA, Bass, Crouch Vale Brewers Gold, Sharp's Eden, Sharp's Doom Bar

If you're wondering about the hot cross buns, the story goes that past landlord Jack Turnell took over the pub on Good Friday, whereupon he nailed a bun to one of the beams; since then, a bun has been added every year – the cement version marking the wartime rationing. The Bell has been run by the same family for the last 50 years, although dates back nearly 12 times that. Drinkers will find themselves at home in the wood-panelled bar, while diners can choose from a beamed area or more formal restaurant. Cooking uses quality produce to create classically based dishes with a modern touch; maybe apple tart with a glass of malted milkshake. Bedrooms are styled after famous Victorian mistresses; those in Hill House display thoughtful extras.

Closing times
Closed 25-26 December and Bank Holiday Mondays

Prices
Meals: a la carte £ 22/33

15 rooms: £ 70/119

Typical Dishes
Smoked haddock Scotch egg, mussel & prawn chowder
Roast Priors Hall suckling pig
Glazed lemon tart

3 mi northeast of Grays by A 1013 off A 13. Parking.

20 The Mistley Thorn

High St,
Mistley, CO11 1HE
Tel.: (01206)392821 – Fax: (01206)390122
e-mail: info@mistleythorn.com
Website: www.mistleythorn.com

VISA MC

Hardwich Bitter, Adnams

Set opposite the River Stour in the small coastal village of Mistley, this early 18C coaching inn has become something of a local institution. Simplicity is the key here: the brightly coloured walls filled with local art create a stylish yet homely feel and the cooking is of a similarly comforting yet flavoursome vein. Tasty foccacia and fruity olive oil kick things off, followed by anything from burgers, fishcakes and steaks through to soufflés, terrines and shellfish – the tempting specials often featuring game or fish. If you look closely, there's the odd reference to owner Sherri's American/Italian childhood and her Mom's Cheesecake with homemade ice cream is now a permanent fixture. Simple, wood-furnished bedrooms; some with river views.

Closing times
Open daily

Prices
Meals: £ 15 and a la carte £ 18/26

5 rooms: £ 60/110

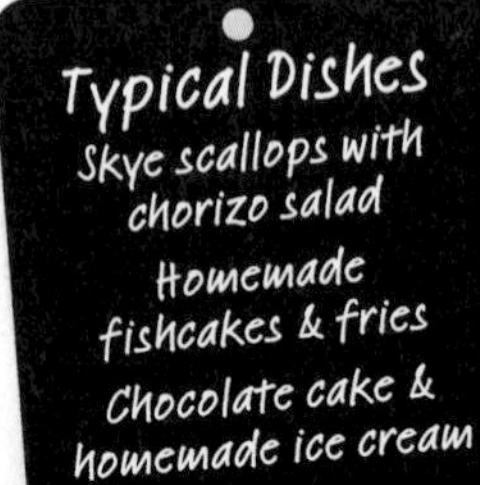

9 mi northeast of Colchester by A 137 and B 1352; not far from Mistley Towers. Parking.

21 The Compasses at Pattiswick

Compasses Rd,
Pattiswick, CM77 8BG
Tel.: (01376)561322 – Fax: (01376)564343
e-mail: info@thecompassesatpattiswick.co.uk
Website: www.thecompassesatpattiswick.co.uk

  MC

 **Adnams Gunhill, Woodforde's Wherry and Everards Tiger**

The Compasses started life as two estate workers' cottages. Now a smart pub, it boasts walls filled with Hugo Fircks artwork and a small counter selling meats, pâté and dips; but it's the cheery staff who really make the place. The best spot is in the barn-style restaurant, although spaces on the terrace are sought after too. Set weekday menus represent the best value but there's also the monthly changing à la carte and daily specials to consider; you might find pork pies or Welsh rarebit at lunchtime and braised lamb shank or seared tuna steak in the evening. Cooking is honest, simple and well done, with a huge amount of effort put into sourcing local ingredients. Venison is from the woods behind; pheasant and partridge, from local shoots.

Closing times
Open daily

Prices
Meals: a la carte £ 22/35

Typical Dishes
Chicken liver parfait & toasted brioche
Grilled plaice & new potatoes
Chocolate fridge cake

 *4 mi east of Braintree by A 120 and a minor road north. Parking.*

22 The Woodmans Arms

Rayleigh Rd,
Thundersley, SS7 3TA
Tel.: (01268)775799 – Fax: (01268)590689
e-mail: thewoodmans@hotmail.co.uk
Website: www.thewoodmansarms.co.uk

VISA MC

Greene King IPA and Black Sheep

Sometimes when a pub starts to serve good food, its drinkers – ergo the locals – get somewhat sidelined; not so at The Woodmans Arms, where at least half the pub is dedicated to those supping pints and sipping wine, with large comfy sofas and bucket chairs to accommodate them. The smart restaurant is decorated with old black and white photos; half screens cleverly separate the drinkers from the diners and a cheery young team see to the needs of all. The seasonal dishes are hearty and flavourful, and whilst traditional in the main – perhaps roast fillet of salmon or beer battered haddock – the menu might also include a Malaysian chicken salad or Cajan spiced whitebait. Lunchtime sees lighter choices such as baked potato or Welsh rarebit.

Closing times
Open daily

Prices
Meals: a la carte £ 18/28

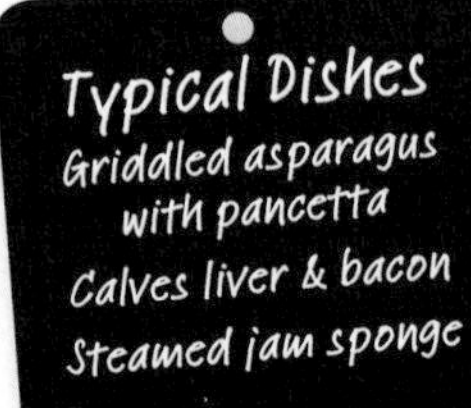

Between Basildon and Southend-on-Sea off A 127. Parking.

23 The Bull of Cottered

Cottered,
SG9 9QP
Tel.: (01763)281243
e-mail: cordell39@btinternet.com

 **IPA and Abbot Ale**

Set right in the heart of the village, it's hard to miss this pub, especially in the summer months when freshly planted tubs shine brightly against its whitewashed walls. Inside there's a warm, homely feel to the place; if you've missed a spot at the coveted alcove table in the bar, head through to the traditional dining room, or still further to the garden, which provides the perfect suntrap. Food at The Bull is satisfyingly unfussy and unpretentious. Lunchtime is geared towards snacks and light bites, featuring particularly tasty homemade burgers and some tempting ploughman's variations; while at dinner the selection of hearty main courses includes Scotch beef and steaks, as well as a daily changing fish dish entitled 'The Blue Plate'.

Closing times
Open daily
Prices
Meals: a la carte £ 25/35

Typical Dishes
Pan-seared King scallops & prawns
Fillet of sea bass with potatoes
Chocolate torte

6 mi southeast of Baldock by A 507; in the centre of the village. Parking at the front of the pub.

24 The Tilbury

Watton Rd,
Datchworth, SG3 6TB
Tel.: (01438)815550 – Fax: (01438)718340
e-mail: info@thetilbury.co.uk
Website: www.thetilbury.co.uk

VISA MC AE

Brakspear Oxford Gold, Bitter and Wychwood

Chef Paul Bloxham now seems to spend more time behind the stoves at The Tilbury than on TV, save for the odd appearance on Market Kitchen – and for the pub, that can only be a good thing. Owners Paul and Paul know where it's at when it comes to local, seasonal produce and the cover of the menu will reassure any sceptic, listing the ingredients that will feature each month, alongside their provenance and other ethical considerations they take into account when sourcing produce. The menu itself is a real mix, ranging from classical aged rib-eye to more adventurous stuffed lobster and scallop sea bass. If you like getting involved, they run cookery classes; if not, just sit back among the modern artwork or beside the roaring fire and enjoy.

Closing times
Closed Sunday dinner

Prices
Meals: £ 18/23
and a la carte £ 24/35

Typical Dishes

Scallop, chorizo & Jerusalem artichoke bruschetta

Guinea fowl in a jar & sauerkraut

Chocolate pot with doughnuts

4 mi southeast by A 602 from Stevenage and minor road south. Parking.

25 The Bricklayers Arms

Hogpits Bottom,
Flaunden, HP3 0PH
Tel.: (01442)833322 – Fax: (01442)834841
e-mail: goodfood@bricklayersarms.com
Website: www.bricklayersarms.com

VISA MC AE

Fuller's London Pride, Greene King IPA, Rebellion Nuts, Jack O' Legs and Tring

This pub is tucked away by itself on the outer reaches of a small hamlet, so you'll need a good navigator when trying to find it. Part-built in 1722, it was originally two cottages, before becoming a butcher's, a blacksmith's and later, an alehouse. Inside it's rather smart, with polished tables and fresh flowers everywhere; the areas to the side of the bar being more formally laid than those in front. This isn't the place for a quick snack (a glance at the menu will show there are none), but somewhere serving good old-fashioned, French-inspired dishes. The home-smoked meats and fish have become signature dishes and Sunday lunch is a real family affair. If you've only time for a fleeting visit, have a hearty pudding on the spacious terrace.

Closing times
Open daily
Prices
Meals: a la carte £ 24/35

4 mi north of Rickmansworth by A 404 and a minor road north. Parking.

Frithsden

26 The Alford Arms

Frithsden,
HP1 3DD
Tel.: (01442)864480 – Fax: (01442)876893
e-mail: info@alfordarmsfrithsden.co.uk
Website: www.alfordarmsfrithsden.co.uk

VISA MC AE

Marston's Pedigree, Flowers Original, Brakspear, Marlow Rebellion and Sharp's Doom Bar

Set among the network of paths that run across the Chilterns, this attractive Victorian pub is a popular destination for hikers – and when you're trying to squeeze your car into a tight space on the narrow country lane, arriving by foot may suddenly seem the better option. A pleasant garden overlooks the peaceful village green – where you might spot the odd Morris dancer or two – and the warm bar welcomes four-legged friends as equally as their owners. The traditional menu has a strong British stamp and follows the seasons closely, so you're likely to find salads and fish in summer and comforting meat or game dishes in winter; these might include belly pork with sticky parsnips, lamb and rabbit shepherd's pie or a tempting blackboard special.

Closing times
Closed 25-26 December

Prices
Meals: a la carte £ 20/27

Typical Dishes
Herb-crusted Ashridge rabbit croquettes
Chicken & black pudding suet pudding
Lemon & thyme posset with crème fraîche ice-cream

4.5 mi northwest of Hemel Hempstead by A 4146.
By the village green. Parking.

27 Fox and Hounds

2 High St,
Hunsdon, SG12 8NH
Tel.: (01279)843999
e-mail: info@foxandhounds-hunsdon.co.uk
Website: www.foxandhounds-hunsdon.co.uk

  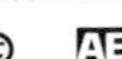

Adnams Bitter, Adnams Broadside and guest ale Red Squirrel Brewery

London to Hertfordshire isn't the biggest of moves but swapping the hustle and bustle of crowded streets for the peace and quiet of the countryside is a move that childhood sweethearts James and Bianca – now husband and wife – believe is well worth making. They play a very hands-on role, with him hard at work in the kitchen and her leading the team our front. If the weather's good, sit in the garden or on the terrace; if not, find a spot in the pleasant bar or dining room. Menus are short and simple, displaying unfussy, cleanly prepared dishes which arrive in generous portions. Styles range from braised oxtail to mackerel teriyaki – and there are always a few options available in two sizes. They serve some rather good organic fruit juices too.

Closing times
Closed 26 December, Sunday dinner and Monday except bank holiday lunch

Prices
Meals: £ 14 and a la carte £ 25/40

5 mi east of Ware by B 1004 to Widford and B 180 south. Parking.

28 **The Sun at Northaw**

1 Judges Hill,
Northaw, EN6 4NL
Tel.: (01707)655507
e-mail: info@thesunatnorthaw.co.uk
Website: www.thesunatnorthaw.co.uk

Adnam's Broadside, Red Squirrel Conservation, Gluntingford Golden Plover and Buntingford Highwayman

This restored 16C pub sits by the village green. Deceptively spacious, it's contemporary in style, with a traditional edge. Cooking is hearty and classical, with a comfort food element, so expect to find dishes like ham hock terrine or fish pie, as well as half lobsters and steaks on the seasonal menu. There's a regional slant here: an East England map shows the provenance of various ingredients, there are local ales and ciders behind the bar, as well as some English bottles on the wine list and the toilet walls are even papered with Ordnance Survey maps of the area. Service is friendly but lacks any real sense of urgency – although the pub's affectionate spaniel, Smudge, might well wander over and welcome you if the staff are too busy.

Closing times
Closed Sunday dinner and Monday

Prices
Meals: £ 29 (Sunday) and a la carte £ 25/35

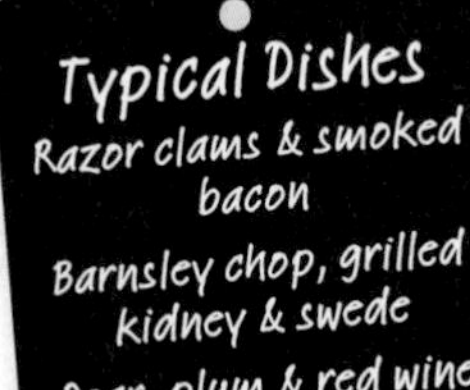

Beside village green on main road through the village. Parking.

29 The Cabinet at Reed

High St,
Reed, SG8 8AH
Tel.: (01763)848366
e-mail: thecabinet@btconnect.com
Website: www.thecabinetatreed.co.uk

VISA MC AE

Woodforde's Wherry, Fullers London Pride, Timothy Taylor and regularly changing guest beer

Set foot in Reed and you'll be transported back to days of old, when houses were surrounded by moats and the pub was the hub of the village. The houses are now ringed by large grass verges but all roads still lead to The Cabinet. Behind its white clapperboard exterior this pub hides a delightful brick-floored snug, a cosy open-fired bar and a small, simply laid restaurant. There's an air of informality about the place which is echoed in the menus, so you'll find a list of dishes that the owners would like to eat themselves. Cooking is flavoursome but dishes aren't always what they seem, as traditional recipes are given a more modern twist. The set lunches provide particularly good value and the warming casseroles and pies are a hit in winter.

Closing times
Closed 26 December, 1 January and Monday

Prices
Meals: £ 15/25
and a la carte £ 25/45

Typical Dishes
Home-smoked salmon
Pan-fried duck with garlic beans & potato galette
Rhubarb crème brûlée

3 mi south of Royston by A 10 and side road east. Parking.

30 **The Blue Anchor**

145 Fishpool St,
St Albans, AL3 4RY
Tel.: (01727)855038
e-mail: info@theblueanchorstalbans.co.uk
Website: www.theblueanchorstalbans.co.uk

 **McMullens IPA, McMullens Country bitter and Rusty Anchor**

The Blue Anchor is a relative newcomer to the Hertfordshire pub scene; although owner Paul Bloxham – TV chef and owner of sister pub, The Tilbury – is no stranger to the trade. The pub is nicely set, close to the historic city centre, opposite Verulamium Park, and boasts a pleasant pub-meets-bistro style. The front bar is the most atmospheric of the rooms but on a sunny day head for the lovely garden, which runs right down to the River Ver. Paul has a passion for seeking out the best local producers and letting the seasons inform his cooking, so you'll find top notch ingredients and plenty of homemade and home-smoked products. Dishes are rustic and robust, and even the simplest offerings are taken seriously. Service is chirpy and swift.

Closing times
Closed Sunday dinner and Monday

Prices
Meals: a la carte £ 20/29

Typical Dishes
Razor clams with chilli, lemon & garlic
South Devon sirloin steak & chips
Jelly & ice cream

 *Off the High St past the cathedral. Parking.*

31 **The Fox**

Willian,
SG6 2AE
Tel.: (01462)480233 – Fax: (01462)676966
e-mail: info@foxatwillian.co.uk
Website: www.foxatwillian.co.uk

  VISA

 **Adnam's Best Bitter, Woodforde's Wherry, Fuller's London Pride and Buntingford Polar Star**

Set right in the heart of the village, this bright, airy pub is extremely popular. At lunchtime, drinkers and diners vie for tables in the bar, while in the evenings the local drinkers pull rank and those wanting a meal head for the dining room. Light wood floors and matching furniture feature throughout and the keener eye will notice a host of subtle references to Norfolk – home to the owner's other two pubs. Crisps and olives are provided while you study the menu and tasty homemade chocolates finish things off. There's plenty of seafood on offer here, with the likes of haddock rarebit, black bream or herb-crusted cod and always a good choice of game in season. For those who just can't decide, 'The Fox Slate' provides the perfect solution.

Closing times
Closed Sunday dinner

Prices
Meals: a la carte £ 20/34

Typical Dishes
Sacombe Hill farm rabbit & confit chicken ballottine
Butter-roasted fillet of brill
Chocolate dessert trio

 *3 mi northeast of Hitchin by A 505 and side road. Parking.*

Blakeney

32 **The White Horse**

4 High St,
Blakeney, NR25 7AL
Tel.: (01263)740574
e-mail: info@blakeneywhitehorse.co.uk
Website: www.blakeneywhitehorse.co.uk

   AE

Adnams, Adnams Broadside, Woodforde's Wherry, Yetmans

Maybe you've spent the afternoon wandering the beautiful north Norfolk coastline, spotting the various species of bird that flock along the marshes, or on a boat trip out to Blakeney Point to see the seals basking on the sandbanks. The invigorating sea air will no doubt have stoked your appetite, so head for something hearty to eat at this brick and flint former coaching inn. The same à la carte menu is served in all areas and changes according to what's freshly available and in season. Dishes might include grilled lemon sole or pot roast suckling pig, with puddings like hot chocolate fondant or crème brûlée. Bedrooms have modern facilities and come in various shapes and sizes; some decorated in the bright blues and yellows of the seaside.

Closing times
Closed 25 December
Prices
Meals: a la carte £ 20/35
9 rooms: £ 60/140

Typical Dishes
Smoked eel & ham hock terrine
Lamb shoulder confit
Baked espresso cheesecake

Off A 149 following signs for the Quay, beside the church. Parking.

33 The Jolly Sailors

Brancaster Staithe,
PE31 8BJ
Tel.: (01485)210314
e-mail: info@jollysailorbrancaster.co.uk
Website: www.jollysailorbrancaster.co.uk

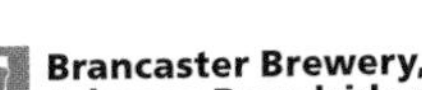

Brancaster Brewery, Woodeforde's Wherry, Adnams Broadside and various guest beers

Already the owner of two successful pubs, Clifford Nye decided to add a more casual younger sister to his collection. Arranged around a central courtyard, The Jolly Sailors is a refreshing break from the norm – retaining much of its original rustic character despite having been spruced up. The open fire provides a focal point and the 'Children, Dogs and Well Behaved Parents' sign reminds you all are welcome. The menu is simple but it works well: there's a selection of baguettes, ploughman's and light bites, as well as freshly made pizzas – with a create your own option – and a selection of main dishes that could include curry or liver and bacon. There's also a pie and fish of the day, and usually some local oysters from the beds out front.

Closing times
Open daily

Prices
Meals: a la carte £ 14/25

2 mi west of Burnham Market by A 149. Parking.

34

The White Horse

Brancaster Staithe,
PE31 8BY
Tel.: (01485)210262 – Fax: (01485)210930
e-mail: reception@whitehorsebrancaster.co.uk
Website: www.whitehorsebrancaster.co.uk

VISA

Woodforde's Wherry, Adnam's Best Bitter, Brancaster Best

With glorious views over the Brancaster Marshes and Scolt Head Island, a seat on this pub's sunny back terrace or in the spacious rear conservatory is a must. If the tables here are all taken, then the landscaped front terrace may not have the views, but it's got the parasols, the heaters and the lights to make up for it. Foodwise, the oft-changing menus provide ample choice, with a seafood slant that takes in local Cromer crab, Brancaster oysters, mussels and fish from the boats at the end of the car park. The pub's popularity means that service can sometimes suffer under the strain but with the coastal views to provide a distraction you might not even notice. Bedrooms are comfy; those in the rear extension each have their own terrace.

Closing times
Open daily
booking essential

Prices
Meals: a la carte £ 19/31
15 rooms: £ 75/130

Typical Dishes
Local Oysters, natural or tempura
Homemade bouillabaisse & saffron new potatoes
White Horse lemon tart

On A 149 Hunstanton to Wells rd. Parking.

35 The Hoste Arms

The Green,
Burnham Market, PE31 8HD
Tel.: (01328)738777
e-mail: emma@hostearms.co.uk
Website: www.hostearms.co.uk

VISA

Woodforde's Wherry and Nelson's Revenge, Abbot Ale

This extended 17C inn has plenty of space in which to dine, including a rustic bar with leather sofas, an informal conservatory and an enclosed rear garden and terrace. Menus are classically based but have global influences, so expect dishes like Thai fish broth or Natal lamb curry with basmati rice alongside roasted rack of lamb or steak and kidney pudding. Local produce is well used, so you'll find the oysters are from Loose's in nearby Brancaster, the steak comes from Arthur Howell butchers and the seafood and fish are from Lowestoft. The young staff are friendly and polite but when the place gets busy service can slow quite dramatically. Stylish, comfortable bedrooms in and around the hotel include the eye-catching Zulu wing.

Closing times
Open daily
booking essential

Prices
Meals: a la carte £ 23/37

Overlooking the green. Parking.

36 **The Crown Inn**

The Green,
East Rudham, PE31 8RD
Tel.: (01485)528530
e-mail: reception@thecrowninnnorfolk.co.uk
Website: www.thecrowninnnorfolk.co.uk

VISA

Adnams

The owner of this 15C pub may be a Kiwi but he is well aware of what a rich seam there is to be mined in Norfolk in terms of food supplies, so as you tuck into generous helpings of tasty dishes like seared sea bass or honey glazed pork fillet, you can rest assured that none of the ingredients had to travel too far to reach your plate; perhaps from Wells-next-the-Sea, like the fresh fish, or neighbouring West Rudham, like the asparagus. Original features including a 14ft fireplace sit alongside more contemporary comforts like large leather sofas, perfect for pre-dinner drinks in the snug. For a private gathering, the upstairs Buffalo Room, with its vast collection of books, is ideal. Comfortable bedrooms with modern bathrooms complete the look.

Closing times
Open daily

Prices
Meals: a la carte £ 21/30
6 rooms: £ 70/150

Between King's Lynn and Fakenham on A 148. Parking.

37 **The Hunny Bell**

The Green,
Hunworth, NR24 2AA
Tel.: (01263)712300
e-mail: hunnybell@animalinns.co.uk
Website: www.hunnybell.co.uk

Adnam's Best, Woodforde and Green King

Following a sympathetic renovation and extension, this 18C whitewashed pub with its smart country interior looks the bee's knees. Exposed brickwork, stone flooring and restored wooden beams are offset by bold modern feature walls, and there's an appealing conservatory and smart wood-furnished patio overlooking the green. The owners' experience really shines through, resulting in a keenly priced, seasonal menu that's modern-European meets traditional pub. For main course you might discover local pork sausages or sage-roast chicken breast, while at either end of the meal the chef proudly presents homemade breads and sorbets. The baby of the Animal Inns family, it is as sound as a bell and 'Hunny' is sure to be the buzz word for miles around.

Closing times
Closed 25 December

Prices
Meals: a la carte £ 20/30

2.5 mi south by B 1149 from Holt. Parking.

Ingham

38 The Ingham Swan

Sea Palling Rd,
Ingham, NR12 9AB
Tel.: (01692)581099
e-mail: dt.smith@live.co.uk
Website: www.theinghamswan.co.uk

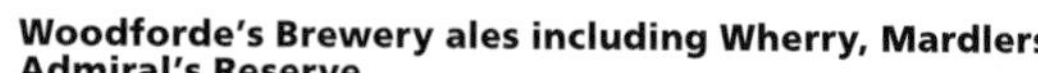

Woodforde's Brewery ales including Wherry, Mardlers, Admiral's Reserve

This attractive thatched pub, dating from the 14C and sitting in the shadow of a fine 11C church, lies in a small hamlet known for its delightful cricket field – all in all, a charming scene of English pastoral splendour. The cosy beamed interior is equally characterful and while this is clearly more of a dining pub, drinkers are still welcome. The one area which does break with tradition is the cooking, which is far from straightforward but clearly skilled; dishes are made up of many ingredients, albeit in classic combinations, and presentation adopts a contemporary style; even the simple burger is elevated to something a lot more exotic. Bedrooms are a little too modest for us to recommend at this stage.

Closing times
Closed Sunday dinner and Monday lunch
booking essential at dinner

Prices
Meals: £ 16/20
and a la carte £ 20/38

Typical Dishes
Ràs al-hànout pork belly
Fillet of sea bass with asparagus & sautéed potatoes
Cheesecake panna cotta & white chocolate sorbet

In the centre of the village. Parking.

39 **The Walpole Arms**

The Common,
Itteringham, NR11 7AR
Tel.: (01263)587258 – Fax: (01263)587074
e-mail: goodfood@thewalpolearms.co.uk
Website: www.thewalpolearms.co.uk

 **Adnams Bitter and Broadside, Woodforde's Wherry and one weekly changing guest ale**

This red-brick inn has all the old-fashioned charm of one who has been providing hospitality since the 18C. The Mediterranean-influenced menus are modified daily, as dictated by suppliers and seasons, with tasty, well-prepared dishes such as baby octopus in red wine and tomato sauce or escabeche of red mullet to start, followed by fillet of salmon with saffron mash, Morston mussels or sauté of veal with potato gratin. The formal restaurant, with its low ceilings and clothed tables, makes a becoming backdrop for a dinner date; the gardens and terrace are great come summer, while the rustic, beamed bar is definitely the most characterful seat in the house. If you're after something light to eat, the snack menu of pub classics will oblige.

Closing times
Closed 25 December and Sunday dinner

Prices
Meals: a la carte £ 21/28

Typical Dishes
Crab & filo tart, pickled cucumbers & pea shoots
Confit of duck leg with potatoes & pancetta
Strawberry royal tart & frozen strawberry yoghurt

 *5 mi northwest of Aylsham by B 1354; signed The Common. Parking.*

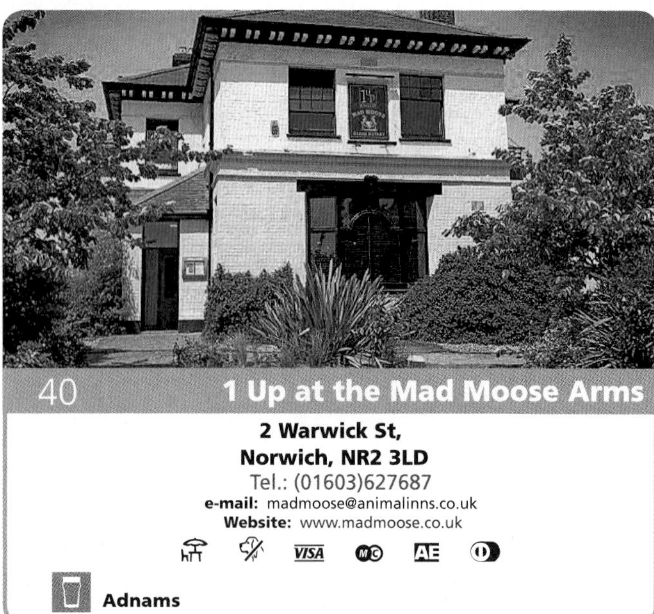

40 1 Up at the Mad Moose Arms

2 Warwick St,
Norwich, NR2 3LD
Tel.: (01603)627687
e-mail: madmoose@animalinns.co.uk
Website: www.madmoose.co.uk

VISA MC AE

Adnams

The Mad Moose Arms is very much a neighbourhood haunt and you're likely to find the locals in their droves as you step through the doorway. It's a 'proper' pub, with cosy burgundy walls, plenty of tables and a busy, buzzy atmosphere; even more so during match times, when you'll find excited groups clustered around the TVs. Large blackboards list an enticing array of dishes that range from light bites to substantial pub favourites – but if you're after something a little more formal, head upstairs. Here you'll find period chairs set around smartly laid tables, bold silvery wallpaper, gilt chandeliers and an interesting menu of more ambitious, classically based dishes. Presentation is modern; amuse bouches and pre-desserts also feature.

Closing times
Closed 25 December

Prices
Meals: £ 28 (dinner) and a la carte £ 20/30

Typical Dishes
Potted Suffolk pork & toasted brioche
Wild mushroom & Jerusalem artichoke millefeuille
Dark chocolate terrine with glazed bananas

Off Unthank road. Local on street parking.

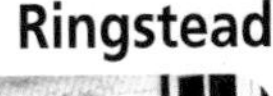

41 **The Gin Trap Inn**

6 High St,
Ringstead, PE36 5JU
Tel.: (01485)525264
e-mail: thegintrap@hotmail.co.uk
Website: www.gintrapinn.co.uk

  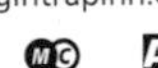

 **Woodforde's Wherry, Adnams Bitter and various rotating guests ales - Tom Woods, Elgoods**

Two ploughs hanging on the front walls of this attractive whitewashed inn remind you of its 17C origins, as does the cosy front bar with its traditional quarry tile floor, wood burner and beams. Locals still congregate here with their dogs, but it's no longer packed with gin traps, as once was the case; the link to the pub's name now provided by the more modern juniper berry logo. Another contemporary addition is the spacious wood-floored conservatory with its stylish wood tables and leather-effect chairs, which overlooks the garden. Dishes are well-presented, flavoursome and good value, with choices such as game terrine, sausage and mash, pot roasted lamb shoulder or fried sea bass. Bedrooms boast wrought iron beds and roll top baths.

Closing times
Open daily
Prices
Meals: a la carte £ 20/28
3 rooms: £ 49/140

Typical Dishes
Thornham oysters
Beer-battered haddock fillet, handcut chips
Buttermilk panna cotta & mulled wine berries

 *3.5 mi east of Hunstanton by A 149. Parking.*

Snettisham

42 The Rose and Crown

Old Church Rd,
Snettisham, PE31 7LX
Tel.: (01485)541382 – Fax: (01485)543172
e-mail: info@roseandcrownsnettisham.co.uk
Website: www.roseandcrownsnettisham.co.uk

Adnams Best, Broadside, Woodforde's Wherry and one regularly changing guest ale

Its warren of rooms and passageways, uneven floors and low beamed ceilings place the Rose and Crown squarely into the quintessentially English bracket of inns; the larger dining rooms, the paved terrace and the children's play area in the garden add some 21C zing to the pub's 14C roots. Cooking is gutsy by nature and makes good use of local produce, with neatly presented dishes such as peppered tuna carpaccio or pan-roast salmon on offer alongside trusty classics like sausage and mash or steak and chips. Service is efficient, they are well used to being busy and a good crowd of locals from the village can often be found enjoying a tipple or two at the bar. Bedrooms are quite a contrast to the rustic pub: light, airy and modern in style.

Closing times
Open daily

Prices
Meals: a la carte £ 20/30
16 rooms: £ 75/130

In the middle of the village. Parking.

43 Wildebeest Arms

82-86 Norwich Rd,
Stoke Holy Cross, NR14 8QJ
Tel.: (01508)492497 – Fax: (01508)494946
e-mail: wildebeest@animalinns.co.uk
Website: www.thewildebeest.co.uk

Inspectors' favourites

   AE

 **Adnams Best Bitter**

With its wicker fence and chairs, tribal tree trunk tables and wild animal artefacts, this pub offers a taste of the African savannah in the unlikely setting of Norfolk. Despite the pub's exotic undertones, the food is more European in flavour, with seasonal main courses such as seared pigeon breast, rump of English lamb, and butternut squash, leek and parmesan risotto and desserts like vanilla panna cotta. Cooking is distinctly modern in style, with neatly presented dishes in well judged portions. The set lunch and dinner menus represent very good value for money and service comes from friendly, well organised staff who handle busy periods with aplomb. Should it begin to approach balmy African temperatures, head for the pleasant terrace.

Closing times
Closed 25-26 December
booking essential

Prices
Meals: £ 17/22
and a la carte £ 25/33

Typical Dishes
Confit duck & pancetta cake
Chargrilled farm chicken breast
Raspberry & almond Bakewell tart

 *Just off the A 140 5.5 mi south of Norwich. Parking.*

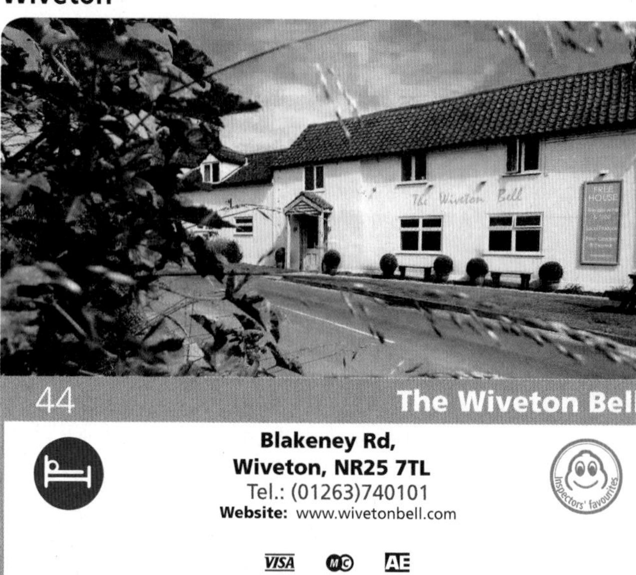

44 The Wiveton Bell

Blakeney Rd,
Wiveton, NR25 7TL
Tel.: (01263)740101
Website: www.wivetonbell.com

Inspectors' favourites

VISA MC AE

Woodforde's Wherry, Yetmans, Adnams Broadside

Situated in a beautiful area surrounded by salt marshes and nature reserves, The Wiveton Bell makes the ideal stop off point for walkers following the coastal path. The neatly kept garden provides a fantastic location for stargazing at night and hosts an attractive flower display by day; while inside the pub there's a comfy, modern bar leading to an airy conservatory – which is brightened yet further by a convivial atmosphere and the cheery team. Traditional menus offer salads, light meals and largely British-based dishes, alongside a few more international influences; you might find Thai fish cakes, Briston pork belly or fisherman's pie. Charming bedrooms come complete with a continental tuckbox, so keep your PJs on and have breakfast in bed.

Closing times
Closed 25 December
booking advisable

Prices
Meals: a la carte £ 18/30
2 rooms: £ 90/120

Typical Dishes
Morston mussels
Kelling Hall roast partridge
Chocolate torte

1 mi southeast by A 149 on Wiveton Rd from Blakeney. Parking.

45 **Queen's Head**

The Street,
Bramfield, IP19 9HT
Tel.: (01986)784214
e-mail: qhbfield@aol.com
Website: www.queensheadbramfield.co.uk

   AE

Adnams Bitter and Adnams Broadside

Run by a dedicated husband and wife team, this characterful, cream-washed pub has been in the family for more than 11 years. Set in the heart of a small country village beside an attractive thatched church, it boasts three rooms; the largest, with its high beamed ceiling and scrubbed tables opening out onto a flower-filled garden. The central bar has lots to catch the eye, with shelves crammed full of books and a selection of homemade preserves, chutneys and cakes for sale. There's a blackboard snack menu and a daily changing, classically based à la carte, which is formed around the latest local, seasonal and organic produce. Some Fridays you'll find local bands playing, while others are 'Paupers' evenings, when they offer a good value set menu.

Closing times
Open daily

Prices
Meals: a la carte £ 19/26

 *3 mi south of Halesworth on A 144. Parking.*

Bungay

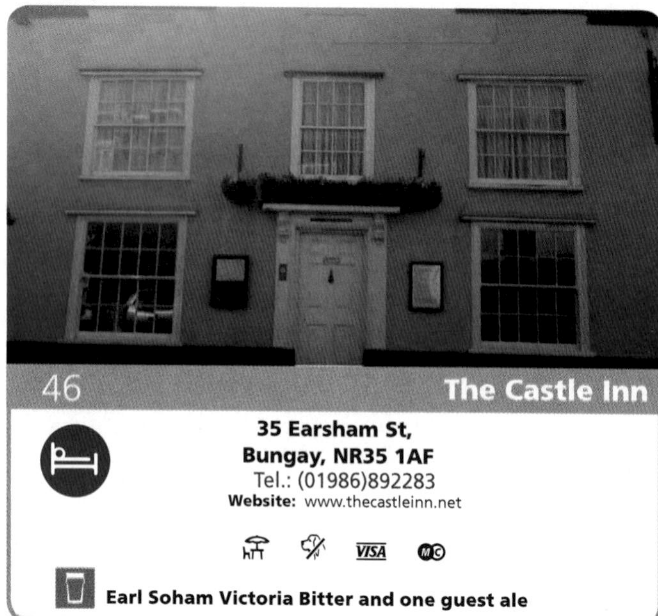

46 **The Castle Inn**

35 Earsham St,
Bungay, NR35 1AF
Tel.: (01986)892283
Website: www.thecastleinn.net

VISA

Earl Soham Victoria Bitter and one guest ale

This sky-blue pub's cosy interior takes in two main dining rooms and an intimate rear bar – perfect for a postprandial coffee, with its leather sofas and foodie magazines. Cooking is country based; fresh, simple and seasonal, and while lunchtime might see sausage and mash or fisherman's pie on offer alongside sandwiches, the evening menu might include pan-seared pigeon breast or duck leg confit. The Innkeeper's platter is a perennial favourite and showcases local produce, including a great pickle made by the Rocking Grannies – keep an eye out for the cake stands too, with their homemade cakes and cookies. Themed evenings include pie and wine night and film and food night, complete with popcorn. Bedrooms are homely, warm and comfortable.

Closing times
Closed Sunday dinner

Prices
Meals: £ 17 (lunch) and a la carte £ 17/30

4 rooms: £ 65/85

Typical Dishes
Brancaster mussels
Cassoulet of duck leg & Topcroft sausages
Date & sticky toffee pudding

5.5 mi west of Beccles by B 1062. Parking.

47 The Buxhall Crown

Mill Rd,
Buxhall, IP14 3DW
Tel.: (01449)736521
e-mail: thebuxhallcrown@hotmail.co.uk
Website: www.thebuxhallcrown.co.uk

Greene King IPA and Abbot, Old Speckled Hen, Olde Trip and fortnightly changing guest ales

This part-16C country pub is set off the beaten track, with a bright, yellow-painted dining room which looks out to Buxhall Windmill. Head down into the cosy, low beamed bar for beer straight from the barrel – while you're here take a look over the blackboard menu of seasonal dishes. These tend towards the classics so expect choices like rack of English lamb or steak and chips alongside pub favourites such as sausage and mash; at the weekends, when it's busier, they step things up a gear, adding a few more modern touches. There's a great value, weekly changing 2 course set menu, a decent selection of Suffolk cheeses and classic desserts like lemon tart; release your inner child with some fun puds featuring space dust and penny chews.

Closing times
Closed 25-26 December, Sunday dinner and Monday

Prices
Meals: £ 16 (lunch) and a la carte £ 20/35

Signposted off the B 1115 3.5 mi west of Stowmarket. Parking.

Levington

48 The Ship Inn

Church Ln,
Levington, IP10 0LQ
Tel.: (01473)659573 – Fax: (01473)659151

 **Adnams Best, Broadside and guest ales- Oyster, Mayday and Gunhill**

There may well be a new captain at the helm but it's steady as she goes for The Ship Inn. Reputedly built from ships' timbers, and crammed with nautical memorabilia, the small rooms of this characterful 14C pub soon fill up with customers but, as they don't take bookings, it's wise to arrive early. Start with dishes like stilton and leek tart or seared scallops, followed by pan-fried lemon sole or salmon and tiger prawn brochette. With its emphasis on local seafood, the menu changes daily, but there's always plenty of non-fish dishes too, from belly of Blythburgh pork to char-grilled rib-eye steak. On a warm day, the picnic tables are a great place from which to watch the distant boats; if it gets too draughty, try the rear terrace instead.

Closing times
Closed 25-26 December
bookings not accepted

Prices
Meals: a la carte £ 20/30

Typical Dishes
Sautéed tiger prawns & fregola pasta
Steak & Suffolk ale pie & roasted root vegetables
Pear & frangipane tart

 *Midway between Ipswich and Felixstowe signposted off A 14. Parking.*

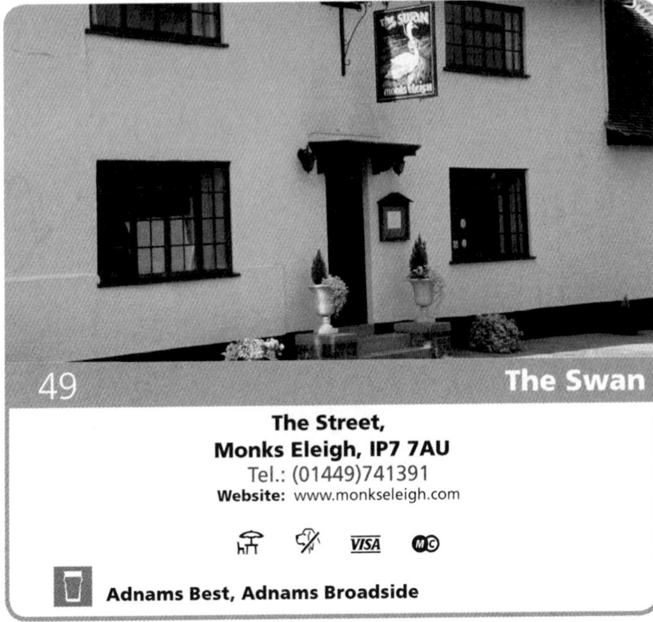

49 **The Swan**

The Street,
Monks Eleigh, IP7 7AU
Tel.: (01449)741391
Website: www.monkseleigh.com

VISA MC

Adnams Best, Adnams Broadside

The Swan's owners may originally hail from the north, but they have fully embraced their adopted home of East Anglia, and the wealth of produce the area offers provides ample inspiration for the frequently changing, seasonal menu of generous, flavourful dishes. Depending on the ingredients fresh in, these might include smoked haddock fish pie with creamy mash or lamb tagine with apricots, almonds and couscous, and – thanks to Nigel's background – often include a smattering of Italian influences. Everything is made on-site; from the bread and terrines to the classic British puddings and ice creams. The thatched pub's beamed interior is fresh and bright, and the bubbly Carol serves locals and newcomers alike with warmth and efficiency.

Closing times
Booking essential in summer and closed 25-26 December, Sunday dinner and Monday

Prices
Meals: £ 18 and a la carte £ 19/30

3.5 mi southeast of Lavenham on A 1141. Parking.

50 **The Crown Inn**

Bridge Rd,
Snape, IP17 1SL
Tel.: (01728)688324
e-mail: snapecrown@tiscali.co.uk
Website: www.snape-crown.co.uk

VISA MC AE

Adnams Bitter, Broadside and seasonal ales

With its low ceilings, open fires and mismatched wooden chairs, this characterful 400 year old building on the outskirts of the village really is a true country pub. It's not just local ingredients that you'll find on the menu but produce that's recently been picked from the owner's garden or plucked off his trees – and the eggs, milk and meats are equally as fresh, as they keep pigs, calves, goats, turkey, quail and rescued battery hens out the back. As you would expect, cooking is seasonal and simply done, with light bites on offer at lunch and more substantial dishes such as confit duck or rib-eye steak at dinner. The blackboard specials always include a market fish of the day and to finish, there's a selection of tasty nursery puddings.

Closing times
Open daily
Prices
Meals: a la carte £ 20/30

5 mi west of Aldeburgh by A 1094. Parking.

51 **The Crown**

90 High St ,
Southwold, IP18 6DP
Tel.: (01502)722275 – Fax: (01502)727263
e-mail: crown.hotel@adnams.co.uk
Website: www.adnams.co.uk

VISA AE

Adnams - Bitter, Broadside, Explorer

This 17C former coaching inn sits on the high street of a charming town, near to the brewery and only a hop, skip and a jump away from the sea. Its traditionally styled bar and dining room are often buzzing with diners and the small, oak-panelled, nautically themed locals bar is a great place for a leisurely pint or two of Adnams of an afternoon. The same modern, seasonal menu is served throughout: choose from dishes such as pan-fried sea bass, Cromer crab cakes, sausage and mash or cottage pie, with perhaps a sticky toffee pudding or some homemade ice cream for dessert. Arrive early to avoid disappointment, however, as they don't take bookings. Individually styled bedrooms have a contemporary feel; those towards the rear are the quietest.

Closing times
Open daily

Prices
Meals: a la carte £ 25/30

14 rooms: £ 95/165

Typical Dishes

Seared pigeon breast & golden raisin purée

Plaice, crushed celeriac & pickled wild mushrooms

Chocolate & beetroot ganache

In the town centre. Parking.

Stoke-by-Nayland

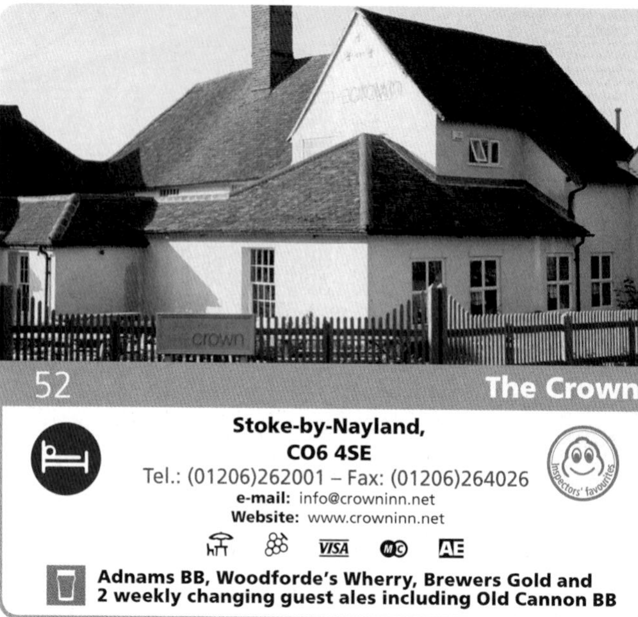

52 **The Crown**

Stoke-by-Nayland,
CO6 4SE
Tel.: (01206)262001 – Fax: (01206)264026
e-mail: info@crowninn.net
Website: www.crowninn.net

Inspectors' favourites

VISA AE

Adnams BB, Woodforde's Wherry, Brewers Gold and 2 weekly changing guest ales including Old Cannon BB

Set overlooking the Box and Stour river valleys, in a hillside village in the Dedham Vale, this substantial 16C pub is a lovely place to visit, with its large lawned gardens and a smart wood-furnished patio. Step inside and you'll find various little rooms and semi open-plan snugs, where wood and flag flooring gives way to boldly coloured walls. If you're into wine, there are over 30 by the glass; while a large glass-fronted room displays a selection of top quality bottles. Menus change every three weeks and feature the latest seasonal produce sourced from nearby farms and estates, supplemented by a daily catch and seafood specials. Spacious bedrooms take on either contemporary or country cottage styles; some have French windows and a terrace.

Closing times
Closed 25-26 December

Prices
Meals: a la carte £ 20/33
11 rooms: £ 75/200

In the centre of the village. Parking.

53 The Anchor

Main St,
Walberswick, IP18 6UA
Tel.: (01502)722112 – Fax: (01502)724464
e-mail: info@anchoratwalberswick.com
Website: www.anchoratwalberswick.com

VISA MC AE

Adnam's Bitter, Adnam's Broadside

Unusually for a pub, The Anchor is housed in an Arts and Crafts building. It's a welcoming, relaxing place, run by an enthusiastic, friendly team; there's a pleasant terrace and a path leading directly from the garden to the beach. But enough about the pub – for it's all about the food, wine and beer here. Owners Sophie and Mark are passionate about sourcing local, seasonal produce – with some ingredients even coming from their own allotment. Dishes are prepared with real care and global flavours punctuate the menu, so alongside British classics like fish and chips, you'll find Asian dressings, Indian spicing, tapas platters and risottos. Simple chalet bedrooms; breakfast like a king on choices such as smoked haddock and jugged kippers.

Closing times
Closed 25 December

Prices
Meals: a la carte £ 23/35
8 rooms: £ 85/110

In the centre of the village. Parking.

Westleton

54 **The Westleton Crown**

The Street,
Westleton, IP17 3AD
Tel.: (01728)648777 – Fax: (01728)648239
e-mail: info@westletoncrown.co.uk
Website: www.westletoncrown.co.uk

VISA

Adnams and two weekly changing guest ales including Nethergate

This good-looking red-brick 17C former coaching inn, set in a pretty little village, delivers what you'd expect and a little bit more. The bar welcomes you with its beams and open fires but venture a little further in and you'll find an attractive and surprisingly modern conservatory, as well as an appealing terrace and garden. Mercifully, the same seasonally pertinent menu is offered throughout, so you can eat your suet pudding or the more sophisticated breast of guinea fowl with confit spring roll anywhere you choose. Those staying overnight not only have their own pleasant sitting room but will find that the bedrooms, which are named after birds, come in a crisp, uncluttered style and have particularly luxurious bathrooms.

Closing times
Open daily

Prices
Meals: a la carte £ 23/36
34 rooms: £ 95/165

Typical Dishes
Blythburgh ham terrine & duck liver paté
Guinea fowl breast & confit spring roll
Pineapple & star anise tarte Tatin

In the centre of the village. Parking.

55 The White Horse

Rede Rd,
Whepstead, IP29 4SS
Tel.: (01284)735760
e-mail: di@whitehorsewhepstead.co.uk
Website: www.whitehorsewhepstead.co.uk

 **Adnam's BItter and guest ales including Broadside and Woodforde's Wherry**

The attractive copper-topped bar is the hub of this cheerfully run 17C village pub, not long refurbished. There are three further areas to choose from: to the left is a beamed and characterful room which fills up quickly; to the right the brighter Gallery, so named as its shows local artists' work; and, thirdly, a back room for larger parties which leads out to the large garden. But everyone likes to assemble in the bar to look at the large menu with each dish displayed on a separate blackboard. The kitchen's strength lies in the more conventional dishes like liver and bacon, grilled kippers and the pub's own homemade sausages. It's owned by a couple who established their reputation at The Beehive in nearby Horringer.

Closing times
Closed 25-26 December and Sunday dinner

Prices
Meals: a la carte £ 20/25

 *Well signposted off the A 143, 4.5 mi south of Bury St Edmunds. Parking.*

Woodbridge

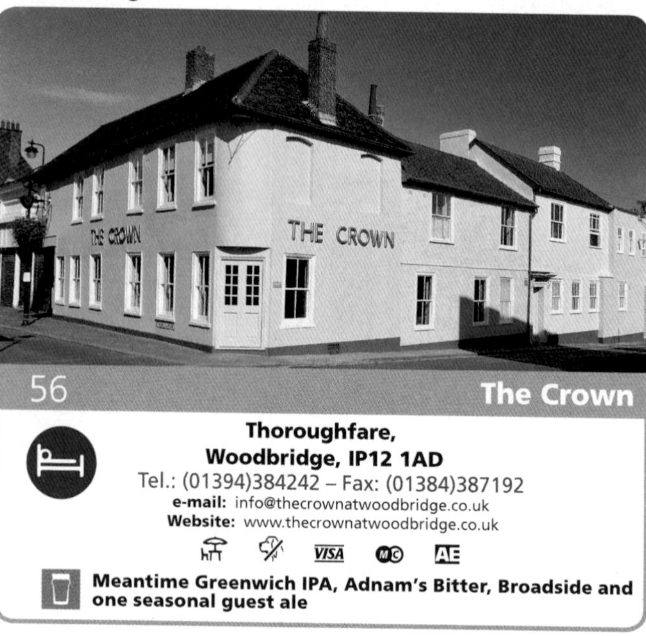

56 **The Crown**

Thoroughfare,
Woodbridge, IP12 1AD
Tel.: (01394)384242 – Fax: (01384)387192
e-mail: info@thecrownatwoodbridge.co.uk
Website: www.thecrownatwoodbridge.co.uk

VISA MC AE

Meantime Greenwich IPA, Adnam's Bitter, Broadside and one seasonal guest ale

With its farmers' markets and a main street full of restaurants and cafés, the delightful riverside town of Woodbridge is up there with the best of them when it comes to foodie credentials; and all the more so since the arrival of The Crown. After a top-to-toe, 21C makeover, this colourfully painted pub retains little evidence of its 17C roots; a glass-roofed, granite-floored bar sits at its centre, with four smart dining areas set around it. Bedrooms are stylish, with good facilities and service is polite and friendly, coping well when busy. The extensive menu offers everything from salads and starters like cockle and samphire fritters through to main dishes like meatballs, fish pie or duck. Look out for the skiff and the sporks.

Closing times
Closed dinner 25 December

Prices
Meals: a la carte £ 22/35

10 rooms: £ 95/180

Typical Dishes
Southend cockle & samphire fritters
Twice-cooked pig's cheeks & spinach
Cardamom panna cotta

At town centre crossroads. Parking.

Twenty-first century London may truly be called the definitive world city. Time zones radiate from Greenwich, and global finances zap round the Square Mile, while a vast smorgasbord of restaurants is the equal of anywhere on the planet. A stunning diversity of population now calls the capital its home, mixing and matching its time between the urban sprawl and enviable acres of green open space. From Roman settlement to banking centre to capital of a 19C empire, London's pulse has rarely missed a beat. Along the way, expansion has gobbled up surrounding villages, a piecemeal cocktail with its ingredients stirred to create the likes of Kensington and Chelsea, Highgate and Hampstead, Twickenham and Richmond. Apart from the great range of restaurants, London boasts over three and a half thousand pubs, many of which now see accomplished, creative cooking as an integral part of their existence and appeal. And you can find them sprinkled right the way across from zones one to five…

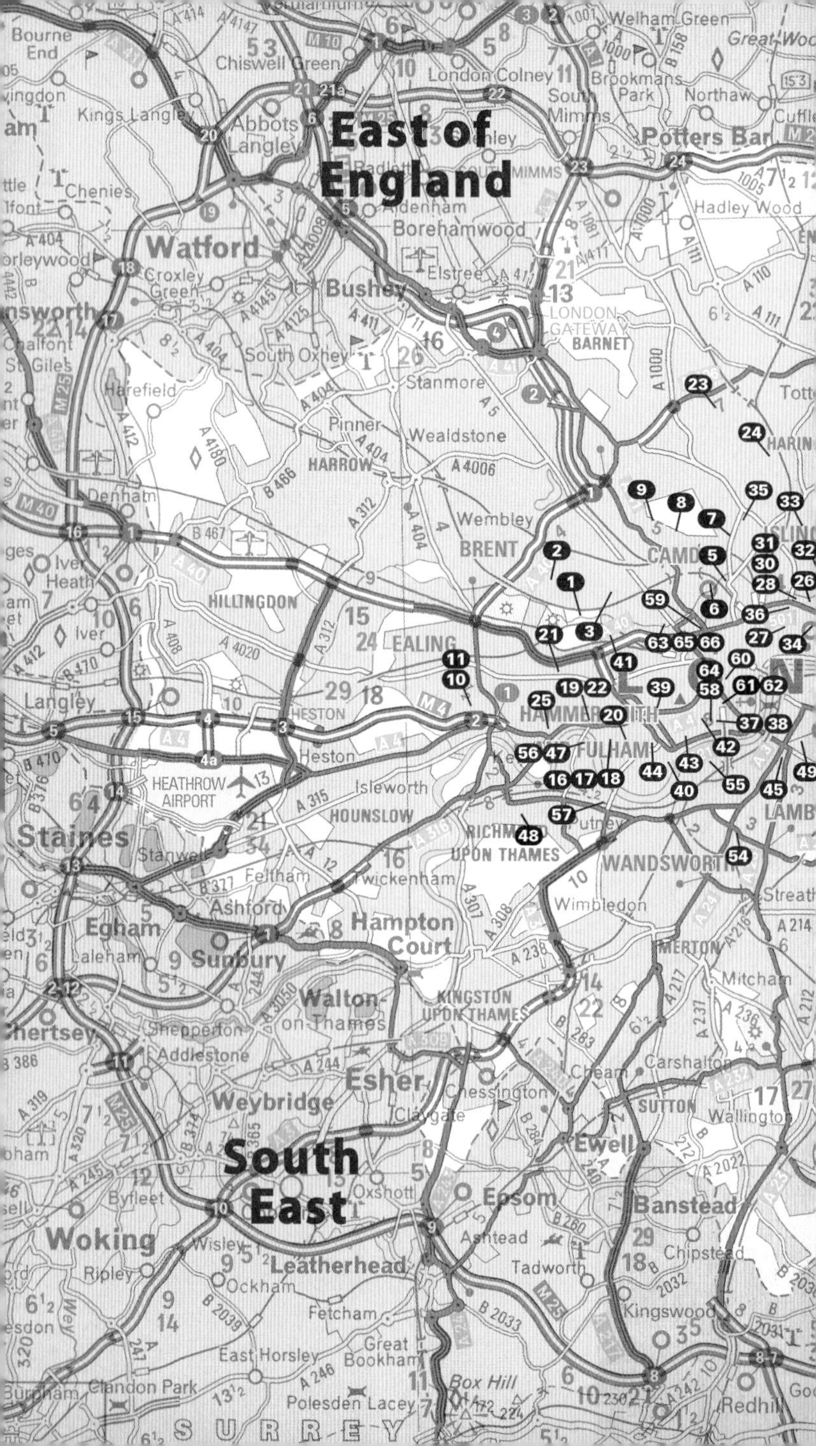

East of England
South East
Watford
Bushey
Borehamwood
Elstree
Potters Bar
Hadley Wood
London Colney
Chiswell Green
Kings Langley
Abbots Langley
Radlett
Aldenham
Chenies
Croxley Green
South Oxhey
Stanmore
Harefield
Pinner
Wealdstone
HARROW
Wembley
BRENT
Denham
HILLINGDON
EALING
Iver
Iver Heath
Langley
HESTON
Heston
HEATHROW AIRPORT
Isleworth
HOUNSLOW
Staines
Stanwell
Feltham
Twickenham
Ashford
Egham
Sunbury
Laleham
Hampton Court
Walton-on-Thames
Shepperton
Chertsey
Addlestone
Weybridge
Esher
Chessington
Claygate
KINGSTON UPON THAMES
RICHMOND UPON THAMES
WANDSWORTH
Wimbledon
Putney
HAMMERSMITH
FULHAM
CAMDEN
MERTON
Mitcham
Carshalton
SUTTON
Wallington
Cheam
Ewell
Epsom
Oxshott
Byfleet
Woking
Wisley
Ripley
Ockham
Leatherhead
Ashtead
Tadworth
Banstead
Chipstead
Kingswood
Fetcham
East Horsley
Great Bookham
Clandon Park
Polesden Lacey
Box Hill
Redhill
SURREY
LONDON GATEWAY
BARNET
Welham Green
Brookmans Park
Northaw
South Mimms
Cuffley
Bourne End
Chalfont St Giles
Streatham
LAMBETH

East of England
LONDON
South East
Epping
Cheshunt
Waltham Abbey
Loughton
Chigwell
Brentwood
Ilford
Hornchurch
Upminster
Dartford
Grays Thurrock
Northfleet
Swanscombe
Sidcup
Swanley
Orpington
Sevenoaks
Westerham
Oxted
Caterham
Warlingham
Biggin Hill
New Addington
West Wickham
Croydon
Bromley
Greenwich
Woolwich
Bexley
Erith
Dagenham
Barking
Havering
Sydenham
Lewisham
Hackney
Newham
Beckton
Blackwall Tunnel
Wrotham
Ightham
Borough Green
Mereworth
Shipbourne
Knole
Ightham Mote
Chartwell
Limpsfield
Crockham
Woldingham
Farningham
Eynsford
Wilmington
Darenth
Longfield
Hartley
Meopham
Ash
West Kingsdown
Otford
Sundridge
South Ockendon
Aveley
Bulphan
Ingrave
Pilgrims Hatch
Stapleford Abbotts
Abridge
Theydon Bois
N. Weald Bassett
High Ongar
Fyfield
Blackmore
Fryerning
Ingatestone
Chipping Ongar
Istead Rise
Dartford Crossing
Thurrock
Tilbury

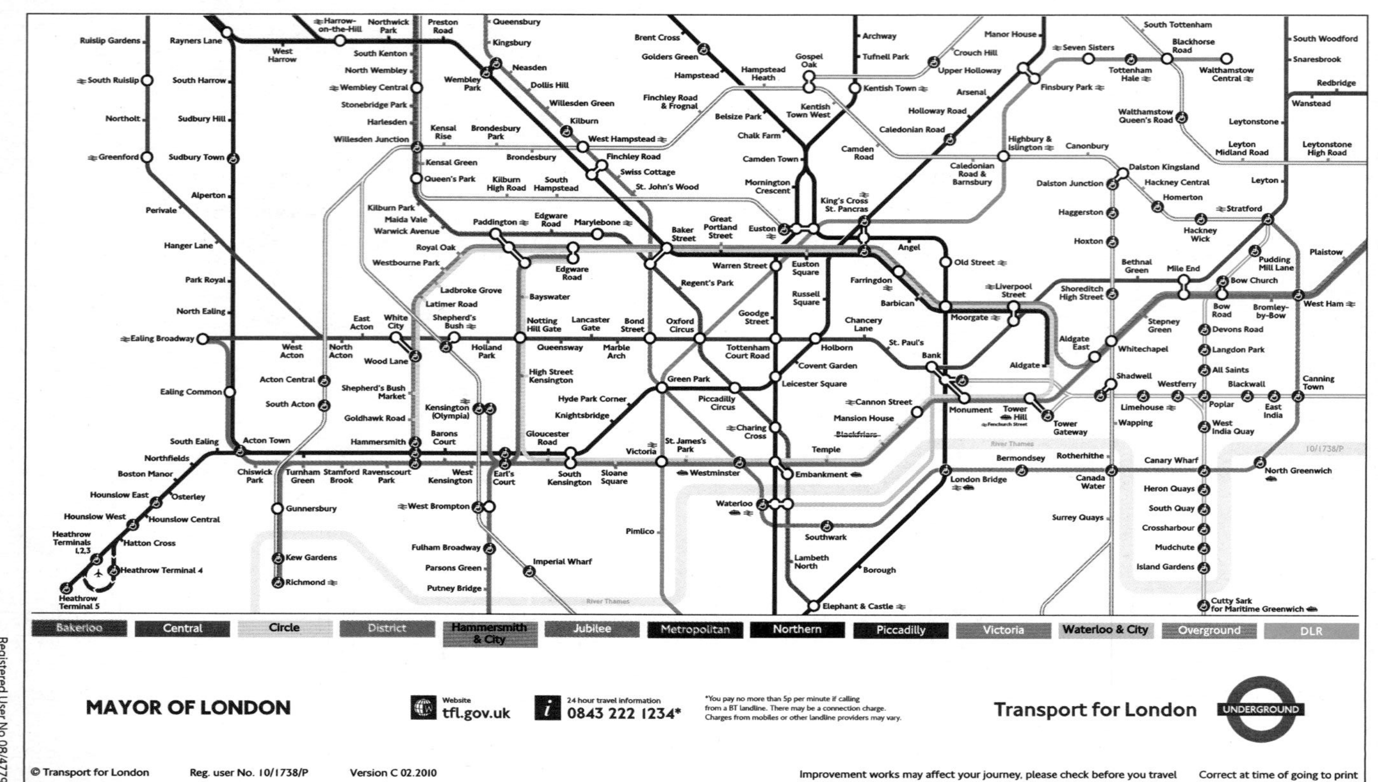

Registered User No 08/4779

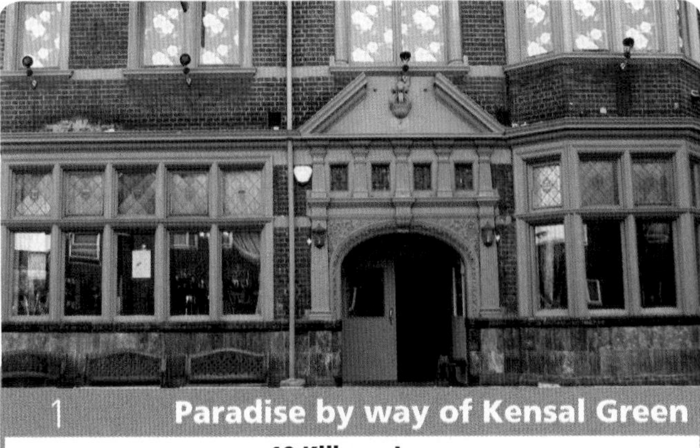

1 Paradise by way of Kensal Green

19 Kilburn Ln,
Kensal Green, W10 4AE
Tel.: (020)89690098
e-mail: caroline@thecolumbogroup.com
Website: www.theparadise.co.uk

VISA   

 **Charles Wells's Bombardier**

Their slogan is 'They love to party at Paradise' and, frankly, who can blame them? This is so much more than just a pub, it's a veritable fun palace – upstairs plays host to everything from comedy nights to film clubs and you can even 'host your own roast' with friends in a private room. If you're coming in to eat then grab a squashy sofa in the Reading room off the bar and share some of the terrific snacks; or sit in the dining room where the French-influenced cooking is showy but satisfyingly robust. Whether it's potted meats, terrines, chateaubriand or poached turbot, it's clear that this is a very capable kitchen. The atmosphere throughout is great and helped along in no small way by a clued-up team who know their food.

Closing times
Open daily

Prices
Meals: £ 25/30
and a la carte £ 28/40

Typical Dishes
Goosnargh smoked duck & celeriac remoulade
Pan-fried plaice & mash potatoes
Sticky toffee pudding

⊖ *Kensal Green.*

2 The Queensbury

110 Walm Ln,
Willesden Green, NW2 4RS
Tel.: (020)84520171
e-mail: info@thequeensbury.net
Website: www.thequeensbury.net

Young's London Gold, Eagle IPA, Winter Warmer, Directors, Castle Rock's Elsie Mo and Jennings' Snecklifter ales

The Conservative Club of Willesden Green have displayed a questionable lack of fiscal foresight because it's hard to sell off your building to a property developer when you've already offloaded the half that housed your snooker room and seen it turned into a pub. The inside hasn't changed much from when this was called The Green: a long narrow bar leading into a bright and open dining room, complete with antique mirrors. The blackboard menu blends pub numbers like pies and jerk chicken burgers with the more adventurous pork belly with chorizo; Parma ham with celeriac remoulade comes on a wooden board and desserts appear to be a strength of the kitchen. There's brunch at weekends and further snacky choices available in the bar.

Closing times
Open daily

Prices
Meals: a la carte £ 20/30

⊖ Willesden Green.

3 **The Salusbury**

50-52 Salusbury Rd,
Queen's Park, NW6 6NN
Tel.: (020)73283286
e-mail: thesalusburypub@btconnect.com

VISA 

 **Adnam's Broadside, Adnam's Bitter**

The Salusbury is a pleasingly down-to-earth pub; one side is for drinking, the other hosts a laid-back dining room. The Italian menu is a model of understatement and it's not until the food arrives that one realises how seriously this pub takes its cooking. There's plenty of choice, including about five pasta dishes that can be taken as starters or main courses. Dishes are as generous in size as they are in flavour. The crisp Sardinian guttiau bread comes with aubergine and pecorino and is a great way of starting proceedings; the pappardelle with the tender duck ragu is very tasty; an impressive array of fish go into the fritto misto and the tiramisu would shame many a smart Italian restaurant. The wine list offers plenty for under £20.

Closing times
Closed 25-26 December, 1 January and Monday lunch

Prices
Meals: £ 22/25

⊖ *Queens Park.*

4 Crown

**46 Plaistow Ln,
Sundridge Park, BR1 3PA**
Tel.: (020)84661313
e-mail: dine@thecrownsundridgepark.co.uk
Website: www.thecrownsundridgepark.co.uk

    VISA

 **Adnams Broadside, Meantime Brewery**

The owners have been moving steadily south: having started in Battersea, they then bought the Rosendale in West Dulwich and now it's Bromley's turn. The Crown is a stout and fetching Victorian fellow who has been transformed into a slick, contemporary dining pub. Midweek the menu is fairly unremarkable, in an understandable bid to avoid being labelled as a 'special occasion' destination – the death knell of many an establishment. At weekends the kitchen is allowed to express itself a little more and this is when you'll see rillettes and risottos, brûlées and parfaits. The owner is also passionate about wine and his list has over 300 bottles. The only shame is that you enter through the side – the main corner entrance is just for show.

Closing times
Closed Sunday dinner and Monday

Prices
Meals: £ 20 and a la carte £ 23/33

 ⊖ *Sundridge Park (rail).*

5 **Bull and Last**

168 Highgate Rd,
Dartmouth Park, NW5 1QS
Tel.: (020)72673641
e-mail: info@thebullandlast.co.uk
Website: www.thebullandlast.co.uk

 **Sharp's Doom Bar, Mad Goose, Deuchar's IPA and Black Sheep**

You'll be thankful that Parliament Hill is so close because you'll need the exercise – portions at the reinvigorated Bull and Last are man-sized and that man was clearly hungry. It was taken over in 2008 by the team behind Putney's Prince of Wales and they've kept plenty of character. It's bright and breezy and hugely popular so book first. Suppliers are name-checked on boards behind the bar which tells you they take their food seriously. Animals are taken whole and butchered accordingly so expect lots of terrines and homemade charcuterie, along with everything from oysters to smoked eel; the menu can change twice a day depending on available produce. There's an upstairs room used at weekends that's like a taxidermist's showroom.

Closing times
Closed 25 December
booking essential

Prices
Meals: a la carte £ 25/32

 *⊖ Tufnell Park. Free parking in the neighbourhood.*

6 The Engineer

65 Gloucester Ave,
Primrose Hill, NW1 8JH
Tel.: (020)77220950 – Fax: (020)74830592
e-mail: info@the-engineer.com
Website: www.the-engineer.com

 **Charles Wells Bombardier, St Peters Organic and Meantime Pale Ale**

Although speculation remains as to the identity of the original engineer, what is certain is that this is a great local, which is at the heart of the local community. It's divided equally between bar and dining room, with a terrific garden terrace to boot; and it's always busy, with occasional live music on Sundays adding to the fun. The reverse of the menu name checks the suppliers – always a reassuring act – and there are usually a couple of vegetarian options along with a separate menu of the day's specials. The steak and fabulous baker fries are a constant and cooking is wholesome and generally gutsy. The wine list is printed within old cartoon annuals; wines are decently priced and divided up according to their character.

Closing times
Open daily

Prices
Meals: a la carte £ 24/32

 *⊖ Chalk Farm. On street parking meters.*

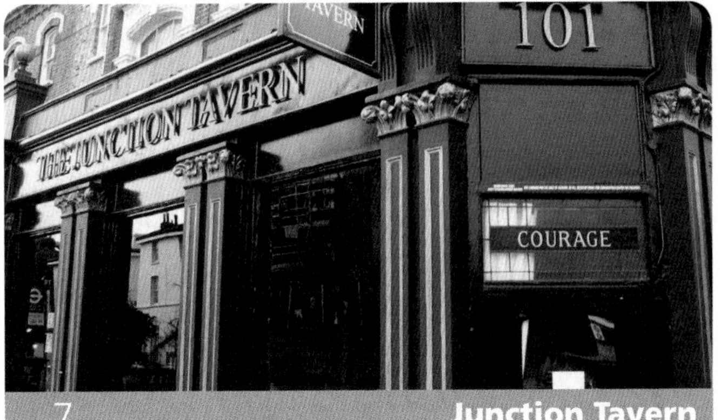

7 Junction Tavern

101 Fortess Rd,
Tufnell Park, NW5 1AG
Tel.: (020)74859400 – Fax: (020)74859401
Website: www.junctiontavern.co.uk

 **Sambrook's Wandle and 10-15 guest beers per week from independent regional brewers**

Over the years, Tufnell Park has appealed to young urban professionals because, along with its pretty Victorian terraces, it has a belligerent edge to add a little credibility. The Junction Tavern fits in well. The menu changes daily and portion size has been slightly reduced to give more balance to the menu as a whole; the cooking remains unfussy and relies on good flavours. There's plenty of choice, from light summer dishes such as grilled sardines and seared tuna to the more robust rib-eye and pork belly. Staff are a chatty bunch whose know their beers – they offer weekly changing guest beers and hold a popular beer festival; the 'pie and a pint' choice remains a favourite. Commendably, they also offer tap water without being prompted.

Closing times
Closed 24-26 December and 1 January

Prices
Meals: a la carte £ 23/30

 ⊖ *Tufnell Park. Pay & display parking in nearby streets.*

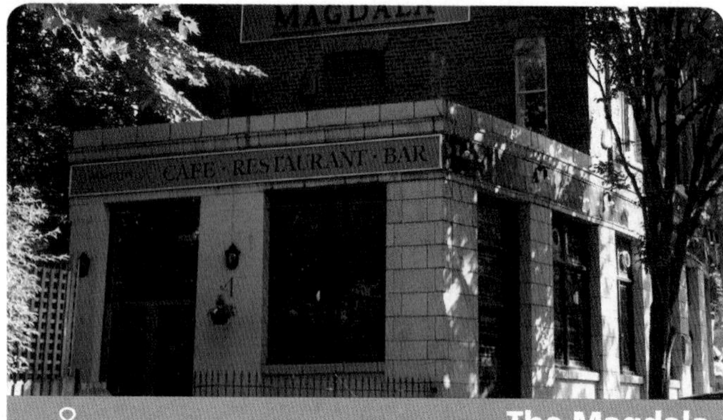

8 **The Magdala**

2A South Hill Park,
Hampstead, NW3 2SB
Tel.: (020)74352503 – Fax: (020)74356167
e-mail: themagdala@hotmail.co.uk
Website: www.the-magdala.com

 **Greene King IPA, Fuller's London Pride and twice weekly changing guest ales**

The Magdala is divided into three: on the right-hand side is the locals bar – you can eat here but not many do as it's a little dark and you'll feel like an impostor. Just go left, grab a seat anywhere and you'll be served. The third part of the operation is the upstairs, used as an extension at weekends or for hosting the monthly comedy club or fortnightly quiz. There's nothing on the menu to frighten the horses: there are burgers, sausages, paella and charcuterie plates or meze to share. However, the cooking is undertaken with greater care than you expect and you end up feeling as though you're in a country pub miles from the city. The owner certainly found a novel solution to the problem of keeping her chef – Reader, she married him.

Closing times
Open daily
Prices
Meals: a la carte £ 19/28

Typical Dishes
Confit Guinea fowl leg & mash
Oxtail & pearl onion pie
Sticky toffee pudding

 *⊖ Belsize Park. Pay & display parking outside the pub; heath car park 5 min walk.*

9

The Wells

30 Well Walk,
Hampstead, NW3 1BX
Tel.: (020)77943785
e-mail: info@thewellshampstead.co.uk
Website: www.thewellshampstead.co.uk

 **Adnams Broadside and Black Sheep**

London pubs can be loud, hysterical affairs but The Wells is a more sober beast, as one would expect from a pub in the middle of Hampstead village. Being so near the Heath makes it feel like a country pub but, then again, it's equally close to the High Street which adds a dose of urban poise. Downstairs is usually pretty busy but head up to the neat, first floor dining room that's divided into three, with the brightest - the blue room - looking down over the spring blossom. The cooking reflects the pub: it's hearty but with a sophisticated finish. You'll find duck confit or rump of lamb, scallops and wood pigeon but also veggie shepherd's pie and Sunday roasts. Puddings are big and they do a good apple and rhubarb crumble.

Closing times
Open daily

Prices
Meals: a la carte £ 28/38

Typical Dishes
Pork belly & pomme purée
Blackface Barnsley lamb chop
Apple & rhubarb crumble

 ⊖ Hampstead. Parking in Well Road.

10 The Bollo

13-15 Bollo Ln,
Acton Green, W4 5LR
Tel.: (020)89946037
e-mail: thebollohouse@btconnect.com
Website: www.thebollohouse.co.uk

Greene King - IPA, Abbot Ale and seasonal ales

The Bollo is a large, handsome Victorian pub whose glass cupola and oak panelling give it some substance and personality in this age of the generic pub makeover. Tables and sofas are scattered around in a relaxed, sit-where-you-want way. The menu changes as ingredients come and go; the kitchen appeals to its core voters by always including sufficient numbers of pub classics be they the Bollo Burger, the haddock or the fishcakes. But there is also a discernible southern Mediterranean influence to the menu, with regular appearances from the likes of chorizo, tzatziki, bruschetta and hummus. This is a pub where there's always either a promotion or an activity, whether that's the '50% off a main course' Monday or the Wednesday quiz nights.

Closing times
Open daily

Prices
Meals: a la carte £ 20/30

⊖ Chiswick Park. Parking meters.

11 **Duke of Sussex**

75 South Par,
Acton Green, W4 5LF
Tel.: (020)87428801
e-mail: thedukeofsussex@realpubs.co.uk

 **3 regularly changing guest ales**

This grand old Victorian Duke has been given a new lease of life by an enthusiastic pair of gastropub specialists. They've done it all up and, most importantly, introduced some very appealing menus. The best place to eat is in the back room, which was once a variety theatre and comes complete with proscenium arch and chandeliers. The menu is printed daily and the Spanish influence highlights where the chef's passions lie. Rustic and satisfying stews, whether fish or fabada, suit the place perfectly, as does a plate of cured meats or a tortilla; there are often dishes designed for sharing and on some evenings the kitchen will roast a boar or suckling pig. The wine list is short but affordable, with plenty available by the glass or carafe.

Closing times
Closed Monday lunch

Prices
Meals: a la carte £ 20/28

Typical Dishes
Duck hash cake & poached egg
Galician fish stew
Chocolate caramel tart

 *⊖ Chiswick Park. Parking on adjacent street.*

12 **Cat & Mutton**

76 Broadway Mkt,
Hackney, E8 4QJ
Tel.: (020)72545599 – Fax: (020)79861444
e-mail: catandmutton@yahoo.co.uk
Website: www.catandmutton.co.uk

VISA MC AE

Old Speckled Hen, Adnams Broadside, Bombardier

Four sets of doors provide your first challenge at this Victorian corner pub (clue: it's the smallest that allows access). Inside, the high counter means the bar staff tower over you when you're ordering a drink and the place has a worn and slightly scruffy feel that seemingly appeals to a young crowd, many of whom are often accompanied by their dogs and/or laptops. The relatively concise menu changes weekly; the cooking is straightforward but is also undertaken with more care than you expect. So you'll find the dishes deliver on flavour, whether it's a pie, crumble, pan-fried fish or something on toast. Quiz nights and art classes in an upstairs room, reached via the spiral staircase, add to the neighbourhood feel.

Closing times
Closed 25-26 December

Prices
Meals: a la carte £ 20/31

Typical Dishes

Creamed leeks with morcilla

Mussels with smoked haddock & bacon

Orange marmalade bread and butter pudding

⊖ *Bethnal Green.*

13 The Empress of India

130 Lauriston Rd,
Victoria Park, Hackney, E9 7LH
Tel.: (020)85335123
e-mail: info@theempressofindia.com
Website: www.theempressofindia.com

    AE

 **Adnams BItter and Broadside**

Built in the 1880s, The Empress of India has enjoyed a variety of incarnations over the years which include time as a nightclub and print works. But in 2006 it was restored by the Martin brothers and now it's hard to imagine the place being anything other than this family-friendly pub with a stoutly British menu. As well as restoring the pub's original name, they have kitted it out with mosaics, murals and photos commemorating Queen Victoria and the British Raj – but just beware of that Bengal tiger. The menu triumphs the British provenance of its meats, poultry and game, many of which are spit-roasted. Hams are cured in-house and while some dishes don't always deliver on the promise of the menu, the more robust choices won't disappoint.

Closing times
Closed 25 December

Prices
Meals: a la carte £ 24/35

 ⊖ *Mile End. On-street parking meters.*

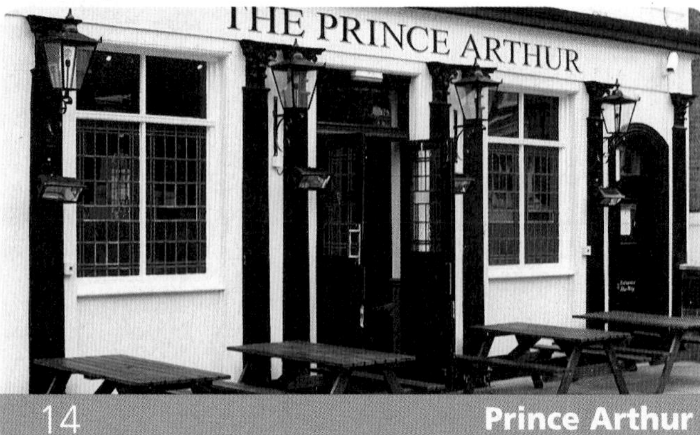

14 Prince Arthur

95 Forest Rd,
Hackney, E8 3BH
Tel.: (020)72499996 – Fax: (020)72497074
e-mail: info@theprincearthurlondonfields.com
Website: www.theprincearthurlondonfields.com

   AE

 **Fuller's London Pride, Deuchar's IPA**

Those who judge by first impressions will probably walk on by as this slightly scruffy corner pub would struggle to entice anyone on looks alone. To be honest, the inside isn't much keener on the eye, apart from the stuffed animals and the postcard collection, but then this isn't about appearances, more about good food and convivial company. Sit anywhere in the U-shaped room and the amiable staff will be quick to come over. The menu reads appealingly: smoked salmon, terrines, fish and chips, sausage and mash – but the cooking is done with unexpected care and more than a little skill; fish from Billingsgate is handled particularly deftly. Just thinking about the deep-fried jam or cherry sandwich for dessert will be enough to seal an artery.

Closing times
Closed 25 December and Monday-Thursday lunch

Prices
Meals: a la carte £ 22/32

 ⊖ *Bethnal Green.*

15 The Princess of Shoreditch

76-78 Paul St,
Shoreditch, EC2A 4NE
Tel.: (020)77299270
e-mail: info@theprincessofshoreditch.com
Website: www.theprincessofshoreditch.com

VISA MC AE

Meantime London Pale Ale and Sambrooks Wandle

The old girl may change hands now and then but she remains as popular as ever. The ground floor is your proper pub; drinkers are the mainstay but they get an appealing and appropriate menu where platters of sausage, charcuterie and cheese are the highlights, along with pies of the cottage or pork variety. For more mellow surroundings follow the fairy lights up to a warm, candlelit room. Here, the menu displays greater ambition. The cooking is more European in its influence and, despite the occasional affected presentation, it's clear the kitchen has confidence and ability. Flavours are good, techniques are sound and parfaits are a real highlight. The pub prides itself on the friendliness of its staff and upstairs is no different.

Closing times
Closed 25-26 December

Prices
Meals: £ 20 and a la carte £ 25/35

Typical Dishes
Hand-dived Shetland scallops & borlotti beans
Loin and shoulder of Rhug Estate lamb
Warm chocolate fondant

⊖ *Old Street. On street meters.*

16 Anglesea Arms

35 Wingate Rd,
Hammersmith, W6 0UR
Tel.: (020)87491291
e-mail: anglesea.events@gmail.com
Website: www.anglesea-arms.com

Ringwood 49er, Timothy Taylor Landlord, Otto, St Austell Tribute, Harveys, Sharp's Doom Bar

Anglesea Arms proves that you can update a pub while still respecting its heritage. Its windows are etched with the inviting words 'Pies and Hams' and 'Stout and Oysters' and above the door is 'Mon Mam Cymru', Mother of Wales, as the Isle of Anglesey is known. The wood-floored, wood-panelled bar has a cluttered, lived-in feel and gets very crowded, so if you're in for eating head for the brighter rear dining room, with its part-glass ceiling and exposed kitchen. The blackboard menu might change between services and can be a little unbalanced with lots of starters, fewer mains and a limited number of puddings but the cooking is robust and has a strong British bias, with the likes of pig's head terrine, smoked eel and game featuring.

Closing times
Closed 25 December

Prices
Meals: a la carte £ 17/46

⊖ *Ravenscourt Park.*

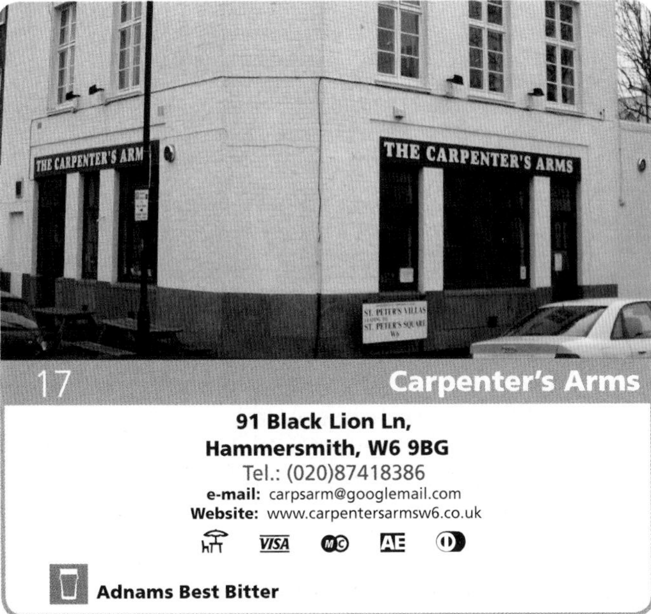

17 **Carpenter's Arms**

91 Black Lion Ln,
Hammersmith, W6 9BG
Tel.: (020)87418386
e-mail: carpsarm@googlemail.com
Website: www.carpentersarmsw6.co.uk

VISA MC AE

Adnams Best Bitter

The Carpenter's Arms is a civilised sort of place that doesn't look like much from the outside and indeed inside has made a virtue of its pared down, somewhat plain decorative style. Apart from allowing passers-by to have a good gawp in, the windows let in plenty of light during the day; while at night the gas fires make it cosier. The atmosphere is always convivial, helped along by the efforts made with the service. Despite the relatively compact size of the place, the menu is quite extensive and offers something for all tastes and appetites, from foie gras terrine to a bowl of soup; hotpot to halibut; ice cream to clafoutis. Add game in season and some Mediterranean flavours and you have a pub that knows how to satisfy its customers.

Closing times
Open daily
booking essential

Prices
Meals: £ 16 (lunch)
and a la carte £ 30/55

Typical Dishes
Clams with bacon & smoked paprika
Venison chops & Swiss chard
Spiced prunes, yoghurt and pistachio

⊖ Stamford Brook.

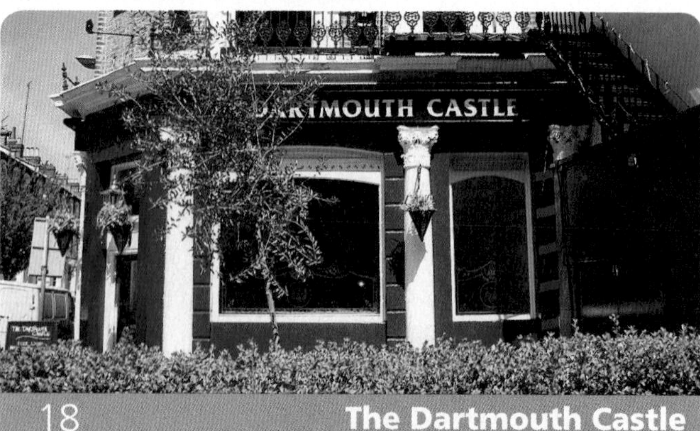

18 The Dartmouth Castle

26 Glenthorne Rd,
Hammersmith, W6 0LS
Tel.: (020)87483614 – Fax: (020)87483619
e-mail: dartmouth.castle@btconnect.com
Website: www.thedartmouthcastle.co.uk

   AE

 **Fuller's London Pride and 2 rotating guests ales**

The view one way is of offices, the other, smart Victorian terraced houses, so this pub has to satisfy a wide variety of customers and their differing needs – and it does so with aplomb. Plenty just come in for a drink but you can eat on either of the two floors, although the ground floor has the better atmosphere, despite its somewhat over-enthusiastic lighting; just order at the bar and leave them your credit card. The Mediterranean exerts quite an influence on the large menu, whose prices are more than fair. Pasta dishes appear to come in two sizes – big or even bigger – and the antipasti dish for two is great for sharing over a bottle of wine. Sandwiches use ciabatta, and dishes like tiramisu or panna cotta finish things off nicely.

Closing times
Closed 24 December to 1 January and 2nd Monday in August

Prices
Meals: a la carte £ 18/30

Typical Dishes
Sautéed wild mushrooms with cream & polenta croutons
Tuscan sausages & roast garlic mash
Chocolate parfait & passion fruit

 ⊖ *Hammersmith.*

19 The Harwood Arms

Walham Grove,
Fulham, SW6 1QP
Tel.: (020)73861847
e-mail: admin@harwoodarms.com
Website: www.harwoodarms.com

Fuller's London Pride, Sambrooks Wandle and Hook Norton Old Hooky

More chefs should eat here so they can see that great food doesn't always have to be served in lavish surroundings to whispering diners. The Harwood Arms is a proper, noisy pub and just as welcoming to drinkers as it is to diners – it's just that the food is the sine qua non of the operation. While not wholly traditional pub food, it does offer appropriately robust flavours in recognisable combinations. There are usually a couple of sharing dishes, such as shoulder of cider-braised Roe deer on the bone, and plenty of great seasonal produce like Jersey Royals, Herefordshire snails and Berkshire pheasant. Prices are also down to earth, service is chatty and the place is as refreshingly uncomplicated as it looks.

Closing times
Closed 24-28 December, 1 January and Monday lunch

Prices
Meals: a la carte £ 28/32

Typical Dishes
Herefordshire snails with oxtail braised in stout
Braised beef cheeks & celeriac purée
Camp coffee ice cream

⊖ Fulham Broadway.

Hammersmith and Fulham

20 **The Havelock Tavern**

57 Masbro Rd,
Brook Grn, Shepherd's Bush, W14 0LS
Tel.: (020)76035374
e-mail: info@thehavelocktavern.co.uk
Website: www.thehavelocktavern.com

   AE

Wandle, Purity, Sharp's Doom Bar and several monthly changing guest ales

Head straight for the bar where smiley, somewhat dishevelled looking staff will organise a drink, open a tab and add your name to the list of those waiting for a table, which are allocated on a first-come-first-served basis. This actually appears to add to the atmosphere as everyone is forced to rub shoulders in the bar first, where you'll find bowls of pistachios and olives while waiting. The blackboard menu changes with each service and cooking is on the stout side so you're better off sharing a nibble like chipolatas and mustard or pickled quail egg, before choosing a pie or a steak; only if your appetite is really healthy will you have room for crumble and custard. The busier the place gets, the better the service.

Closing times
Closed 25 December

Prices
Meals: a la carte £ 21/26

Typical Dishes
Brawn with sour apple chutney & toast
Rib of beef & chips
Apple & treacle tart with ice cream

 ⊖ *Kensington Olympia. On-street pay & display parking.*

21 Princess Victoria

217 Uxbridge Rd,
Shepherd's Bush, W12 9DH

Tel.: (020)87495886 – Fax: (020)87494886
e-mail: info@princessvictoria.co.uk
Website: www.princessvictoria.co.uk

   MC

 **Fuller's London Pride, Timothy Taylor Landlord and Harvey's Sussex Best Bitter**

From tramstop to live music venue, this magnificent Victorian gin palace has seen it all. A chef and a sommelier then took it over, gave it a top-to-toe revamp and the old girl has since had a whole new lease of life. The large dining room is dominated by a grand centre table. The stunning wine list has over 350 bottles, with a focus on Rhône, Pinot Noir and Riesling. Food-wise, it's a mix of classics, with the odd Asian or Mediterranean influence. The Pork Board starter, which includes pig's cheek and Bayonne ham, has become a favourite, and you'll always find the Angus rib-eye. Sausages are homemade and the kitchen knows its butchery. More nostalgia comes courtesy of the pudding menu, with the appearance of coupes and sundaes.

Closing times
Closed 2 weeks at Christmas

Prices
Meals: £ 15 (lunch) and a la carte £ 22/32

Typical Dishes
Potted Dorset crab
Chargrilled rib-eye steak, triple cooked chips
Caramelised chocolate & peanut tart

 *⊖ Shepherd's Bush.*

22 Sands End

135-137 Stephendale Rd,
Fulham, SW6 2PR
Tel.: (020)77317823
e-mail: thesandsend@hotmail.co.uk
Website: www.thesandsend.co.uk

 VISA MC AE

Black Sheep, Hook Norton Hooky and St Austell's Tribute

Urbanites will consider the look to be junkshop chic while those who head westwards at weekends will insist it's more Cirencester. But what all agree on is the appeal of the food. We're all aware of the seismic improvements in the standard of pub dining but this has also had a knock-on effect on that most British of nibble – the bar snack. The choice is no longer between flavours of crisps: here drinkers are offered homemade sausage rolls, Scotch eggs and Welsh rarebit soldiers. Those who prefer sitting when eating will also find much to savour from the concise menu. Snails come in garlic butter or as an accompaniment to rib-eye; steak and kidney pie sits alongside guinea fowl, and rice pudding competes for your attention with panna cotta.

Closing times
Open daily
booking advisable

Prices
Meals: £ 13 (lunch)
and a la carte £ 24/30

Typical Dishes
Truffled duck egg & parmesan beignets
28-day aged rib-eye
Carrot cake & ginger ice cream

 ⊖ *Fulham Broadway.*

23 **Clissold Arms**

115 Fortis Green,
Fortis Green, N2 9HR
Tel.: (020)84444224

Timothy Taylor Landlord, Fuller's London Pride, Harveys Sussex

Such is the growing reputation of The Clissold Arms that it may soon be better known for the quality of its cooking than its more longstanding claim to fame – that of having played host to The Kinks' first gig. Come at lunch and the menu and atmosphere make you feel you're in a proper pub where you can expect classics like fishcakes or steak sandwiches. At dinner it all looks more like a restaurant, with loftier prices and slightly more ambitious, but still carefully prepared, dishes. The place is a lot bigger than you expect and, while staff could do with a little more guidance, it's often busy with locals grateful to have somewhere other than chain restaurants in their neighbourhood. The decked terrace has recently been extended.

Closing times
Closed 1 January

Prices
Meals: a la carte £ 22/35

Typical Dishes

Duo of asparagus with truffle vinaigrette

Cod viennoise & steamed spinach

Lemon & lavender crème brûlée

 *East Finchley. Parking.*

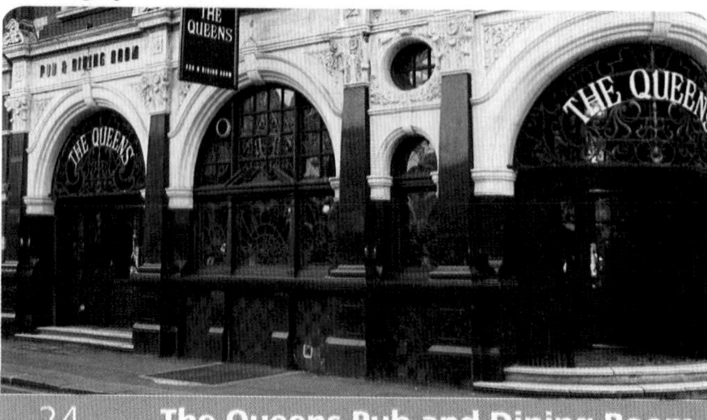

24 The Queens Pub and Dining Room

26 Broadway Par,
Crouch End, N8 9DE
Tel.: (020)83402031
e-mail: queens@foodandfuel.co.uk
Website: www.thequeenscrouchend.co.uk

VISA MC AE

Adnams Gunhill and two weekly changing guest ales

It would be hard to find a more striking example of Victoriana than The Queens Pub and Dining Room. From the original mahogany panelling to the beautiful stained glass windows and ornate ceiling, this pub has it all. The dining room is particularly stunning – ask for tables 105 or 106 on the raised section. The open kitchen recognises that some will only want classic pub food in this environment – so you'll find beef and mushroom pie, rib-eye, plaice goujons and various sausages – while others want something slightly more ambitious, hence the likes of risotto, plates of smoked meats, sea bass and assorted choices of a more Mediterranean persuasion. Selected dishes are highlighted to form part of the affordable 'This week we love…' menu.

Closing times
Open daily
Prices
Meals: a la carte £ 25

Typical Dishes
Duck liver parfait with apple chutney
Grilled lamb leg & sweet potato gratin
Eton mess

On-street parking meters.

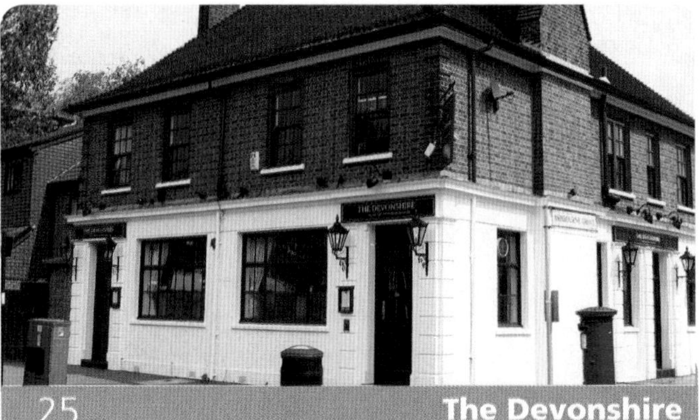

25 The Devonshire

126 Devonshire Rd,
Chiswick, W4 2JJ
Tel.: (020)75927962
e-mail: thedevonshire@gordonramsay.com
Website: www.gordonramsay.com

Inspectors' favourites

 **Fuller's London Pride, Twickenham Bitter**

The Devonshire is an attractive and appealingly restored Edwardian pub in a typical London street where contrasting styles of housing seemingly sit happily together. Whether having a pint in front of the fire or eating at one of the simple tables down one side of the bar, you'll find the atmosphere warm and friendly. Food is available in a variety of forms: from a bucket of chips, a ploughman's, a club sandwich or devilled kidneys at the bar to the classic British dishes from the main menu such as wild boar and apple sausages, braised salt marsh lamb or grilled Old Spot pork. This pub closed as we went to print.

Closing times
Open daily
booking advisable

Prices
Meals: £ 22 and a la carte £ 23/30

Typical Dishes
Crisp fried quail & cured pork belly
Roasted Durnoch lamb rump & rosemary potatoes
Steamed treacle pudding

 ⊖ *Turnham Green.*

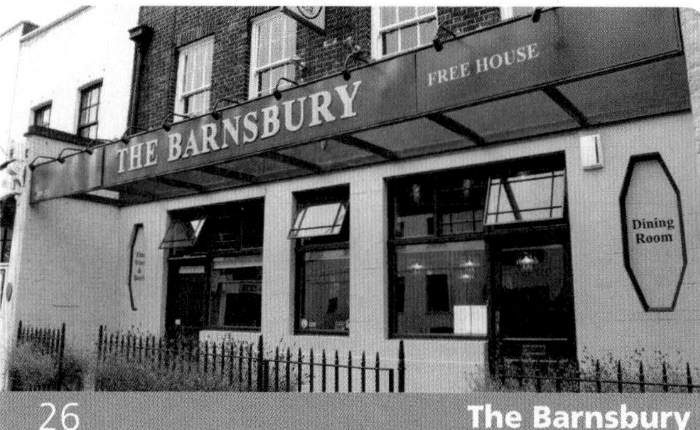

26 The Barnsbury

209-211 Liverpool Rd,
Islington, N1 1LX
Tel.: (020)76075519 – Fax: (020)76073256
e-mail: info@thebarnsbury.co.uk
Website: www.thebarnsbury.co.uk

VISA MC AE

Gravesend Shrimpers, Whitstable Kentish Reserve and weekly changing guest beer

The young new owner may have a background in some of London's more fashionable dining establishments, but he's keen to turn The Barnsbury back into a proper local pub as he felt it had become too much like a restaurant. That being said, the food is still done well and the menu is appealing, with tarts, salads, potted shrimps and mussels jostling for attention alongside Toulouse sausages, risottos and steaks served with the ubiquitous triple-cooked chips; the homemade puds are especially good. Lunch trade is not big in these parts so the midday menu is more limited. Chandeliers fashioned from wine glasses are dotted around the place and add character; but do sit in the more atmospheric front bar rather than in the dining area at the back.

Closing times
Closed 24-26 December, 1 January and Monday lunch

Prices
Meals: a la carte £ 25/35

⊖ *Highbury and Islington. On-street parking meters.*

27 The Coach & Horses

26-28 Ray St,
Clerkenwell, EC1R 3DJ
Tel.: (020)78371336
e-mail: info@thecoachandhorses.com
Website: www.thecoachandhorses.com

   AE

Adnams Bitter, Fuller's London Pride, Timothy Taylor Landlord

This is one of those small, warm and cosy pubs that provide such a welcome retreat on a winter's night. Restored rather than renovated, its wood panelling, engraved windows and mirrors add to the traditional feel. There are also vestibules at both entrances – a rare sight as most pubs removed them to create more space. Diners have their own area separated by a wooden partition but there is also a back room which adjoins the terrace. The kitchen keeps things as British and straightforward as they can; even the charcuterie board contains home-cured Wiltshire ham with piccalilli. Dishes could include devilled crab, smoked haddock fish pie, and apple and almond crumble; all prepared with care, sensibly proportioned and fairly priced.

Closing times
Closed 24 December-3 January, Easter, Saturday lunch, Sunday dinner and bank holidays

Prices
Meals: £ 16 (Sunday lunch) and a la carte £ 20/29

⊖ Farringdon. Parking meters across the road.

28 **The Compass**

58 Penton St,
Islington, N1 9PZ
Tel.: (020)78373891
e-mail: info@thecompassn1.co.uk
Website: www.thecompassn1.co.uk

VISA

No real ales offered

The Compass is another Victorian pub that has been rescued from a life of seedy anonymity and turned into a lively local known for the quality of its food. Most of the original features remain, such as the tiling, floorboards and ceiling lights, but the fact that the chefs are also on display gives a clue as to where the emphasis now lies. Decent olives and homemade bread kick things off and recognisable favourites from the gastropub canon, such as fishcakes, rib-eye and rump of lamb are combined with other dishes of more European provenance. Lighter classics and a good value set menu feature at lunch and the cooking is accurate and clearly confident. The wine list is concise but offers a good few choices by the glass and carafe.

Closing times
Closed lunch Monday-Tuesday

Prices
Meals: a la carte £ 22/30

Typical Dishes
Ham Hock 'trifle' with apple jelly
Roasted Barbary duck with chutney
Melting chocolate pudding

⊖ Angel.

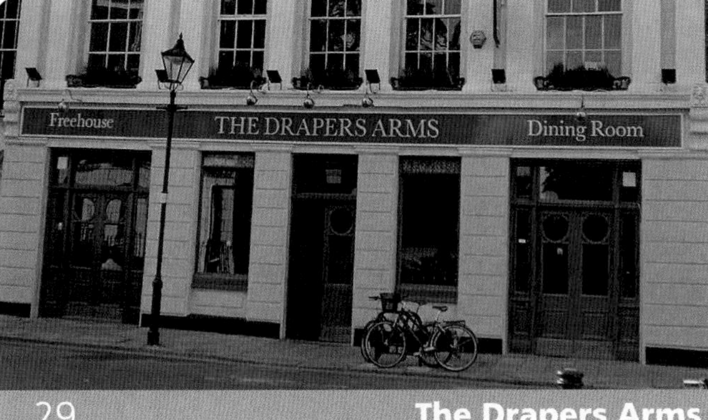

29 The Drapers Arms

44 Barnsbury St,
Islington, N1 1ER
Tel.: (020)76190348
e-mail: info@thedrapersarms.com
Website: www.thedrapersarms.com

Butcombe, Harvey's and Sambrooks' Wandle

This handsome Georgian pub was rescued, revived and reopened a couple of years ago by new owners, one of whom is the son of restaurant critic Fay Maschler. The chef is an alumnus of St John but, while his experience informs his cooking, that doesn't make it a facsimile. It does place the same emphasis on seasonality, on unfussy 'proper' British cooking and on the use of less familiar cuts, but there's also an acknowledgement that this is a local pub first and foremost. Reservations are only taken for the somewhat starkly decorated upstairs dining room but you'll find the same menu in the bar, where it's more fun, with its shelves of Penguin Classics and board games as well as a further menu of dishes such as oysters, devils on horseback and whelks.

Closing times
Open daily

Prices
Meals: a la carte £ 22/29

⊖ Highbury and Islington.

30 **The Fellow**

24 York Way,
King's Cross, N1 9AA
Tel.: (020)78334395
e-mail: info@thefellow.co.uk
Website: www.thefellow.co.uk

   AE

Gales HSB, Brains Reverend James and Young's

It was just a matter of time before a few decent pubs opened around the rapidly developing area of King's Cross. The Fellow is one of the busiest, attracting a youthful and local clientele; it also manages to give the impression it's been here for years. Eating happens on the dark and atmospheric ground floor, with drinkers heading upstairs to the even more boisterous cocktail bar. The menu is quite a sophisticated little number but the kitchen is up to the task. Start with ham hock terrine or potted crab, followed by roast rump of lamb or grilled haddock with champ. Desserts such as apple tart display a lightness of touch. The serving team are a bright, capable bunch. There is an outdoor terrace but you'll be surrounded by smokers.

Closing times
Closed Sunday dinner

Prices
Meals: a la carte £ 27/32

⊖ *King's Cross. 2 min walk from Tube and Mainline station.*

31 The Green

29 Clerkenwell Gn,
Finsbury, EC1R 0DU
Tel.: (020)74908010
e-mail: info@thegreenec1.co.uk
Website: www.thegreenec1.co.uk

Adnams, East India Pale, Barnstormer

29 Clerkenwell Green dates from 1580 and had become a tavern by 1720. It's therefore fitting that, after decades being used firstly as offices and then as a restaurant, The Green is now back to being known as a pub. Appetising and imaginative bar snacks like hog shank on toast are to be had in the ground floor bar, but the intimate upstairs is where the real eating goes on. Here you'll find an appealing menu of fresh, seasonal ingredients which might include Devon crab, Cornish mackerel, Wiltshire trout or Suffolk pork. The traditional fish pie is a favourite of many and the puds on the blackboard continue the British theme. Lunches get pretty busy with those wearing suits but dinner is more relaxed and the clientele in less of a hurry.

Closing times
Open daily

Prices
Meals: a la carte £ 21/30

Typical Dishes
Grilled Cornish mackerel & pickled cucumber
Roast rib-eye of beef with braised peas & bacon
Bread & butter pudding

 ⊖ *Farringdon.*

32 **The House**

63-69 Canonbury Rd,
Canonbury, N1 2DG
Tel.: (020)77047410 – Fax: (020)77049388
e-mail: info@inthehouse.biz
Website: www.thehouse.islington.com

Inspectors' favourites

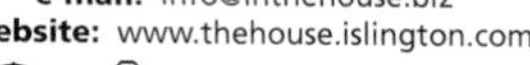

 **Adnams**

The House is one of the smarter pubs around; indeed, with its attractive terrace it can look more like a restaurant from the outside but step inside and you'll find sufficient numbers of regulars relaxing around the bar exuding a general sense of localness. Even the eating area towards the rear has that reassuringly hotchpotch feel and, while the service is clearly on the button, it is also friendly and chatty. The menu covers all corners, from the classics like shepherd's pie and apple crumble to other more elaborate choices such as sea bass with artichoke purée and peppered venison with spiced red cabbage. Cooking is clean, crisp and confident and there's an emphasis on good quality, organic ingredients.

Closing times
Closed Monday lunch

Prices
Meals: £ 18 (lunch)
and a la carte £ 26/35

Typical Dishes
Seared scallops & risotto
Wild sea trout with Jersey Royals & cockles
Passion fruit & strawberry pavlova

 ⊖ *Highbury and Islington.*

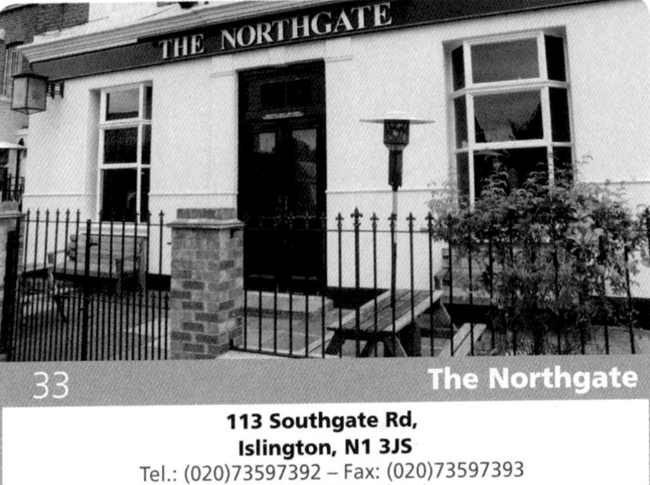

33 **The Northgate**

113 Southgate Rd,
Islington, N1 3JS
Tel.: (020)73597392 – Fax: (020)73597393
e-mail: jspt@hotmail.co.uk

VISA

Deuchar's IPA, Fuller's London Pride and Greene King IPA

The Northgate is decked out in the usual gastropub aesthetic of mismatched furniture and local artists' work for sale on the walls; at the back you'll find tables laid up for dining and an open kitchen. You'll also find an extraction fan that's so strong you can feel its tug. Staff are pretty laid back, at times almost to the point of somnolence; go with a similarly relaxed frame of mind to avoid irritation. Where the pub scores is in the food: there's a strong Mediterranean influence on the vast blackboard. You'll find merguez and chorizo sausages, assorted pastas, a bit of Greek and some French – all in generously sized proportions with the emphasis on flavour. Finish with something a little closer to home like treacle tart.

Closing times
Closed 25 December
dinner only and lunch at weekends

Prices
Meals: a la carte £ 20/27

Typical Dishes
Potted salt beef
Wild mushroom risotto
Apple strudel with crème anglaise

⊖ *Dalston Kingsland (rail). Free on-street parking after 6.30pm.*

34 **The Peasant**

240 St John St,
Finsbury, EC1V 4PH
Tel.: (020)73367726 – Fax: (020)74901089
e-mail: eat@thepeasant.co.uk
Website: www.thepeasant.co.uk

  AE

Crouch Vale Brewers Gold, Wells Bombardier, Skinners Betty Stogs and one weekly changing guest ale

Come along too early in the evening and you'll find the bar four deep with city boys having a quick pint on the way home. However, things do quieten down later and, when it does, you'll notice what a characterful spot this is. Most of the eating gets done upstairs in the dining room with its dimmed chandeliers, open fire and circus-themed posters. The cooking has been simplified and returned to a core of British dishes accompanied by the occasional Mediterranean note. The result is that it is far more satisfying and the well-judged dishes –whether braised rib of beef with horseradish mash or roast pollock with shrimps – all largely deliver on flavour. You will need a side dish or two with your main course, which can push up the final bill.

Closing times
Closed 25 December to 2 January
booking essential

Prices
Meals: £ 35 and a la carte £ 18/38

Typical Dishes
Homemade Scotch egg
Beef & Guinness pie with carrots, kale and mash
Peasant bread & butter pudding with toffee sauce

⊖ Farringdon. On-street parking meters nearby; also free parking at weekends after 1.30pm.

35 St John's Tavern

91 Junction Rd,
Archway, N19 5QU
Tel.: (020)72721587 – Fax: (020)72721587
Website: www.stjohnstavern.com

VISA MC AE

Timothy Taylor Landlord, Black Sheep, Jenning's Cocker Hoop, Adnam's Broadside and Brakspear's Gold

Too many diners arrived expecting Clerkenwell's St John restaurant – hence the addition of 'tavern' to the name of this pub, which has long been a beacon of hope on drab old Junction Road. The dark colours and fireplace in the dining room may make it look like somewhere for a winter's night but staff keep things light and perky throughout the year. The menu changes daily and the open kitchen puts some thought into the vegetarian choices, be they the courgette and cheddar tart or the squash and halloumi parcels; but they also know how to fire up the heat when cooking a pork chop or rib-eye. The wine list is sensibly priced, with enough carafes to make up for the 125ml glasses, although Black Sheep bitter is a popular alternative.

Closing times
Closed 25-26 December and lunch Monday-Thursday

Prices
Meals: a la carte £ 23/30

Typical Dishes
Pig's head terrine with parsley & gherkin purée
Duck confit & black pudding
Panettone eggy bread

⊖ Archway. Pay & display parking bays; free after 6.30pm.

36

The Well

180 St John St,
Finsbury, EC1V 4JY
Tel.: (020)72519363 – Fax: (020)72539683
e-mail: james@downthewell.co.uk
Website: www.downthewell.com

    AE

 **Meantime Pale Ale**

The Well is perhaps more of a locals' pub than many others found around these parts. It's all quite small inside but, thanks to some huge sliding glass windows, has a surprisingly light and airy feel, and the wooden floorboards and exposed brick walls add to the atmosphere of a committed metropolitan pub. Monthly changing menus offer modern dishes ranging from potted shrimps, to foie gras and chicken liver parfait, or sea trout and samphire, as well as classic English puddings like Eton Mess and some particularly good cheeses. The downstairs bar with its seductive lighting and fish tank is only available for private hire; check out the picture of a parched desert and a well which follows the curve of the wall on your way down.

Closing times
Open daily

Prices
Meals: a la carte £ 30/60

Typical Dishes

Grilled Irish black & white pudding, pig's ear & onion purée

Roast rack of lamb, black truffle jus

Forced Yorkshire rhubarb & custard posset

 ⊖ *Farringdon. On-street parking meters.*

37 The Admiral Codrington

17 Mossop St,
Chelsea, SW3 2LY
Tel.: (020)75810005 – Fax: (020)75892452
e-mail: theadmiralcodrington@333holdingsltd.com
Website: www.theadmiralcodrington.com

VISA AE

Black Sheep and Spitfire

The Admiral Codrington is a smart, dependable affair as befits an establishment named after a hero of the Battles of Trafalgar and Navarino. What was once the HQ of the Sloane Ranger movement is now known for the quality of its food, although it still attracts a well turned-out crowd. The main bar and terrace are quite subdued during the day but get busy in the evening when all the eating is done in the neat, comfortable restaurant with its sliding glass roof. The menu can't quite decide whether this is a pub or a restaurant and so covers all bases from chilli salt squid to roast beef; coq au vin to fish and chips and includes some baguettes at lunch. Service can sometimes lack a little personality but the young team do get the job done.

Closing times
Open daily

Prices
Meals: a la carte £ 24/30

Typical Dishes
Chilli salt squid
The Admiral's cod
Rhubarb crumble with vanilla custard

⊖ South Kensington. Parking in the adjacent streets.

Kensington and Chelsea

38 **Builders Arms**

13 Britten St,
Chelsea, SW3 3TY
Tel.: (020)73499040
e-mail: buildersarms@geronimo-inns.co.uk
Website: www.geronimo-inns.co.uk

VISA MC AE

Fuller's London Pride, Adnams Bitter, Sharp's Cornish Coaster

The Builders Arms is very much like a packed village local - the only difference being that, in this instance, the village is Chelsea. They adopt a simple but effective approach to cooking – there's an easy to read menu, supplemented by a daily specials blackboard, which always includes a soup and fresh fish. Dishes range from devilled kidney on toast to herb-crusted lamb; others, such as the corn-fed peri-peri chicken are designed for sharing. Presentation has an appealingly rustic edge; portions are appropriately pub-size and prices are kept realistic. There's a weekly Bordeaux selection as well as regular wine promotions. Bookings are only taken for larger parties but just tell the staff that you're here to eat and they'll sort you out.

Closing times
Closed 25-26 December

Prices
Meals: a la carte £ 25/30

⊖ South Kensington.

39 The Cadogan Arms

298 King's Rd,
Chelsea, SW3 5UG
Tel.: (020)73526500
e-mail: nadia@etmgroup.co.uk
Website: www.thecadoganarmschelsea.com

  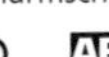

Fullers London Pride, Adnams Bitter and one regularly changing guest ale including Adnams Gunhill

The Martin brothers seem to have the King's Road covered, with The Botanist dominating the Sloane Square end and The Cadogan Arms doing its thing at the other. The tiled entrance step reads 'Luncheon, bar and billiards' which sounds appealingly like a lost afternoon and it is clear that this is still a proper, blokey pub. The upstairs billiard tables are available by the hour and, while you eat, you'll feel the beady eyes of the various stuffed and mounted animals on the walls staring at you. The cooking is appropriately gutsy. Juicy Aberdeen Angus rib-eye, golden-fried haddock, Dexter Beef and Welsh lamb are all staples of the menu. Starters and desserts are a little showier – perhaps something for the ladies? Staff catch the mood just so.

Closing times
Closed 25-26 December
booking advisable at dinner

Prices
Meals: a la carte £ 24/37

 ⊖ *South Kensington.*

40 Chelsea Ram

32 Burnaby St,
Chelsea, SW10 0PL
Tel.: (020)73514008
e-mail: bookings@chelsearam.co.uk

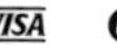

 **Youngs Bitter and Wells Bombardier**

It's easy to see why the Chelsea Ram is such a successful neighbourhood pub: it's somewhat secreted position means there are few casual passers-by to upset the peace, the locals appreciate the relaxed and warm feel of the place and the pub provides them with just the sort of food they want. That means proper pub grub, with highlights being things on toast, like chicken livers or mushrooms, and the constant presence of favourites like The Ram burger or haddock and leek fishcake; prices are fair and portions large. They do take bookings but somewhat reluctantly, as they always want to keep a table or two for that spontaneous visit. The Chelsea Ram's winning formula is that it's comfortable just being what it is – a friendly, reliable local.

Closing times
Closed Sunday dinner

Prices
Meals: a la carte £ 18/30

Typical Dishes
Goat's cheese with spring onion & spinach tart
Pork belly & crackling with crushed potato mash
Apple & pear crumble

 ⊖ *Fulham Broadway. On-street parking meters and single yellow lines.*

41 **The Fat Badger**

310 Portobello Rd,
North Kensington, W10 5TA
Tel.: (020)89694500
e-mail: helen@thefatbadger.com
Website: www.thefatbadger.com

VISA MC AE

Butcombe and one regularly changing guest ale including Ruddles

The Fat Badger treads the line between being worn in and worn out. Stuffing sprouts from sofas and chips and scuffs abound but the locals seem to like the general raggedness. Use of the upstairs restaurant is largely dependent on enough punters requesting it and, besides, the same menu is served in the bar. The one decorative element that really stands out is the patterned wallpaper which only reveals its true nature on close inspection. Service can be hit and miss as not all members of staff share the same attitude towards customer service. But the food is good: the kitchen doesn't try to reinvent anything but also displays a light touch, whether in the crisp cuttlefish and chorizo, the roast chicken breast or the panna cotta.

Closing times
Open daily
Prices
Meals: £ 25 (lunch)
and a la carte £ 20/29

Typical Dishes
Organic English asparagus & confit of tomatoes
Fillet of sea bream
Mango parfait with coconut crème anglaise

⊖ *Ladbroke Grove. On-street parking meters.*

42 Lots Road Pub & Dining Room

114 Lots Rd,
Chelsea, SW10 0RJ
Tel.: (020)73526645
e-mail: lotsroad@foodandfuel.co.uk
Website: www.lotsroadpub.com

  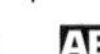 AE

 **Sharp's Doom Bar, Adnam's Gunhill and one regularly changing guest ale**

Lots Road and its customers are clearly happy with one another as the pub has introduced a customer loyalty scheme, whereby anyone making their fifth visit is rewarded with a discount. Lunch is geared more towards those just grabbing a quick bite but dinner sees a choice that could include oysters, mussels or a savoury tart of the day; the Perthshire côte de boeuf is the house speciality. There are also pies and casseroles, in appropriate pub-like sizes, and even salads for those after something light. Service remains bright and cheery, even on those frantic Thursday nights when the pub offers 'Thursday Treats' with wine tasting and nibbles. The only disappointment is the somewhat ordinary bread for which they make a not insubstantial charge.

Closing times
Open daily

Prices
Meals: a la carte £ 20/31

 ⊖ *Fulham Broadway.*

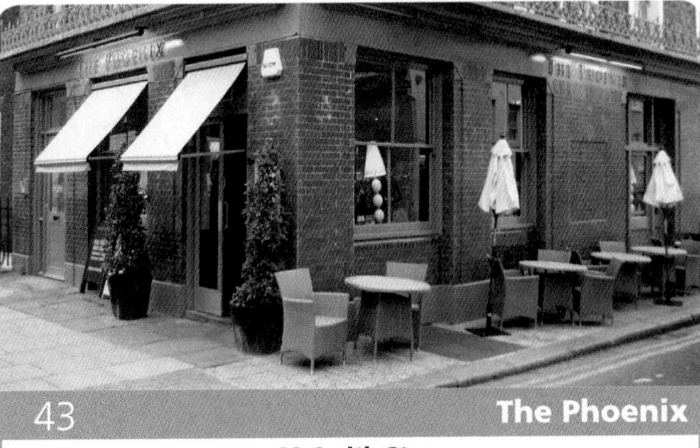

43 The Phoenix

23 Smith St,
Chelsea, SW3 4EE
Tel.: (020)77309182
e-mail: thephoenix@geronimo-inns.co.uk
Website: www.geronimo-inns.co.uk

   AE

 **Adnams, Sharp's Doom Bar**

The same menu is served throughout and, while the bar has plenty of seating and a civilised feel, head to the warm and comfortable dining room at the back if you want a more structured meal or you're impressing a date. Blackboard specials supplement the menu which keeps things traditional: fish on a Friday, a pasta of the day and the likes of fishcakes or sausage and mash with red onion jam. For lunch, you'll find some favourites for late-risers, like eggs Benedict and, in winter, expect the heartening sight of crumbles or plum pudding. Wines are organised by their character, with nearly 30 varieties offered by the glass. The side dishes can bump up the final bill but The Phoenix remains a friendly and conscientiously run Chelsea local.

Closing times
Closed 25-26 December

Prices
Meals: a la carte £ 23/30

 ⊖ *Sloane Square. On-street parking meters.*

44 **The Pig's Ear**

35 Old Church St,
Chelsea, SW3 5BS
Tel.: (020)73522908 – Fax: (020)73529321
e-mail: thepigsear@hotmail.co.uk
Website: www.thepigsear.com

Greene King IPA, Sharp's Doom Bar and Fuller's London Pride

This Chelsea pub may not look much like a foodie spot from the outside, or indeed from the inside, but it does have a refreshing honesty to it. Lunch is in the rough-and-ready ground floor bar, decorated with everything from 'Tintin' pictures to covers of 'Sounds' newspaper. There's a decent choice of 5-6 main courses and a wine list on a blackboard. With its wood panelling and dressed tables, the upstairs dining room provides quite a contrast, but the atmosphere is still far from starchy. Here the menu displays a little more ambition but cooking remains similarly earthy and the wine list has plenty of bottles under £30. The kitchen knows its way around an animal: slow-cooked dishes such as pork cheeks are done particularly well.

Closing times
Closed 2 weeks at Christmas and Sunday dinner

Prices
Meals: a la carte £ 22/35

⊖ *Sloane Square. 25 min on foot.*

45 **Canton Arms**

177 South Lambeth Rd,
Stockwell, SW8 1XP
Tel.: (020)75828710
e-mail: thecantonarms@googlemail.com
Website: www.cantonarms.com

Skinners Brewery and three regularly changing guest ales

Its appreciative audience prove that the demand for fresh, honest, seasonal food is not just limited to smart squares in Chelsea or Islington. The oval-shaped bar dominates the room, with the front half busy with drinkers and the back laid up for diners, although it's all very relaxed and you can eat where you want. The kitchen's experience in places like the Anchor & Hope and Great Queen Street is obvious on their menu which features rustic, earthy British food, the sort that suits this environment so well. Lunch could be a kipper or tripe and chips, even a reinvented toasted sandwich. Dinner sees a short, no-nonsense menu offering perhaps braised venison or grilled haddock, with daily specials which could be a steak and kidney pie for two.

Closing times
Closed 25-26 December, 31 December, 1 January, Monday lunch, Sunday dinner and bank holidays

Prices
Meals: a la carte £ 20/26

Typical Dishes
House terrine with toast & chutney
Wild rabbit with cider & bacon
Little chocolate pot

 ⊖ *Stockwell. Free parking in the evening.*

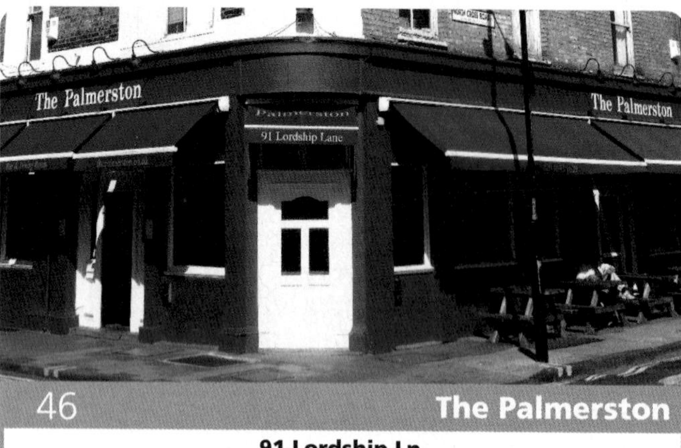

46

The Palmerston

91 Lordship Ln,
East Dulwich, SE22 8EP
Tel.: (020)86931629
e-mail: info@thepalmerston.net
Website: www.thepalmerston.net

 **Sharps' Doom Bar, Harvey's, Timothy Taylor Landlord and Hogs Back Spring ale**

It's not just for the locals – those passing through for a visit to the Horniman Museum or Dulwich Picture Gallery must also be pleased to have somewhere so welcoming in which to extend their stay in SE22. You can sit anywhere, although there is a section at the back with wood panelling and a mosaic floor which they call 'the dining room'. The menus tend to evolve on a monthly basis, with influences ranging from the Med to Asia. The bread is good, which usually augurs well and, refreshingly, the dishes come with just the ingredients described on the menu. Add a well-priced weekday menu and a host of engaging young staff and it's little wonder the pub attracts such a wide range of ages, which in turn creates a pleasant atmosphere.

Closing times
Open daily

Prices
Meals: £ 15 (lunch)
and a la carte £ 22/29

Typical Dishes
Sautéed sweetbreads with pancetta
Blanquette of veal with Jersey Royals & asparagus
Baked peach & mascarpone

 ⊖ *East Dulwich (rail). Free on street parking in the evening.*

47 The Brown Dog

28 Cross St,
Barnes, SW13 0AP
Tel.: (020)83922200
Website: www.thebrowndog.co.uk

   AE

 **Westerham Brewery Grasshopper, Twickenham Original, Wandle Sam Brown Brewery**

Thankfully, changes of ownership don't appear to mean much here – perhaps you really can't teach an old dog new tricks – because The Brown Dog remains a terrific neighbourhood pub and the locals clearly love it just the way it is. Mind you, this pretty Victorian pub is so well hidden in the maze of residential streets that it's a wonder any new customers ever find it anyway. The look fuses the traditional with the modern and service is bubbly and enthusiastic. Jugs of iced water arrive without prompting and the cleverly concise menu changes regularly. A lightly spiced crab salad or pint of prawns could be followed by a succulent rump of lamb, while puddings not only display a great lightness of touch but are also very commendably priced.

Closing times
Closed 25-26 December

Prices
Meals: a la carte £ 20/50

Typical Dishes
Grilled cuttlefish and chorizo salad
Sea bream fillet with crushed Jersey Royal potatoes
Lemon & strawberry posset

 ⊖ *Barnes Bridge (Rail).*

48

The Victoria

10 West Temple Sheen,
East Sheen, SW14 7RT
Tel.: (020)88764238 – Fax: (020)88783464
e-mail: bookings@thevictoria.net
Website: www.thevictoria.net

VISA

Fuller's London Pride, Timothy Taylor Landlord

Many pubs claim to be genuine locals – The Victoria is the real deal: it sponsors local clubs and the chef is patron of the local food festival and holds cookery workshops at the school next door. This is a beautifully decorated pub, with a restored bar with a wood burning stove and plenty of nooks and crannies; a few steps down and you're in the more formal conservatory overlooking the terrace. The cooking is modern British with the odd international note. Warm homemade bread could be followed by Scotch egg with roast beetroot, cod with a white bean stew and, to finish, blood oranges with rhubarb sorbet. Produce is local where possible: veg is from Surrey and honey from Richmond. Service is engaging and there are simple bedrooms available.

Closing times
Closed 2 days between Christmas and New Year

Prices
Meals: a la carte £ 25/35

7 rooms: £ 112/148

Typical Dishes
Oak-smoked eel fillet on caramelised apple
Steamed sea bass on mussel butter broth
Yorkshire rhubarb Eton mess

⊖ Mortlake (Rail). Just off Upper Richmond Rd. West (A205) by Coval St and Temple Sheen

49 The Anchor & Hope

36 The Cut,
Southwark, SE1 8LP
Tel.: (020)79289898 – Fax: (020)79284595
e-mail: anchorandhope@btconnect.com

Youngs Ordinary, Wells Bombardier and guest ales such as Brains SA

The Anchor & Hope is still running at full steam and its popularity shows no sign of abating. It's not hard to see why: combine a menu that changes with each service and is a paragon of seasonality with cooking that is gutsy, bold and wholesome, and you end up with immeasurably rewarding dishes like suckling kid chops with wild garlic, succulent roast pigeon with lentils or buttermilk pudding with poached rhubarb. The place has a contagiously congenial feel and the staff all pull in the same direction; you may spot a waiter trimming veg or a chef delivering dishes. The no-reservation policy remains, so either get here early or be prepared to wait – although you can now book for Sunday lunch when everyone sits down at 2pm for a veritable feast.

Closing times
Closed 2 weeks at Christmas, Easter, May and August bank holidays, Sunday dinner and Monday lunch

Prices
Meals: £ 30 (lunch Sunday) and a la carte £ 22/35

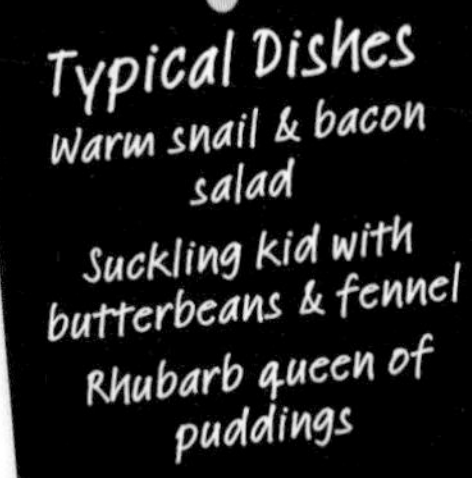

 ⊖ *Southwark. On-street parking meters.*

50 The Garrison

99-101 Bermondsey St,
Bermondsey, SE1 3XB
Tel.: (020)70899355
e-mail: info@thegarrison.co.uk
Website: www.thegarrison.co.uk

 **Adnams Bitter and St Peter's Organic Ale**

'Sweet' is not an adjective that could apply to many of London's pubs but it does seem to fit The Garrison. The service has a certain natural charm and the place has a warm, relaxed vibe, while its mismatched style and somewhat vintage look work well. Open from 8am for smoothies and breakfast, it gets busier as the day goes on – and don't bother coming for dinner if you haven't booked. Booth numbers 4 and 5, opposite the open kitchen, are the most popular while number 2 at the back is the cosiest. The menu has a distinct Mediterranean flavour; salads dominate the starters and steaks and braised meats sit alongside pasta and fresh fish options. Puddings are more your classic pub variety. The owners' other place, Village East, is down the street.

Closing times
Open daily
booking essential at dinner

Prices
Meals: £ 14 (early dinner) and a la carte £ 30/40

Typical Dishes
Beetroot carpaccio & soft goat's cheese
Smoked haddock & champ potatoes
Warm chocolate brownie

 ⊖ *London Bridge.*

51 The Gun

27 Coldharbour,
Canary Wharf, E14 9NS
Tel.: (020)75155222 – Fax: (020)75154407
e-mail: info@thegundocklands.com
Website: www.thegundocklands.com

   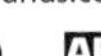 AE

Several monthly changing guest ales including Fuller's London Pride, Adnams Bitter and Meantime Pale Ale

The 18C Gun may have had a 21C makeover but that doesn't mean it has forgotten its roots: its association with Admiral Lord Nelson, links to smugglers and ties to the river are all celebrated in its oil paintings and displays of assorted weaponry. The dining room and the style of service are both fairly smart and ceremonial yet The Gun is a pub where this level of formality seems appropriate. Dockers have now been replaced by bankers, the majority of whom rarely venture beyond the 35-day aged steak. This is a shame as the menu cleverly combines relatively ambitious dishes such as game or John Dory with more traditionally local specialities like eel and oysters. Even the dessert menu offers a mix, from soufflés to stewed plums.

Closing times
Closed 25 December

Prices
Meals: a la carte £ 21/30

⊖ Blackwall (DLR). Marsh Wall car park; on-street parking meters.

52 The Morgan Arms

43 Morgan St,
Bow, E3 5AA
Tel.: (020)89806389
e-mail: themorgan@geronimo-inns.co.uk
Website: www.geronimo-inns.co.uk

Sharp's Doom Bar, Adnam's Best Bitter and Redemption Pale Ale

This former boozer's clever makeover respects its heritage while simultaneously bringing it up to date. The bar's always busy while the dining area is more subdued. You'll find the kitchen keeps its influences mostly within Europe but also understands just what sort of food works well in a pub. The daily-changing menu usually features pasta in some form and staples like whitebait - which come devilled in this instance - assorted tarts and the perennial favourite, fishcakes accompanied by a poached egg. What's more, prices are kept at realistic levels which, together with their policy of not taking bookings, makes this pub appealing to those who live nearby and who like a little spontaneity in their lives.

Closing times
Closed 25-26 December

Prices
Meals: a la carte £ 19/35

Typical Dishes
Scallops & black pudding
Roast cod with potatoes dauphinoise & wild mushrooms
Chocolate brownie tart

⊖ Bow Road. Parking meters in Tredegar Square until 6.30pm; after 6.30pm parking outside.

53 The Narrow

44 Narrow St,
Limehouse, E14 8DP
Tel.: (020)75927950 – Fax: (020)75921603
e-mail: thenarrow@gordonramsay.com
Website: www.gordonramsay.com

 **Meantime London Pale Ale and Adnams Oyster**

Despite receiving some negative publicity just over a year ago when it was revealed that certain dishes in Gordon Ramsay's pubs are prepared in a central kitchen, The Narrow does not seem any less frenetic. This 'logistical cooking', as they describe it, is used for dishes requiring a lengthy cooking process, such as the slow-roasted pork belly or beef braised in Guinness. However it gets there, the food on the plate is tasty, seasonal and laudably British, be it devilled kidneys, Morecambe Bay brown shrimps, a chicken pie or a sherry trifle. What is also certain is that no other London pub has better views, as one would expect from a converted dockmaster's house; just be sure to request a table in the semi-permanent conservatory.

Closing times
Open daily
booking essential

Prices
Meals: £ 22 and a la carte £ 21/27

Typical Dishes
English asparagus & fried duck egg
Braised neck of lamb with pearl barley & bacon risotto
Sticky toffee pudding

 *⊖ Limehouse (DLR). Parking.*

54 The Avalon

16 Balham Hill,
Balham, SW12 9EB
Tel.: (020)86758613
e-mail: info@theavalonlondon.com
Website: www.theavalonlondon.com

 **Timothy Taylor Landlord, Sharp's Doom Bar and Otter ales**

A full renovation has turned The George into a slick and imaginatively styled pub, where Sir Edward Coley Burne-Jones prints add a suitably mythical edge to the aesthetic. The rear dining room's walls are covered in cream tiles but any resemblance to a morgue is thankfully undone by the general bustle and those eye-catching chandeliers. The menu combines British and Mediterranean influences, sometimes, as in the case of the kedgeree risotto, in the same dish. Expect roasted veal marrow bones, crab linguine, venison carpaccio, lamb cutlets and crème brûlée, but also crumble, appropriately of the apple variety. The concise wine list is appealingly priced and there's beer aplenty. Those locals still can't quite believe that Avalon really exists.

Closing times
Open daily
booking advisable
Prices
Meals: £ 18 and a la carte £ 20/25

Typical Dishes
Goat's cheese in pecan crust, baby spinach & beetroot
Roast lamb with garlic mash & peas
Chocolate, hazelnut & raisin torte

 ⊖ *Clapham South.*

55 The Bolingbroke

174 Northcote Rd,
Battersea, SW11 6RE
Tel.: (020)72284040
e-mail: thebolingbrokepub@renaissancepubs.co.uk
Website: www.thebolingbroke.com

Timothy Taylor Landlord and St Austell's Proper Job

The influx of professionals with young families is such that this end of Northcote Road is now known as 'Nappy Valley'. A Cath Kidston shop? Check. Artisan food markets? Check. Antique emphoria? Check. Now it's time for a decent pub and here's where The Bolingbroke comes in. Its glass roof makes the fairly small dining room feel bigger, although the romantically inclined should ask for the table under the stairs. The menus change weekly, with more choice at dinner. British influences lead the way, from the asparagus and cheddar tart, to the lamb shoulder and apple crumble. Steaks and burgers are perennials but you'll also find additional Euro stars like ravioli and a niçoise salad. Unsurprisingly, there's also a children's menu.

Closing times
Open daily
Prices
Meals: £ 19 and a la carte £ 25/33

⊖ *Clapham Junction (Rail).*

56 **Prince of Wales**

138 Upper Richmond Rd,
Putney, SW15 2SP
Tel.: (020)87881552
e-mail: info@princeofwalesputney.co.uk
Website: www.princeofwalesputney.co.uk

Fuller's London Pride, Sharp's Doom Bar and Mad Goose

You'll feel the warmth as soon as you enter. The bar, whose walls are lined with tankards, is usually packed with a mix of drinkers and diners, perhaps enjoying homemade scotch eggs or fish with triple-cooked chips; you'll feel as though you just want to join in the fun. There is a quieter space behind the bar but if you want something completely different then go down a few steps and you'll find a grand and lavishly kitted out baronial style dining room. The daily changing menu is full of seasonality and diversity. Oysters, Asian salads or charcuterie can be followed by beef Bourguignon or some terrific game, and there's usually a great selection of ice creams to finish. Sunday lunch is a family affair, with spit-roast chicken a speciality.

Closing times
Open daily

Prices
Meals: a la carte £ 30/40

Typical Dishes

Prawn, pea and broad beans salad

Pan-fried plaice, trompette risotto & Jerusalem artichoke velouté

Chocolate fondant & poppy seed sorbet

⊖ *East Putney.*

57 The Spencer Arms

237 Lower Richmond Rd,
Putney, SW15 1HJ
Tel.: (020)87880640 – Fax: (020)87882216
e-mail: info@thespencerarms.co.uk
Website: www.thespencerarms.co.uk

VISA MC AE

Sharp's Doom Bar, Fuller's London Pride and one monthly changing guest ale from Sharp's Brewery

The Spencer Arms is one of those classic Victorian pubs that have a likeably unassuming manner and unstructured layout. The etched windows proclaim the offer of "Gutsy Grub" which is no word of a lie: food here is of the what-you-see-is-what-you-get variety which means it's satisfying and wholesome. They also offer small plates of what could be referred to – for lack of an alternative – as 'English tapas'. These can act as starters, bar nibbles or just as shared plates and include Scotch egg, smoked mackerel or black pudding sausage rolls; order too many, however, and your bill will quickly climb. Traditionalists can still order their three-courser and there are more Mediterranean flavours too, in the form of chorizo, ratatouille and panna cotta.

Closing times
Closed 25 December and 1 January

Prices
Meals: a la carte £ 18/25

Typical Dishes
Chicken liver parfait
Duck confit with flageolets à la crème
Mango & passion fruit cheesecake

⊖ *East Putney.*

58 The Ebury

11 Pimlico Rd,
Victoria, SW1W 8NA
Tel.: (020)77306784 – Fax: (020)77306149
e-mail: info@theebury.co.uk
Website: www.theebury.co.uk

VISA MC AE D

Fuller's London Pride

Grab a passing waiter to get yourself seated otherwise they'll assume you've just come for a drink at the bar and will ignore you. Once you've got your feet under one of the low-slung tables, however, you'll find everything moves up a gear. This is a rather smart affair and provides an object lesson in how to draw in punters. That means a varied menu, from burger to black bream, assorted salads that show some thought, three vegetarian dishes and main courses that display a degree of originality. Add to that a conscientious kitchen, a wine list that offers plenty by the glass and carafe, and weekend brunch that goes on until 4pm and it's little wonder the place is always so busy. The waiters come with French accents and self-confidence.

Closing times
Closed 25-26 December

Prices
Meals: £ 20 (lunch and early dinner) and a la carte £ 30/45

Typical Dishes
Goat's cheese beignets
Chargrilled poussin, asparagus, lemon & pecorino
Chocolate fondant & pistachio ice cream

⊖ *Sloane Square. Pay & display in the street.*

59 The Larrik

32 Crawford Pl,
Marylebone, W1H 5NN
Tel.: (020)77230066
e-mail: info@thelarrik.com
Website: www.thelarrik.com

VISA MC AE

Regularly changing guest ales including Charles Wells' Bombardier, Sharp's Doom Bar and Hook Norton

Its airy feel and capable service means that The Larrik has always been popular with larger groups and now, thanks to the obvious ambition of the owner, it's attracting plenty more customers for the quality of its food; so it's no surprise to find the place packed by 1pm on a daily basis. Try to sit at the front where it's brighter and more fun. Freshly made and substantial salads, a luxurious chicken liver parfait, plump salmon and haddock fishcakes with hollandaise and rewardingly rich desserts like chocolate brownies confirm a kitchen that's well grounded in the basics and aware of what people want from a pub. Add regularly changing real ales and you have a pub that's set to be part of the local landscape for some time to come.

Closing times
Closed 25 December

Prices
Meals: a la carte £ 20/27

Typical Dishes

Chicken liver parfait & onion chutney

Fishcake with poached egg & hollandaise sauce

Chocolate brownie & vanilla ice cream

⊖ *Edgware Rd. On-street parking meters.*

60 The Only Running Footman

5 Charles St,
Mayfair, W1J 5DF
Tel.: (020)74992988 – Fax: (020)76298061
e-mail: manager@therunningfootmanmayfair.com
Website: www.therunningfootmanmayfair.com

VISA MC AE

Fuller's London Pride, Wells Bombardier, Youngs

Apparently the owners added 'only' to the title when they found out that theirs was the only pub in the land called 'The Running Footman'. Spread over several levels, it offers cookery demonstrations and private dinners along with its two floors of dining. Downstairs is where the action usually is, with its menu offering pub classics from steak sandwiches to fishcakes, but you can't book here and it's always packed. Upstairs is where you'll find a surprisingly formal dining room and here they do take reservations. Its menu is far more ambitious and European in its influence but the best dishes are still the simpler ones, with desserts being a strength. But you can't help feeling that you would be having a lot more fun below stairs.

Closing times
Open daily

Prices
Meals: a la carte £ 26/35

Typical Dishes
Confit of wild rabbit terrine with truffle jelly on toast
Roast rump of veal, capers and mint
Strawberry & champagne jelly

⊖ Green Park.

61 The Orange

37-39 Pimlico Rd,
Victoria, SW1W 8NE
Tel.: (020)78819844
e-mail: reservations@theorange.co.uk
Website: www.theorange.co.uk

  AE

 **Harvey's and Adnams Bitters**

The Belgravia-Victoria-Pimlico quarter is clearly working for the team behind The Thomas Cubitt and Pantechnicon Rooms because their latest pub, The Orange, is within shouting distance of their other two and appears to be equally busy. But there are a couple of differences: this pub has bedrooms, nicely decorated and named after the local streets, and the food is a little more down-to-earth and family-friendly. Pizza in the bar from their wood-fired oven is always a popular choice; there's Film Night on Mondays and, unusually, the first floor restaurant is noisier than the bar. The building's stucco-fronted façade may be quite grand but the colonial feel inside and the particularly friendly service create a pleasantly laid-back atmosphere.

Closing times
Open daily

Prices
Meals: a la carte £ 23/26

4 rooms: £ 189/212

Typical Dishes

Shoulder of pork with figs & chestnut

Torn chicken with sage & pecorino pizza

Rice pudding & winter berry jam

 ⊖ *Sloane Square.*

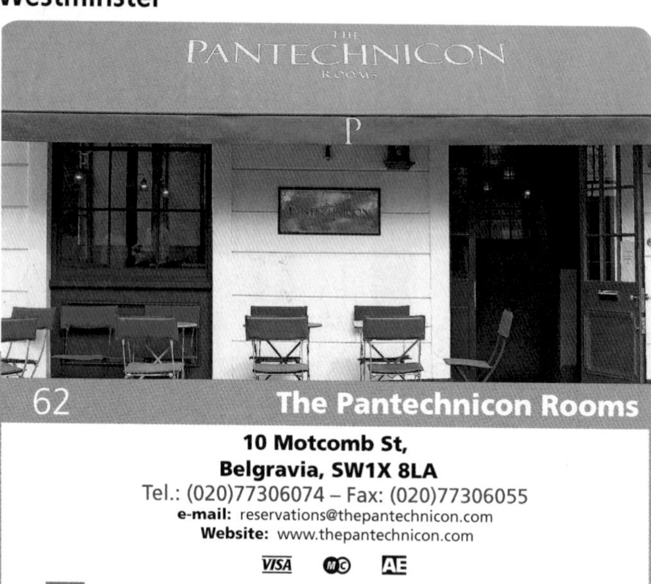

62 **The Pantechnicon Rooms**

10 Motcomb St,
Belgravia, SW1X 8LA
Tel.: (020)77306074 – Fax: (020)77306055
e-mail: reservations@thepantechnicon.com
Website: www.thepantechnicon.com

VISA MC AE

Adnams Southwold Bitter

The name 'Pantechnicon' either refers to a large removal wagon or the antique repository which once sat on Motcomb Street until it was destroyed by fire in the 1870s. It's no clearer inside, as you'll find both sepia photos of assorted removal vehicles as well as a painting depicting the fire. But one thing is certain: this is the antithesis of a spit 'n' sawdust pub. The ground floor is first-come-first-served and is always lively but upstairs is an altogether more gracious affair, designed for those who like a little formality with their pheasant. The cooking is traditional but with a twist. Oysters are a perennial; there's a decent salad selection and they set their stall by the traceability of their mature Scottish steaks.

Closing times
Open daily

Prices
Meals: a la carte £ 30/45

⊖ *Knightsbridge .*

63 Prince Alfred & Formosa Dining Room

5A Formosa St,
Maida Vale, W9 1EE
Tel.: (020)72863287
e-mail: princealfred@youngs.co.uk
Website: www.theprincealfred.com

VISA MC AE

 **Youngs Bitter and Charles Wells' Bombardier**

Original plate glass, panels and snugs make The Prince Alfred a wonderful example of a classic Victorian pub. Unfortunately, the eating is done in the Formosa Dining Room extension on the side but at least it's a lively room with capable cooking. There's a rustic theme running through the menu, with a strong British accent, so traditionalists will enjoy the fish pie, potted trout, steak and ale pie and calves liver but there are also risottos, parfaits and terrines for those of a more European bent. The open kitchen is not averse to sprucing up some classics, for example your burger arrives adorned with foie gras and truffles. Prices are realistic, even with a charge made for bread, and the friendly team cope well under pressure.

Closing times
Open daily

Prices
Meals: a la carte £ 21/35

Typical Dishes
Crayfish tail Caesar salad
Crispy pork belly
Passion fruit and mango cheesecake

 *⊖ Warwick Avenue. Parking by Warwick Avenue station (2min on foot).*

64 The Thomas Cubitt

44 Elizabeth St,
Victoria, SW1W 9PA
Tel.: (020)77306060 – Fax: (020)77306055
e-mail: reservations@thethomascubitt.co.uk
Website: www.thethomascubitt.co.uk

  AE

Adnams' Southwold BItter and IPA

The Thomas Cubitt is a pub of two halves: on the ground floor it's perennially busy and you can't book which means that if you haven't arrived by 7pm then you're too late to get a table. However, you can reserve a table upstairs, in a dining room that's a model of civility and tranquillity. Here, service comes courtesy of a young team where the girls are chatty and the men unafraid of corduroy. Downstairs you get fish and chips; here you get pan-fried fillet of brill with oyster beignet and truffled chips. The cooking is certainly skilled, quite elaborate in its construction and prettily presented. So, take your pick: upstairs can get a little pricey but is ideal for entertaining the in-laws; if out with friends then crowd in downstairs.

Closing times
Open daily
booking essential

Prices
Meals: a la carte £ 30/45

Typical Dishes
Seared Loch Crinan scallops
Peppered wild venison fillet
White chocolate crème brûlée

⊖ Sloane Square. Parking meters in Elizabeth Street.

65 The Warrington

93 Warrington Cres,
Bayswater, W9 1EH
Tel.: (020)75927960 – Fax: (020)75921603
e-mail: thewarrington@gordonramsay.com
Website: www.gordonramsay.com

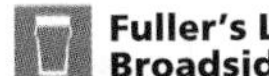 **Fuller's London Pride, Greene King IPA, Adnams Broadside**

The British pub appears to be steadily breaking up into two rival camps: there's the traditional pub, where you can stand at the bar with a sausage roll in one hand and a pint in the other; and the modern one, where you're given a table and someone serves you pork belly and a glass of Pinot Noir. The joy of The Warrington is that both types are available under one roof. The wood-panelled ground floor with its friezes and mosaic is full of atmosphere and the menu here includes fish pie and bangers. Upstairs is altogether smarter and the mood a little more subdued. Here the menu is much more sophisticated, as you'd expect from a Gordon Ramsay restaurant, although it's still commendably British and could include braised duck or pan-fried bream.

Closing times
Closed lunch Monday-Wednesday

Prices
Meals: £ 22 (lunch and early dinner) and a la carte £ 20/30

 ⊖ *Maida Vale. Parking meters in Sutherland Avenue; on-street parking in Warrington Crescent.*

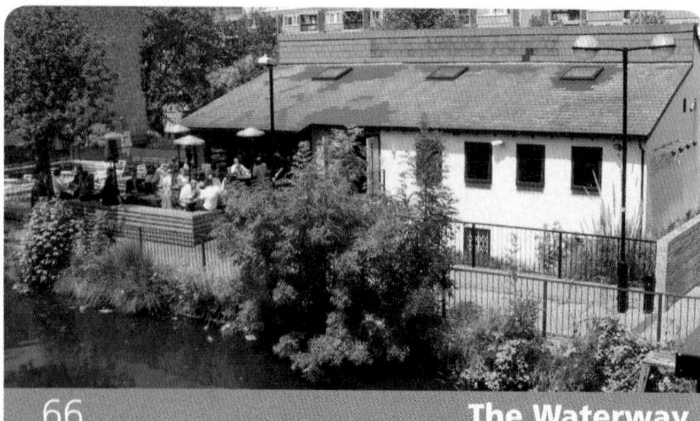

66 The Waterway

54 Formosa St,
Maida Vale, W9 2JU
Tel.: (020)72663557 – Fax: (020)72663547
e-mail: info@thewaterway.co.uk
Website: www.thewaterway.co.uk

VISA MC AE

Fullers London Pride and guest ale Summer Lightning

Strictly speaking, The Waterway is not really a pub but it does always have lots of people standing outside with drinks in their hands. To see it at its best you have to arrive by narrowboat as the terrific canalside terrace is one of its great selling points. The dining area is beyond the bar and has a nicely balanced menu. For starters expect squid, scallops or risotto; main courses could include beef Bourguignon or duck breast with okra and dishes are executed with a certain degree of vim. There are more accessible choices available too, especially on the terrace, like the house burger, Caesar salad and rib-eye steak. The young team of servers can sometimes place too much emphasis on functionality at the expense of personality.

Closing times
Open daily

Prices
Meals: £ 17 (lunch)
and a la carte £ 30/45

Typical Dishes
Truffled asparagus & egg beignet
Rump of salt marsh lamb & ratatouille
Raspberry panna cotta

⊖ *Warwick Avenue.*

This region cradles some of England's wildest and most dramatic scenery typified by Northumberland National Park, a landscape of rolling purple moorlands and roaring rivers bursting with salmon and trout. Kielder Forest's mighty wilderness has been called "the country's most tranquil spot" while Bill Bryson has waxed lyrical upon the glories of Durham Cathedral. Those who love the wind in their hair are equally effusive about the eleven-mile footpath that accompanies the pounding waves of Durham's Heritage Coast; further north are the long, dune-backed beaches of Northumberland. Rambling across the region is Hadrian's Wall, 73 miles of iconic Roman history, while a modern slant on architectural celebrity is proffered by the Millennium Bridge, BALTIC Centre and Angel of the North. The famously bracing air whets hearty appetites for local Cheviot lamb, Coquetdale cheese or Holy Island oysters. And what could be more redolent of the North East than a breakfast of Craster kippers?

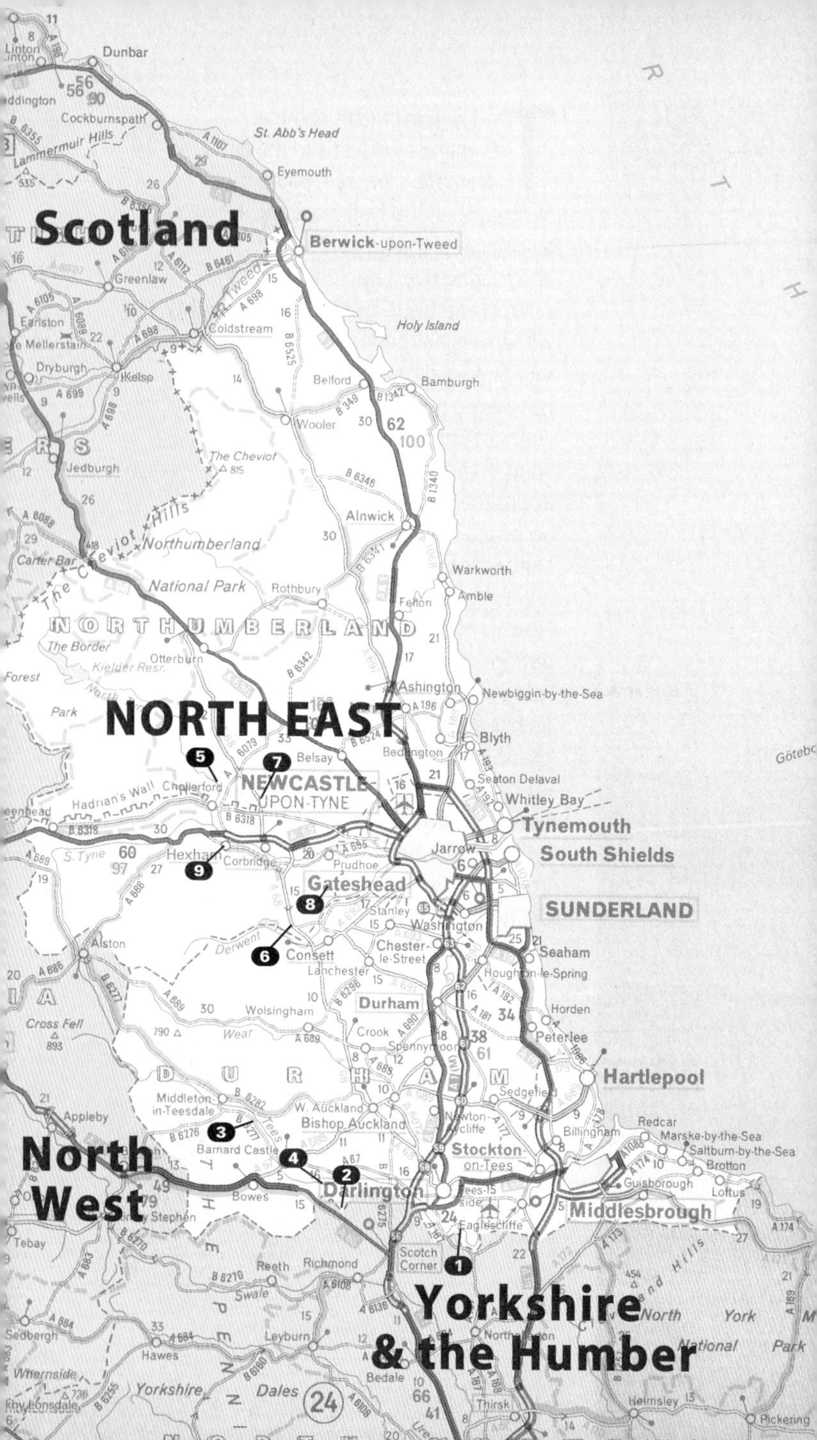

Scotland
NORTH EAST
North West
Yorkshire & the Humber
Dunbar
Cockburnspath
Lammermuir Hills
St. Abb's Head
Eyemouth
Berwick-upon-Tweed
Greenlaw
Coldstream
Earlston
Mellerstain
Dryburgh
Kelso
Holy Island
Belford
Bamburgh
Wooler
Jedburgh
The Cheviot
Cheviot Hills
Carter Bar
Northumberland
National Park
Alnwick
Warkworth
Amble
Felton
Rothbury
NORTHUMBERLAND
The Border
Otterburn
Kielder Resr.
Forest
Park
Ashington
Newbiggin-by-the-Sea
Blyth
Bedlington
Belsay
Seaton Delaval
Whitley Bay
Chollerford
Hadrian's Wall
NEWCASTLE-UPON-TYNE
Tynemouth
South Shields
Jarrow
Hexham
Corbridge
Prudhoe
S. Tyne
Gateshead
SUNDERLAND
Stanley
Washington
Chester-le-Street
Seaham
Houghton-le-Spring
Alston
Derwent
Consett
Lanchester
Durham
Horden
Peterlee
Cross Fell
Wolsingham
Wear
Crook
Spennymoor
Hartlepool
DURHAM
Sedgefield
Middleton-in-Teesdale
W. Auckland
Bishop Auckland
Appleby
Newton Aycliffe
Billingham
Redcar
Marske-by-the-Sea
Saltburn-by-the-Sea
Brotton
Loftus
Barnard Castle
Stockton-on-Tees
Darlington
Bowes
Guisborough
Middlesbrough
Tees-side
Eaglescliffe
Tebay
Scotch Corner
Richmond
Reeth
Swale
North York Moors National Park
Sedbergh
Hawes
Leyburn
Northallerton
Whernside
Yorkshire Dales
Bedale
Thirsk
Helmsley
Pickering
Kirkby Lonsdale
1
2
3
4
5
6
7
8
9

1 **The Bay Horse**

45 The Green,
Hurworth on Tees, DL2 2AA
Tel.: (01325)720663 – Fax: (01325)729840
e-mail: mail@thebayhorsehurworth.com
Website: www.thebayhorsehurworth.com

Inspectors' favourites

Bitter & Twisted, Stafford's Stallion, Cumberland

Set on a long grassy street in an attractive village, this early 18C creamwashed pub is framed by colourful planters and hanging baskets, and boasts a pleasant rear terrace and garden. Drinkers and diners mingle amongst antique chairs, low stools and leather banquettes in the open-fired bar area and the relaxed, informal atmosphere continues through into the dining room. For special occasions the private first floor room definitely adds some style, with its 20 foot Victorian table and adjoining lounge. Menus offer something for everyone, featuring classics such as moules marinierè, daube of beef or omelette Arnold Bennett, as well as familiar pub favourites. Dishes range in their presentation from simple and rustic to modern and intricate.

Closing times
Closed Sunday dinner

Prices
Meals: £ 15 (weekday lunch) and a la carte £ 22/38

Typical Dishes
Wild duck with pistachio terrine
Beef and ale suet pudding
Baked ginger and treacle sponge with Calvados custard

2 mi south of Darlington; signed off A 167; in the middle of the village. Parking.

Hutton Magna

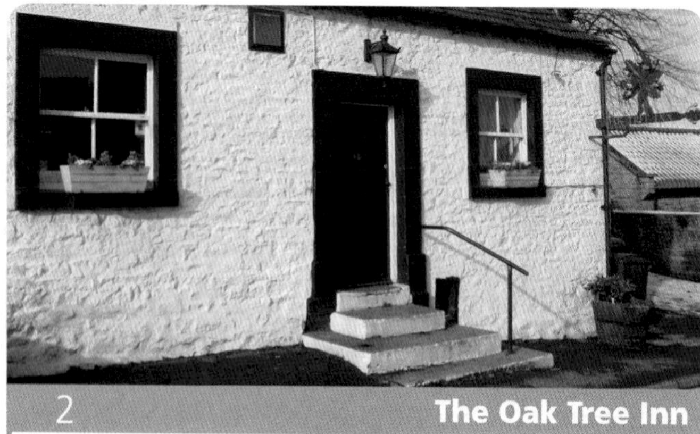

2

The Oak Tree Inn

Hutton Magna,
DL11 7HH
Tel.: (01833)627371

Black Sheep Best, Wells Bombardier, Timothy Taylor Landlord

They say good things come in small packages and that's definitely the case with this charming whitewashed pub. Found on the main street of a small hamlet, it consists of a single room with a proper old-fashioned counter, six wooden tables flanked by green settles and a bench table for the locals. Claire – who both serves the drinks and delivers the food – provides a warm welcome at the bar, while behind the scenes in the kitchen, Alastair single-handedly holds the fort. The menu takes on a fairly formal format, offering generous portions of hearty, flavoursome cooking with a rustic French feel: you might find confit belly pork, onion and thyme tart or best end of lamb. More wide-ranging flavours such as cumin and chilli often appear too.

Closing times
Closed 25-27 December and 1-2 January
dinner only
booking essential

Prices
Meals: a la carte £ 26/33

Typical Dishes
Onion & thyme tart with salmon
Lamb with feta cheese & olive pasty
Hot chocolate fondant

7 mi southeast of Barnard Castle off A 66. Parking.

3 Rose and Crown

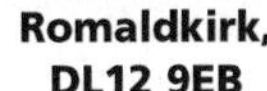

Romaldkirk,
DL12 9EB
Tel.: (01833)650213 – Fax: (01833)650111
e-mail: hotel@rose-and-crown.co.uk
Website: www.rose-and-crown.co.uk

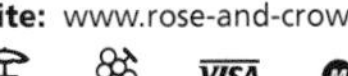

Theakston Best Bitter, Black Sheep Bitter and Allendale' s Best (Guest)

Set next to a Saxon church in the middle of three village greens – looking out over a water pump and some stocks – is this quintessential 18C English village inn. There's a wonderfully atmospheric front bar displaying plenty of brass, a warmly decorated brasserie and, tucked away to the rear, a cosy lounge boasting an impressive grandfather clock. Between the bar and brasserie menus there's a good range of dishes, with a core of classics and some more substantial offerings at dinner. In the evening, residents tend to favour the traditional linen-laid dining room with its china-filled dresser and seasonally changing four course menu. Split between the inn and the courtyard, bedrooms are cosy and classical, but boast modern TVs and Bose radios.

Closing times
Closed 24-26 December

Prices
Meals: a la carte £ 17/29
12 rooms: £ 92/165

3.5 mi southeast of Middleton-in-Teesdale on B 6277; on the village green, next to the church. Parking.

Whorlton

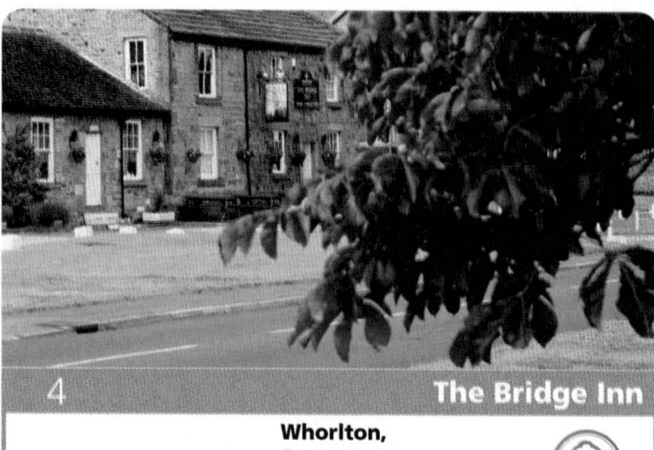

4 **The Bridge Inn**

Whorlton,
DL12 8XD
Tel.: (01833)627341 – Fax: (01833)627995
e-mail: info@thebridgeinnrestaurant.co.uk
Website: www.thebridgeinnrestaurant.co.uk

Adnams Bitter, Timothy Taylor Landlord, Theakston Black Bull

The flat screen television delivering live broadcasts of all the kitchen action to the dining room speaks volumes about how seriously the chefs at The Bridge Inn take their work. The resulting dishes are accomplished and full of flavour, and the kitchen knows what goes with what, be it smoked eel fillet with roast beetroot and horseradish or winter fruits with cinnamon ice cream. Its two rooms contrast in style: the bar is traditional, with beams, horse brasses and an open fire, while the spacious white dining room, with its contemporary edge, feels faintly stark in comparison. The beautiful Teeside village of Whorlton is a grand spot for a post-prandial stroll; keep an eye out for the suspension bridge after which the pub is named.

Closing times
Closed first 2 weeks in January, Sunday and Monday lunch

Prices
Meals: £ 17 and a la carte £ 22/37

Typical Dishes
Pigeon breast with nettle risotto
Halibut with mushy peas and chips
Iced cinder toffee parfait

5 mi east of Barnard Castle by A 67 and minor road south. Parking.

5 Barrasford Arms

Barrasford,
NE48 4AA
Tel.: (01434)681237
e-mail: contact@barrasfordarms.co.uk
Website: www.barrasfordarms.co.uk

 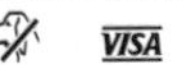  

 **Gold Tankard, Grannys Sock and Humble Heifer**

Set right in the heart of the Northumbrian countryside, close to Kielder Water and Hadrian's Wall, this personally run 19C stone inn provides an ideal base for exploring the North Tyne Valley. Retaining its traditional character, this pub provides the perfect home from home. The cosy fire is a huge draw, as are the regular vegetable, darts and quoits competitions, but the star attraction here really is the food. Menus differ between lunch and dinner; the former being a touch less formal. Pub classics such as steak pie or gammon and fat cut chips give way to more substantial offerings such as cheese soufflé or grilled rabbit, followed by local shoulder of lamb or chicken with truffle risotto. Comfortable bedrooms take on a modern style.

Closing times
Closed 25 December, 1 January, Sunday dinner and Monday lunch

Prices
Meals: £ 13 (lunch) and a la carte £ 22/30

7 rooms: £ 45/85

 *7 mi north of Hexham signed off A 6079. Parking.*

Carterway Heads

6 **Manor House Inn**

Carterway Heads,
DH8 9LX
Tel.: (01207)255268
Website: www.themanorhouseinn.com

Old Speckled Hen, Banks's, Timothy Taylor Landlord, Copper Dragon and Wychwood Hobglobin

High up on the hills between the Tyne Valley and Consett sits this stone-built pub, with Derwent Reservoir just visible in the valley below. There's a room to suit your every mood, from the rustic, wood-floored locals bar, complete with dartboard and muzak, to the traditional lounge bar with its countryside views; or perhaps one of the two dining rooms; the smaller one more cosy, with an open fire. The main menu offers classic dishes like braised lamb shank, steak and ale pie or slow braised oxtail, while the hanging slate specials boards offer more variety and can change several times a day, depending on what is fresh in at any given time. 'The Gables' offers space for private parties, and four comfortable bedrooms boast pleasant views.

Closing times
Open daily

Prices
Meals: a la carte £ 13/37
4 rooms: £ 45/75

Typical Dishes
Homemade chicken liver paté & onion marmalade
Slow roasted belly pork
Sticky toffee pudding

3 mi west of Consett at junction of B 6278 and A 68. Parking.

7 Queens Head Inn

Great Whittington,
NE19 2HP
Tel.: (01434)672267
Website: www.the-queens-head-inn.co.uk

  VISA MC

 **Tyneside Blonde and Deuchars IPA**

A wonderful mural above the fire in the bar depicts the Queens Head Inn as it once was; in fact, this cosy room was at one time all that existed of what is considered by some to be the oldest inn in Northumberland. Its 400 year old thick brick walls have now been breached and the rear extension houses a dining room filled with bookshelves, old farming implements and general bric à brac. The lunchtime menu offers anything from filled stotties to duck spring rolls, while the evening menu might mean homemade game terrine, twice-baked soufflé, lambs liver and bacon or honey-roast Barbary duck; with lamb and Galloway beef supplied by the farm next door. Service is as friendly as it comes, and a couple of courses shouldn't break the bank.

Closing times
Closed 25 December

Prices
Meals: a la carte £ 17/28

Typical Dishes
Spiced pork belly & pan-seared scallops
Great Whittington rump steak
Traditional banoffee pie

 *6 mi north of Corbridge by A 68 off B 6318. Parking.*

Hedley on the Hill

8 **The Feathers Inn**

Hedley on the Hill,
NE43 7SW
Tel.: (01661)843607
e-mail: info@thefeathers.net
Website: www.thefeathers.net

Inspectors' favourites

Mordue Workie Ticket, Cumberland Brewery's Corby, Consett Red Dust

Bookshelves crammed with cookbooks suggest that this is a place which takes its food seriously; words like 'homemade', 'local' and 'Northumbrian' pepper the daily changing menu, while the map printed on the back, showing the provenance of the various ingredients, provides further proof of the pub's foodie credentials. Traditional pub dishes such as sausage and mash sit alongside bar snacks like whitebait, but the highlight here are the old-fashioned British classics like devilled lamb, potted hare or leek and cheese pie. Thanks to its enthusiastic owners, this community pub always has something going on; be it a quiz, a theme night or the annual beer barrel race. It's set on a steep hill and affords great views over Newcastle and Gateshead.

Closing times
Closed first 2 weeks in January and Monday lunch

Prices
Meals: a la carte £ 16/25

6 mi north of Consett by A 694, B 6309 and minor road. Parking.

9 The Rat Inn

Anick,
Hexham, NE46 4LN
Tel.: (01434)602814
e-mail: info@theratinn.com
Website: www.theratinn.com

Bass Draught, Deuchar's, Nel's Best, Wylam Gold, Allendale Curlew's Return and other regularly changing ales

A) Rat catchers once used this as a meeting place, B) It was once home to a large rat, C) The local snitch lived here during the Jacobite rebellion. Unfortunately nobody knows the answer as to how this 18C drover's inn got its name, so just sit back and enjoy the pleasant Tyne valley views and tasty, wholesome cooking. Situated in a small hillside hamlet, it's the perfect place to escape the rat race of the city, with its multi-levelled garden boasting arbours and picnic sets, and a traditional interior displaying wooden beams and an open range. The daily blackboard menu is concise but covers a good range of dishes, from pub classics such as cottage pie to more ambitious rack of lamb for two. Produce is fresh, good quality and locally sourced.

Closing times
Closed Sunday dinner and Monday

Prices
Meals: a la carte £ 18/30

Typical Dishes
Terrine of local game
Roast Northumbria rib of beef
Sticky toffee pudding

1.45 mi north of Hexham off A 69. Parking.

England • North East • Northumberland

Energised by Liverpool's swagger as 2008's European City of Culture, the north west feels like a region reborn. Dovetailed by the confident sophistication of a reinvigorated Manchester, the country's oldest industrial heartland boasts an impressive cultural profile. And yet arty urban centres are a million miles away from the rural grandeur of the region: trails and paths criss-cross the area all the way from the Solway Firth to Cheshire. Cumbria is a walker's paradise: from Hadrian's Wall to the glories of the Lake District, and along the vast shoreline of Morecambe Bay with its rich gathering of waders and wildfowl, there's a vivid contrast in scenery. The architectural landscape of the region covers the ages, too. Lancaster Castle reverberates to the footsteps of ancient soldiers, while Chester's walled city of medieval buildings is a true gem. Blackpool is now Europe's biggest seaside resort while the flavour of the north west is hotpot, black pudding and Morecambe Bay shrimps.

Scotland
North East
NORTH
Yorkshire & the Humber
CUMBRIA
ISLE OF MAN
Dumfries
New Galloway
Cairnryan
Stranraer
Newton Stewart
Glenluce
Wigtown
Castle Douglas
Gatehouse of Fleet
Ringford
Kirkcudbright
Dalbeattie
New Abbey
Auchencairn
Port William
Whithorn
Isle of Whithorn
Drummore
Luce Bay
Wigtown Bay
Burrow Head
Mull of Galloway
Solway Firth
Annan
Gretna
Canonbie
Longtown
Bowness-on-Solway
Carlisle
Brampton
Greenhead
Hadrian's Wall
Chollerford
Hexham
Corbridge
NEWCASTLE UPON TYNE
Belsay
Park
North Tyne
S. Tyne
Alston
Consett
Wolsingham
Wear
Cross Fell
Silloth
Abbey Town
Wigton
Thursby
Aspatria
Bothel
Maryport
Cockermouth
Workington
Whitehaven
St. Bees Head
Frizington
Egremont
Gosforth
Keswick
Derwent water
Skiddaw
Buttermere
Cumbrian Mountains
Lake District
Scafell Pikes
Penrith
Eden
Ullswater
Patterdale
Grasmere
Ambleside
Windermere
Coniston
Bowness
Kendal
Broughton-in-Furness
Greenodd
Millom
Ulverston
Dalton
Barrow-in-Furness
Grange-Over-Sands
Carnforth
Morecambe
Appleby
Orton
Tebay
Brough
Kirkby Stephen
Sedbergh
Whernside
Ingleton
Middleton-in-Teesdale
Barnard Castle
Bowes
Tees
Reeth
Swale
Leyburn
Hawes
Yorkshire Dales
Threshfield
Point of Ayre
Ramsey
Ballaugh
Snaefell
Peel
Douglas
Port Erin
Port St. Mary
Castletown
Ronaldsway
Belfast

IRISH SEA
BLACKPOOL
LIVERPOOL
WEST
MANCHESTER
East Midlands
West Midlands
Wales
LANCASHIRE
CHESHIRE
GWYNEDD
ANGLESEY
Fleetwood
Cleveleys
Lytham St. Anne's
Southport
Preston
Blackburn
Clitheroe
Burnley
Nelson
Keighley
BRADFORD
Halifax
Rochdale
Bolton
Bury
Wigan
Oldham
Huddersfield
St. Helens
Warrington
Stockport
Altrincham
Wilmslow
Macclesfield
Knutsford
Northwich
Chester
Wrexham
Crewe
Congleton
Leek
STOKE-ON-TRENT
Newcastle-under-Lyme
Birkenhead
Wallasey
Bootle
Rhyl
Colwyn Bay
Llandudno
Conwy
Bangor
Caernarfon
Holyhead / Caergybi
Pwllheli
Bala
Llangollen
Oswestry
Snowdonia

Alderley Edge

1 The Wizard

Macclesfield Rd,
Alderley Edge, SK10 4UB
Tel.: (01625)584000 – Fax: (01625)585105
e-mail: wizardrestaurant@googlemail.com
Website: www.ainscoughs.co.uk

VISA

Thwaites Original and fortnightly changing Storm Brewery guest ales

With its flag floors, wood beams and open fires, this 200 year old pub is full of character and charm. Being dog friendly, it attracts its fair share of walkers, and its mix of drinkers and diners – and the resulting vibrant atmosphere – make it feel like a proper pub. Small tapas-style plates like grilled halloumi or devilled chipolatas give drinkers something to nibble on. There are lunchtime sandwiches and pub favourites like pies, burgers and beef dripping chips, as well as more substantial dishes like lamb hotpot or roast pork belly, with the occasional Mediterranean influence. Cooking makes good use of seasonal, local produce and is flavourful, straightforward and very good value. Service is polite and attentive, if rather too formal.

Closing times
Closed 25 December
Prices
Meals: a la carte £ 20/40

Typical Dishes
Seared scallops & truffled mash
Roast saddle & leg of rabbit
Bread & butter pudding

1.25 mi southeast of Alderley Edge on B 5087.

2 The Pheasant Inn

Higher Burwardsley,
CH3 9PF
Tel.: (01829)770434 – Fax: (01829)771097
e-mail: info@thepheasantinn.co.uk
Website: www.thepheasantinn.co.uk

 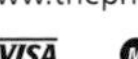 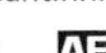 AE

Weetwood - Best, Eastgate, Old Dog and one changing guest ale

Set on a large sandstone outcrop in the middle of the Cheshire plains, this characterful stone pub boasts great views over the surrounding area. Popular with walkers following the Sandstone Trail, it boasts reclaimed beams, stone columns and gas fires. One room is fairly pubby with a leather-furnished snug; the other, similar in style but with more formal seating. The huge windows are a real feature – and tables by them are extremely sought-after – but the best place to sit is on the terrace itself. Extensive daily menus offer refined pub favourites, as well as some Mediterranean-influenced dishes, and sandwiches are available throughout the afternoon. Spacious, beamed bedrooms in the main building; more modern rooms with views in the barn.

Closing times
Closed 25 December

Prices
Meals: a la carte £ 21/33

12 rooms: £ 70/145

 *2.5 mi southeast of Tattenhall. Parking.*

Lach Dennis

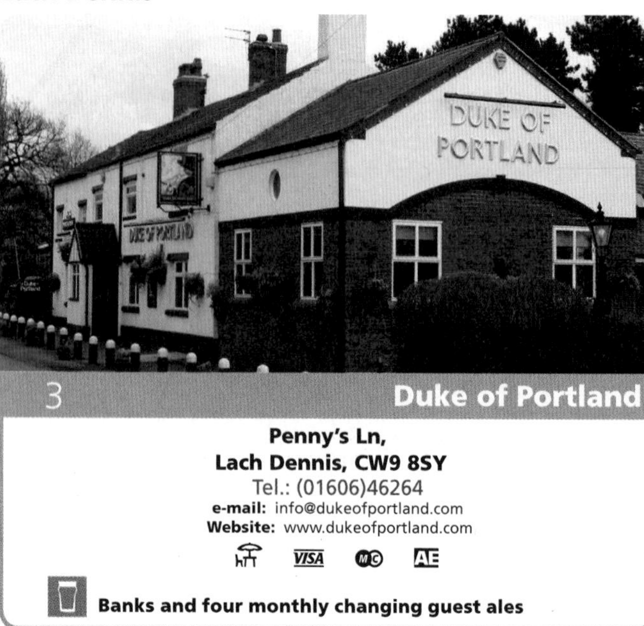

3 **Duke of Portland**

Penny's Ln,
Lach Dennis, CW9 8SY
Tel.: (01606)46264
e-mail: info@dukeofportland.com
Website: www.dukeofportland.com

VISA MC AE

Banks and four monthly changing guest ales

This cream-washed inn sits on the main road through the village, welcoming drinkers and diners alike. The former tend to gather in the high-ceilinged main bar or the relaxing, leather-furnished lounge. The latter have two choices: a raised area close to the bar and – the more popular option – a smart, contemporary side room which houses a mounted stag's head, shot in 1931 by the Duke of Portland. The lengthy à la carte menu offers dishes that won't scare the horses; the daily specials provide a little more interest. Good quality, organic ingredients are sourced from local farmers and artisan suppliers, who are proudly name-checked on the menu. A paved rear terrace offers an appealing alfresco option should the weather choose to acquiesce.

Closing times
Open daily

Prices
Meals: £ 16 (lunch and Monday-Thursday dinner)) and a la carte £ 22/35

Typical Dishes
Black pudding & Old Spot pork belly
Confit of lamb & mini shepherd's pie
Treacle tart

3.5 mi west of Northwich by B 5082. Parking.

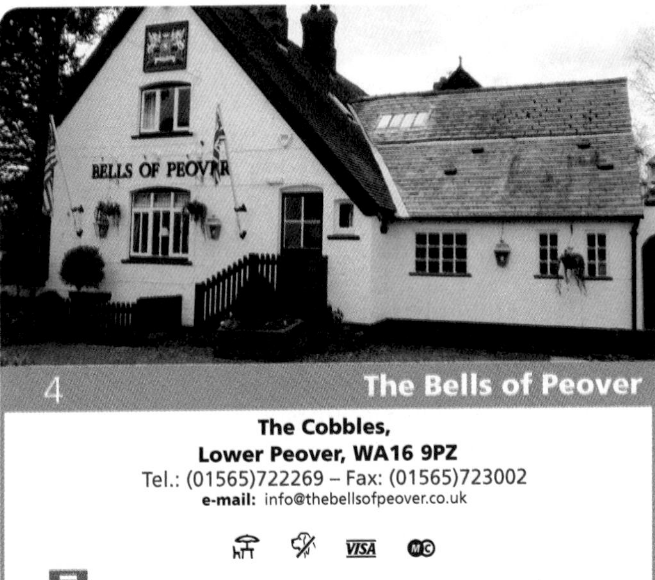

4 The Bells of Peover

The Cobbles,
Lower Peover, WA16 9PZ
Tel.: (01565)722269 – Fax: (01565)723002
e-mail: info@thebellsofpeover.co.uk

VISA

Dizzy Blonde and Theakston's XB

So, why does this refurbished 16C former coaching inn have the Stars and Stripes flying over it? Because, apparently, Generals Eisenhower and Patton were stationed nearby and were regulars. And the Bells? No, not from the church tower but the name of a family who once owned it. These days the pub offers a range of options: from scrumpy and snacks to a full culinary extravaganza. In the bar and the two ground floor dining rooms you'll find a large, appealing menu of classic pub dishes, done well. Up three steps and you enter into 'fine dining' territory, where the ingredients are of a more luxurious (and pricey) nature. Service can be a little over formal, particularly downstairs, but should relax a little over time.

Closing times
Open daily

Prices
Meals: a la carte £ 19/34

Off the B 5081 road through the village. Parking.

Lymm

5 **The Church Green**

Higher Ln,
Lymm, WA13 0AP
Tel.: (01925)752068
e-mail: aidenbyrne@thechurchgreen.co.uk
Website: www.thechurchgreen.co.uk

VISA MC AE

 **Two weekly changing regional ales**

Standing on the green next to St Mary's Church, the original inn burnt down and was later replaced by this double gable-fronted Victorian pub beside Lymm Dam. The experienced chef-owner, Aiden Byrne (who appeared on BBC2s the Great British Menu) is supported by a pleasant, well-structured team, and takes pride in the pub's kitchen garden, which supplies everything from beetroot to soft fruits. The open-plan bar and restaurant are decorated in modern browns and creams and there's a pleasant conservatory and attractive decked terrace to the rear. Throughout the afternoon, the lounge-bar offers simple, pub-style dishes but things step up a gear in the evening with more ambitious offerings such as pork with scallops or beetroot poached salmon.

Closing times
Closed 25 December
booking essential
Prices
Meals: £ 25 (lunch) and a la carte £ 30/38

 *7 mi west of Altrincham by A 56. Parking.*

6 **The Bull**

Worthenbury Rd,
Shocklach, SY14 7BL
Tel.: (01829)250239
e-mail: info@thebullshocklach.com
Website: www.thebullshocklach.com

    AE

 **Stonehouse Station Bitter**

You've got petrol, supermarket and coffee loyalty cards; well now you can get one for your local pub too – if you live in Shocklach, that is. As the only pub in the village, it's very much a part of the local community and you'll often see people popping in to buy some bread or milk. Inside, low beams and eye-catching, hand-painted quarry tiles are offset by contemporary greys, creams and silvers, and an eclectic mix of old posters and modern artwork cover the walls. You can order either at the bar or your table, whether you're after the full three courses or simply a soup or pie of the day – or even just a pint of the local ale. Cooking is refined, flavoursome and generous of portion, with ingredients sourced locally and game a speciality.

Closing times
Closed 25 December

Prices
Meals: a la carte £ 22/30

Typical Dishes
Duck terrine confit with sultana purée
Braised blade of beef with horseradish mash potato
Toffee apple bread & butter pudding

 5 mi northwest of Malpas, off B 5069 in village. Parking.

Ambleside

7 **Drunken Duck Inn**

Barngates,
Ambleside, LA22 0NG
Tel.: (01539)436347 – Fax: (01539)436781
e-mail: office@drunkenduckinn.co.uk
Website: www.drunkenduckinn.co.uk

VISA

Barngates Brewery : Gold, Chesters Strong & Ugly, Taglag, Cracker, Mothbag, Pride of Westmorland and Red Bull Terrier

Situated in the heart of the beautiful Lakeland countryside, this attractive inn takes its name from an old legend about a landlady, some ducks and a leaky beer barrel. The popular fire-lit bar is the cosiest place to sit, among hop bines, pictures of the hunt and old brewery advertisements; but there are also two more formal dining rooms. The same menu is served throughout, offering simple lunches and much more elaborate dinners, with prices to match; cooking is generous and service, attentive. Ales come from the on-site micro-brewery and are made with water from their own tarn. Boutique, country house bedrooms – some with patios – boast extremely comfy beds and country views. Afternoon tea can be taken in the lounge or residents' garden.

Closing times
Closed 25 December
booking essential
Prices
Meals: a la carte £ 20/40
17 rooms: £ 72/275

3 mi southwest of Ambleside by A 593 and B 5286 on Tarn Hows road. By the crossroads at the top of Duck Hill. Parking.

8 George and Dragon

Clifton,
CA10 2ER
Tel.: (01768)865381
e-mail: enquiries@georgeanddragonclifton.co.uk
Website: www.georgeanddragonclifton.co.uk

 VISA MC AE

Lancaster Blonde, Hawkshead Gold and Loweswater Gold

Enter The George and Dragon and you'll soon realise you've come somewhere a bit special. It's owned by prominent Cumbrian landowners, the Lowther family, and the food is as fresh as it gets, with organic meats including lamb and Shorthorn beef from their estate's farms, seasonal game from the surrounding woods and moors, and vegetables from the kitchen gardens. Dishes might include fish pie, chicken livers on toast or grilled local black pudding, and cooking is simple and effective. Although fully refurbished, the 18C coaching inn has lost none of its traditional character, helped along nicely by flagstones, fires, hop bines, rugs and sofas; plus photos which tell tales of the Lowther Estate from days long past. Smart, modern bedrooms.

Closing times
Open daily

Prices
Meals: a la carte £ 20/30
10 rooms: £ 67/135

Southeast : 3 mi on A6. Parking.

9 **The Punch Bowl Inn**

Crosthwaite,
LA8 8HR
Tel.: (01539)568237 – Fax: (01539)568875
e-mail: info@the-punchbowl.co.uk
Website: www.the-punchbowl.co.uk

Inspectors' favourites

Barngates' Tag Lag, Coniston's Bluebird and Stout, Ulverston's Another Fine Mess

Nestled among the hills in the heart of the picturesque Lyth Valley, this attractive 17C inn enjoys a truly delightful setting. The views are glorious, but the pub itself is charming too, boasting cosy open fires, exposed wooden beams and trailing hop bines. Dining takes place in the rustic bar and more formal restaurant; lunch features some interesting takes on classical dishes, such as venison sausage and mash or macaroni cheese with truffles – but the kitchen's ambition is most evident at dinner, where dishes display a degree of complexity that you wouldn't usually find in a pub. Individually styled bedrooms boast quality linen and smart bathrooms with roll-top baths and fluffy towels; 'Noble' features twin tubs and 'Danson', the best views.

Closing times
Open daily

Prices
Meals: a la carte £ 30/40

9 rooms: £ 95/310

Typical Dishes
Confit of sea bass & violet potatoes
Haunch of venison
Baked pear & chocolate sauce

5.25 mi west of Kendal by All Hallows Lane; next to the church. Parking.

10 **Sun Inn**

6 Market St,
Kirkby Lonsdale, LA6 2AU
Tel.: (015242)71965 – Fax: (015242)72485
e-mail: email@sun-inn.info
Website: www.sun-inn.info

VISA MC

Timothy Taylor Landlord, Hawkshead Best Bitter, Twaithes Wainwrights

'Sourced locally' means exactly that at the 17C Sun Inn: meat regularly comes from the butcher down the road; cheese comes from the famous Churchmouse cheese shop next door and if lamb is on the menu, you can be pretty certain it recently frolicked in a nearby field. Everything you would look for in a pub is here; from the rustically refurbished restaurant with its seasonal menu of appealingly presented, generously proportioned dishes, to the busy locals bar with its scrubbed wooden floors, comfy seats and open fire; from the splendid selection of real ales and the cleverly formulated wine list to the hands-on owners and their competent staff. Immaculately kept bedrooms have a modern feel, with great lighting and good quality linen.

Closing times
Closed Monday lunch

Prices
Meals: a la carte £ 24/31
11 rooms: £ 70/150

5.5 mi southwest of Junction 36 on M6. Long stay car park in Booth Rd.

11 **The Black Swan**

Kirkby Stephen,
CA17 4NG
Tel.: (01539)623204 – Fax: (01539)623204
e-mail: enquiries@blackswanhotel.com
Website: www.blackswanhotel.com

 **Black Sheep Bitter, Black Sheep Ale, John Smith's Cask and 2 guest ales**

This part-Victorian, family-run inn really is at the centre of the local community – it's not just the only pub, but also the only shop in this pleasant village; and it's so remotely set that the staff are trained as the first response team for local 999 calls too. The pub itself boasts a bar, two dining rooms and a linen-laid restaurant, while over the road, a huge garden stretches down to Scandal Beck – providing the location for their annual music festival. The same menu is served throughout and features filling pub classics, with more restaurant-style specials appearing in the evening. Staff are polite and friendly but can go a little AWOL at times. Cosy bedrooms are largely antique-furnished; one is more modern and boasts a four-poster.

Closing times
Closed 25 December

Prices
Meals: a la carte £ 17/26
15 rooms: £ 47/125

 *5 mi southwest of Brough by A 685. Parking.*

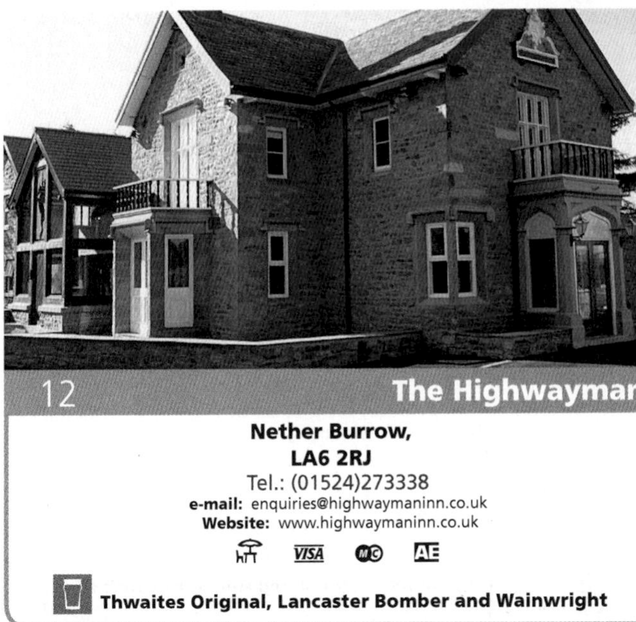

12 **The Highwayman**

Nether Burrow,
LA6 2RJ
Tel.: (01524)273338
e-mail: enquiries@highwaymaninn.co.uk
Website: www.highwaymaninn.co.uk

VISA AE

Thwaites Original, Lancaster Bomber and Wainwright

It's rumoured that this sizeable 18C coaching inn with its lovely terrace was once the midnight haunt of the local highwaymen. Set on the border of three counties – Cumbria, Lancashire and Yorkshire – it makes the most of its setting, with produce so local that a meal almost constitutes a geography lesson. The extensive menu notes the provenance of every ingredient, while on the back page a large map locates and names suppliers. Cooking is hearty and rustic with a comforting feel; you might find Thornby Moor Dairy cheese on toast with Sillfield Farm sweet-cured bacon, followed by heather-reared Lonk lamb Lancashire hotpot and then jam roly poly. Order from the efficient team at the open-fired, stone-floored bar or at any of the pay points.

Closing times
Closed 25 December

Prices
Meals: a la carte £ 16/30

2 mi south of Kirkby Lonsdale by A 65 and A 683. Parking.

Sizergh

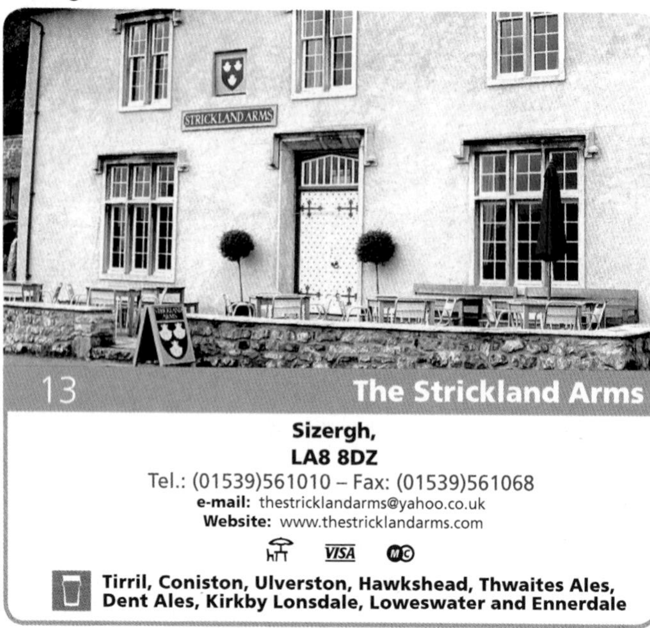

13 **The Strickland Arms**

Sizergh,
LA8 8DZ
Tel.: (01539)561010 – Fax: (01539)561068
e-mail: thestricklandarms@yahoo.co.uk
Website: www.thestricklandarms.com

VISA

Tirril, Coniston, Ulverston, Hawkshead, Thwaites Ales, Dent Ales, Kirkby Lonsdale, Loweswater and Ennerdale

Originally the coach house for next door Sizergh Castle, this sizeable building dates back over 250 years and attracts a diverse range of clientele, from local workers, to visitors from the nearby caravan park and even the Strickland family from the aforementioned castle. There's a characterful, shabby-chic feel to the place and always a few tables reserved by the bar for the locals, who like to sit over a real ale or two. Menus feature classical pub dishes, with daily specials chalked on the board; maybe goat's cheese tart, potted shrimps or steak and ale pie – and all in generous portions. Thursdays are fish nights, Sundays often feature live music and there's a popular beer festival in August with a hog roast, folk music and entertainers.

Closing times
Closed 25 December

Prices
Meals: a la carte £ 20/30

3 mi southwest of Kendal by A 391. Parking.

14 The Queen's Head

Troutbeck,
LA23 1PW
Tel.: (01539)432174 – Fax: (01539)431938
e-mail: reservations@queensheadtroutbeck.co.uk
Website: www.queensheadtroutbeck.co.uk

Dizzy Blonde, Cumbria Way, Hartley's XB, Double Hop, Old Tom and one guest beer every 2 months

This passionately run pub is found in the most delightful setting and makes a great stop off point if you're heading for the Kirkstone Pass. It's amazingly characterful inside, consisting of a beamed bar with an unusual 'four-poster' counter (lined with a huge selection of whiskies), and several interlinking rooms which boast a vast array of memorabilia. Seating varies from heavy wooden settles to high-backed leather chairs but the best spot has to be the terrace with its fantastic hill views. The extensive menu changes six times a year and ranges from nibbles and their fun signature dish, a chip butty with homemade tomato sauce, through to cottage pie and fillet steak. Smart bedrooms boast strong comforts. Rooms 10 and 11 have the best views.

Closing times
Closed dinner 25 December

Prices
Meals: a la carte £ 23/40

15 rooms: £ 80

Typical Dishes

Homemade soup of the day

Real ale battered fish and chips with tartare sauce

Sticky toffee pudding with caramel sauce and ice cream

4 mi north of Windermere by A 592. Parking.

15

Brown Horse Inn

Winster,
LA23 3NR
Tel.: (01539)443443
e-mail: steve@thebrownhorseinn.co.uk
Website: www.thebrownhorseinn.co.uk

 **Lancaster Amber, Moorhouses Pride of Pendle and Bewdley's Old School**

This simple coaching inn has always been popular with the locals; but even more so since the creation of its on-site brewery. It has a shabby-chic style, with flagged floors, antique dressers and a real mix of furniture. In one corner, a miniature model of the bar (made by one of the regulars) and a London Underground map of local pubs provide talking points; while the split-level terrace is a real draw. Seasonal menus feature produce from the fields out back and game comes from shoots they organise themselves. Dishes are designed with hungry walkers in mind; the blackboard specials are a little more adventurous and often include home-reared pork. Bedrooms are a mix of classical and boutique styles; the latter have French windows and terraces.

Closing times
Open daily

Prices
Meals: a la carte £ 19/30

9 rooms: £ 50/100

Typical Dishes

Pressed ham hock terrine

Roast curried cod, crispy potatoes & Puy lentils

Warm chocolate fondant with caramel & sea salt ice cream

 *4 mi south of Windermere by A 5074. Parking.*

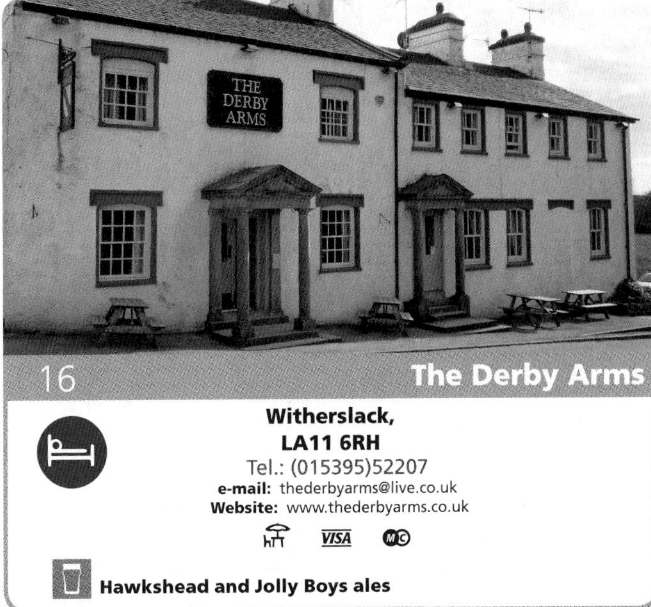

16 **The Derby Arms**

Witherslack,
LA11 6RH
Tel.: (015395)52207
e-mail: thederbyarms@live.co.uk
Website: www.thederbyarms.co.uk

VISA MC

Hawkshead and Jolly Boys ales

This substantial 19C coaching inn is named after the owners of the nearby Halecat Estate, who have been the Earls of Derby since 1485. Located on the main road from Kendal to Ulverston, it was rescued after several years standing empty, and is now a characterful shabby-chic style of place, with rug-covered floors, open fires and hop-hung beams. A bowl of water welcomes your four-legged friends, there's a small community shop filled with local produce to the rear and theme nights are common. Cooking is rustic yet refined, offering the likes of pâté or black pudding followed by steak pie or sausage and mash; with treacle tart or sticky toffee pudding to follow. Classical bedrooms display antique furniture; some boast views or roll-top baths.

Closing times
Open daily

Prices
Meals: a la carte £ 17/25

6 rooms: £ 65/85

In centre of hamlet off the main A 590 Grange over Sands to Kendal road. Parking

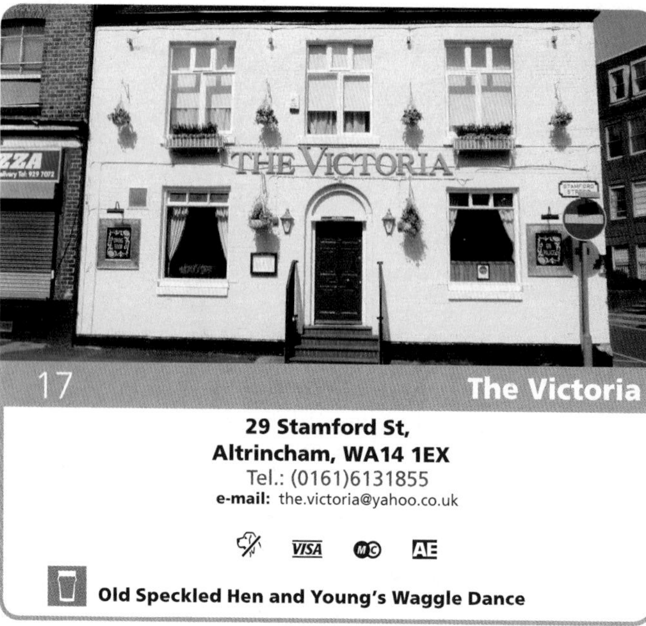

17 **The Victoria**

29 Stamford St,
Altrincham, WA14 1EX
Tel.: (0161)6131855
e-mail: the.victoria@yahoo.co.uk

VISA MC AE

Old Speckled Hen and Young's Waggle Dance

The Victoria is a very traditional looking pub, set in a quiet part of the town centre, with flower pots on the windowsills and a few pavement tables. Its appealing interior comes as a pleasant surprise; a single room with a wooden bar at its centre and half the tables left for drinkers; the other half laid up for diners. There are sandwiches and light bites available on the bar menu, while the à la carte offers classic dishes with a modern twist; perhaps smoked duck crumpet, steak and kidney pudding or jugged wild rabbit. The emphasis here is on locally sourced ingredients, so expect beef from Ashlea Farm, Pendrill's cheese and Dunham Massey Farm ice cream. There's a good value early evening set menu and friendly service from a young team.

Closing times
Closed 26 December, 1 January and Sunday dinner

Prices
Meals: £ 16 (dinner) and a la carte £ 23/32

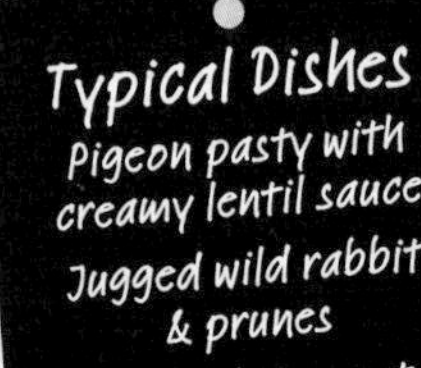

Pay & display parking outside; free at night.

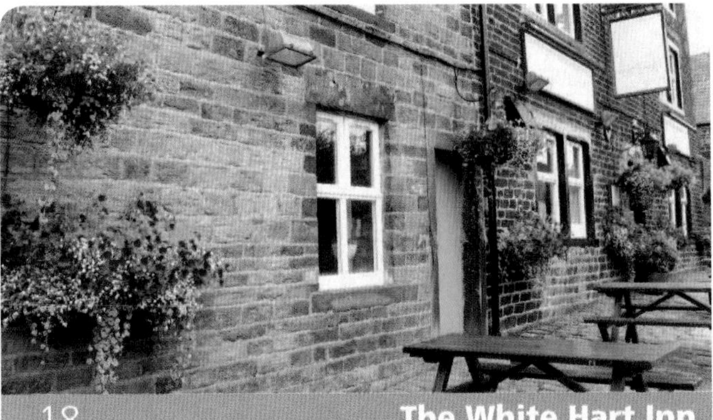

18 The White Hart Inn

51 Stockport Rd, Lydgate, Oldham, OL4 4JJ
Tel.: (01457)872566 – Fax: (01457)875190
e-mail: bookings@thewhitehart.co.uk
Website: www.thewhitehart.co.uk

VISA  AE

 **Timothy Taylor's Best and Landlord, J.W. Lees and weekly changing local guest ales**

Set overlooking Saddleworth Moor, this stone-built inn has undergone various sympathetic extensions over the years; which are now home to a private dining room, a formal restaurant, a function room and 12 antique-furnished bedrooms. The bar boasts a dark wood counter, exposed beams and open fires, while photos of the owner's travels to various mountains in the Highlands, Rockies, China and Tibet hang on the walls; ironically, he once got thrown out of this pub for underage drinking before eventually buying it himself. Menus are fairly lengthy, displaying modern, brasserie-style dishes and a few classics – you might find chicken liver parfait, goat's cheese salad, pot-roast chicken or local sausages and mash – and all at very reasonable prices.

Closing times
Closed 26 December and 1 January

Prices
Meals: a la carte £ 22/35
12 rooms: £ 95/128

Typical Dishes
King scallops & cauliflower purée
Duck breast & lentils
Prune & Armagnac parfait

 *3 mi east of Oldham by A 669 on A 6050. Parking.*

Bashall Eaves

19 **The Red Pump Inn**

Clitheroe Rd,
Bashall Eaves, BB7 3DA
Tel.: (01254)826227
e-mail: info@theredpumpinn.co.uk
Website: www.theredpumpinn.co.uk

VISA

Moorhouse's, Lancaster Ales and Black Sheep

Dine in this pub's traditional restaurant or in the rustic bar. The fire-lit snug is a charming place to idle away an hour or two, while the valley sunsets make the terrace a fantastic place for a drink. Local produce features highly on the seasonal menus, with dishes like super-slow-roasted Pendle belly pork or hot-smoked Dunsop trout paté. With local shoots in and around the Forest of Bowland, game is the speciality, so you'll also see dishes like venison ravioli and pan-fried breast of pheasant. Dessert might mean steamed lemon sponge pudding or a selection of regional cheeses; beers include local and guest ales, with Black Sheep on draught. Sleep in one of the spacious, modern bedrooms; wake up to views of Pendle Hill or Longridge Fell.

Closing times
Closed 2 weeks in February, Tuesday in winter and Monday

Prices
Meals: £ 15 and a la carte £ 17/26

3 rooms: £ 60/115

3 mi northwest of Clitheroe by B 6243 and minor road northwest. Parking.

20 The Clog & Billycock

Billinge End Rd,
Pleasington , Blackburn, BB2 6QB
Tel.: (01254)201163
e-mail: enquiries@theclogandbillycock.com
Website: www.theclogandbillycock.com

Thwaites Original, Wainwrights, Lancaster Bomber

This popular sandstone pub was originally called the Bay Horse, before being renamed after a fashion trend often sported by the former landlord – who liked to wear the quirky combination of clog shoes and a billycock hat. The addition of a large extension means the pub is now modern and open-plan. The neutrally hued walls are filled with photos of their local suppliers and the extensive menus offer a strong Lancastrian slant; you might find Morecambe Bay shrimps, Port of Lancaster smoked fish or Ribble Valley beef, alongside tasty sharing platters. Most produce comes from within 20 miles and suppliers are plotted on a map on the back of the menu. Cooking is rustic and generous; prices are realistic; and the service is friendly and organised.

Closing times
Closed 25 December

Prices
Meals: a la carte £ 17/26

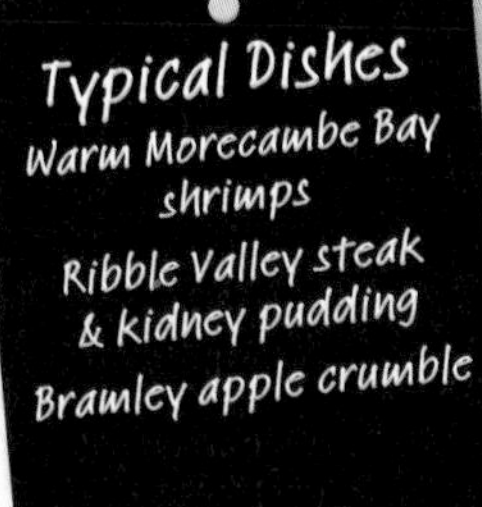

 *2 mi west of Blackburn, signed off A 677. Parking.*

21 The Bay Horse Inn

Bay Horse Ln,
Forton, LA2 0HR
Tel.: (01524)791204
e-mail: yvonne@bayhorseinn.com
Website: www.bayhorseinn.com

  VISA MC AE

Lancaster Red and one weekly changing ale including Hawkshead

Flanked by the A6 and M6, and just a stone's throw away from the main Euston to Glasgow railway line, it's hard to believe how peaceful it is here. Burgundy walls, low beamed ceilings, a stone fireplace and characterful corner bar provide a cosy, welcoming atmosphere, while the rear dining room overlooks an attractive summer terrace and a pleasant wooded garden. The young owner is passionate about sourcing the freshest seasonal produce and you'll always find local offerings such as Andrew Ireland's black pudding, Port of Lancaster smoked salmon and Cumbrian lamb on the menu, with dishes ranging from good old pub classics right through to more modern, sophisticated fare. Beautifully appointed bedrooms are housed nearby in 'The Old Corn Store'.

Closing times
Closed 1 January, Sunday dinner and Monday

Prices
Meals: £ 21 (lunch) and a la carte £ 18/28

3 rooms: £ 89

Typical Dishes
Langoustines
Rabbit cooked in cider with broad beans
Chocolate cake with yoghurt ice cream

1.25 mi north by A 6 on Quernmore Road. Parking.

22

Duke of York Inn

Brow Top,
Grindleton, BB7 4QR
Tel.: (01200)441266
e-mail: info@dukeofyorkgrindleton.com
Website: www.dukeofyorkgrindleton.com

 **Thwaites Original and Black Sheep Bitter**

This ivy-clad pub sits on the main road running through this pleasant hamlet, in the heart of the Trough of Bowland. If its character you're after, dine in the rustic bar with its flag floors and wood burning stove. The more modern alternative is the smart, airy dining room, adorned with wine bottles and a large mirror. There are sandwiches at lunchtime and a great value set lunch and early evening menu; the seasonal à la carte offers plenty of regional choices and a decent selection of fish, often including lobster. Dishes might include steak and Grindleton ale pudding or roast loin and rack of Pendleton lamb; produce is commendably local, with herbs from the chef-owner's garden. Regular events include monthly wine nights and a pudding club.

Closing times
Closed 25 December and Monday except bank holidays

Prices
Meals: £ 11 and a la carte £ 18/28

Typical Dishes
Breast of Bowland wood pigeon with artichoke mousse & black pudding

Chargrilled sirloin of veal

Plate of rhubarb desserts

 *3 mi northwest of Clitheroe signed off A 671. Parking.*

23 **The Borough**

3 Dalton Sq,
Lancaster, LA1 1PP
Tel.: (01524)64170
e-mail: hannah@theboroughlancaster.co.uk
Website: www.theboroughlancaster.co.uk

VISA MC

Thwaites Original, Wainwrights, Hawkshead Best Bitter, Bowland Hen Harrier

Set on the same cobbled square as the town hall, this pub has previously spent time as the mayor's house, a working men's club and a coffee importer's business. At the front is the characterful bar, its walls covered in old pictures of the city; the rear area is for dining and beyond that, there's an enclosed terrace. Extensive menus offer hearty, filling pub dishes like steak, hotpot or pie and peas; the DIY deli boards are a popular choice and, since local artisan producers are well used, you can expect shrimps from Morecambe Bay and fish from Fleetwood. Beer is given due respect, with local bitters, German lager and some unusual bottled ales. Regular comedy nights and a weekly poker class happen in the grand first floor former lounge.

Closing times
Closed 25 December

Prices
Meals: a la carte £ 18/35

Typical Dishes
Cartmel pigeon breast, parsnip purée
Lancashire hotpot
Homemade bread & butter pudding

In Dalton Square adjacent to the Town Hall on the one-way system. Parking in Dalton Square.

24 **The Cartford Inn**

Cartford Ln,
Little Eccleston, PR3 0YP
Tel.: (01995)670166
e-mail: info@thecartfordinn.co.uk
Website: www.thecartfordinn.co.uk

   AE

Moorhouses Pride of Pendle, Theakston Old Peculiar, Hawkshead Lakeland Gold and Bowland Sawley Tempted

A gentle and ongoing makeover is transforming this 17C coaching inn into an attractive dining venue which blends original features with contemporary styling. Gallic touches alert you to the nationality of the owner, who provides friendly, efficient service with his young, local team. Get cosy next to the open fire on a cold winter's evening; come summer, dine alfresco overlooking the River Wyre and the Trough of Bowland. Menus offer something to suit your every mood; from sandwiches and wood platters of local produce to popular pub favourites like oxtail suet pudding, fish pie, lamb hotpot or steak and chips. Bedrooms are a cut above your typical pub: individually styled, with modern facilities, feature walls and antique French furniture.

Closing times
Closed 25 December and Monday lunch except Bank Holidays

Prices
Meals: a la carte £ 19/35
7 rooms: £ 70/120

7 mi west of Blackpool by A 585 and A 586. Parking.

25 The Three Fishes

Mitton Rd,
Mitton, BB7 9PQ
Tel.: (01254)826888
e-mail: enquiries@thethreefishes.com
Website: www.thethreefishes.com

Thwaites Traditional and Bomber, Bowland Hen Harrier

From Morecambe Bay shrimps to Ribble Valley beef and Goosnargh chicken to Fleetwood fish, the menu here reads like a paean to Lancastrian produce. Regional specialities abound and local suppliers are celebrated as food heroes in the striking photos which adorn the pub's walls. The seasonally changing menus are extensive, meaning no matter how many times you come back, you can always try something new, and this a truly family-friendly pub, with children's menus which pay much more than lip service to your little ones. Sunday lunch is popular, when a roast is also available – but this modern country inn is deservedly busy all week long, packed with people keen to try tasty, satisfying dishes made with the best the North West has to offer.

Closing times
Closed 25 December

Prices
Meals: a la carte £ 19/30

Typical Dishes
Treacle-baked middlewhite ribs
Three Fishes pie
Bramley apple & rhubarb crumble

2.5 mi northwest of Whalley on B 6246. Parking.

26 The Inn at Whitewell

Forest of Bowland,
Whitewell, BB7 3AT
Tel.: (01200)448222 – Fax: (01200)448298
e-mail: reception@innatwhitewell.com
Website: www.innatwhitewell.com

Moorhouse's Blonde Witch, Skipton Brewery Copper Dragon, Bowland Brewery Hen Harrier, Timothy Taylors

This 14C creeper-clad inn sits high on the banks of the River Hodder, in prime shooting and fishing country, in the heart of the Trough of Bowland. Antique furniture and a panoramic view of the valley make the spacious bar the most atmospheric place to sit. Other similarly styled rooms boast the character but not the view; for a more formal meal, head for a linen-laid table in the raised-level, valley-facing restaurant. Classic menus offer wholesome, regionally inspired dishes like Lancashire hotpot or fillet of local beef. Spacious bedrooms are split between the inn and nearby coach house. Some are traditional in style with four-posters and antique baths; others are more contemporary. A well-stocked vintners also sells cookbooks and guides.

Closing times
Open daily

Prices
Meals: a la carte £ 25/40

23 rooms: £ 83/189

Typical Dishes

Chicken liver pâté à la Ballymaloe

Loin of Burholme Lonk lamb

Chocolate brownie

6 mi northwest of Clitheroe by B 6243. Parking.

Wiswell

27 The Freemasons Country Inn

8 Vicarage Fold,
Wiswell, BB7 9DF
Tel.: (01254)822218
e-mail: enquiries@freemasonswiswell.co.uk
Website: www.freemasonswiswell.co.uk

Inspectors' favourites

Moorhouses, Tirril, Bowland, Bank Top and Copper Dragon

Charming, welcoming, warm and chatty are all adjectives which apply to the staff here, so it's no wonder that they're busy. Of course service counts for little if the food's not right; but, again, here the Freemasons comes up trumps. Chef Steven Smith likes to create modern versions of traditional pub dishes; think good old chicken Kiev reborn as organic chicken breast and Kiev with potato purée, wild mushrooms and thyme; or trifle: not as your mother made it, but with Pedro Ximenez jelly, baked quince and warm Madeleines. Flag floors, low beams and open fires create a cool country house feel downstairs, while the first floor features a more elegant, antique-furnished dining area, a comfortable lounge and two semi-private dining rooms.

Closing times
Open daily

Prices
Meals: £ 15 and a la carte £ 25/32

Typical Dishes
Crispy hens egg with gammon, egg & pineapple
Poached & roasted Goosnargh duck
Apple trifle with hot cinnamon doughnuts

3.75 mi southwest of the town, on street parking only.

28 **The Mulberry Tree**

9 Wood Ln,
Wrightington Bar, WN6 9SE
Tel.: (01257)451400 – Fax: (01257)451400
e-mail: info@themulberrytree.info
Website: www.themulberrytree.info

 **Flowers IPA, Welsh Smooth Bitter**

Such are the choices available at this spacious 19C pub, you may find yourself frozen in the grip of indecision. Firstly, where to sit: at one of the linen-clad tables in the formal dining area? Or in the more laid-back bar area? Next comes the tricky bit: what to eat. The menu is virtually the same in both parts of the pub, but with more than twenty starters and even more main courses to choose from you might need more than the customary five minutes to decide. There's something for everyone, from Sichuan chicken livers, oysters and fishcakes, to steaks, suet pudding and mushroom risotto, with plenty of pubby classics like fish and chips and sausage and mash. Dishes come in generous portions and at prices that won't break the bank.

Closing times
Open daily
Prices
Meals: a la carte £ 21/35

 *3.5 mi northwest of Standish by A 5209 on B 5250. Parking.*

The south east abounds in handsome historic houses once lived in by the likes of Disraeli and the Rothschilds, and it's no surprise that during the Plague it was to leafy Chalfont St Giles that John Milton fled. It is characterised by rolling hills such as the Chilterns with its ancient beechwoods, and the lilting North and South Downs, which cut a rural swathe across busy commuter belts. The film and television worlds sit easily here: Hambleden and Turville, in the Chilterns, are as used to the sound of the autocue as to the crunch of ramblers' boots. Meanwhile, James Bond's Aston Martin glistens in Beaulieu's Motor Museum, in the heart of the New Forest. Spinnaker Tower rivals HMS Victory for dominance of the Portsmouth skyline, while in Winchester, the Great Hall, home for 600 years to the Arthurian round table, nods acquaintance with the eleventh century Cathedral. Good food and drink is integral to the region, from Whitstable oysters and Dover sole to established vineyards.

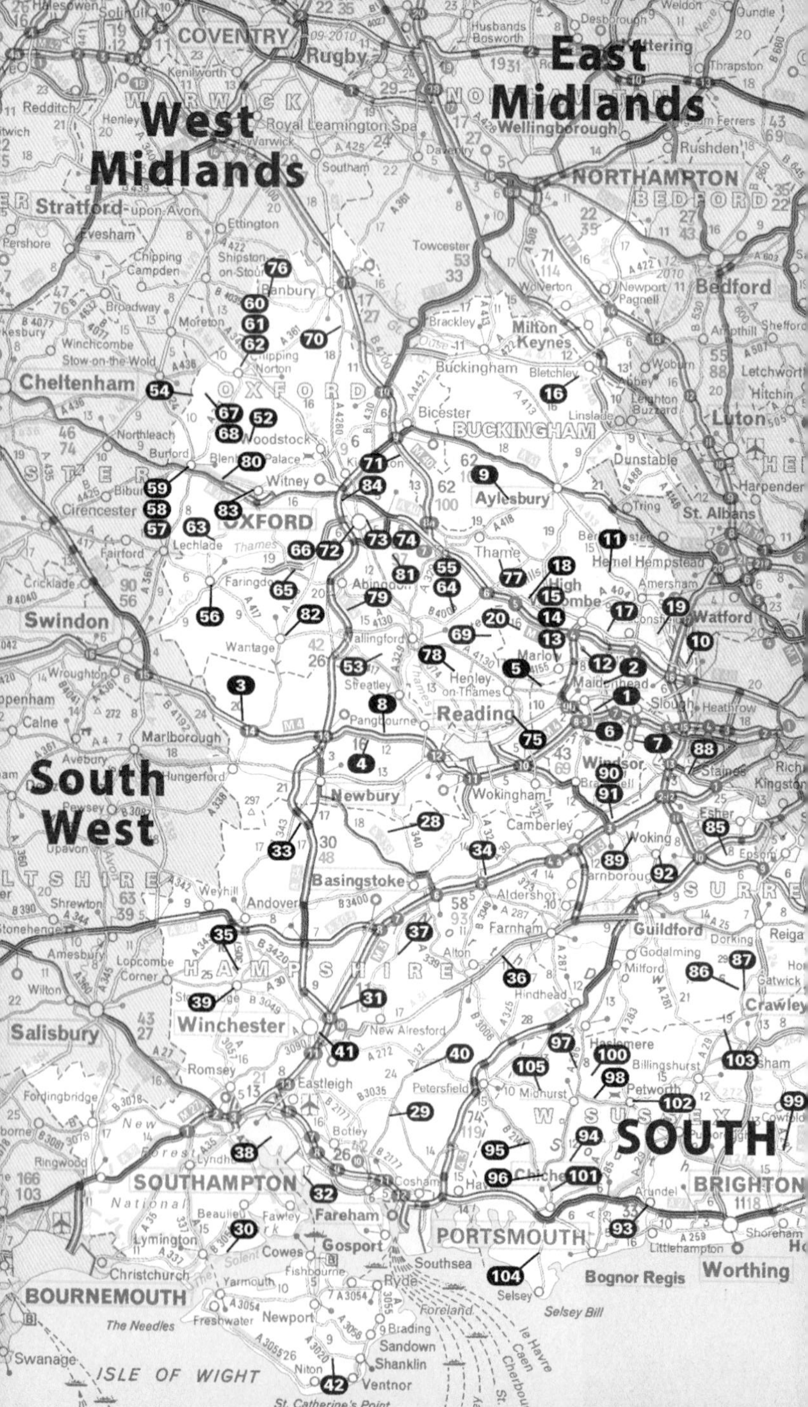
West Midlands
East Midlands
South West
SOUTH
COVENTRY
Rugby
Bedworth
Lutterworth
Husbands Bosworth
Desborough
Kettering
Weldon
Oundle
Thrapston
Halesowen
Solihull
Kenilworth
Redditch
Henley
Royal Leamington Spa
Warwick
Southam
Daventry
Wellingborough
Rushden
NORTHAMPTON
BEDFORD
Stratford-upon-Avon
Pershore
Evesham
Ettington
Shipston-on-Stour
Chipping Campden
Towcester
Wolverton
Newport Pagnell
Bedford
Banbury
Broadway
Moreton
Winchcombe
Stow-on-the-Wold
Chipping Norton
Brackley
Milton Keynes
Buckingham
Bletchley
Woburn
Ampthill
Shefford
Letchworth
Hitchin
Cheltenham
OXFORD
Northleach
Woodstock
Blenheim Palace
Bicester
BUCKINGHAM
Linslade
Leighton Buzzard
Luton
Dunstable
Harpenden
Burford
Witney
Cirencester
Aylesbury
Tring
St. Albans
Fairford
Lechlade
OXFORD
Thames
Thame
Hemel Hempstead
Cricklade
Faringdon
Abingdon
High Wycombe
Amersham
Watford
Swindon
Wantage
Wallingford
Marlow
Maidenhead
Slough
Heathrow
Wroughton
Streatley
Henley-on-Thames
Reading
Pangbourne
Calne
Marlborough
Avebury
Hungerford
Newbury
Wokingham
Windsor
Staines
Kingston
Pewsey
Camberley
Esher
Upavon
Woking
Epsom
Basingstoke
Farnborough
Aldershot
WILTSHIRE
SURREY
Weyhill
Andover
Farnham
Guildford
Dorking
Reigate
Shrewton
Stonehenge
Amesbury
Lopcombe Corner
HAMPSHIRE
Alton
Godalming
Milford
Gatwick
Crawley
Wilton
Winchester
Hindhead
Salisbury
New Alresford
Haslemere
Billingshurst
Romsey
Eastleigh
Petersfield
Midhurst
Petworth
Fordingbridge
Botley
WEST SUSSEX
Ringwood
New Forest
Lyndhurst
SOUTHAMPTON
Cosham
Arundel
BRIGHTON
National
Beaulieu
Fawley
Fareham
PORTSMOUTH
Shoreham
Lymington
Cowes
Gosport
Littlehampton
Worthing
Christchurch
Fishbourne
Southsea
Bognor Regis
BOURNEMOUTH
Yarmouth
Ryde
Selsey
Selsey Bill
The Needles
Freshwater
Newport
Foreland
Brading
Sandown
Shanklin
Swanage
ISLE OF WIGHT
Niton
Ventnor
St. Catherine's Point
Le Havre
Caen
Cherbourg

East of England
London
EAST
Chatteris
Ramsey
Littleport
Brandon
Thetford
Bungay
Harleston
Diss
Scole
Halesworth
Waveney
Ely
Huntingdon
Earith
Soham
St. Ives
Godmanchester
St. Neots
Eltisley
Potton
Newmarket
Bury St. Edmunds
Ixworth
Dennington
Saxmundham
Stowmarket
Lavenham
Haverhill
Clare
Sudbury
IPSWICH
Woodbridge
Hadleigh
Stour
Felixstowe
Harwich
The Naze
Walton-on-the-Naze
Frinton-on-Sea
Clacton-on-Sea
Brightlingsea
W. Mersea
Colchester
Biggleswade
Royston
Saffron Walden
Baldock
Buntingford
Finchingfield
Halstead
Braintree
Great Dunmow
Stevenage
Puckeridge
Stansted
Bishop's Stortford
Hertford
Welwyn Garden City
Ware
Sawbridgeworth
Harlow
Hatfield
Hoddesdon
Epping
Cheshunt
Chelmsford
Witham
Maldon
Bradwell-on-Sea
Burnham-on-Crouch
Foulness Point
Potters Bar
Brentwood
Billericay
Wickford
Rayleigh
Basildon
Benfleet
Southend-on-Sea
Canvey Island
Grays Thurrock
Tilbury
Dartford
R. Thames
Grain
Sheerness
Isle of Sheppey
Queenborough
Leysdown-on-Sea
Gravesend
Rochester
Gillingham
Chatham
Swanley
Orpington
Croydon
Sittingbourne
Whitstable
Herne Bay
Birchington
Margate
North Foreland
Broadstairs
Ramsgate
Faversham
Canterbury
Sandwich
Deal
Sevenoaks
Knole
Redhill
Maidstone
Tonbridge
Southborough
KENT
Ashford
Terminal
Dover
South Foreland
Royal Tunbridge Wells
Biddenden
East Grinstead
Crowborough
Tenterden
Hythe
Folkestone
Tunnel
Cuckfield
Haywards Heath
Hawkhurst
Uckfield
Heathfield
E. SUSSEX
New Romney
Lydd
Rye
Winchelsea
Dungeness
Hailsham
Battle
Lewes
Polegate
Bexhill
Hastings
Newhaven
Seaford
Eastbourne
Beachy Head
Dieppe
PAS DE CALAIS
Cap Gris Nez
Wimereux
Boulogne
le Portel
Hardelot-Plage

Bray

1 The Hinds Head

High St,
Bray, SL6 2AB
Tel.: (01628)626151 – Fax: (01628)623394
e-mail: info@hindsheadbray.co.uk
Website: www.hindsheadhotel.co.uk

 **Marlow Rebellion ales**

Our Pub of the Year 2011 sits at the heart of the pretty village of Bray, its dark panelling and log fires giving it a characterful, almost medieval feel. Although not far from its alma mater, The Fat Duck, it's light years away in terms of its menu. Heston Blumenthal might be famous for molecular gastronomy, but at The Hinds Head, the food is down-to-earth, with classic, comforting dishes like pea and ham soup or heartwarming oxtail and kidney pudding, and traditional desserts such as Eton mess or strawberry trifle. Dishes are fiercely British and big on flavour; rich, simple and satisfying. This is a proper pub and, as such, is busy with drinkers; the bar is the most atmospheric place to sit, although they don't take bookings here.

Closing times
Closed 25-26 December and Sunday dinner
booking essential

Prices
Meals: a la carte £ 25/40

Typical Dishes
Potted shrimps with watercress salad
Oxtail & kidney pudding
Chocolate wine with millionaire shortbread

 *1 mi south of Maidenhead by A 308. Parking in 2 village car parks and opposite the pub.*

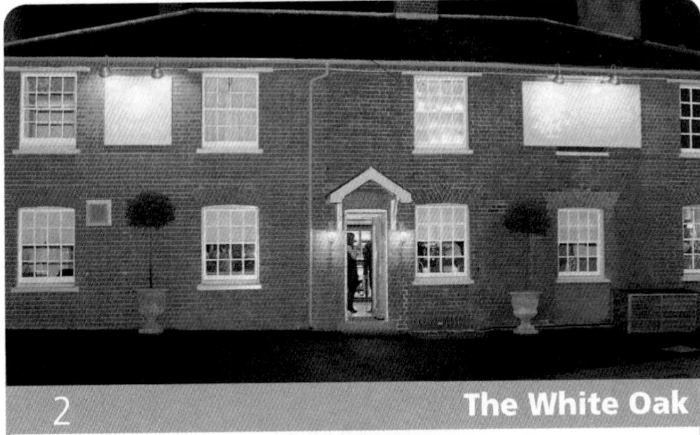

2 The White Oak

Pound Ln,
Cookham, SL6 9QE
Tel.: (01628)523043
e-mail: info@thewhiteoak.co.uk
Website: www.thewhiteoak.co.uk

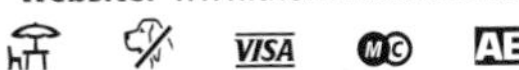

Greene King - Abbot Ale and Old Speckled Hen Smooth

Having cut his teeth in some of London's original gastropubs, Henry Cripps decided to expand his repertoire by looking further afield. His latest rural venture, The White Oak, is set in a picturesque village and boasts a smart terrace with neat planters and a light, bright, neutrally hued interior; the result of a large-scale contemporary makeover. The cooking here is straightforward and generously proportioned, featuring simple pub-style dishes which consist of quality meats and unfussy accompaniments. There are several options for two, including assiettes of starters and seafood, a charcuterie board and, on Sundays, various roasts to share. Service is cheery and there's a good drinks selection, which includes plenty of wines by the glass.

Closing times
Closed Sunday dinner

Prices
Meals: £ 15/19
and a la carte £ 22/39

Across the common. Parking.

East Garston

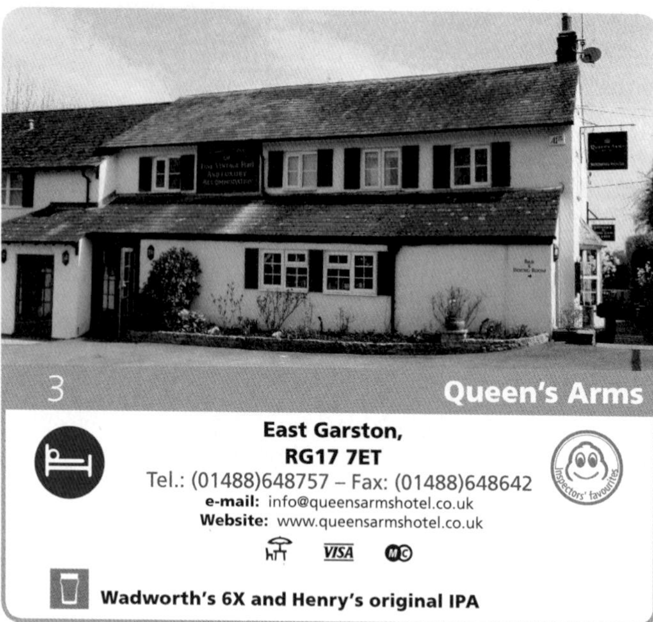

3 **Queen's Arms**

East Garston,
RG17 7ET
Tel.: (01488)648757 – Fax: (01488)648642
e-mail: info@queensarmshotel.co.uk
Website: www.queensarmshotel.co.uk

VISA

Wadworth's 6X and Henry's original IPA

Situated in the heart of the Valley of the Racehorse, The Queen's Arms is a true thoroughbred among pubs. With its country pursuits theme, it celebrates all things English; catch up with the day's racing results in the atmospheric, antique-furnished bar; its walls lined with fantastic photos of riders and shooters. Rustic British dishes might include shepherd's pie or rib-eye steak with fat cut chips, with the lunch menu providing particularly good value. Superb bedrooms are sponsored by purveyors of country equipment and clothing; for the ultimate extravagance, book 'Miller's Club,' which comes with its own honesty bar and poker table. Don't forget to order your copy of The Racing Post to accompany your generous breakfast the next morning.

Closing times
Closed 25 December

Prices
Meals: £ 20 (Monday-Saturday) and a la carte £ 24/32

8 rooms: £ 95/130

3 mi southeast of Lambourn via Eastbury on Newbury Rd. Parking.

Frilsham,
RG18 0XX
Tel.: (01635)201366 – Fax: (01635)201366
e-mail: info@potkiln.org
Website: www.potkiln.org

   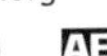 AE

 **Brick Kiln, Mr Chubbs, Maggs' Mild and guest ales**

Part of the old brickworks, The Pot Kiln originally provided refreshment for the workers digging clay from the surrounding fields. Head for the cosy bar and order a pint of specially commissioned Magg's Mild, Mr Chubbs or Brick Kiln beer, then follow the deliciously tempting aromas through to the dining area, where flavoursome British dishes arrive in unashamedly gutsy portions. Chef-owner Mike Robinson takes advantage of the pub's situation in the middle of prime hunting territory and shoots much of the game himself; so you might find pigeon salad followed by pavé of Lockinge fallow deer on the menu. If meat's not your thing, there's plenty of fish too, including local pike, trout and River Kennet crayfish. Service is particularly clued-up.

Closing times
Closed 25 December and Tuesday

Prices
Meals: £ 20 (weekday lunch) and a la carte £ 26/30

Typical Dishes
Woodpigeon and black pudding salad
Pavé of local venison
Sticky toffee pudding

6 mi northeast of Newbury by B 4009 to Hermitage and minor road. Parking.

5 **Black Boys Inn**

Henley Rd,
Hurley, SL6 5NQ
Tel.: (01628)824212
e-mail: info@blackboysinn.co.uk
Website: www.blackboysinn.co.uk

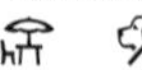 VISA  AE

 **Brakspear ales**

The owners of the Black Boys have plenty of experience in the hospitality industry – and even came out of retirement in order to purchase, refurbish and reopen this 16C pub. They are avid Francophiles, which is evident as soon as you approach the building, as the brasserie-style blinds evoke a quirky Gallic feel. Inside, exposed beams and wood floors create a homely atmosphere, yet it's more of a dining than a drinking kind of a place. Dishes are classically based but some more modern touches creep in when it comes to the presentation. Simply prepared, good quality ingredients provide plenty of flavour: tasty fresh fish comes from the Cornish day boats and desserts are of the good old-fashioned variety. Bedrooms are unfussy and well-kept.

Closing times
Closed Sunday dinner

Prices
Meals: a la carte £ 26/38

8 rooms: £ 85/120

Typical Dishes
Salcombe crab
Confit of goose with caramelised pear
Parfait of Cluizel chocolate & griottines

 *4 mi east of Henley-on-Thames by A 4130. Parking.*

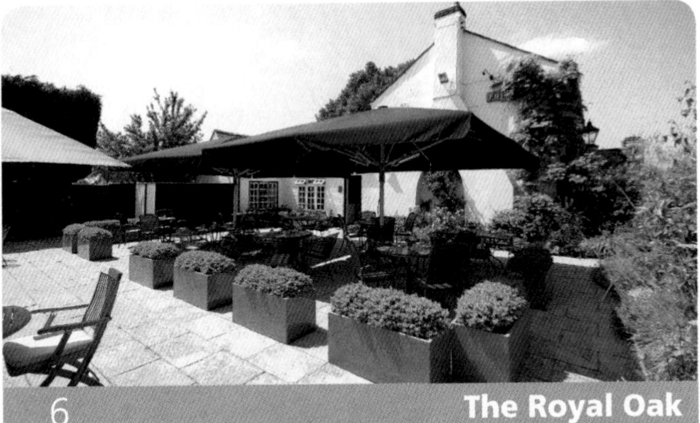

6 **The Royal Oak**

Paley St,
Paley Street, SL6 3JN
Tel.: (01628)620541
e-mail: info@theroyaloakpaleystreet.com
Website: www.theroyaloakpaleystreet.com

VISA AE

Fuller's London Pride

Nick Parkinson is your host and his ability to put guests at ease is clearly one family trait he's inherited from his father, Sir Michael, whose famous encounters are captured in the photos that decorate the place. Boris the dog is usually found snoozing at the front bar, while the rest of the beamed room is given over to dining. The chef is Dominic Chapman, son of West Country hotelier Kit, and, like his father, he champions British food. His cooking displays confidence and a commitment to quality, seasonal ingredients but also suits the place. Fish is handled with particular aplomb, whether it's roast halibut with spicy aubergine or smoked eel with beetroot. He's also likes his game. Service is very pleasant and gets the tone just right.

Closing times
Closed dinner Sunday and bank holiday Mondays

Prices
Meals: £ 22 (lunch) and a la carte £ 30/45

Typical Dishes

Rabbit lasagna & chervil sauce

Peppered haunch of venison

Eton mess

3.5 mi southwest of Bray by A 308, A 330 and B 3024. Parking.

7 **The Greene Oak**

Oakley Grn,
Windsor, SL4 5UW
Tel.: (01753)864294 – Fax: (01753)621185
e-mail: info@thegreeneoak.co.uk
Website: www.thegreeneoak.co.uk

Greene King IPA, Abbott Ale and Old Speckled Hen Smooth

It's set on a busy lorry route to Twyford and may not look like much from the outside, but step inside The Greene Oak and it's a different story. There are contemporary soft furnishings and appealing décor in soothing shades of botanical green, a relaxed feel prevails and a warm welcome at the bar is assured. Older sibling to the White Oak in Cookham, it boasts an experienced owner with a background in London pubs, while the chef previously cooked at The Hind's Head in nearby Bray. Dishes might include comforting coq au vin, smoked fish pie or steak with the works, while both the braised Jacob's Ladder and the breaded scallops with pea purée and pancetta come highly recommended. Alfresco dining on the terrace is a delight come summer.

Closing times
Closed 25 December, Sunday and dinner bank holiday

booking advisable

Prices
Meals: £ 15 lunch (except Friday and Sunday) and a la carte £ 22/39

Typical Dishes
Breaded scallops with pea purée & pancetta crisps
Braised Jacob's ladder & roasted potatoes
Honey panna cotta & spiced pear

3 mi west of Windsor by A 308 on B 3024 Dedworth Rd. Parking.

8

The Royal Oak

The Square,
Yattendon, RG18 0UF
Tel.: (01635)201325
e-mail: info@royaloakyattendon.com
Website: www.royaloakyattendon.com

 **West Berkshire Brewery - Good Old Boy, Mr Chubbs**

A beautiful former coaching inn bursting with country charm, The Royal Oak manages to pull off the tricky feat of being both a true locals pub and a popular destination for foodies. While the picture perfect village and its proximity to the M4 could account in part for the pub's attraction to visitors, it's the cooking which really gets them travelling here from a distance. Honest British dishes might include devilled kidneys, potted shrimps or fish pie, while traditional puddings might be of the bread and butter or sticky toffee varieties. The beamed bar with its blazing log fires is at the pub's hub. There's also a lesser-used restaurant and a pleasant vine-covered terrace at the rear. Comfortable bedrooms boast a country house style.

Closing times
Open daily
booking advisable

Prices
Meals: £ 15 (weekday lunch) and a la carte £ 20/30
5 rooms: £ 85

Typical Dishes
Potted shrimps
Halibut fillet & lyonnaise potatoes
Peach parfait

 *6 mi northeast of Newbury by B4009 and minor road; in the village centre. Parking opposite and in village car park.*

Cuddington

9 **The Crown**

Aylesbury Rd,
Cuddington, HP18 0BB
Tel.: (01844)292222
e-mail: davidberry@googlemail.com
Website: www.thecrowncuddington.co.uk

   AE

Fuller's London Pride, Adnams and one guest ale

Set in the charming village of Cuddington, this Grade II listed 16C building is the very essence of a proper English pub. Whitewashed walls and an attractive thatched roof hide a traditionally styled interior with welcoming open fires, dancing candlelight and a multitude of bygone artefacts; while a loyal band of locals keep up the drinking trade and a friendly serving team help set the tone. There's a blackboard of daily specials and an à la carte that changes with the seasons: so you'll find hearty comfort food in winter – maybe lamb shank or glazed duck breast – and lighter sandwiches and salads in the summer; arrive early if you fancy one of these in a spot in the sun. 'Pie and Pud' nights take place every Wednesday and go down a storm.

Closing times
Closed Sunday dinner

Prices
Meals: £ 17 (lunch) and a la carte £ 21/28

Typical Dishes
Tomato, olive and goat's cheese tartlet
Smoked haddock Welsh rarebit
Raspberry & vanilla cheesecake

 *West of Aylesbury by A 418. Parking.*

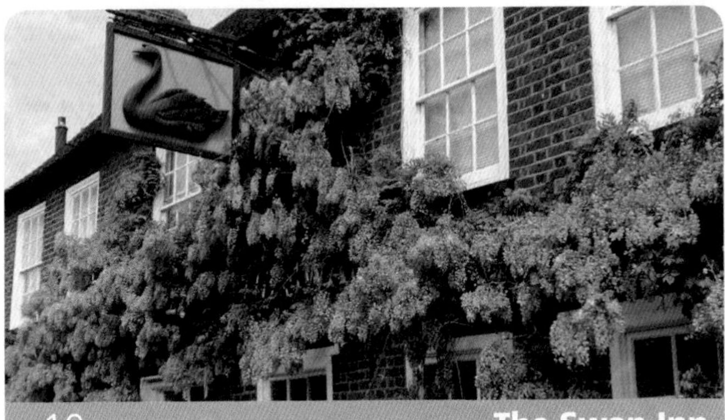

10 The Swan Inn

Village Rd,
Denham, UB9 5BH
Tel.: (01895)832085 – Fax: (01895)835516
e-mail: info@swaninndenham.co.uk
Website: www.swaninndenham.co.uk

   AE

Courage Best, Wadworth 6X, Marlow Rebellion IPA

If you want to escape the hustle of London, this pub may well be the tranquil haven you're after. Close to the A40, M40 and M25 but in a secluded little world of its own, The Swan takes up prime position in this delightful village. Number three in the owner's collection, the Georgian red-brick building is fronted by beautiful cascades of wisteria and framed by manicured trees, with a secluded terrace and gardens to the rear. Menus change with the seasons but their signature bubble & squeak and rib-eye steak are mainstays. This is more just than typical pub food, so you might find confit duck with nutmeg boxty potato and sides such as such as leek, pancetta and parsley crumble. Satisfyingly, they open early for pre-Ascot or Wimbledon champagne.

Closing times
Closed 25-26 December
booking essential

Prices
Meals: a la carte £ 20/27

Typical Dishes
Cauliflower gnocchi & artichoke ragoût
Slow-cooked Stockings Farm pork belly
Rich chocolate fondant

6 mi northeast of Slough by A 412; in the centre of the village. Small car park.

Great Missenden

11 **The Nags Head**

London Rd,
Great Missenden, HP16 0DG
Tel.: (01494)862200 – Fax: (01494)862945
e-mail: goodfood@nagsheadbucks.com
Website: www.nagsheadbucks.com

VISA   

Fuller's London Pride, Tring, Marlow and Vale Breweries

This traditional 15C inn is run by the same team behind the Bricklayers Arms in Flaunden and is proving just as popular, so be sure to book ahead, especially at weekends. It has been made over, yet retains a wealth of original features: the two main dining areas have thick brick walls and exposed oak beams, while an extra helping of rusticity comes courtesy of the inglenook fireplace. Original menus mix Gallic charm with British classics, so you'll find things like foie gras or mushroom feuillette alongside eggs Benedict or sausage and mash; food is flavourful and service cheerful and keen. Stylish, modern bedrooms provide a comfortable night's sleep – number one is the best – and the tasty breakfast ensures you leave satiated in the morning.

Closing times
Open daily

Prices
Meals: a la carte £ 25/35
5 rooms: £ 90/110

Typical Dishes
Chicken liver & Serrano ham ballottine
Best end of lamb with shredded lamb leg
Vanilla cheesecake

 *Between Wendover and Amersham on A 413. Parking.*

12 **The Queens Head**

Pound Ln,
Little Marlow, SL7 3SR
Tel.: (01628)482927
e-mail: tqhlittlemarlow@yahoo.co.uk
Website: www.marlowslittlesecret.co.uk

  MC

 **Fuller's London Pride, Brakspear and regularly changing ales**

Head towards Little Marlow's 12C church and, tucked away down a lane opposite the village's restored cattle pound, you'll find The Queens Head; a popular pub, with keen young partners at its helm and staff who provide poised, friendly service. Once a spit and sawdust sort of a place, its snug bar used to be a salting room and its priest hole makes it a popular place for filming. The garden gets into full swing during the summer months when hungry walkers gather to refuel; the lunch menu provides a quick fix with sandwiches, ploughman's and dishes like steak or fish and chips, while the dinner menu sets the bar a little higher, with starters such as duck liver parfait or peppered squid and main courses like lamb rump and pan-fried sea bass.

Closing times
Closed 25 and 26 December
Prices
Meals: a la carte £ 22/32

 *3 mi east of Marlow on A 4155 by Church Rd. Parking.*

13 **The Cheerful Soul**

Henley Rd,
Marlow, SL7 2DF
Tel.: (01628)483343
e-mail: hello@thecheerfulsoulrestaurant.co.uk
Website: www.thecheerfulsoul.com

Marlow Rebellion including IPA and occasional special ales

Within walking distance of the charming riverside town of Marlow and run by a smiley team, this 17C pub really lives up to its name. Enthusiastic owners Russell and Michele – with a bit of help from Raymond Blanc – opened their doors in 2009, following their success on BBC2's 'The Restaurant'. Set over two levels, with original beams, lightly hued walls and wooden floors, the place has a fresh, clean feel; the simple but well-executed menus providing the perfect match. Dishes are classically based, the steaks are a favourite and the crab and clotted cream tart is fast becoming their signature dish. 'Fish Fridays' add a couple of specials – often battered in local Rebellion Ale – while the midweek 'Nip and Tuck' lunch provides the best value.

Closing times
Closed Sunday dinner and Monday
booking advisable

Prices
Meals: £ 16 (lunch) and a la carte £ 19/35

Typical Dishes
Barkham blue soufflé
Beef shin with kidney pudding & spring cabbage
Mulled pear & warm gingerbread

 *1 mi southwest of Marlow on A 4155. Parking.*

14 The Hand and Flowers

126 West St,
Marlow, SL7 2BP
Tel.: (01628)482277 – Fax: (01628)401913
e-mail: theoffice@thehandandflowers.co.uk
Website: www.thehandandflowers.co.uk

Inspectors' favourites

VISA

 **Greene King IPA**

With its softly lit interior, The Hand and Flowers glows enticingly but it's not often you can drop in on the off-chance, as this is Marlow's not-so-well-kept secret. Low beamed ceilings, flagstone floors and a proper bar counter hint at its history, while the formal serving team are a clue as to the quality of the food. Cooking is of the highest order and the chef puts as much care and passion into a lasagne on the set lunch menu as a fillet of beef on the evening à la carte. The selection may be concise but dishes are refined and flavoursome, ingredients marry perfectly and the simple really is turned into the sublime. Characterful cottage bedrooms are equally meticulous, boasting feature baths or showers. Some even have outdoor jacuzzis.

Closing times
Closed 24-26 December,
1 January dinner
and Sunday dinner
booking essential

Prices
Meals: a la carte £ 31/42
4 rooms: £ 140/190

Typical Dishes
Moules marinière with warm stout & brown bread
Slow-braised shin of Essex beef with glazed carrot, red wine & beef marrow
Lavender panna cotta with whiskey jelly and honeycomb

From town centre follow Henley signs west on A 4155; pub on right after 350 metres. Parking.

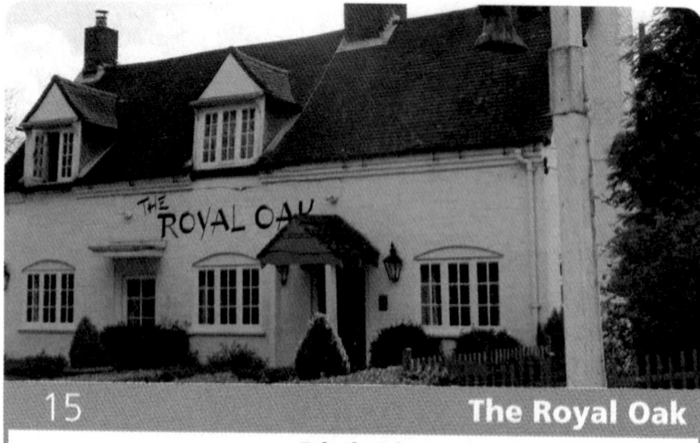

15 **The Royal Oak**

Frieth Rd,
Bovingdon Green, Marlow, SL7 2JF
Tel.: (01628)488611 – Fax: (01628)478680
e-mail: info@royaloakmarlow.co.uk
Website: www.royaloakmarlow.co.uk

 **Brakspear, Marlow Rebellion IPA and Smuggler**

Set less than 15mins from the M40 and M4, this part-17C pub is the ideal escape from the busy streets of London. As you approach, pleasant scents drift up from the herb garden, gentle 'chinks' emanate from the petanque pitch and the world feels at once more peaceful. While away the warmer days on the pleasant terrace or snuggle into pretty cushions beside the wood burning stove in winter, where rich fabrics and heritage colours provide a country-chic feel and freshly cut flowers decorate the room. Not surprisingly, it's extremely popular and the eager team are often stretched to their limit. Cooking is mainly British-led, with the odd Asian influence; you might find pan-roast pork chop with salt and pepper squid or slow-cooked ox cheek pasty.

Closing times
Closed 25-26 December

Prices
Meals: a la carte £ 20/27

Typical Dishes
Old Spot ham hock terrine
Oxfordshire shin of beef Bourguignon
Iced hokey-pokey soufflé

From Marlow town centre head towards Bovingdon Green: pub is on the left as you leave the woods. Parking.

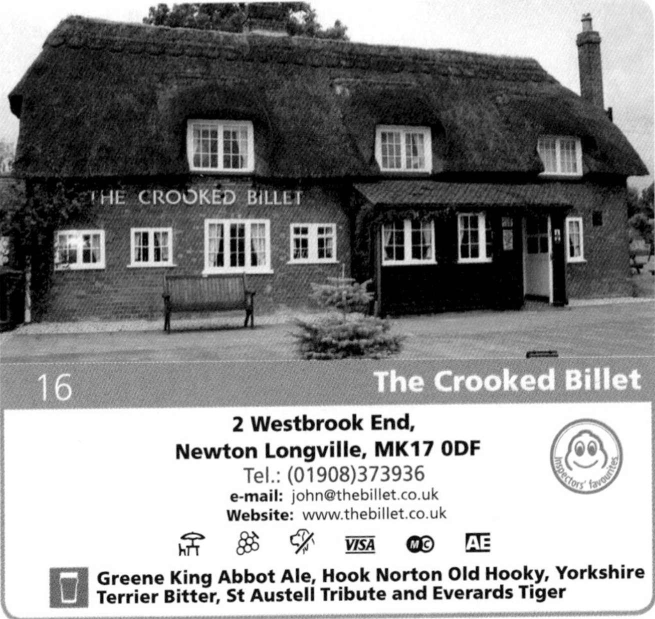

16 **The Crooked Billet**

2 Westbrook End,
Newton Longville, MK17 0DF
Tel.: (01908)373936
e-mail: john@thebillet.co.uk
Website: www.thebillet.co.uk

Inspectors' favourites

VISA MC AE

Greene King Abbot Ale, Hook Norton Old Hooky, Yorkshire Terrier Bitter, St Austell Tribute and Everards Tiger

This charming 17C thatched pub is the last place you expect to find on the outskirts of Milton Keynes. Starting life as a farmhouse and later providing refreshments for passing farmers, it eventually evolved into the village pub. The interior is smart yet informal; the owner's artwork adorns the walls and a cheery bunch of locals prop up the bar. Over the last decade it's built up quite a reputation – so much so that you'll need to book. Emma heads the dedicated kitchen team, who create modern, seasonal dishes; lunch offers sandwiches or a three course à la carte and dinner introduces a 7 course tasting menu. Provenance is noted on the menu, as are wine recommendations, and ex-sommelier John happily guides you through the 200-strong wine list.

Closing times
Closed Monday lunch
booking advisable
Prices
Meals: £ 21/23
and a la carte £ 25/40

6 mi southwest of Milton Keynes by A 421. Parking.

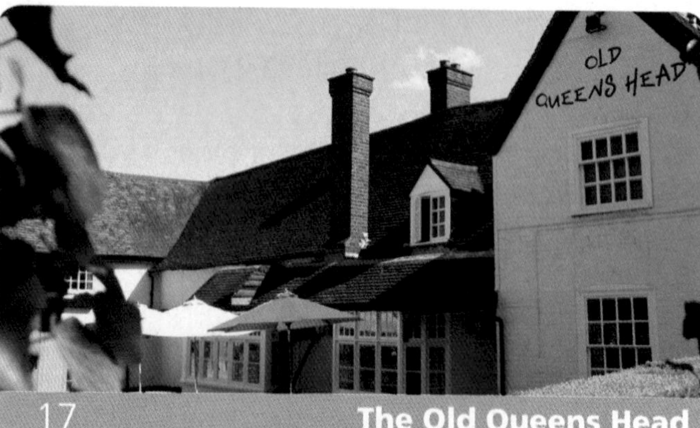

17 **The Old Queens Head**

Hammersley Ln,
Penn, HP10 8EY
Tel.: (01494)813371 – Fax: (01494)816145
e-mail: info@oldqueensheadpenn.co.uk
Website: www.oldqueensheadpenn.co.uk

 **Greene King IPA, Ruddles County**

This pub may not be quite as old as the ancient beech woodlands that surround it but it does have a part to play in the area's history. Legend has it that Lord Penn inherited the pub when he won a game of cards against Charles II. Whether this is true or not, no one knows but it can be proved from the 1666 deeds that it was purchased by one of the King's physicians. Boasting weathered beams and good views the dining room – formerly a barn – is the oldest part; while the surrounding rooms, although slightly newer, continue the rustic theme with their characterful open fires and cosy nooks. Big, hearty dishes are the order of the day, so you might find pigeon breast on red onion tarte tatin, followed by beef bourguignon with oxtail dumplings.

Closing times
Closed 25-26 December

Prices
Meals: a la carte £ 20/27

4 mi north of A 40, Junction 2, via Beaconsfield by B 474. Parking.

18 The Three Horseshoes Inn

Bennett End,
Radnage, HP14 4EB
Tel.: (01494)483273 – Fax: (01494)485464
e-mail: threehorseshoe@btconnect.com
Website: www.thethreehorseshoes.net

Inspectors' favourites

VISA MC AE

Marlow Breweries - IPA and Fat Cat

This 18C red-brick pub is set in a fantastic hillside location, deep in the countryside. The cosy bar with its attractive flag floor and inglenook fireplace is the place to be – although with space being limited, you might want to head to the restaurant, with its stunning beams and smart, minimalist feel; or in warmer weather, the terrace, which boasts pleasant views over the duck pond to the hills beyond. Menus reflect the chef's background, so you'll find classically prepared dishes with the odd French touch. Lunch consists mainly of soups, salads and pâtés, while dinner offers a more formal à la carte and some lighter tapas dishes; the latter served in the bar and garden. Bedrooms are contemporary and lavish; the Molières suite is the best.

Closing times
Closed Sunday dinner and Monday lunch

Prices
Meals: £ 18 (lunch) and a la carte £ 19/36

6 rooms: £ 75/145

5 mi west of High Wycombe by A 40 and minor road north. Parking.

Seer Green

19 The Jolly Cricketers

24 Chalfont Rd,
Seer Green, HP9 2YG
Tel.: (01494)676308

  AE

 **Marlow Rebellion and Chilton Brewery Vale**

Somehow it's hard to imagine a pub called The Jolly Footballers. Indeed, no sport does nostalgia or evokes a spirit of bonhomie quite like cricket and this charming Victorian pub certainly does its bit for the gentleman's game: there's memorabilia aplenty, including signed cricket bats and Test Match programs, and even the menu comes divided into 'Openers, Main Play and Lower Order'. But this is also a pub where people come to eat. The kitchen nicely balances classic dishes with more modern choices, so seasonal asparagus could be followed by monkfish with Moroccan spices and, for dessert, a generously sized and satisfyingly filling fruit crumble. In winter, sit by the fireplace and count down the months until summer comes around again.

Closing times
Closed dinner Sunday and Monday

Prices
Meals: a la carte £ 22/32

Typical Dishes
Asparagus with potatoes & poached duck egg
Roasted rump of lamb & aubergine purée
Raspberry soufflé & lemon thyme sorbet

 *2.5 mi northeast of Beaconsfield off A355*

20 The Bull & Butcher

Turville,
RG9 6QU
Tel.: (01491)638283 – Fax: (01491)638836
e-mail: info@thebullandbutcher.com
Website: www.thebullandbutcher.com

  VISA

 **Brakespear's Bitter, Oxford Gold and Hooky Dark Mild**

Nestled peacefully in the Chilterns, it's hard to believe that the small village of Turville has so many claims to fame: over the years it's provided the setting for The Vicar of Dibley, featured in several Midsomer Murders and had its 18C windmill reincarnated as Caractacus Potts' workshop in Chitty Chitty Bang Bang. Down the hill from the windmill you'll find the characterful Grade II listed Bull and Butcher, which boasts open fires, wood beams and even an old well; not forgetting a large garden with lovely views. Cooking is generous and robust, and theme nights feature everything from sushi to game; the latter offering tempting dishes such as roast pheasant with Calvados and apple or saddle of fallow deer stuffed with pine nuts and rosemary.

Closing times
Open daily
booking advisable

Prices
Meals: a la carte £ 20/32

5 mi north of Henley-on-Thames by A 4130 off B 480. Parking.

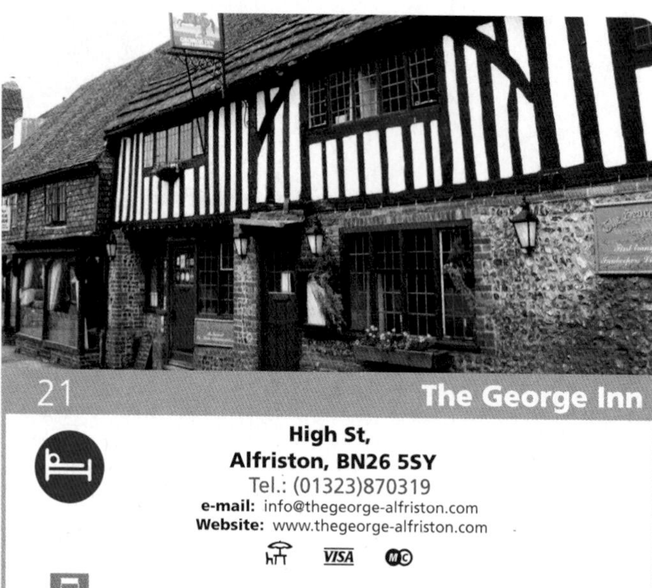

21 The George Inn

High St,
Alfriston, BN26 5SY
Tel.: (01323)870319
e-mail: info@thegeorge-alfriston.com
Website: www.thegeorge-alfriston.com

VISA

Greene King IPA and Abbot Ale

If it's character you're after, you're in the right place. The picturesque village of Alfriston is on the Southdown Way and boasts its own cricket club, a group of bell ringers and this delightful 14C stone and timber pub. As characterful inside as out, it has vast inglenook fireplaces and more beams than you've ever seen before; there's even one on the floor. For dining, there's the choice between the rustic bar and another spacious, slightly more formal room. The menu offers sharing boards and restaurant-style dishes such as knuckle of lamb or mushrooms with bacon and goat's cheese, and pub classics appear as the specials. Comfy, simply furnished bedrooms are named after scholars; Bob Hall with its 13C wattle and daub murals is the best.

Closing times
Closed 25-26 December

Prices
Meals: a la carte £ 20/30

6 rooms: £ 60/130

Typical Dishes
Pan-fried scallop & chorizo
Rump of lamb with dauphinoise potatoes
Chocolate cake with black cherries & cream

Two public car parks (1min walk) and street parking.

22 The Ginger Dog

12 College Pl,
Brighton, BN2 1HN
Tel.: (01273)620990
e-mail: info@gingermanrestaurants.com
Website: www.gingermanrestaurants.com

  AE

 **Harvey's Sussex Best Bitter, Sharp's Doom Bar**

The latest addition to the locally based 'Ginger' empire is this shabby-chic, canine-themed pub, with a welcoming atmosphere and relaxed feel. Many of the original architectural features – such as the ornate wood – are juxtaposed with contemporary design touches; note the bowler hats used as lampshades. Tables are smartly laid up behind the bar but you can eat anywhere. Fresh produce is to the fore on the menu, which is mostly British but with the odd nod to Italy, and could include local Rye Bay plaice with shrimps, Scotch quail egg and black pudding salad or a proper trifle .Water and excellent bread are not only brought to the table without hesitation but are not charged for either; and a ginger 'dog' biscuit is served with coffee.

Closing times
Open daily
Prices
Meals: a la carte £ 30/40

 *In heart of Kemp Town, just off Marine Parade (A259) towards Lewes. Metered parking nearby.*

23

Coach & Horses

School Ln,
Danehill, RH17 7JF
Tel.: (01825)740369 – Fax: (01825)740369
e-mail: coachandhorses@danehill.biz
Website: www.coachandhorses.danehill.biz

   AE

 **Harveys Best and Dark Star Best**

Set on the edge of Ashdown Forest, this characterful stone building has been serving the local community since 1847, when it first opened as an ale house. Inside it's tiny, with simple, open-fired bars to either side – one leading to a small dining room with characterful stone walls, flagged floor and exposed rafters; while outside, a pleasant garden and 'child free' terrace boast lovely views over the South Downs. The locals remain the backbone of this pub, so you'll find weekly changing guest ales in the bar, alongside light lunch dishes and a menu of straightforward, hearty classics like steak and kidney pie. The concise evening menu displays the best of what's available locally, with dishes arriving in satisfying, flavoursome portions.

Closing times
Closed 26 December and Sunday dinner except summer

Prices
Meals: a la carte £ 22/27

Typical Dishes
Local game offal pie
Crown of local pigeon
Hazelnut & muscovado tart, espresso sabayon

 *0.45 mi northeast on Chelwood Common Rd. Parking.*

24 The Jolly Sportsman

Chapel Ln,
East Chiltington, BN7 3BA
Tel.: (01273)890400 – Fax: (01273)890400
e-mail: info@thejollysportsman.com
Website: www.thejollysportsman.com

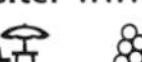  

 **Dark Star Hophead and regularly changing guest ales**

Down a myriad of country lanes, in a small hamlet, this grey clapperboard pub attracts locals in their droves, so even midweek you'll have to book. You're greeted by smoky aromas from an open fire and a bubbly team; often even by the owner himself. Choose a spot in the cosy bar, warmly decorated red room, rear extension or large garden and terrace – and prepare for just as much choice when it comes to the food. There are good value set menus, a rustic, European-based à la carte and interesting bar bites such as Cabezada and Guindillas. Blackboard specials quickly come and go but there's always plenty of local meats, offal and fish to be found on the main menu. A very good wine list and plenty of cask ales, cider and perry are offered too.

Closing times
Open daily
booking essential

Prices
Meals: £ 16 (weekday lunch) and a la carte £ 22/29

Typical Dishes
Pig's head terrine & celeriac remoulade
Rump of Ditchling lamb
Chocolate tart

5.5 mi northwest of Lewes by A 275 and B 2116 off Novington Lane. Parking.

25 **The Griffin Inn**

Fletching,
TN22 3SS
Tel.: (01825)722890 – Fax: (01825)722810
e-mail: info@thegriffin.co.uk
Website: www.thegriffininn.co.uk

Inspectors' favourites

 **Harvey's Best Bitter, Kings of Horsham, Hepworth and Dark Star**

Under the same ownership for over 30 years, this hugely characterful red and white brick coaching inn is the kind of place that every village wishes for. It boasts a linen-laid dining room, traditional wood-panelled bar and comfy 'Club Room' adorned with cricketing memorabilia, as well as a sizeable garden and terrace – with wood burning oven for sophisticated summer Sunday barbeques. A large freestanding blackboard in the bar offers a huge range of British and Italian classics and there's a more structured à la carte available in the dining room. If you live locally, work it off by joining one of the pub's cricket teams; if not, follow narrow, sloping corridors to one of the individually decorated bedrooms which are dotted about the place.

Closing times
Closed 25 December
meals in bar Sunday dinner

Prices
Meals: £ 30 (Sunday lunch) and a la carte £ 25/36

13 rooms: £ 70/160

Typical Dishes
Ham hock & apricot terrine
Portland crab linguine
Lemon polenta cake

 *Between Uckfield and Haywards Heath off A 272. Parking.*

26 The Ginger Pig

3 Hove St,
Hove, BN3 2TR
Tel.: (01273)736123
e-mail: info@gingermanrestaurants.com
Website: www.gingermanrestaurants.com

VISA AE

Harvey's Sussex Bitter

Set just off the seafront, this smart building displays a mortar relief of a ship above the entrance and a beautifully restored revolving door, harking back to its former days as the Ship Hotel. Inside you'll find a long wood-floored bar and large dining room, and although they take bookings it's worth arriving early, especially at weekends. The à la carte offers precisely prepared, flavoursome British dishes – including plenty of vegetarian options – and there are great value set menus at both lunch and dinner, along with some good wine deals; order a coffee and it'll arrive with a quirky pig-shaped shortbread. They're used to being busy and service copes well under pressure, the only drawback being that it can lack a more personal touch.

Closing times
Open daily

Prices
Meals: a la carte £ 25/30

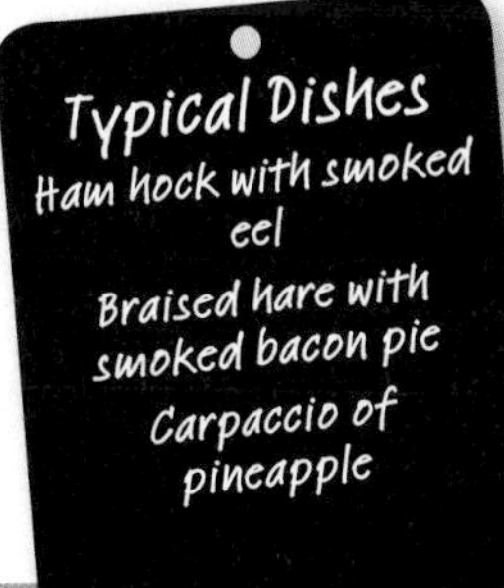

Off north side of shore road, Kingsway, A 259. NCP car park (2min walk) & parking meters (2hr maximum during day).

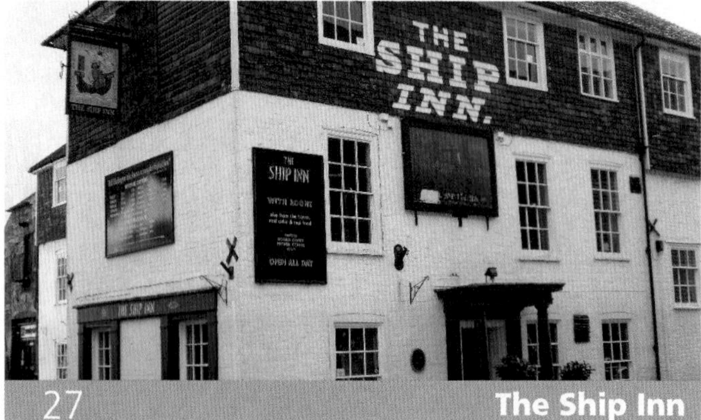

27 The Ship Inn

The Strand,
Rye, TN31 7DB
Tel.: (01797)222233
e-mail: info@theshipinnrye.co.uk
Website: www.theshipinnrye.co.uk

Harvey's Best Bitter, Whistable Bay Oyster Ale and Rother Valley Boadicea

Fittingly located at the bottom of Mermaid Street, The Ship Inn dates back to 1592, when it was used as a warehouse for impounding smuggled goods. This is a place that proves that smart surroundings aren't a prerequisite for good food. Modern pop art and boars' heads are dotted about the rooms, fairy lights are draped everywhere and if you sit on one of the battered sofas, don't be alarmed if you end up at a quirky angle or even falling through. The quality of the food then, comes as a surprise. Ingredients are well-sourced and preparation is careful. The result: flavoursome, rustic dishes that arrive in generous portions – maybe baked cod or soy-braised pork belly. Compact bedrooms display similarly wacky wallpapers and painted floors.

Closing times
Open daily
Prices
Meals: a la carte £ 16/30
10 rooms: £ 70/100

Typical Dishes
Smoked haddock soup
Rabbit stew
Hot chocolate fondant

Close to the Quayside. Local car park close by.

28 The Wellington Arms

Baughurst Rd,
Baughurst, RG26 5LP
Tel.: (0118)9820110
e-mail: hello@thewellingtonarms.com
Website: www.thewellingtonarms.com

 **Wadworth 6X, Good Old Boy and Andwell's King John**

If success relies on the effort put into sourcing local produce and making, growing and rearing everything possible, then The Wellington is a sure-fire winner. A smart, cream-washed building with box hedges framing the doorway, it boasts its own herb and vegetable beds, as well as its own pigs, chickens and bees; it comes as no surprise then, to discover homemade honey, preserves and teas for sale in the bar. It's a cosy, welcoming kind of place, with quarry-tiled floors, low beams and just eight tables on offer. Blackboard menus feature 6 dishes per course – which are rubbed off and replaced as produce runs out – and cooking is generous and satisfying, featuring dishes such as goat's cheese soufflé and beef from a farm just over the fields.

Closing times
Closed Sunday dinner
booking essential

Prices
Meals: £ 18 (weekday lunch) and a la carte £ 18/34

Typical Dishes
Crispy pumpkin flowers with ricotta
Home-reared rack of roast pork
Rhubarb jelly & raspberries

 *8 mi north of Basingstoke by A 339 and minor road through Ramsdell and Pound Green; south of village on the Kingsclere / Newbury rd. Parking.*

Droxford

29 The Bakers Arms

High St,
Droxford, SO32 3PA
Tel.: (01489)877533
e-mail: enquiries@thebakersarmsdroxford.com
Website: www.thebakersarmsdroxford.com

Bowman Ales - Swift One & Wallops Wood

The owners of this pub met whilst working abroad on private yachts, eventually returning to their roots to run this roadside inn. Their experience, effort and enthusiasm have stood them in good stead: cooking is unfussy and filling, with an emphasis on locally sourced ingredients. Main dishes might include venison steak or slow cooked Hampshire beef, with puddings like apple crumble or treacle tart. The pub itself is pleasingly traditional with an open-plan bar, Chesterfield sofas and a roaring log fire; interesting decorative oddments include beer adverts, Victorian photographs and stag heads. Staff are friendly and polite, and the prevalence of local produce continues with the beer, which comes from Droxford-based brewery, Bowman Ales.

Closing times
Closed Sunday dinner and Monday

Prices
Meals: a la carte £ 23/29

Typical Dishes
Hampshire pigeon salad
Grilled gurnard & brown shrimps
Treacle tart, vanilla ice cream

6 mi north of Fareham by A 32. Parking.

30 East End Arms

Lymington Rd,
East End, SO41 5SY
Tel.: (01590)626223
Website: www.eastendarms.co.uk

 VISA 

 **Ringwood Best and Fortyniner**

Owned by John Illsley, bass guitarist of Dire Straits, this traditional country pub boasts a great display of black and white photos of legendary singers, musicians and celebrities from his personal collection. When he bought the place in the late '90s, the locals petitioned for him to keep the place the same, so you'll find a slightly shabby bar with cushioned pews, open fire and dart board, and a slightly smarter pine-furnished dining room behind. Menus are fairly concise, featuring local produce in satisfying, British-based dishes, which are listed in order of price. You might find whitebait followed by pigeon breast, maybe even shark loin. Service is polite if a little lack-lustre. Modern, cottage-style bedrooms provide a smart contrast.

Closing times
Closed Sunday dinner

Prices
Meals: a la carte £ 19/27

5 rooms: £ 68/115

Typical Dishes
Wild mushroom risotto
Catch of the day
Rib-eye steak & fries

 *3 mi east of Lymington by B 3054. Parking.*

Easton

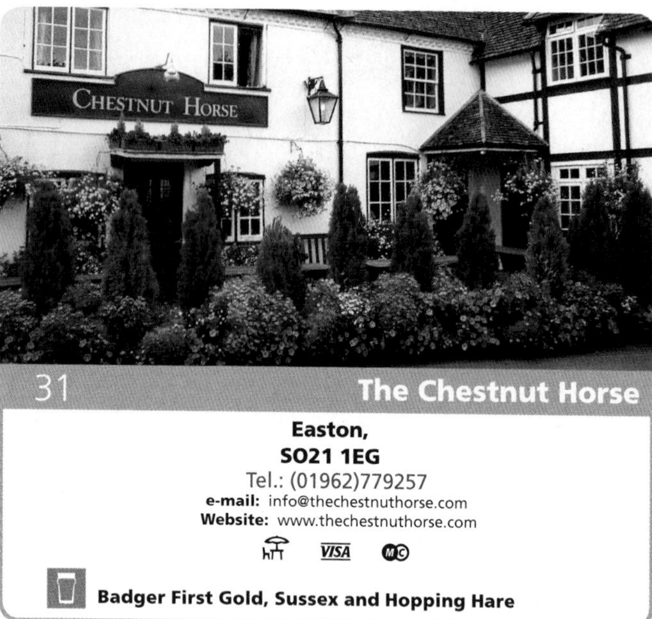

31

The Chestnut Horse

Easton,
SO21 1EG
Tel.: (01962)779257
e-mail: info@thechestnuthorse.com
Website: www.thechestnuthorse.com

VISA

Badger First Gold, Sussex and Hopping Hare

Hidden away in the peaceful village of Easton, in the Itchen Valley countryside, The Chestnut Horse provides a warm welcome. It dates back to 1564 and offers the choice of two rustic bars – boasting exposed beams hung with tankards and teapots – and two candlelit dining rooms; the 'Red' and 'Green' rooms, each one boasting the corresponding décor. Menus are similar at lunch and dinner, and offer traditional dishes with a French edge, so you might find a trio of brioche parcels, followed by smoked cheese glazed ratatouille crêpes or lamb medallions with boulangère potatoes and bacon. Seasonal specials might include Alresford watercress and trout ravioli or watercress iced tea parfait, which, on a sunny day, are ideal taken on the terrace.

Closing times
Closed Sunday dinner

Prices
Meals: a la carte £ 30/36

4 mi northeast of Winchester by A 3090 off B 3047. Parking.

32 **The Bugle**

High St,
Hamble, SO31 4HA
Tel.: (023)80453000 – Fax: (023)80453051
e-mail: manager@buglehamble.co.uk
Website: www.buglehamble.co.uk

 **Courage Best**

This attractive whitewashed pub is set down a cobbled street in the coastal village of Hamble. It's popular with the sailing community – and is owned by a keen seafarer – and its terrace has pleasant views over Southampton Water. The pub menu is served in the bar and offers sandwiches, small plates such as salt and pepper squid or devilled white bait – and pub classics like ale-battered fish and chips or home-cooked honey roast ham. The à la carte is available in the dining room and features more ambitious dishes such as seared local wood pigeon breast, slow-roast pork belly or whole roasted local plaice. Sporting events are popular thanks to the flat screen TVs; equally well-liked are the regular quiz nights and themed food evenings.

Closing times
Closed 25 December
booking essential

Prices
Meals: a la carte £ 17/28

7 mi southeast of Southampton by A 3024 or A 3025 and B 3397. Parking.

Highclere

33 **The Yew Tree**

Hollington Cross,
Andover Rd, Highclere, RG20 9SE
Tel.: (01635)253360 – Fax: (01635)255035
e-mail: info@theyewtree.net
Website: www.theyewtree.net

Inspectors' favourites

VISA MC AE

Timothy Taylor Landlord, Adnams Southwold, Black Sheep, Wadworth 6X, Butts Brewery Barbus Barbus

Anyone expecting darts and a bit of spit and sawdust should think again: Marco Pierre White doesn't do casual and, sure enough, every table in his inn comes dressed in crisp linen; even the bar is a wondrous marble topped affair. The menu reads like Marco Pierre White's CV, from Box Tree apprentice to grandee of the London dining scene, and only the terminally indecisive will struggle to make a choice from a menu that blends French sophistication with British frankness. Dishes like parfait of foie gras or omelette Arnold Bennett jostle for your attention with more pub-like offerings, such as pies of the steak and ale, shepherd or fish variety. There are six bedrooms available for those wishing to make a night of it; ask for the Cartoon Room.

Closing times
Closed dinner
25-26 December

Prices
Meals: £ 16 (Sunday supper)/23 and a la carte £ 30/50

6 rooms: £ 110

5 mi south of Newbury by A 343. Parking.

34 The Hogget

London Rd,
Hook, RG27 9JJ
Tel.: (01256)763009
e-mail: inbox@hogget.co.uk
Website: www.hogget.co.uk

Ringwood Best Bitter, Marston's Pedigree and Wychwood Hobgoblin

Its unusual name refers to a boar of between one and two years of age – hence the rather cute sign. Were he still with us, former owner Cornelius Byford, whose picture hangs inside, would no doubt be pleased with the bay windows and heated terrace; the customers certainly seem to like the pub and, despite its location at the junction of the A30 and A287 (with no in-built community to serve), it has become mightily popular. Its success is down to wholesome food and sensible prices; all dishes are homemade using local produce, and choices range from fish and chips or rib-eye steak through to pan-fried fillets of bream or pea and ham risotto. There are breakfasts most mornings and roasts on a Sunday. Polite service comes from cheery staff.

Closing times
Closed 25-26 December and Sunday dinner

Prices
Meals: a la carte £ 23/28

At the junction of A 30 and A 287. Parking.

Longstock

35 **The Peat Spade Inn**

Village St,
Longstock, SO20 6DR
Tel.: (01264)810612 – Fax: (01264)811078
e-mail: info@peatspadeinn.co.uk
Website: www.peatspadeinn.co.uk

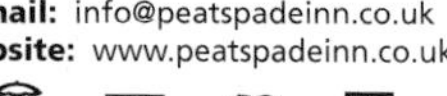

Ringwood - Best and 49er and weekly changing guest ale`

Just north of Stockbridge, in the heart of the Test Valley, you'll come across the pretty village of Longstock and this charming 19C inn, where period furnishings and flickering candlelight are accompanied by warming winter fires. Country pursuits are the name of the game, so you'll find plenty of shooters and fishermen inside, alongside local farm workers and those leisurely passing through. Menus offer classically based dishes that have been brought up-to-date; there might be black pudding Scotch egg with apple purée and crispy bacon, followed by roast halibut with squid ink risotto. Stylish bedrooms are split between the main building and the annexe, there's an open-fired residents' lounge and shooting and fishing trips can be arranged.

Closing times
Closed 25 December
booking essential

Prices
Meals: a la carte £ 24/34
6 rooms: £ 130

1.5 mi north of Stockbridge on A 3507. Parking.

36 **The Anchor Inn**

Lower Froyle,
GU34 4NA
Tel.: (01420)23261
e-mail: info@anchorinnatlowerfroyle.co.uk
Website: www.anchorinnatlowerfroyle.co.uk

VISA AE

Inspectors' favourites

Alton's Pride and Bowland's Quiver

With its origins firmly in the 14C, this part-whitewashed, part-tile hung pub boasts much more in the way of history than sister establishment, The Peat Spade Inn. Pretty countryside and a little pond set the scene and the interior doesn't disappoint, boasting characterful low-beamed olive green rooms and a pleasing mix of cushioned pews, benches and old chairs. Good-sized menus offer classic pub dishes with a refined edge and cooking is hearty and flavoursome; you might find jellied ham hock, followed by sirloin steak and jam roly poly to finish. Service is fittingly keen and friendly, and there's a concise but well-chosen wine list. Bedrooms are characterful but if you retire before closing, you may be able to hear a gentle hum from the bar.

Closing times
Closed 25 December
Prices
Meals: a la carte £ 25/35
5 rooms: £ 90/120

5 mi northeast of Alton by A 31. Parking.

Preston Candover

37 **Purefoy Arms**

Preston Candover,
RG25 2EJ
Tel.: (01256)389777
e-mail: info@thepurefoyarms.co.uk
Website: www.thepurefoyarms.co.uk

 **Timothy Taylor Landlord and Itchen Brewery's Hampshire Rose**

Don't be fooled by the somewhat austere façade; a charming young couple have totally restored this once crumbling pub, which was last rebuilt in the 1860s. It now comes with an attractive contemporary feel, although many of the original features have been retained. The daily changing menu, with its hints of Spain – especially in the bar nibbles – is very appealing. Some luxury ingredients may appear at weekends but the philosophy is tasty food at competitive prices and everything's homemade, including the bread. There are also dishes to share, such as the suckling pig, which requires pre-ordering. And the chocolates in the bar are courtesy of the owner's father, a retired chocolatier who has set up a studio in one of the barns.

Closing times
Open daily

Prices
Meals: a la carte £ 19/25

6,5 mi north of New Alresford on B 3046 in centre of village. Parking

38 White Star Tavern, Dining and Rooms

28 Oxford Street,
Southampton, SO14 3DJ
Tel.: (023)80821990 – Fax: (023)80904982
e-mail: manager@whitestartavern.co.uk
Website: www.whitestartavern.co.uk

VISA AE

Ringwood and monthly changing guest ales

You can't miss this striking black pub with its oversized windows and smart pavement terrace. Set in the lively maritime district, it's provided nourishment and shelter for seafarers since the 19C, although you'll find a much more diverse mix of visitors nowadays. It's a spacious place, made up of several different areas organised around a central bar, and displays an eclectic combination of furniture. The à la carte offers a good choice of modern British main courses – finished off with proper old-fashioned puddings – but there's also a selection of tapas-style small plates on offer throughout the day; and they even open early for breakfast. Smart, modern bedrooms boast good facilities; bathrooms are named after legendary White Star Liners.

Closing times
Closed 25-26 December

Prices
Meals: a la carte £ 20/28

13 rooms: £ 89/119

Southeast of West Quay shopping centre, off Bernard Street. Parking meters directly outside and College St car park (2min walk).

39 **The Greyhound**

31 High St,
Stockbridge, SO20 6EY
Tel.: (01264)810833
e-mail: enquiries@thegreyhound.info
Website: www.thegreyhound.info

VISA MC

Butcombe Bitter and summer guest beers

It may not be as smart on the outside as some of the other properties in the street but its interior is far nicer than its façade suggests. The bar boasts a low-beamed ceiling and large French bistro posters on the walls, while the comfy lounge makes a great place for coffee and homemade cake. If you fancy a picnic, ask for one of the popular hampers and head for the garden, which runs down to the River Test. Served only inside, the lunch menu offers sandwiches and dishes aimed at people wanting just one course; while dinner consists of a concise à la carte selection featuring old pub recipes but with refined presentation and some restaurant-style touches. Service can sometimes be a little functional. Spacious bedrooms come with huge showers.

Closing times
Closed 3 days Christmas, 31 December-1 January and Sunday dinner

Prices
Meals: a la carte £ 25/40
8 rooms: £ 70/125

15 mi east of Salisbury by A 30. Parking.

40 The Thomas Lord

High St,
West Meon, GU32 1LN
Tel.: (01730)829244
e-mail: enjoy@thethomaslord.co.uk
Website: www.thethomaslord.co.uk

VISA MC

All ales from Hampshire breweries

This pub is named after the founder of Lord's Cricket Ground, who retired to and is buried in this village – so if you know your stump from your swing and your grubber from your googly, you should feel at home among the bats, county caps and other memorabilia making its home here. Three rooms display a worn, shabby-chic style, with open fires and soft seating; the snug has shelves of second-hand books for sale, with the proceeds going to community projects. Produce is almost exclusively local, with herbs and vegetables from the pub's kitchen garden. The concise menu of British dishes changes at least once a day, depending on what's freshly available and might include crab cakes, Hampshire rarebit, braised lamb or slow-cooked pork belly.

Closing times
Closed Monday

Prices
Meals: a la carte £ 22/29

9 mi west of Petersfield by A 272 and A 32 south.

41 **The Wykeham Arms**

75 Kingsgate St,
Winchester, SO23 9PE
Tel.: (01962)853834 – Fax: (01962)854411
e-mail: wykehamarms@fullers.co.uk
Website: www.fullers.co.uk

VISA MC AE

Fuller's London Pride, HSB and Chiswick

This 18C red-brick inn might be hidden away but that doesn't stop a diverse collection of people from finding it. Tucked away on a cobbled street between the college and cathedral, it's named after Bishop William of Wykeham, who founded the former of these two establishments in the 14C. Made up of various characterful rooms, it's deceptively spacious, with an appealingly shabby style and interesting display of curios; from old school uniform and ex-college desks to Nelson memorabilia, Bishop Pike's mitre and 1,700 tankards. Menus range from soups, pies and pastas through to more elaborate dishes such as lobster. Individually styled bedrooms boast good facilities; those upstairs are the most characterful, those opposite, the most peaceful.

Closing times
Open daily
booking essential
Prices
Meals: a la carte £ 25/35
14 rooms: £ 70/119

Near (St Mary's) Winchester College. Access to car park via Canon Street only. Parking or street parking with permit.

42 The Taverners

High Street,
Godshill, PO38 3HZ
Tel.: (01983)840707 – Fax: (01983)840517
Website: www.thetavernersgodshill.co.uk

 **Taverners Own Ale, Sharps Doom Bar, Guest ale**

In a pretty – and often busy – little village, stands The Taverners, a pleasant whitewashed pub with a cosy, characterful bar and two deceptively large dining rooms. It's the kind of place that's all about the latest island ingredients and handmade, homemade everything. Out front, a blackboard asks for any surplus home-grown produce (in return for a local Taverners beer or two); to the rear, a large garden is home to chickens, herbs and veg; and inside, various boards display food miles and tables of what's in season and when. Cooking is fresh and tasty, mixing traditional pub classics such as lamb burgers with more ambitious daily specials like sea bass fillets. The hand-raised pork pie is a speciality, as is "my nan's" lemon meringue pie.

Closing times
Closed 3 weeks early January, Sunday dinner except bank holiday weekends and school holidays

Prices
Meals: a la carte £ 18/25

4 mi west of Shanklin by A 3020. Parking.

43 The Three Chimneys

Hareplain Rd,
Biddenden, TN27 8LW
Tel.: (01580)291472
Website: www.thethreechimneys.co.uk

  VISA

 **Adnams Best and Broadside, Harvey's Old in winter and monthly guest ales**

This delightful pub dates back to 1420 and has all the character you would expect of a building its age. The low-beamed, dimly lit rooms have a truly old world feel and for sunnier days there's a conservatory, garden and charming terrace. Menus feature largely British dishes such as smoked haddock, finished off with classics like apple crumble, and there are some tempting Biddenden wines, ciders and cask ales on offer. The story surrounding the pub's name goes that French prisoners held at Sissinghurst Castle during the Seven Years' War were allowed to wander as far as the three lanes but were forbidden to pass the junction where the pub was sited. 'Les trois chemins' (the three roads) was then later mistranslated into 'The Three Chimneys'.

Closing times
Closed 25 and 31 December
booking essential

Prices
Meals: a la carte £ 25/32

 *1.5 mi west by A 262. Parking.*

44 **The Dove**

Plum Pudding Ln,
Dargate, ME13 9HB
Tel.: (01227)751360
e-mail: phillip.macgre@btconnect.com

Shepherd Neame's Masterbrew, Late Red and Amber Ale

Set in the heart of a sleepy hamlet, in the delectable sounding Plum Pudding Lane, this attractive red-brick Victorian pub boasts well-tended gardens and three cosy rooms set with scrubbed pine tables. It's very much a locals pub and villagers pop in and out all day, especially at lunchtime and after work. Phillip, the chef-owner, began his training here at the age of 17 and returned over 10 years later to take the helm. Weekdays he offers a hugely appealing menu of enticing nibbles, pub classics and dishes like smoked cod macaroni: cooking is simple but executed with care and a light touch. Friday and Saturday things step up a gear with a concise, more ambitious menu and prices to match; you might find crab risotto or Gurnard with chorizo.

Closing times
Closed Sunday dinner and Monday
booking advisable at weekends

Prices
Meals: a la carte £ 18/34

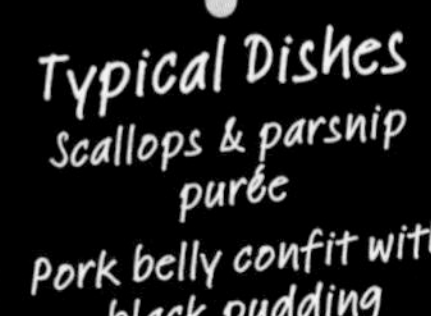

Typical Dishes
Scallops & parsnip purée
Pork belly confit with black pudding
Bitter chocolate tart

Between Faversham and Whitstable, south of A 299. Parking.

45 The Fitzwalter Arms

The Street,
Goodnestone, CT3 1PJ
Tel.: (01304)840303
e-mail: thefitzwalterarms@g.mail.com
Website: www.thefitzwalterarms.co.uk

Shepherd Neame, Late Red

This attractive pub really is in the middle of nowhere but follow the signs for Goodnestone House and Gardens and you can't go far wrong. The village belongs to the Fitzwalter estate – which was owned by relatives of Jane Austen – and this unusual brick building with its castellated exterior and mullioned windows was, reputedly, the keep for the manor house. Consisting of two small rooms, it has a shabby yet characterful feel, with welcoming open fires and dried hops hanging from the beams. The concise blackboard menu features flavoursome country dishes – with plenty of fish in summer and locally shot game in winter – as well as some more modern, European-influenced offerings. The rabbit tagliatelli and baked chocolate mousse are favourites.

Closing times
Closed 25 December, 1 January, Sunday dinner and Tuesday

Prices
Meals: £ 16 (lunch) and a la carte £ 20/25

Typical Dishes
Pheasant with lentils and bacon soup
Confit of pork belly
Clementine sorbet

The village is signposted off B 2046 south of Wingham. Parking in front of pub.

46 The Granville

Street End,
Lower Hardres, CT4 7AL
Tel.: (01227)700402 – Fax: (01227)700925
e-mail: info@thegranvillecanterbury.com
Website: www.thegranvillecanterbury.com

 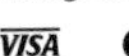 

 **Masterbrew and Late Red seasonal ale**

This pub may not look as impressive as the Tudor warship it's named after but it definitely has the size. Set on a small village crossroads, it's a real family affair, with the owner's sister out front and her partner in the kitchen – and, like their other pub, The Sportsman, you can guarantee it'll be busy. With a high ceiling, exposed rafters and an open-plan layout, the interior is a touch Scandinavian; the sofas making a great spot for a quick snack, the hotchpotch of tables beyond being better for a proper meal. A constantly evolving blackboard menu offers unfussy dishes which arrive in generous, flavoursome portions; mostly on chunky wooden platters. Warm oiled pumpkin seeds come with the bread and veg originates from their allotment.

Closing times
Closed Sunday dinner and Monday

Prices
Meals: a la carte £ 21/34

 *3 mi south of Canterbury on B 2068. Parking.*

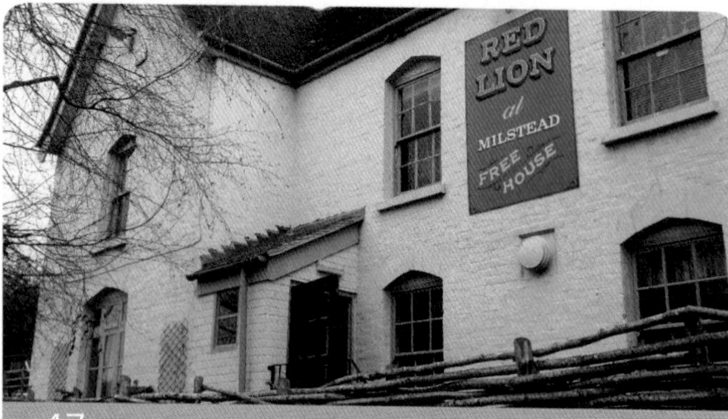

47

Red Lion

Rawling St,
Milstead, ME9 0RT
Tel.: (01795)830279 – Fax: (01795)830279
e-mail: patrickcoevoet@frecuk.com
Website: www.theredlionmilstead.co.uk

Adnams, Harvey's Best, Whistable Native Bitter and one monthly changing guest ale

A 'Red Lion' pub has stood on this spot since Victorian times; the current one belonging to a very capable and experienced couple, who have run numerous pubs in the area over the years. They like to get involved, so you'll find him hard at work in the kitchen and her leading the friendly, engaging service. It's a simple place, featuring a cosy, open-fired bar where the locals tend to gather and a dining room with rich red walls, benches and Lloyd Loom chairs. The ever-changing blackboard menu offers plenty of choice and the Gallic roots of the chef are clear to see; you might find French onion soup, homemade bouillabaisse, cassoulet of lamb shank and Provençale sauces. In true country style, dishes are honest, wholesome and richly flavoured.

Closing times
Closed Sunday and Monday
booking advisable at weekends

Prices
Meals: a la carte £ 20/26

Typical Dishes
Chicken liver & walnut salad
Bouillabaisse
Pistachio crème brûlée

South of Sittingbourne signposted off the A2. Parking.

48 Three Mariners

2 Church Rd,
Oare, ME13 0QA
Tel.: (01795)533633
e-mail: info@thethreemarinersoare.co.uk
Website: www.thethreemarinersoare.co.uk

Shepherd Neame's Masterbrew, Early Bird and Late Red

If you've been negotiating the Saxon Shore Way, this 500 year old pub is the perfect place to refresh yourself, as there's a certain warmth and quirkiness about it, from the roaring fires to the smiley team. A constantly evolving à la carte offers an appealing mix of carefully prepared, flavoursome dishes like smoked pigeon salad or skate cheeks; while the two-choice set menus represent great value – the Walkers' Lunch might include potted duck, chicken pie and homemade ice cream, and the Business Lunch, Parma ham, sea bass and artisan cheeses. From starters to desserts, there's always plenty of local produce. Set in a sleepy hamlet, next to a small marina in the Swale channel, it offers pleasant views over the marshes to the estuary beyond.

Closing times
Closed Sunday dinner and Monday

Prices
Meals: £ 11/20
and a la carte £ 22/32

1 mi northwest of Faversham by minor road or A 2 and B 2045. Parking.

49 George & Dragon

Speldhurst Hill,
Speldhurst, TN3 0NN
Tel.: (01892)863125 – Fax: (01892)863216
e-mail: info@speldhurst.com
Website: www.speldhurst.com

 **Larkins Traditional, Harveys Best and Westerham Georges Marvellous Medicine**

Dating back to 1212, this timbered Wealden Hall house boasts an impressive beamed ceiling and displays an unusual Queen's post in the upstairs dining room (unfortunately only used at busier times). It's thought to be the second oldest pub in the country and has even provided refreshment for the soldiers returning from Agincourt. It's a hugely appealing place, with several rooms, characterful flag floors, vast inglenook fireplaces and a contrastingly modern, landscaped terrace. Cooking is generous and strives to keep things local and organic. Lunch offers largely pub classics, while dinner sees more elaborate offerings such as Kentish ham hock and Turners Hill pheasant. The Groombridge belly pork and Ashdown Forest venison are best sellers.

Closing times
Closed 1 January and Sunday dinner

Prices
Meals: a la carte £ 20/28

Typical Dishes
Seared pigeon breasts
Roast belly of Groombridge pork
Kentish apple crumble

 *3.5 mi north of Royal Tunbridge Wells by A 26. Parking.*

50 **The Sportsman**

Faversham Rd,
Seasalter, CT5 4BP
Tel.: (01227)273370
e-mail: contact@thesportsmanseasalter.co.uk
Website: www.thesportsmanseasalter.co.uk

Shepherd Neame - Masterbrew Bitter, Early Bird, Whitstable Bay and Late Red

Set on the edge of town, close to the sea wall, the unassuming-looking Sportsman proves that you should never judge a book by its cover; for while both its façade and its interior appear rather modest, its top-class food really steals the show. The daily blackboard menu might read simply but dishes are rarely as straightforward as they seem; true, they may only feature two or three ingredients but they are top quality, locally sourced and prepared with precision. Flavours are extremely well-judged and presentation is original; the homemade bread, butter and salt remain a highlight and the crispy duck and roasted pork belly are favourites. Arrive early if you want the full choice, as dishes disappear off the menu as produce is used up.

Closing times
Closed 24 dinner to 26 December, Sunday dinner and Monday
booking advisable

Prices
Meals: a la carte £ 30/40

Typical Dishes
Crab risotto
Monkshill farm lamb
Lemon tart & meringue ice cream

2 mi southwest of Whitstable by B 2205 following the coast road. Parking.

51 **Pearson's Arms**

The Horsebridge,
Sea Wall, Whitstable, CT5 1BT
Tel.: (01227)272005
e-mail: pearsonsarms@hotmail.co.uk
Website: www.pearsonsarms.com

Gadds - No.5 and No.7 Bitter ales and Harvey's

Some pubs have a beautiful setting; some boast a buzzing atmosphere, whilst others serve delicious home-cooked food. The Pearson's Arms is one of those rare gems which tick all the boxes. You'll find drinkers on the squashy sofas downstairs; dining happens in the bright, heavily beamed upstairs room with its fantastic sea views; service is friendly and there's a lively, informal ambience throughout. Cooking shows care and consideration, without over-complication; the flavours are big and the portions, generous. Dishes are as diverse as they are tasty, ranging from beer battered ling with dripping chips or 9-hour salt marsh lamb hotpot, to roast wild halibut in crab oil with artichoke, fennel and crab. Watch the sun set over the sea as you dine.

Closing times
Open daily

Prices
Meals: a la carte £ 23/35

Typical Dishes
Salt Marsh lamb ham
Local bass baked in sea salt
Caramelised pear & cobnut praline ice cream

In centre of town on seafront. Street parking nearby.

52

The Swan Inn

4 Shipton Rd,
Ascott-under-Wychwood, OX7 6AY
Tel.: (01993)832332
e-mail: ricky@swanatascott.com
Website: www.swanatascott.com

 **Brakspear, Hook Norton, Wadworth**

The owner of this 400 year old inn's dream was to create a traditional community pub and his vision has been well and truly realised: it is now a mainstay of the village, with the glorious sort of atmosphere anyone would wish for in their local. The team in the kitchen share his philosophy: the food is traditional, with nothing too fancy, but its quality speaks for itself – and from the stock and the bread to the ice cream and even the chips, everything is made on the premises. Dishes might include pork belly with black pudding and potato fritter, sausage and mash or omelette Arnold Bennett, with delicious desserts like dark chocolate cheesecake or apple and orange crumble. Bedrooms are contemporary in style, with more planned for the future.

Closing times
Closed Sunday dinner and Monday
booking advisable at dinner

Prices
Meals: a la carte £ 21/30
5 rooms: £ 75/125

Typical Dishes
Smoked salmon with halibut
Cod with pea and mint potatoes
Raspberry panna cotta

 *Between Burford and Chipping Norton by A 361. Parking.*

Aston Tirrold

53 The Sweet Olive at The Chequers Inn

Baker St,
Aston Tirrold, OX11 9DD
Tel.: (01235)851272
Website: www.sweet-olive.com

 **Brakspear, Fuller's London Pride**

A red-brick Victorian pub at the heart of an English village; cosy, welcoming and frequented by locals. What sets it apart is its decidedly Gallic feel, attributable in no small part to its French owners. One of the owners also happens to be the chef, so expect to see dishes like Mediterranean fish soup and onglet of beef on the menu; other staples include the more globally influenced tiger prawns in tempura or crispy duck salad, and the thoroughly British ox cheeks and mash or treacle sponge and custard. The old French wine boxes which bedeck the bar offer a clue as to wine list: most are from France, with many from the Alsace region. Oenophiles, or those celebrating, will find plenty to get excited about on the separate fine wine list.

Closing times
Closed 2 weeks February, 1 week July, 25 December, Sunday dinner and Wednesday
booking essential

Prices
Meals: a la carte £ 24/30

Typical Dishes
Tempura tiger prawns
Escalope of roe deer
Treacle sponge

4 mi southwest of Wallingford by minor road through South Moreton. Parking.

54 **The Kings Head Inn**

The Green,
Bledington, OX7 6XQ
Tel.: (01608)658365 – Fax: (01608)658902
e-mail: kingshead@info.net
Website: www.kingsheadinn.net

VISA MC

Hook Norton, Wye Valley, Stroud, Cottage and Purity

This warmly welcoming 15C inn is set on the pretty village green with a stream running alongside. Seats by the fire in its low ceilinged, beamed bar are popular; the dining room is just as comfortable, if perhaps not quite as atmospheric, while the paved terrace is great for alfresco dining in the sun. The same menu is served in all areas and you'll find traditional dishes such as pan-fried lamb cutlets or homemade steak, ale and root vegetable pie, with the odd international influence thrown in. Cooking is robust and rustic in style, with local ingredients well used. Bedrooms are smart, with good facilities and some antique furniture; those in the pub itself are older and more characterful, while the others have a more stylish feel.

Closing times
Closed 25-26 December

Prices
Meals: a la carte £ 20/35
12 rooms: £ 65/125

4 mi southeast of Stow-on-the-Wold by A 436 and B 4450. Parking.

Britwell Salome

55 **The Goose**

Britwell Salome,
OX49 5LG
Tel.: (01491)612304
e-mail: info@thegoosebritwellsalome.com
Website: www.thegoosebritwellsalome.com

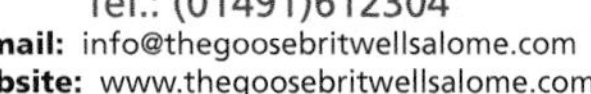

Brakspear Bitter and occasional local ales

The Goose has gone back to its roots as a community pub; albeit one that's still doing darn good food. More importantly, the locals are returning too, and they appear to be especially pleased about the reintroduction of hand-drawn ales. This handsome brick and flint pub has a tree-lined terrace to one side and the local cricket pitch behind; the interior is bright and quite contemporary and service is relaxed and endearing. There's a pleasing range of eating options; from tasty blackboard snacks like Scotch eggs or salt beef sandwiches through to a full menu of modern, seasonal and confidently prepared dishes which demonstrate the chef's pedigree and invention. Much of the top quality produce comes from the village farm across the road.

Closing times
Closed Sunday dinner and Monday

Prices
Meals: £ 18/26
and a la carte £ 27/40

Typical Dishes
Wood pigeon and goat's cheese sandwich
Lemon sole with parsnip and samphire
Chocolate tart, stout ice cream

In village centre on B4009. Parking.

56 The Trout at Tadpole Bridge

Buckland Marsh,
SN7 8RF
Tel.: (01367)870382 – Fax: (01367)870912
e-mail: info@troutinn.co.uk
Website: www.troutinn.co.uk

 **Youngs, Ramsbury, London Pride and guest ales including Old Hooky and White Horse Bitter**

If you fancy trying your hand at boating, then The Trout could be the pub for you. Set just off the Thames Path, it boasts a pleasant garden running down to the river, where, upon request, you'll find an electric punt, complete with picnic hamper; and six private moorings. It's a smart place but manages to retain a loyal band of drinkers, who congregate in the characterful flagstone bar; the diners sat beside them or in the airy back room. The concise main menu consists of classical Gallic dishes with the odd contemporary touch, supplemented by a blackboard of daily specials that often include seafood or game. It's a popular place, so you'll need to book but the cheery staff cope well under pressure. Comfortable bedrooms exceed expectations.

Closing times
Closed Sunday dinner November-April except bank holidays

Prices
Meals: a la carte £ 20/35
6 rooms: £ 80/120

Typical Dishes
Lamb sweetbreads with champagne & mushroom sauce
Venison & chestnut pie
Fig tarte Tatin

 *4.5 mi northeast of Faringdon by A 417, A 420 on Brampton road. Parking.*

57 The Carpenter's Arms

Fulbrook Hill,
Burford, OX18 4BH
Tel.: (01993)823275
e-mail: info@thecarpentersarmsfulbrook.com
Website: www.thecarpentersarmsfulbrook.com

 **Greene King - IPA, Abbot Ale and Old Speckled Hen**

Most people are in such a headlong rush to Burford that they'll drive straight past The Carpenter's Arms without a moment's notice, oblivious to its charms. This is a shame because the pub could be one of the best things about this market town; although, to be honest, its outer appearance gives little clue as to its inside, which mixes the contemporary with the rustic. The owners, having emigrated for a while to Gloucestershire, have returned to take up the reins once again and they understand what works in a pub: robust dishes, priced competitively. Freshly baked breads are cut on an old butcher's block, while the menu successfully mixes classics like grilled bacon chop with more original choices such as cod with Catalan chickpea stew.

Closing times
Closed Sunday dinner and Monday

Prices
Meals: a la carte £ 20/27

 *0.5 mi northeast of Burford on A361. Parking.*

58 The Highway Inn

117 High St,
Burford, OX18 4RG
Tel.: (01993)823661
e-mail: info@thehighwayinn.co.uk
Website: www.thehighwayinn.co.uk

Hook Norton Best Bitter, Vale Brewery, Wye Valley Brewery and Prescott Brewery

You might say that the Highway Inn's owners were meant to be: a local boy, he met his wife when she came over from Australia to visit her grandmother. They married in Burford, and even spent their wedding night at the 15C inn. Fast forward a few years, and it belongs to them. Twinkly lights in the bay trees draw you in; grab a table under the ticking clock, close to the roaring fire and take a look at the menu. Pub dishes like fish and chips and sausage and mash are the staples here, with maybe a lamb or pork burger and specials such as risotto, calves liver or lamb shank. Desserts are delicious and far from dainty, with choices like bread and butter pudding. Cooking is as it should be: simple, honest and fresh. Classic, cosy bedrooms.

Closing times
Closed 25-26 December and first 2 weeks January

Prices
Meals: a la carte £ 20/35
9 rooms: £ 79/140

Parking unrestricted in the town centre.

Burford

59 **The Lamb Inn**

Burford,
OX18 4LR
Tel.: (01993)823155 – Fax: (01993)822228
e-mail: info@lambinn-burford.co.uk
Website: www.cotswold-inns-hotels.co.uk

 **Hook Norton, Wadworth 6X**

Set in picture perfect Burford, once famous for its wool and sheep fairs, it's no coincidence that this 1420s weavers' cottage is set on Sheep Street. You can't fail to be impressed by the cosiness of the place, with its characterful flag-floored bar, elegant columned restaurant, courtyard terrace and cottage garden. As well as main dishes and a fresh fish board, the bar offers nibbles, light bites and afternoon tea; while the restaurant offers more substantial daily market menus and a set selection. Cooking is robust and classical but isn't afraid of pushing boundaries; you might find trio of beef, or scallops and langoustines with vanilla sauce. It's rightly popular and, at times, staff can struggle to keep up. Bedrooms are warm and cosy.

Closing times
Open daily

Prices
Meals: a la carte £ 35/45
17 rooms: £ 81/265

Typical Dishes
Pork belly & scallops with cauliflower purée
Fillet of beef & brisket pastille
Apple Pithivier

 *Parking at Bay Tree Hotel.*

60 **The Masons Arms**

Banbury Rd,
Swerford, Chipping Norton, OX7 4AP
Tel.: (01608)683212 – Fax: (01608)683105
e-mail: admin@masons-arms.com
Website: www.masons-arms.com

Inspectors' favourites

 **Hook Norton Best**

This stone-built inn is the perfect place to be on a lazy summer's day, when you can kick back in the garden, survey the surrounding countryside and linger over a real ale. Don't be out off if the car park looks busy, as although it's a popular destination, there's plenty of room for one and all. They also have the service well and truly sussed, so you'll never have to wait too long. Good value menus present an eclectic mix of unfussy dishes, ranging from the traditional to the more exotic; so you could find anything from a ploughman's to tempura battered squid or maybe a chicken Jalfrezi. Ingredients are traceable, meats are rare breed, poultry is free range and fish is delivered daily; while terrines, breads and desserts are all homemade.

Closing times
Closed 24-26 December

Prices
Meals: £ 18 (lunch)
and a la carte £ 21/35

Typical Dishes

Salad of smoked duck, quail's eggs & raspberries

18 hour shoulder of Old Spot pork

Rich Belgian chocolate pot with pistachio ice cream

 *5 mi northeast of Chipping Norton by A 361. Parking.*

Church Enstone

61

The Crown Inn

Mill Ln,
Church Enstone, OX7 4NN
Tel.: (01608)677262

 **Hooky Best, Timothy Taylor Landlord, Fuller's London Pride and Ramsbury Deer Hunter**

Found in a picturesque village on the edge of the Cotswolds, among pretty stone houses, this 17C inn boasts a welcoming slate-floored conservatory, a beamed dining room and a rustic stone-walled bar; as well as a front terrace and a secluded garden for sunnier days. The chef-owner has built up quite a reputation for his seafood in these parts, so you'll find fishcakes and king scallop and bacon salad as permanent fixtures, alongside beer-battered cod and some more unusual varieties of fish such as Red Gurnard. The daily lunchtime blackboard reads like a top ten of old pub favourites, with the likes of sausage and mash and homemade steak and Hooky ale pie. Meats, fruit and vegetables are sourced from local farms and puddings are made on-site.

Closing times
Closed 26 December, 1 January and Sunday dinner

Prices
Meals: £ 18 (Sunday lunch) and a la carte £ 19/28

Typical Dishes
Scallop & bacon salad
Steak & Hooky ale pie
Vanilla panna cotta

 *3.5 mi southeast of Chipping Norton by A 44. Parking.*

62 The Chequers

Church Rd,
Churchill, OX7 6NJ
Tel.: (01608)659393

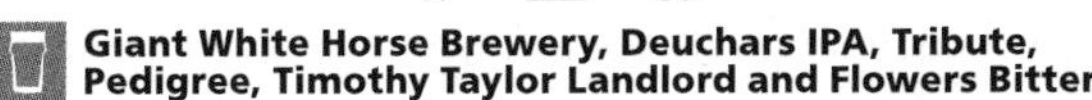

Giant White Horse Brewery, Deuchars IPA, Tribute, Pedigree, Timothy Taylor Landlord and Flowers Bitter

If you're after a brush with local life, then a visit to this attractive Cotswold stone pub is a must. The first clue as to its position at the centre of the community is its sign, which proudly states 'Village Pub'. The second, is the fact that there's always a trusty band of villagers – often alongside the local book club or church group – to be found in the bar. It's surprisingly stylish, with the flag floors, exposed stone walls and inglenook fireplace all adding to the atmosphere. The menu, however, is firmly rooted in the traditional, with dishes ranging from pies through to sea bass; and satisfyingly old school puddings to finish it all off. Thursday is roast duck night and regular events include paella and beef Wellington evenings.

Closing times
Closed 25 December

Prices
Meals: a la carte £ 18/23

Typical Dishes
Black pudding & mango salad
Rack of lamb with cocotte potatoes
Lemon & raspberry posset

 *3 mi southwest of Chipping Norton by B 4450. Parking.*

Clanfield

63 The Clanfield Tavern

Bampton Rd,
Clanfield, OX18 2RG
Tel.: (01367)810223
e-mail: info@clanfieldtavern.com
Website: www.clanfieldtavern.com

Banks's Bitter, Ringwood's Boondoggle and Brakspear's Hooray Henley

Set beside a babbling stream, this charming 17C mellow stone pub oozes character, from its charming gardens to the open-fired sitting room and sizeable conservatory. It boasts its fair share of history too, having been used for everything from club meetings and society auctions to parish elections and court inquests. The landlord is passionate about beer, so you'll find beer pairings on the menu and three regularly changing ales behind the bar – and for those who just can't decide, specially crafted 1/3 pint glasses. The à la carte consists of wholesome, seasonal pub dishes and tasty, good old-fashioned puddings. Thursday Steak Nights offer a variety of breeds – maybe Dexter or Belted Galloway – and a platter of rib, sirloin and rump for two.

Closing times
Closed 25 December and Monday

Prices
Meals: £ 16 and a la carte £ 19/34

In centre of village. Parking.

64 **The Half Moon**

Cuxham,
OX49 5NF
Tel.: (01491)614151
e-mail: info@thehalf-moon.com
Website: www.thehalf-moon.com

Brakspear, Brakspear Organic Oxford

Behind the unassuming façade of this thatched pub, it's clear that 'The Good Life' is alive and well. Bounding with almost as much energy as Harry, their Springer Spaniel, its enterprising young owners grow their own vegetables, herbs and salad leaves and have reared various animals including pigs, geese, turkeys and chickens. They make their own pork scratchings and crisps, smoke their own salmon and sell their own pickles, chutneys and jams. Unsurprisingly, the menu here is focused on local produce; beasts are brought in whole to be butchered and nothing goes to waste, with the more unusual cuts made into pies and faggots. The pub's interior blends 17C beams with contemporary furnishings and its laid back atmosphere adds to the charm.

Closing times
Closed Sunday dinner September-May and Monday

Prices
Meals: a la carte £ 16/30

Typical Dishes
Home smoked salmon
Confit pork belly with lentils
Iced raspberry parfait with chocolate shortbread

 *In village centre on B 480. Parking.*

Fyfield

65 **The White Hart**

Main Rd,
Fyfield, OX13 5LW
Tel.: (01865)390585
e-mail: info@whitehart-fyfield.com
Website: www.whitehart-fyfield.com

Hook Norton Hooky Bitter, Sharp's Doom Bar, Marlow Rebellion's Zebedee and Ferryman's Gold Bitter

A 15C former chantry house, this intriguing building displays many original features including a two-storey, flag-floored hall with vaulted ceiling (now the dining room), a minstrels' gallery and a secret tunnel; as well as a pleasant terrace and cosy beamed bar with inglenook fireplace. They make use of the wealth of produce on their doorstep: so you'll find meat from nearby farms or estates; flour – for the homemade bread – from the local mill; and fruit and veg from either the pub or locals' gardens. Catering for all, menus display honest British cooking and some internationally influenced sharing boards, followed by excellent desserts. Service is slick and friendly, and the biannual beer festival and hog roast makes a great day out.

Closing times
Closed Sunday dinner and Monday except Bank Holidays

Prices
Meals: £ 18 (weekday lunch) and a la carte £ 25/32

Typical Dishes
Home-cured salmon gravadlax
Slow roasted pork belly, crackling
Rhubarb & almond tart with goat's cheese ice cream

10 mi southwest of Oxford by A 420. Parking.

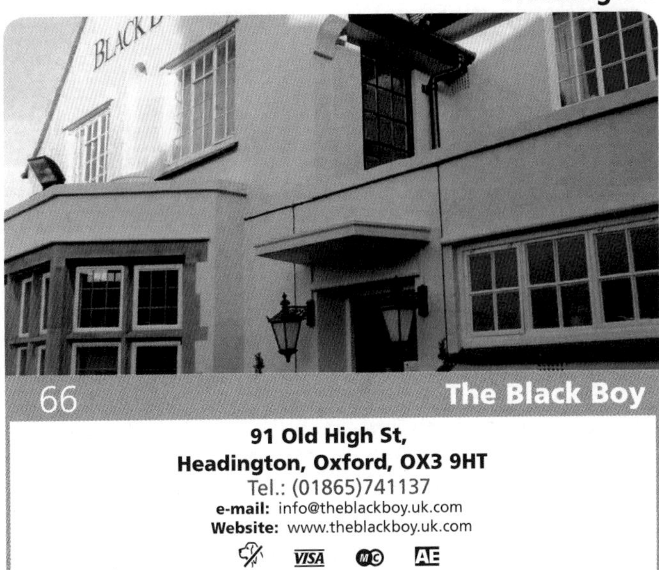

66 **The Black Boy**

91 Old High St,
Headington, Oxford, OX3 9HT
Tel.: (01865)741137
e-mail: info@theblackboy.uk.com
Website: www.theblackboy.uk.com

VISA MC AE

Greene King IPA, Hareraiser, Yorkshire Terrier

It's big and it's bold; it's The Black Boy and it's back to its beautiful best. The chef did a long stint with Raymond Blanc, so it comes as no surprise that there's a French edge to the essentially classic menu, but don't get the wrong idea; this is proper pub food, no messing, with unadorned mains like braised pork belly or sausage and mash for under a tenner. Bring some bling to your Black Boy burger by eating it in the small side restaurant; the low-lit bar is the less popular, but by no means less pleasant, alternative. There are homemade breads and pizzas, a roast goes down a storm for Sunday lunch and Tuesday night is quiz night. Thursday night's for jazz-lovers, and Sunday mornings are when the kids can get creative in the kitchen.

Closing times
Open daily
Prices
Meals: a la carte £ 17/26

East of Oxford off London Rd. Some parking at the front of pub and in nearby streets.

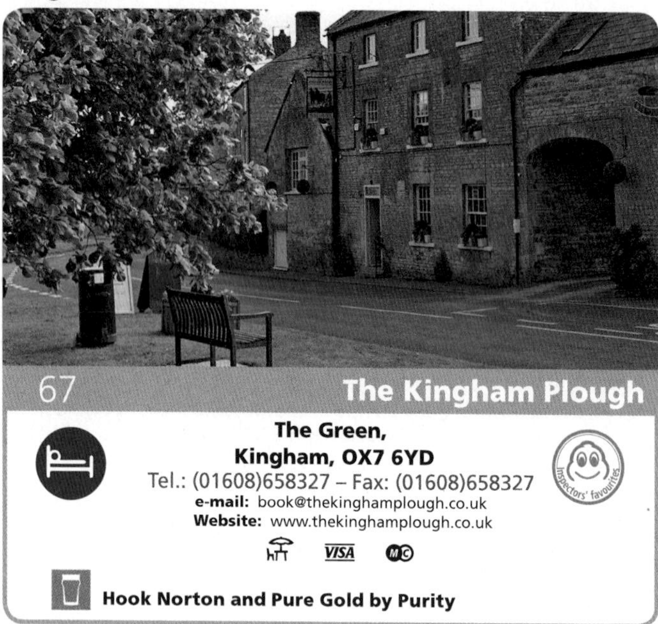

67 **The Kingham Plough**

The Green,
Kingham, OX7 6YD
Tel.: (01608)658327 – Fax: (01608)658327
e-mail: book@thekinghamplough.co.uk
Website: www.thekinghamplough.co.uk

VISA MC

Inspectors' favourites

Hook Norton and Pure Gold by Purity

Set on the green of a beautifully unspoilt village in the Evenlode Valley, this pub boasts a rustic bar, laid-back restaurant and easy-going team. It's owned by Emily Watkins, former sous-chef at The Fat Duck, so you'll find the odd dish such as snails on toast that harks back to her Heston days. The majority of dishes are rooted in the gutsy pub vein, however; albeit a very modern one. The bar menu offers a selection of tasty snacks such as scotched quails' eggs or hand-raised pork pie, while the concise restaurant menu features the latest seasonal produce from foraging expeditions and nearby farms or estates – evolving throughout the evening as ingredients arrive. Preparation is careful and slow cooking reigns. Nearby, comfy bedrooms await.

Closing times
Open daily

Prices
Meals: a la carte £ 20/44

7 rooms: £ 70/125

In village centre. Parking.

68 The Tollgate Inn

Church St,
Kingham, OX7 6YA
Tel.: (01608)658389
e-mail: info@thetollgate.com
Website: www.thetollgate.com

  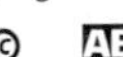 AE

Hook Norton Bitter and one regularly changing guest ale

The owners of the Tollgate Inn used to live next door to it – and loved the pub so much, they bought it. It sits proudly at the centre of this unspoiled village, its front terrace bathed in the midday sun, and attracts passing trade as well as loyal locals. The building is a Grade II listed former Georgian farmhouse which dates back to 1720 but the interior is modern and light, with comfy seating and inglenook fireplaces helping to create a relaxed feel. Food-wise, the choice is more than adequate: while the easy-going lunch menu might offer a Cajun chicken salad or lasagne, the more ambitious dinner menu focuses on dishes like roasted duck breast or pan-fried venison. Modern bedrooms are immaculately kept and have a warm, bright feel.

Closing times
Closed first week in January and Monday

Prices
Meals: a la carte £ 22/35
9 rooms: £ 70/110

3 mi southwest of Chipping Norton by B 4450 to Churchill and minor road west. Parking.

Maidensgrove

69 **The Five Horseshoes**

Maidensgrove,
RG9 6EX
Tel.: (01491)641282
e-mail: admin@thefivehorseshoes.co.uk
Website: www.thefivehorseshoes.co.uk

VISA

Brakspear Bitter, Oxford Gold

Many a walker can be found sat by the crackling log fire in the bar of this charming, part-17C inn, resting their weary feet and refuelling on one of the pub's renowned doorstop sandwiches. Others take a seat in the splendidly sun-soaked restaurant and wine room, or in the garden, with its stunning views out over the countryside. The chef has dipped into many a famous kitchen and his dishes range from comforting classics like Berkshire pork bangers or rib-eye steak with fat chips to more ambitious offerings such as truffle tagliatelle or smoked rainbow trout with chopped goose egg. In summer, the wood-fired oven is used to cook breads, pizzas and various meats. Homely desserts might include apple and rhubarb crumble or sticky toffee pudding.

Closing times
Closed Monday dinner October until March

Prices
Meals: £ 15 (weekdays) and a la carte £ 20/40

Typical Dishes
Homesmoked trout & chopped goose egg
Seabass & clam linguine
Passion fruit soufflé

North of Henley by A 4230 and B 480, then 0.75 mi west; near Stonor Park. Parking.

70 The Black Boy Inn

Milton,
OX15 4HH
Tel.: (01295)722111
e-mail: info@blackboyinn.com
Website: www.blackboyinn.com

Adnams, Greene King, Edwards Beers and Minerals, Abbot Ale and two bi-weekly changing guest ales

The origin of the pub's name remains unclear but suggestions include it being a reference to the swarthy Charles II; an old nickname from its days as a tobacconist's; or in recognition of a young slave found hiding in the cellar. Set back from the road beside the church, this 16C sand-coloured stone building is very much a locals' pub; welcoming children, dogs and all. There's a spacious garden to the front, a traditional bar inside and a conservatory dining room opening out onto a courtyard. The wide-ranging à la carte changes little from lunch to dinner, offering sandwiches, salads and pub classics, as well as a good selection of more substantial starters and main courses. Cooking is proudly British with just the odd international flavour.

Closing times
Closed Sunday dinner

Prices
Meals: £ 15 (Monday-Thursday) and a la carte £ 27/38

4 mi south of Banbury by A 4260 and a minor road west via Adderbury. Parking.

71 **The Nut Tree**

Main St,
Murcott, OX5 2RE
Tel.: (01865)331253
Website: www.nuttreeinn.co.uk

Hook Norton, Spitfire Bitter, Fuller's London Pride, Charles Wells Bombardier and monthly changing Vale Brewery's ales

You want a good old-fashioned thatched pub with a cosy beamed bar, and a tasty, good quality meal: enter The Nut Tree. It's owned by a local and his wife, and apart from the addition of a smart new restaurant, the building itself has altered little since they bought it. Appealing menus change constantly as the latest seasonal ingredients arrive and produce is organic, free range or wild wherever possible. Breads and ice creams are homemade, salmon is smoked on-site and sausages and pork pies are for sale. In the ultimate bid to ensure only the freshest of meats are used, they even rear their own rare breed pigs and Dexter cattle out back. There's always plenty of choice too, with offerings ranging from baguettes to ambitious tasting menus.

Closing times
Closed Sunday dinner in winter and Monday

Prices
Meals: £ 18 (weekdays except Friday dinner) and a la carte £ 29/45

Typical Dishes
Smoked salmon & horseradish cream
Confit pork belly & celeriac purée
Hot chocolate fondant, peanut butter ice cream

5 mi from Bicester by A 41 East and a minor road South via Lower and Upper Arncott; at T-junction beyond the motorway turn right. Parking.

72 **The Fishes**

North Hinksey,
OX2 0NA
Tel.: (01865)249796
e-mail: fishes@peachpubs.com
Website: www.fishesoxford.co.uk

 **Greene King IPA and regularly changing guest ales**

This pub's pretty riverside garden, with its fairytale white benches, is a large part of its charm – kick back with a drink on a lazy afternoon or order a picnic, which comes complete with crockery, cutlery and even a blanket on which to sit. Inside, the décor moves seamlessly between the traditional – think stuffed fish in display cases – and the modern – try colourful abstract artwork and low leather seating. The atmosphere is lively, and, the garden apart, the decked terrace and the conservatory are the best places to sit. Food is fresh, free range and available all day: dishes might include sticky pork ribs, rack of lamb or sausage and mash; some choices come in small or large portions and there are a selection of deli boards for two.

Closing times
Open daily
Prices
Meals: a la carte £ 20/40

 *3 mi west of Oxford city centre by A 420 and minor road south on east side of A 34. Parking.*

73 **The Anchor**

2 Hayfield Rd,
Walton Manor, Oxford, OX2 6TT
Tel.: (01865)510282
e-mail: charlotte@theanchoroxford.com
Website: www.theanchoroxford.com

All Wadworth ales including Bishops Tipple, 6X, Henry's IPA and regularly changing guest ales

Located in a smart residential area by the city, this striking art deco pub is one of a handful of town-based establishments left that understand the true meaning of 'community'. Set beside a lovely old convenience store, just a stone's throw from the canal, it hosts a breakfast club on Fridays, a quiz night on Sundays and is home to the local book club. A careful renovation has retained a lovely atmosphere, with coal fires burning brightly among dark wood panelling and characterful furnishings befitting its age. The chef is keen to promote local, seasonal ingredients and produces tasty, gutsy, carefully presented dishes ranging from snack-sized Worcester sauce glazed cocktail sausages to substantial daily specials like whole roast wood pigeon.

Closing times
Closed 25-26 December

Prices
Meals: £ 19 (lunch)
and a la carte £ 22/30

Typical Dishes
Wood pigeon salad with apricots
Duck leg confit & horseradish mash
Treacle tart & ginger cream

Just north of city centre off Woodstock Rd. Parking.

74 The Magdalen Arms

243 Iffley Rd,
Oxford, OX4 1SJ
Tel.: (01865)243159 – Fax: (01865)724864
e-mail: info@magdalenarms.co.uk

 **Theakston's Best Bitter, Theakston's XB and Deuchars' IPA**

This battleship-grey pub is a relative newcomer to the established Oxford scene but it's already a hit with the locals. The place buzzes – even on a weeknight – and there's always something to keep you entertained, be it a board game or a turn on the bar billiards table. The spacious, open-plan interior boasts deep red walls, quirky old standard lamps and an eclectic collection of 1920s posters, while huge blackboards display nibbles and the twice daily changing menu. Order at the bar for a casual lunch or head through to the curtained-off dining room for table service. The experienced chef uses local ingredients to create tasty, good value dishes; perhaps pork and rabbit rillettes, braised ox cheek or seven hour lamb for five to share.

Closing times
Closed Sunday dinner, Tuesday lunch and Monday

Prices
Meals: a la carte £ 20/28

Typical Dishes
Goat's curd with greens on toast
Braised ox cheek, dumplings & horseradish
Pear & almond tart

 *Southeast of city centre on A4158, on street parking.*

Shiplake Row

75 **Orwells**

Shiplake Row,
RG9 4DP
Tel.: (01189)403673
e-mail: eat@orwellsatshiplake.co.uk
Website: www.orwellsatshiplake.co.uk

VISA

Brakspear, Oxford Gold and Triple

Dating from the 18C – and formerly called The White Hart but renamed in honour of George Orwell who spent his childhood in Shiplake Row – this pub has been leased by the brewery to a local boy with experience in some stellar kitchens. The contemporary interior is neatly divided into three distinct sections: the bar, the cosy conservatory and the imaginatively titled fine dining room, 'The Room'. Food is very much the focus of the operation and the commendable 'use local' ethos is evident throughout: rabbit rissoles or wild garlic risotto could appear on the appealing bar menu, while dishes for the restaurant's dinner menu reveal themselves to be altogether more ambitious and elaborate in design, using modern techniques and styles of presentation.

Closing times
Closed 5 days Christmas-New Year, 2 weeks early January, 2 weeks early September, Sunday dinner and Monday

Prices
Meals: £ 16 (Tuesday-Thursday) and a la carte £ 20/38

3.5 mi south of Henley-on-Thames off A4155 on Peppard road towards Binfield Heath. Parking.

76 The Wykham Arms

Temple Mill Rd,
Sibford Gower, OX15 5RX
Tel.: (01295)788808
e-mail: info@wykhamarms.co.uk
Website: www.wykhamarms.co.uk

St Austell Tinners, Purity Ubu, Wadworth 6X and Fuller's London Pride

If you're after a true village pub, the 17C Wykham Arms may well be it. Set down narrow lanes in the middle of the countryside, this thatched pub certainly plays its role in the community. It boasts attractive sand-coloured stone walls adorned with pretty climbing plants and a pleasant terrace with cast iron furniture. So as not to price out the locals, menus offer a range of dishes right through from light bites and bar snacks to the full three courses; so you might find Salcombe crab and mango salad, Brixham sea bream or baby deer. Suppliers are proudly noted on the blackboard and the chef is only too happy to answer any questions. There's a good choice of wines and what better way to celebrate than with lobster and champagne on the terrace?

Closing times
Closed Sunday dinner and Monday

Prices
Meals: a la carte £ 26/31

8 mi west of Banbury by B 4035. Parking.

77 Sir Charles Napier

Sprigg's Alley,
OX39 4BX
Tel.: (01494)483011 – Fax: (01494)485311
e-mail: info@sircharlesnapier.co.uk
Website: www.sircharlesnapier.co.uk

VISA MC AE

Wadworth IPA and 6X

Set in a small hamlet on the hillside, this attractive 18C flint pub might just have it all. The delightful terrace and gardens buzz with conversation in the warmer months, while sculptures of beasts and figures peer out from behind bushes or lie on the lawn. Inside yet more creatures hide about the place – and all are for sale. It's worth heading to the cosy bar with its open fires and comfy sofas, although the beamed dining room adorned with flowers and art is equally as charming. Cooking is refined and has a strong French accent, offering the likes of eel and foie gras terrine followed by noisette of venison or boeuf bourguignon. Dishes are skilfully prepared and capture flavours to their full. A well-chosen wine list completes the picture.

Closing times
Closed 3 days Christmas, Sunday dinner and Monday except bank holidays

Prices
Meals: a la carte £ 30/40

2.5 mi southeast of Chinnor by Bledlow Ridge rd. Parking.

78 The Cherry Tree Inn

Stoke Row,
RG9 5QA
Tel.: (01491)680430
e-mail: info@thecherrytreeinn.com
Website: www.thecherrytreeinn.com

VISA

Brakspear, Hobgoblin, Oxford Gold

Stoke Row's first claim to fame was as a leading producer of tent pegs during WWII; its second, is as home to an ornate 370ft well and cherry orchard, paid for by the Maharajah of Benares. No longer bearing fruit, the grove is now an ornamental garden but its spirit lives on in the name of the pub. Despite being 400 years old it gives off a slightly funky, just-out-of-London vibe; although a glance at the locals propping up the bar brings you back to Oxford. Menus are fresh and zesty, with dishes ranging from classical slow-roast belly of pork to more adventurous sea bass teriyaki stir fry. Mussels are a permanent fixture and beer plays an important role – both in batter and as a suggested accompaniment. Bedrooms are spacious, bright and modern.

Closing times
Open daily

Prices
Meals: a la carte £ 25/40

4 rooms: £ 95

Between Henley-on-Thames and Goring off B 481. Parking.

79 **The Fish**

4 Appleford Rd,
Sutton Courtenay, OX14 4NQ
Tel.: (01235)848242
Website: www.thefishatsuttoncourtenay.co.uk

VISA MC AE

Moorland Original

Its owners have brought a taste of La France profonde to The Fish, so expect French pictures, French music and a largely French wine list as well as a profusion of French food and charming Gallic service. Feast on meaty terrines, escargots or moules marinière; such dishes mingle merrily on the menu with British pub classics such as steak and kidney pie, as well as dishes like Gressingham duck breast or fillet of lamb. L'entente cordiale continues on the dessert menu, with crème brûlée clamouring for your attention alongside treacle sponge and profiteroles. This is robust country cooking in its most classic form, with pretty much everything homemade using seasonal ingredients. Head to the rear of the pub for the lovely garden and conservatory.

Closing times
Closed January, Sunday dinner and Monday

Prices
Meals: £ 16 (Tuesday-Saturday lunch)
and a la carte £ 23/30

Typical Dishes
Tiger prawns tempura
Venison escalope with creamed cabbage
Homemade meringues

Between Abingdon and Didcot on B 4016. Parking.

80

The Swan Inn

Swinbrook,
OX18 4DY
Tel.: (01993)823339
e-mail: swanninnswinbrook@btconnect.com
Website: www.theswannswinbrook.co.uk

Inspectors' favourites

VISA MC

Hook Norton Best, Sharp's Doom Bar, Adnams Bitter

Set on the banks of a meandering river, The Swan Inn is a delightful place – so booking is a must. Outside, you'll find honey-coloured walls covered in wisteria and a lovely garden filled with fruit trees; while the interior boasts an open oak frame and exposed stone walls covered with old lithographs. A well-versed team serve tasty dishes from the monthly menu, which features the latest seasonal produce from nearby farms and estates. Cooking is fairly modern in style, with some dishes a contemporary take on older recipes; you might find loin of roe deer carpaccio with truffled mayonnaise, followed by fillet of bream with tandoori crushed potatoes, then baked ginger pudding with hot spiced treacle. Well-appointed bedrooms have a luxurious feel.

Closing times
Closed 25-26 December

Prices
Meals: a la carte £ 20/34

6 rooms: £ 100/180

3 mi northeast of Burford by A 40 and minor road north. Parking.

Toot Baldon

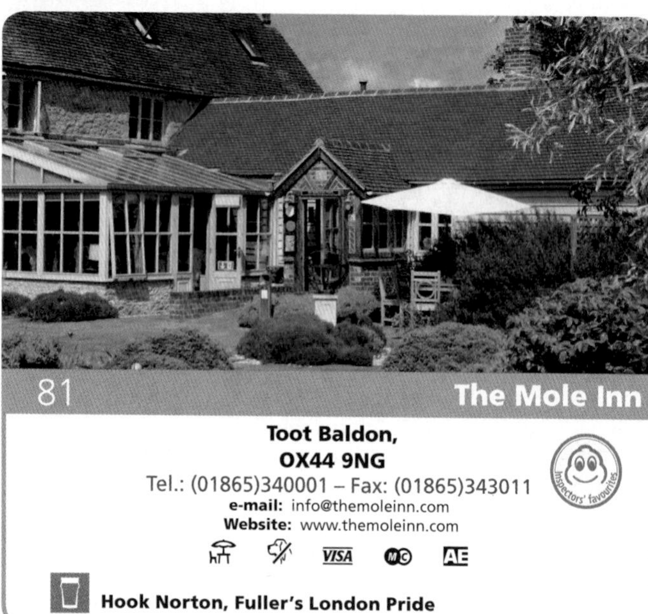

81 **The Mole Inn**

Toot Baldon,
OX44 9NG
Tel.: (01865)340001 – Fax: (01865)343011
e-mail: info@themoleinn.com
Website: www.themoleinn.com

VISA MC AE

Hook Norton, Fuller's London Pride

The Mole has made quite a name for itself in the area and deservedly so. Beautiful landscaped gardens and a pleasant terrace front the building, while inside attractive beamed ceilings and exposed brick walls create a warm and welcoming atmosphere. The menu is equally appealing, catering for all tastes and appetites; you might find sautéed squid with linguine and chorizo, followed by twice-cooked belly of pork with gratin dauphinoise. Sourcing is a serious business and it's a case of 'first come, first served' if you want the full choice. The Tuesday grill and Wednesday fish night menus are decided the day before, so if there's something you've set your heart on, it's worth calling to reserve your dish. Service remains smooth under pressure.

Closing times
Open daily

Prices
Meals: a la carte £ 23/30

6 mi southeast of Oxford; between B 480 and A 4074. Parking.

82 The Boar's Head

Church St,
Ardington, Wantage, OX12 8QA
Tel.: (01235)833254
e-mail: info@boarsheadardington.co.uk
Website: www.boarsheadardington.co.uk

VISA MC AE

No real ales offered

Built by local benefactor Lord Wantage, the picture perfect village of Ardington is, in fact, a Victorian model village. Set in the Vale of the White Horse, the village's centrepiece is the attractive 18C part-timbered Boar's Head, which once paid for the village's lighting through its profits. The pub is now better known as a provider of good food and has built itself quite a reputation in recent years. The central room displays cosy wood floors and a warming fire but the bright, sunny colours and fresh flower displays help to create an airy, informal style. Wide-ranging menus offer something for everyone, from a 'Rapide' lunch to a gourmet dinner selection – and even a seven course tasting menu. Bedrooms are modern, stylish and spacious.

Closing times
Open daily
Prices
Meals: £ 18 (lunch)
and a la carte £ 25/38
3 rooms: £ 80/140

2 mi east of Wantage by A 417. Next to the church. Parking.

83

The Fleece

11 Church Green,
Witney, OX28 4AZ
Tel.: (01993)892270
e-mail: fleece@peachpubs.com
Website: www.fleecewitney.co.uk

VISA

Greene King IPA, Old Speckled Hen

Set overlooking the green, this smart Georgian building is involved in many areas of community life. At breakfast and lunchtime it plays host to business meetings, in the afternoon it provides a sunny spot for mums and their babies and at weekends it keeps the locals entertained with live music. They invest in some worthy values, sourcing ethically produced coffee, locating sustainable timber for their furniture and using local, free range produce in their cooking. The main menu offers interesting 'create you own' deli boards, classics and daily specials, and there's a concise set menu available throughout the day. Staff are well informed and infectiously enthusiastic. Bright, modern bedrooms win over business guests and visitors alike.

Closing times
Open daily

Prices
Meals: a la carte £ 19/30

10 rooms: £ 80/90

Typical Dishes

Sardines with tomato & pumpkin muffin

Parma-ham wrapped chicken

Rhubarb and Ginger Eton mess

11 mi west of Oxford by A 40. Parking.

84 **The Trout Inn**

195 Godstow Rd,
Wolvercote, OX2 8PN
Tel.: (01865)510930
Website: www.thetroutoxford.co.uk

   VISA MC AE

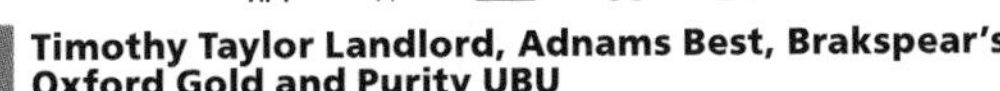

Timothy Taylor Landlord, Adnams Best, Brakspear's Oxford Gold and Purity UBU

The hustle of Oxford feels a million miles away as you sit on the delightful waterside terrace of this idyllically set Cotswold stone inn, watching the greedy chub. The only problem is, so many people know about it, that if you haven't booked, you could have a lengthy wait. The inn dates back to the 17C but it started life as a hospice for the nearby nunnery. It boasts cosy nooks, crannies and roaring fires, as well as an interesting literary history that includes a visit from the fictional Inspector Morse. Menus focus on Italy, featuring sharing antipasti plates, pizza, pasta, Peroni beer-battered fish and tiramisu; but there are plenty of international influences too, with the likes of Greek meze, Moroccan chicken and teriyaki swordfish.

Closing times
Open daily
booking advisable

Prices
Meals: a la carte £ 16/30

3 mi northeast of Oxford off A 4114. Parking.

85 **The Old Bear**

Riverhill,
Cobham, KT11 3DX
Tel.: (01932)862116
e-mail: info@theoldbearcobham.co.uk
Website: www.theoldbearcobham.co.uk

 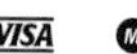 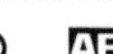 AE

Black Sheep, Sharp's Doom Bar and Hobgoblin

Found at the south end of the high street is this much enlarged 17C coaching inn. The bar is a rustic affair, with an open fire that doesn't always get lit, and is perhaps not the best place in which to eat as you can get blown away by the fearful draughts from the main door. Instead, turn right to find yourself in a snug, rustic room, or left, for the dining room. Staff are easy to spot in their butcher's aprons – appropriate apparel as the highlights of the menu include the more sturdy choices such as sautéed ox heart, homemade terrine and spiced pig's head. In amongst all the period character is a useful piece of 21C technology: a temperature controlled wine dispenser that allows for some pretty decent wines to be served by the glass.

Closing times
Open daily
Prices
Meals: a la carte £ 24/35

Junction 10 of M25 southern end of high street on A245.

86 **Parrot Inn**

Forest Green,
RH5 5RZ
Tel.: (01306)621339
e-mail: drinks@the parrot.co.uk
Website: www.theparrot.co.uk

VISA MC AE

Ringwood Best, Youngs Ordinary and guest ales such as Dorking Ruby, Hog's Back, TEA, Adnams Broadside

When a pub sells its own home-grown and homemade produce – bread, cheese, cakes and preserves, as well as eggs and meat from its own farm – you can be pretty much guaranteed that their cooking is going to be fresh and full of flavour. With well-priced, generously proportioned dishes such as vegetable and stilton pie or pork belly with chorizo and baked butter bean, the Parrot certainly doesn't disappoint. This is a pub where they home-cure their own black pudding and aren't afraid to serve less well-known offerings such as oyster sausages or mutton. The 300 year old pub's interior is traditional, with plenty of character in the form of exposed brick, flag floors and low wooden beams. Sup real ale as you watch a cricket match on the green.

Closing times
Closed 25 December and Sunday dinner

Prices
Meals: a la carte £ 18/28

8 mi south of Dorking by A 24, A 29 and B 2126 west. Parking.

Ockley

87 **Bryce's**

Old School House,
Stane St, Ockley, RH5 5TH
Tel.: (01306)627430 – Fax: (01306)628274
e-mail: bryces.fish@virgin.net
Website: www.bryces.co.uk

VISA MC

 **Fuller's London Pride, Kings Horsham Bitter**

Although it may look like a traditional pub, this is much more of a dining operation, with just a small copper-topped counter and a couple of tables to make up the lounge. There are two similarly styled dining areas boasting high-backed leather chairs – each has its own menu and one of them is linen-laid. You'll always find a couple of meat dishes but it's the fresh seafood from the South Coast day boats that people come for. The cheaper bar menu offers simple dishes such as herring roes or smoked salmon tart, with several options available in two sizes; while the more adventurous restaurant menu might offer red snapper en papillote or herb-crumbed supreme of cod. There's also a 3 course 'menu of the day' and blackboard specials to consider.

Closing times
Closed 25-26 December, 1 January, and Sunday dinner in winter

Prices
Meals: £ 15 (weekdays) and a la carte £ 34/40

Typical Dishes
Loch Fyne queen scallops
Fillets of black bream
Steamed orange & ginger pudding

 *8 mi south of Dorking by A 24 and A 29. Parking.*

88 The Three Horseshoes

25 Shepperton Rd,
Staines, TW18 1SE
Tel.: (01784)469606
e-mail: info@3horseshoeslaleham.co.uk
Website: www.3horseshoeslaleham.co.uk

Ringwood Best, Hogs Back TEA and Sharp's Doom Bar

The sister pub to the Red Lion in Woking is this sturdy 17C inn, which has had a full and sympathetic makeover. It's a pretty thing, with a pleasant enclosed garden and an interior divided into three large dining areas, all of which have their own charm and character. Just order at a bar and hand over your credit card – which they keep in the safe, so there's no need to panic. Staff are a cheery and bunch who patently care about their customers. The menu is unashamedly traditional but the cooking is done with due care and attention. Calf's liver is popular, as are the lighter, tapas-style dishes. There are shared plates, a style of eating which always seems so appropriate in a pub, and the crab sandwiches are also good.

Closing times
Open daily

Prices
Meals: a la carte £ 20/35

Junction 13 on M 25 southeast 2.5 mi by A 30, A 308 and on B 376. Parking.

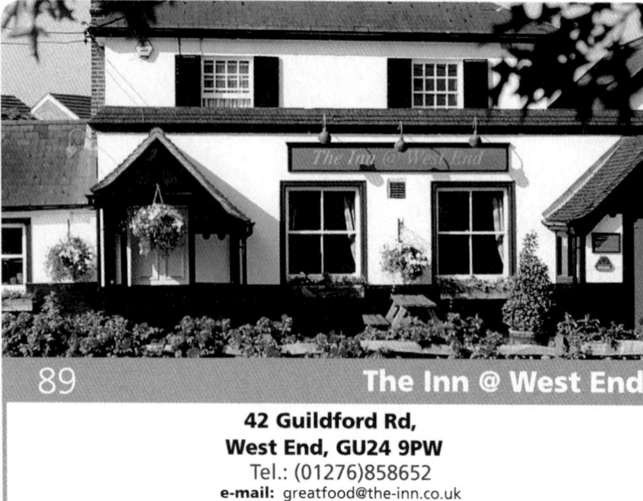

89 **The Inn @ West End**

42 Guildford Rd,
West End, GU24 9PW
Tel.: (01276)858652
e-mail: greatfood@the-inn.co.uk
Website: www.the-inn.co.uk

VISA MC AE

Fuller's London Pride and one guest ale such as Hook Norton and Exmoor Ales

A snug and friendly village pub, with a roaring fire in winter and a pleasant garden for alfresco dining come summer. Blackboards tell you all you need to know: there's a small one listing lunchtime sandwiches, which come in brown, white, dainty or doorstop; on Wednesdays there's a board which offers fresh fish and, Mondays, in season, a board which lists a large selection of game. Event nights are also announced in this manner – with the pub's loyal local following ensuring an impressive turnout. The array of menus means there's something for everyone – perhaps chicken liver and black pudding salad, roast rump of lamb or loin of pork and twice-cooked belly. The owner also has a wine business, so expect a large selection by the glass.

Closing times
Open daily

Prices
Meals: a la carte £ 26/37

2.5 mi southeast of Junction 3 on M 3 by A 322. Parking (40 spaces).

90 The Bee

School Rd,
Windlesham, GU20 6PD
Tel.: (01276)479244
e-mail: eat@thebeepub.co.uk
Website: www.thebeepub.co.uk

Sharp's Doom Bar, Hop Back Summer Lightning, Courage Best, Hogs Back TEA

The espresso machine on the bar is the first clue. Wood floors, eggshell-coloured walls, a mishmash of wooden furniture and a leather Chesterfield make it abundantly clear: this is a pub which has had the gastro treatment – and judging by the number of punters making a beeline for it, it seems to have done the trick. The daily changing menus showcase local, seasonal produce, with precisely cooked dishes such as roast rump of lamb or braised breast of veal; the two course lunch menu is good value, but with starters like pigeon and wild mushroom salad and desserts like sticky toffee pudding, the trouble will be knowing which courses to go for. With a children's play area and regular barbecues, the garden becomes a hive of activity in summer.

Closing times
Closed Sunday dinner

Prices
Meals: £ 16 (lunch)
and a la carte £ 22/35

Typical Dishes
Scallops with chorizo
Beef Wellington
Apple & prune crumble

Just off A 30 on B 386. Parking.

91 **The Brickmakers**

Chertsey Rd,
Windlesham, GU20 6HT
Tel.: (01276)472267 – Fax: (01276)451014
e-mail: thebrickmakers@4cinns.co.uk
Website: www.thebrickmakerswindlesham.co.uk

  AE

Fuller's London Pride, Courage Best and seasonal ales

Thus named because workers from the nearby former brickmaking works used to pop in for a pint on their way home, this red-brick pub may appear quite small from the outside – not hard when it's surrounded by houses as grand as some of those nearby – but it actually goes back a long way. It's set in a pretty location and its narrow, immaculately kept garden is quite a feature in summer. If you're dining inside, choose a seat in the linen-laid restaurant which extends out into the conservatory. The other option is the bar, with its comfy sofas and open fire. Food-wise, the choice is between a simple bar menu and a more interesting à la carte. Dishes, which range from sausage and mash to roasted duck breast, are good value and full of flavour.

Closing times
Open daily

Prices
Meals: £ 20 (Sunday) and a la carte £ 20/30

Typical Dishes
Chicken liver paté
Half shoulder of lamb with rosemary mash
Apple crumble

1 mi east on B 386. Parking.

92 Red Lion

High St, Horsell
Woking, GU21 4SS
Tel.: (01483)768497
e-mail: info@redlionhorsell.co.uk
Website: www.redlionhorsell.co.uk

  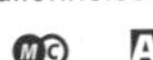

 **Courage Best, Fullers London Pride and Adnams Broadside**

This modern take on the pub is concealed within a residential area but is just five minutes from the centre of Woking. It's made up of a large, contemporary main bar, with sofas and wi-fi for those who've brought along their technological gadgetry, and a plethora of boards advertising the cocktail of the day and menu offers. The two large rooms at the back constitute the dining room but the same menu is served throughout. That means lots of pub classics, the highlights being the supremely fresh fish and the shared dishes. Whole gammons are sometimes roasted at weekends, along with spit-roasted chickens and there are all-day dining options too. Add large outside seating, occasional live music and wine tasting and you have a successful operation.

Closing times
Open daily
booking advisable

Prices
Meals: a la carte £ 15/25

1.5 mi northwest of Woking by Brewery Rd and Church Hill. Parking.

93 George and Dragon

Main St,
Burpham, BN18 9RR
Tel.: (01903)883131
e-mail: mail@burphamgeorgeanddragon.com
Website: www.georgeanddragoninnburpham .com

Dark Star Hop Head, Arundel Pickled Mouse and XB

Standing close to the green in a peaceful hamlet, the George and Dragon boasts delightful views out over the rolling countryside. Such a good old English name is perfectly fitting for a pub that's been trading since 1736 and the associations don't end there. Cooking features British classics – with pub favourites and daily specials on the blackboard, and a concise à la carte featuring the likes of rib-eye steak, rump of lamb and game from the local estate. The laid-back, classically styled interior is divided in two: there's a formal linen-laid dining room and a rustic bar with scrubbed tables and a large brick fireplace. Exposed beams, twinkling church candles and local artwork feature throughout, and theme nights take place all year-round.

Closing times
Open daily

Prices
Meals: a la carte £ 21/32

Typical Dishes
Scallops & celeriac purée
Rump of lamb & creamed cabbage
Chocolate torte, praline cream

 *3 mi northeast of Arundel by A 27. Parking.*

94 **The Fox Goes Free**

Charlton,
PO18 0HU
Tel.: (01243)811461 – Fax: (01243)811712
e-mail: enquiries@thefoxgoesfree.com
Website: www.thefoxgoesfree.com

   AE

Fox Goes Free (special brew), Harveys Sussex Best, Ballards Best

Set in beautiful South Downs countryside, close to Goodwood, this charming 17C flint pub was once the haunt of William III and his Royal Hunting Party. It boasts a pleasant garden with lovely outlook and retains most of its original features, including exposed stone walls, low beamed ceilings, brick floors, inglenook fires and even an old bread oven. There are three dining areas, two with waiter service and one where you order at the bar; behind which you'll find a good selection of hand-pulled ales. Dishes range from simple pub classics on the bar menu to an à la carte of local pork chop, braised venison shank or steak and kidney pie for two. It's deservedly popular, so definitely worth booking ahead. Bedrooms are too modest to recommend.

Closing times
Closed 25 December

Prices
Meals: a la carte £ 20/28

Typical Dishes
Chicken liver parfait
Braised lamb shank
Homemade chocolate brownie

6.45 mi north of Chichester by A 286. Parking.

95 **Fish House**

Chilgrove,
PO18 9HX
Tel.: (01243)519444 – Fax: (01243)519499
e-mail: bookings@thefishhouse.co.uk
Website: www.thefishhouse.co.uk

VISA

Harvey's, Black Sheep and Timothy Taylor Landlord

The Fish House is a stylish, rurally set inn, popular with foodies. With limestone flooring, low beams and a 300 year old fireplace, it retains a characterful sense of history, while contemporary touches like the oyster bar and fish tanks bring it firmly into the 21C. The bar's the most atmospheric place to sit, but if you want a touch more formality, then head for the high-ceilinged dining room. The kitchen focuses on seafood dishes and these range from classics such as potted shrimps or fish and chips to those with a more international flavour such as wok-fried whole bream, with chilli, garlic, spring onions, soy and ginger. Individually styled bedrooms come with every conceivable facility, including espresso machines and iPod docks.

Closing times
Open daily

Prices
Meals: £ 20 (lunch)
and a la carte £ 30/60

15 rooms: £ 90/160

Typical Dishes
Salcombe cock crab
The fruits de mer
Rhubarb panna cotta

6.5 mi north of Chichester by A 286 on B 2141. Parking.

96 The Royal Oak Inn

Pook Ln,
East Lavant, PO18 0AX
Tel.: (01243)527434
e-mail: info@royaloakeastlavant.co.uk
Website: www.royaloakeastlavant.co.uk

 **Sharp's Doom Bar, Dark Star's Hophead, Goodwood Best**

Set in the heart of the village, among some stunning properties, this 18C inn boasts a small outside seating area with immaculately kept planters and a welcoming interior filled with exposed stone, brick and wood. There's a really relaxing feel to the place but you'll have to make like the locals and arrive early if you want to bag a sofa or spot by the fire. Although combinations may be classical, cooking is fairly refined. There are always some interesting vegetarian options, steaks play an important role and there's a good selection of cheese. Produce is delivered from Smithfield, Billingsgate and Covent Garden, and you'll find a fine selection of wines by the glass. Spacious bedrooms are very comfy and well-equipped; breakfast is a treat.

Closing times
Open daily

Prices
Meals: a la carte £ 31/60
10 rooms: £ 60/210

Typical Dishes
Scottish scallops, bacon cream
Pavé of beef with watercress pesto
Cheesecake with Kirsch infused cherry compote

 *Off A 286 after the hump-back bridge. Parking.*

Fernhurst

97 **Duke of Cumberland**

Fernhurst,
GU27 3HQ
Tel.: (01428)652280
e-mail: info@thedukeofcumberland.com
Website: www.dukeofcumberland.com

VISA MC

Harvey's Sussex, Langhams' Best and Hip-Hop

A hidden gem affectionately known as The Duke, this 15C hillside pub nestles in pretty tiered gardens with trickling streams, trout ponds and a splendid view over the South Downs. The pub's interior is as enchanting as the garden, with low beams, flag floors, a huge fireplace, simple wood tables and bench seating; the young serving staff are engaging and the landlord, charming. An appealing menu offers carefully prepared, seasonal dishes; lunch is a two course affair, with choices like pan-seared scallops with rocket or Selsey Crab salad, a selection of organic baguettes and homely puddings like hot chocolate fondant. Dinner offers the full three courses, with dishes that might include potted shrimps, steak and chips or braised lamb shanks.

Closing times
Closed Sunday dinner and Monday

Prices
Meals: a la carte £ 23/35

Typical Dishes
Sussex venison carpaccio
Confit free-range pork belly, thyme jus
Warm chocolate fondant

4.5 mi north of Midhurst off A286 at Fernhurst. Parking.

98 **The Halfway Bridge Inn**

Halfway Bridge,
GU28 9BP
Tel.: (01798)861281
e-mail: enquiries@halfwaybridge.co.uk
Website: www.halfwaybridge.co.uk

Sharp's Doom Bar and Langham's Halfway to Heaven

Set right on the edge of Cowdray Park – famous for its polo – this charming pub has been here so long that the road in front of it has been re-routed, giving the inn a rather back-to-front appearance. Once inside, you'll find several cosy, fire-lit rooms, their walls filled with local maps and country prints. Dishes tend towards the traditional and might include pan-seared calves liver or slow-cooked belly of pork. There's a fine selection of lunchtime baguettes as well as tasty nursery puddings like apple and rhubarb crumble or sticky toffee pudding. Bedrooms are in converted stables a two minute walk away. Like the pub itself, they blend rustic charm with modern facilities – and in the morning, a deliciously fresh cooked breakfast awaits.

Closing times
Closed 25 December

Prices
Meals: a la carte £ 22/37

6 rooms: £ 75/140

Typical Dishes

Pigeon breast, black pepper cream

Steak, ale & Stilton pie

Banana bread & butter pudding

Halfway between Midhurst and Petworth on A 272. Parking.

99 **The Ginger Fox**

Albourne,
Henfield, BN6 9EA
Tel.: (01273)857888
e-mail: info@gingermanrestaurants.com
Website: www.gingermanrestaurants.com

 **Harvey's of Lewes and one guest ale**

The fox in hungry pursuit of a pheasant on the thatched roof of this 17C inn gives a clue as to its charm and character. Inside you'll find beams, open fires and parquet flooring; there's a spacious dining room, a rustic open bar and – the best place to sit – 'The Den.' Cooking is skilful, with a real country flavour; the distinct menu offering unfussy dishes such as duck egg and mushrooms on toast, jellied knuckle of pork, stuffed saddle of rabbit or a whole grilled lemon sole. There's a vegetarian tasting plate, a special children's menu with smaller portions, and puddings with names you will recognise, but which come with a twist. Packed at weekends, the pub is particularly popular with families, who enjoy its spacious garden and slides.

Closing times
Closed 25 December

Prices
Meals: a la carte £ 20/30

Typical Dishes
Wild boar terrine
Ham & mushroom pie
Coconut & lime leaf bavarois

 *8 mi north of Shoreham by A283 and A2037. Parking.*

100 The Lickfold Inn

Lickfold,
GU28 9EY
Tel.: (01798)861285
e-mail: lickfold@evanspubs.co.uk
Website: www.evanspubs.co.uk

Langham's Best BItter and Hog's Back TEA

This rurally set, 16C inn boasts a charming, rustic feel typified by wooden beams, cosy seating and huge open fires. Its appealing menu offers well-priced pub dishes like haddock and chips, classic beef Bourguignon or rack of local lamb. Antipasti boards are popular, as are the starter boards offering tempting morsels like mini scotch eggs, devils on horseback, and baked mini camembert. Desserts might mean a panna cotta or a crumble and great care is taken with the cheese board selection. Real ales come from the next village and there are many wines available by the glass. A loyal local following enjoy the spacious gardens, the suntrap courtyard and the many special events held here – including 'Grumpy Hour' which actually lasts for two.

Closing times
Open daily

Prices
Meals: a la carte £ 25/34

Typical Dishes
Ham hock terrine
Sussex rib-eye steak
Sticky toffee pudding

6 mi northwest of Petworth by A 272. Parking.

Mid Lavant

101 The Earl of March

Mid Lavant,
PO18 0BQ
Tel.: (01243)533993
e-mail: info@theearlofmarch.com
Website: www.theearlofmarch.com

   AE

Fuller's London Pride, Hopback Summer Lightning, Harveys Sussex Bitter and Ringood Best

This 18C inn offers the perfect blend of country character and contemporary styling, boasting a wood burning stove and cosy sofas in the bar, a smart restaurant, and a relaxed feel throughout. Its terrace affords amazing views of the South Downs, with the main stand at Goodwood racecourse in the distance, and its private dining room changes use seasonally; home to shooting parties in winter and serving champagne and seafood in summer. The owner spent time as executive head chef at The Ritz, so expect good quality, seasonal produce; dishes are British and mainly classical in style, and might include vegetable soup, lamb chops, pan-fried fillet of Sussex beef or Gressingham duck breast. Desserts are old favourites like sticky toffee pudding.

Closing times
Closed Sunday dinner

Prices
Meals: £ 22 (early dinner) and a la carte £ 25/35

Typical Dishes
Pan-fried scallops
Loin of venison with roast roots
Vanilla panna cotta & mulled plums

 *3 mi north of Chichester by A 286.*

102 Badgers

Coultershaw Bridge, Petworth, GU28 0JF
Tel.: (01798)342651
e-mail: reception@badgers.co.uk
Website: www.badgers.cc

  MC

 **Youngs, TEA and Fuller's London Pride**

This white-painted pub close to the River Rother has a satisfyingly homely feel. Log fires blaze in the grate, fresh flowers are dotted about the place and in the evening, candles flicker. A beautiful oak-panelled bar boasts carvings from its former 'Badger and Honeypot' days, while black and white photos depict its original railway inn-carnation. You'll also find an attentive, cheery team and a truly intimate single table alcove. Menus are rather eclectic; offering robust, flavoursome cooking with international influences. You could find anything from lamb's liver or bubble and squeak to prawns with Cajun spices or Spanish fish casserole – while in summer, lobsters picked from the tank are a favourite. Bedrooms aren't currently recommendable.

Closing times
Closed Sunday dinner from October to April

Prices
Meals: £ 15 (lunch)
and a la carte £ 20/39

Typical Dishes
Selection of fish tapas
Half shoulder of lamb
Chocolate cheesecake

 *2 mi south of Petworth by A 285 at Coultershaw Bridge. Parking.*

103 The Chequers Inn

Rowhook,
RH12 3PY
Tel.: (01403)790480
e-mail: thechequersrowhook@gmail.com

 **Harvey's Best, Fuller's London Pride and Hepworth of Horsham**

As you step inside you're instantly surrounded by the oaky aroma of an open fire and the murmur of the day's tales being recounted by groups of cheery locals. The origins of this inn can be traced back to the 15C, which comes as no surprise when you look around the charming stone-floored bar, but there's also a slightly unusual corrugated dining room extension (formerly the village hall), a large paved terrace and spacious garden. The experienced chef-owner loves the hands-on approach, so he's often out in the woods foraging for wild mushrooms and tracking down game, or out in the garden gathering the latest yield; maybe artichoke, pears or greengages. Classically based menus display a good understanding of how best to prepare ingredients.

Closing times
Closed 25 December and Sunday dinner

Prices
Meals: a la carte £ 25/35

Typical Dishes
Pigeon & foie gras pasty
Sea bream with fennel purée
Tonka bean panna cotta

 *3 mi west of Horsham by A 281. Parking.*

104 **Crab & Lobster**

Mill Ln,
Sidlesham, PO20 7NB
Tel.: (01243)641233
e-mail: enquiries@crab-lobster.co.uk
Website: www.crab-lobster.co.uk

Inspectors' favourites

    AE

 **Harvey's Sussex Best Bitter and Sharp's Doom Bar**

This historic inn, with its pretty gardens, is superbly located within the striking landscape of Pangham Harbour Nature Reserve; a marshy haven for wildlife, particularly birds. The pub has a light, relaxed feel, with an open main dining room, a snug seating area and a log fire. Cooking places its emphasis on seafood, with starters like sautéed calamari or clam and red mullet chowder and main courses such as fresh cod and chips with homemade tartare sauce or kedgeree with poached egg. Local crab sandwiches go down a storm at lunch and desserts might include deep fried ice cream with butterscotch or a fine selection of English cheeses. Very comfortable bedrooms have a modern, minimalist style; one has its own garden and an open fired stove.

Closing times
Open daily
booking advisable

Prices
Meals: a la carte £ 26/46
4 rooms: £ 80

Typical Dishes
Crab & crayfish parcel
Gloucestershire Old Spot pork belly
Deep-fried vanilla ice cream & butterscotch sauce

6 mi south of Chichester by B 2145, then turn right into Rookery Lane. Parking.

105 The Keepers Arms

Trotton,
GU31 5ER
Tel.: (01730)813724
e-mail: info@keepersarms.co.uk
Website: www.keepersarms.co.uk

 **Dark Star Hophead, Ballard's Best Bitter and Otter Ale**

The Keeper's Arms is a cheery, welcoming, neighbourhood inn, where the customer is king. Set back from the road and perched halfway up a hill, it affords pleasant countryside views if you're dining alfresco; inside, it's quite compact, with low ceilings, an open fire, a Chesterfield sofa and a host of quirky tables. Cooking is good value and honest, with dishes changing regularly; try a nice juicy bowl of olives to kick you off, then perhaps a warm goat's cheese tart, some char-grilled mackerel or duck cooked two ways. Pudding might mean a simple lemon parfait with fresh raspberries or a good old chocolate brownie – and the wine list changes as often as the food; thus ensuring that you can always find a glass to perfectly complement your meal.

Closing times
Closed 25-26 December
Prices
Meals: a la carte £ 23/30

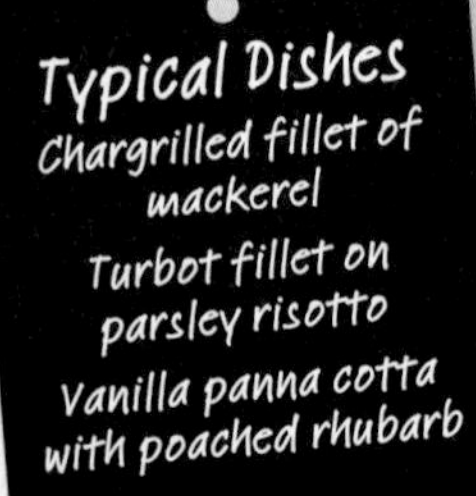

 *4 mi west of Midhurst by A 272. Parking.*

106 **The Cat Inn**

Queen's Sq,
West Hoathly, RH19 4PP
Tel.: (01342)810369
e-mail: thecatinn@googlemail.com
Website: www.catinn.co.uk

 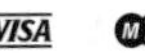

Harvey's Sussex Best, Harvey's Sussex Old and Dark Star's Hop Head

This charming inn is located in the centre of a pleasant hamlet, opposite a lovely 11C church and just two minutes walk from The Priest House museum. The pub itself dates back to the 17C and boasts a part-tiled exterior and a myriad of different rooms filled with pewter tankards and hop bines. These include a semi-panelled bar with huge log fire, a room with delightful glass floor panel looking down into an old well, two intimate, rustic areas and two larger, more formally laid dining rooms. There's also a few tables out the front and a large terrace to the rear. The hands-on owners have plenty of experience and are supported by a bubbly team. Menus feature satisfying country-style classics. Bedrooms are modern and extremely comfortable.

Closing times
Closed Sunday dinner

Prices
Meals: a la carte £ 20/31
4 rooms: £ 80/140

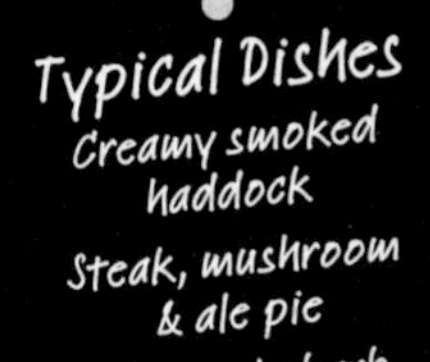

4 mi southwest of East Grinstead by B2110 and B2028. Parking.

Six hundred miles of relentlessly breathtaking coastline pound the majestic South West, assuring it of a dramatic backdrop whatever the season. Its prestige is bolstered by four UNESCO World Heritage sites: one of them is Dorset's spectacular Jurassic Coast, which includes the 180 billion pebbles of Chesil Beach. Further north, Dartmoor and Exmoor embody the region's untamed beauty. The built environment may be of a more recent time line, but examples are still impressive, ranging from thirteenth century Lacock, home of many a filmed costume drama, to Elizabethan Longleat with its Capability Brown designed parkland, and late Victorian Lanhydrock, "the great house of Cornwall". The same county boasts its very own "theatre under the stars", The Minack, where the drama of nature collides with the drama of the written word. Days out in this unforgettable region come complete with pasties and a pint of local ale, or freshly caught lobster, scallops or mussels enjoyed along the quay.

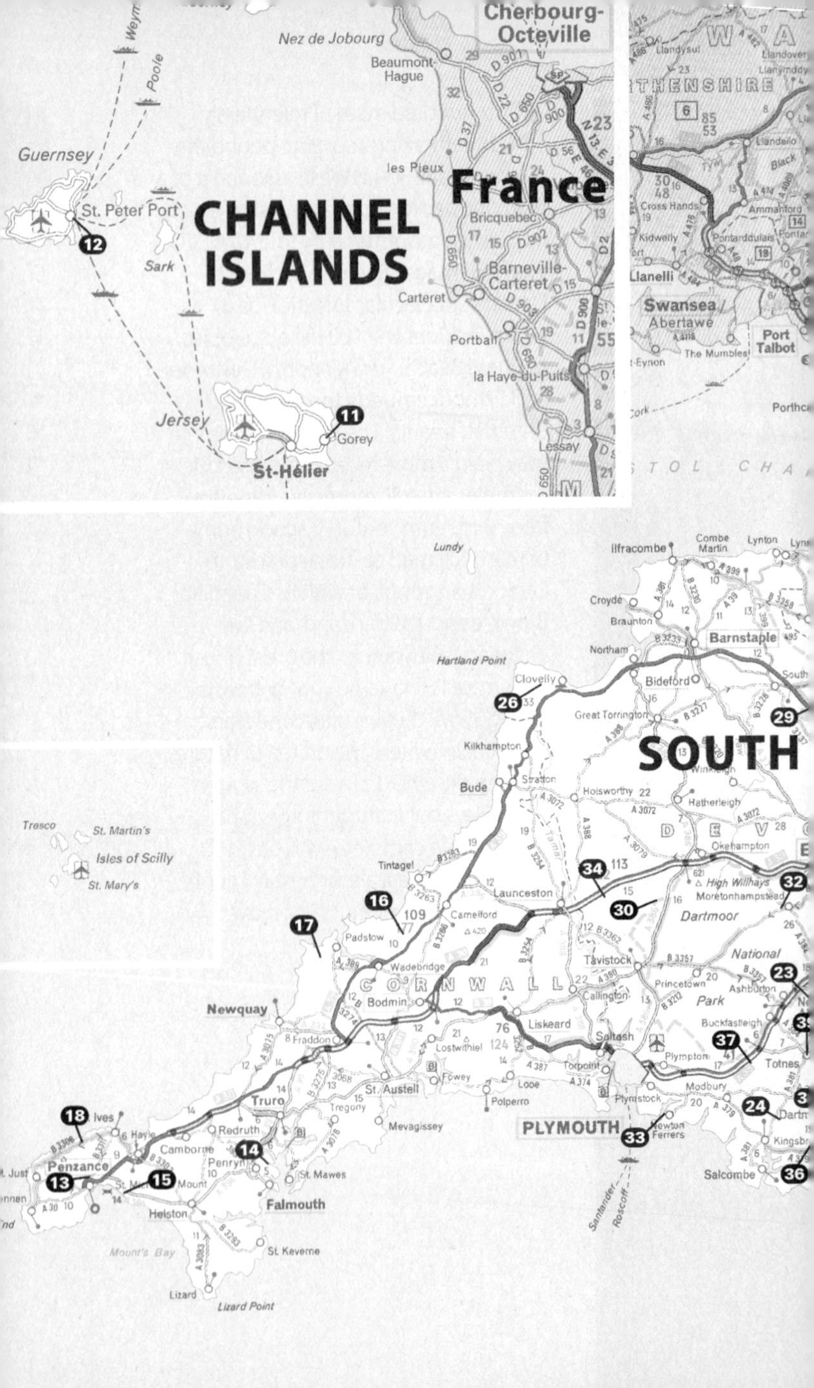

CHANNEL ISLANDS
France
Cherbourg-Octeville
Nez de Jobourg
Beaumont-Hague
les Pieux
Bricquebec
Barneville-Carteret
Carteret
Portbail
la Haye-du-Puits
Lessay
Guernsey
St. Peter Port
Sark
Jersey
Gorey
St-Hélier
Weymouth
Poole
12
11
Llandysul
Llandovery
Llandeilo
Cross Hands
Ammanford
Kidwelly
Pontarddulais
Llanelli
Swansea
Abertawe
The Mumbles
Port Talbot
Cork
Lundy
Ilfracombe
Combe Martin
Lynton
Croyde
Braunton
Barnstaple
Northam
Hartland Point
Clovelly
Bideford
Great Torrington
SOUTH
Kilkhampton
Stratton
Bude
Holsworthy
Hatherleigh
Okehampton
High Willhays
Moretonhampstead
Dartmoor
National
Park
Tresco
St. Martin's
Isles of Scilly
St. Mary's
Tintagel
Camelford
Launceston
Padstow
Wadebridge
CORNWALL
DEVON
Bodmin
Tavistock
Princetown
Ashburton
Callington
Newquay
Fraddon
Lostwithiel
Liskeard
Saltash
Buckfastleigh
Plympton
Totnes
St. Austell
Torpoint
Truro
Tregony
Fowey
Looe
Polperro
Plymstock
Modbury
Mevagissey
Ives
Hayle
Redruth
Camborne
PLYMOUTH
Newton Ferrers
Penzance
Penryn
St. Mawes
Mount
Falmouth
Helston
Salcombe
Kingsbridge
Mount's Bay
St. Keverne
Lizard
Lizard Point
Santander
Roscoff
26
29
34
30
32
16
17
23
37
24
18
14
13
15
33
36

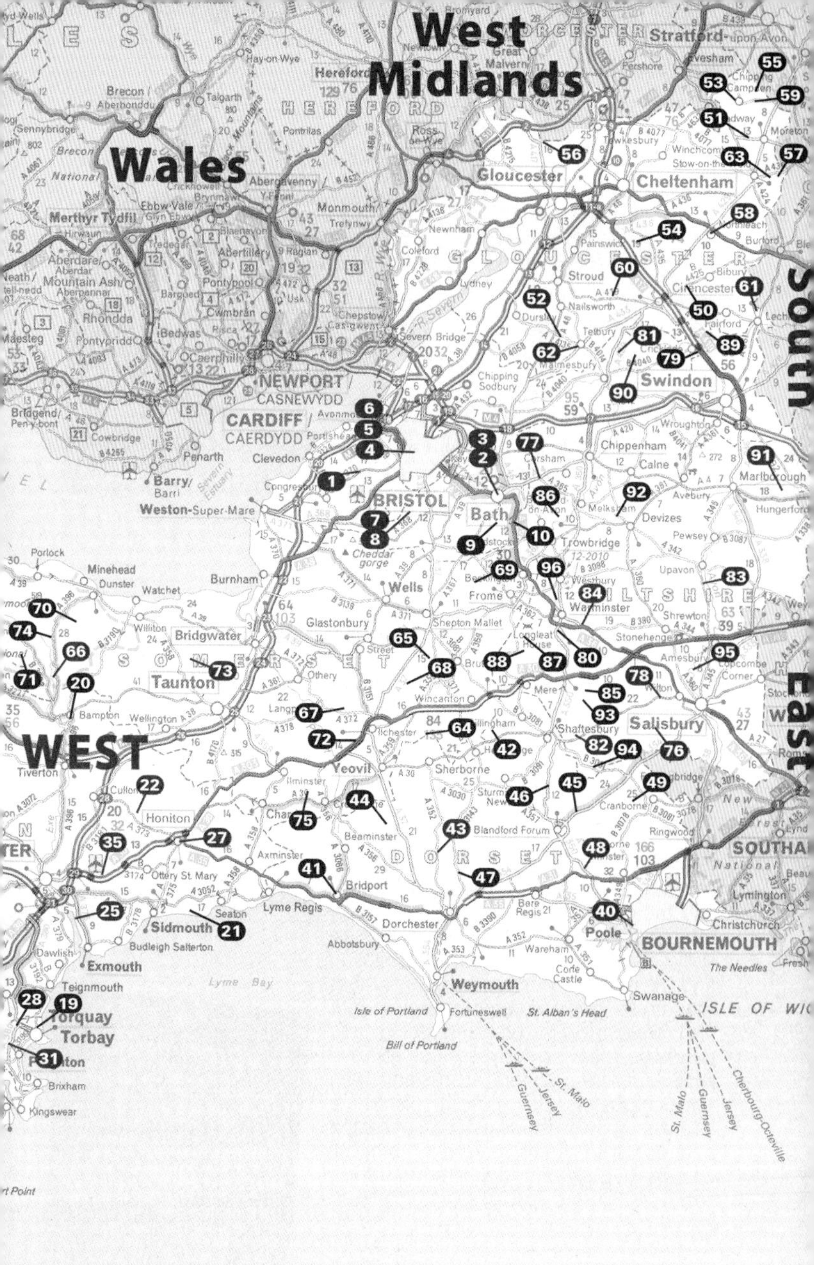
West Midlands
Wales
WEST
South East
Hereford
Gloucester
Cheltenham
Stratford-upon-Avon
Evesham
Tewkesbury
Brecon
Abergavenny
Monmouth
Merthyr Tydfil
NEWPORT / CASNEWYDD
CARDIFF / CAERDYDD
Barry/ Barri
Weston-Super-Mare
Clevedon
Portishead
Avonmouth
BRISTOL
Bath
Chepstow
Severn Bridge
Stroud
Nailsworth
Cirencester
Tetbury
Malmesbury
Swindon
Chippenham
Calne
Marlborough
Devizes
Melksham
Trowbridge
Westbury
Warminster
Frome
Wells
Glastonbury
Shepton Mallet
Bridgwater
Taunton
Minehead
Dunster
Watchet
Burnham
Cheddar gorge
Wincanton
Yeovil
Sherborne
Shaftesbury
Salisbury
Amesbury
Stonehenge
Blandford Forum
Dorchester
Weymouth
Bridport
Lyme Regis
Honiton
Sidmouth
Exmouth
Teignmouth
Torquay
Torbay
Paignton
Brixham
Kingswear
Poole
BOURNEMOUTH
Christchurch
Lymington
Ringwood
Swanage
Wareham
Isle of Portland
Bill of Portland
St. Alban's Head
Lyme Bay
ISLE OF WIGHT
The Needles
St. Malo
Guernsey
Jersey
Cherbourg-Octeville

Backwell

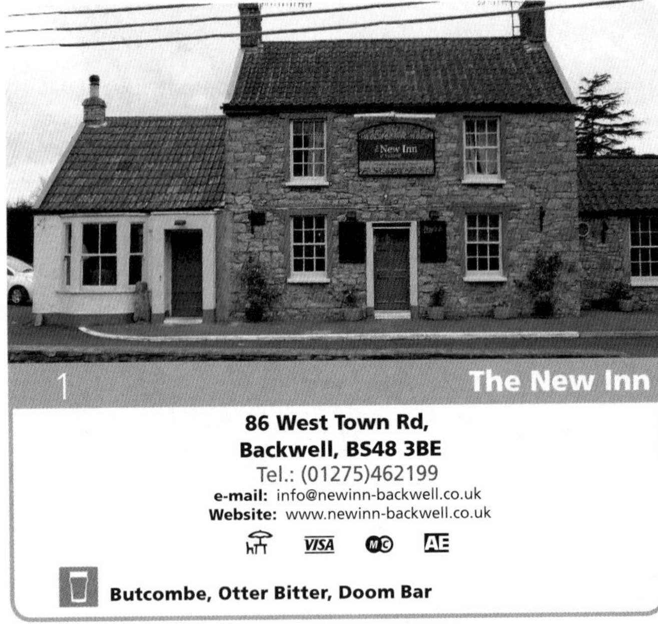

1 **The New Inn**

86 West Town Rd,
Backwell, BS48 3BE
Tel.: (01275)462199
e-mail: info@newinn-backwell.co.uk
Website: www.newinn-backwell.co.uk

VISA MC AE

Butcombe, Otter Bitter, Doom Bar

A pretty 18C stone pub with a warm farmhouse feel, The New Inn boasts a lovely open-fired bar with comfy seating and a slightly more formal dining area with polished pine tables and an almost 'tea room' atmosphere. The pleasant staff are as welcoming as the surroundings and the confident cooking is in a stylishly modern vein. Descriptions on the twice daily changing menu sound appealing and the precisely prepared, elegant dishes that arrive don't disappoint: you might find scallops with pease pudding and pancetta, followed by roast guinea fowl with cauliflower cheese cream and ham hock croquettes. Even the side dishes are interesting, with the likes of salt roasted beetroot with crème fraîche or broccoli with toasted almonds and lemon butter.

Closing times
Open daily
Prices
Meals: £ 20/28
and a la carte £ 20/28

6 mi southwest of Bristol by A370. Parking.

2 The Marlborough Tavern

35 Marlborough Buildings,
Bath, BA1 2LY
Tel.: (01225)423731
e-mail: info@marlborough-tavern.com
Website: www.marlborough-tavern.com

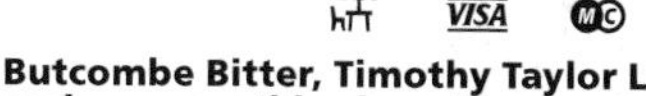

Butcombe Bitter, Timothy Taylor Landlord, Otter Bitter and one monthly changing guest ale

If you're a Londoner looking for a home away from home, then this is probably the place for you. Set next to the Royal Victoria Park, this spacious, modern pub boasts funky flock wallpaper, scrubbed wooden floors and displays local artwork on its walls. The chef is very passionate about his craft and carefully sources his ingredients from nearby farms and small independent producers. He favours organic growing methods and traditional rearing techniques, and strives to find produce that originates from sustainable stocks. Menus have a classical base and dishes are unfussy, straightforward and hearty – the pork belly in particular is a firm favourite. Daily specials are chalked on the blackboard and change as new produce arrives at the door.

Closing times
Closed 25 December
booking advisable

Prices
Meals: a la carte £ 25/35

Typical Dishes
Battered Cornish squid
Slow-roast pork belly
Caramelised apple tart & ice cream

Northwest of city centre on east side of Royal Victoria Park. Parking bays opposite; parking also in the park (50m).

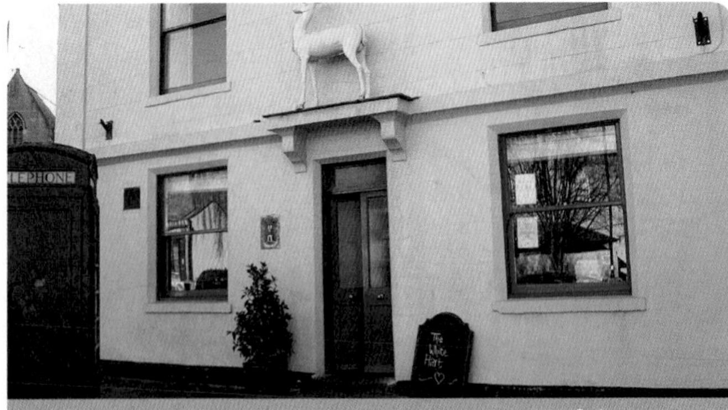

3 **White Hart**

Widcombe Hill,
Bath, BA2 6AA
Tel.: (01225)338053
e-mail: enquiries@whitehartbath.co.uk
Website: www.whitehartbath.co.uk

Butcombe, Sharp's Doom Bar and Pitchfork

Situated close to the railway, just over the river, The White Hart has a real neighbourhood feel. It has attracted a loyal local following, so get here early or book ahead as it fills up quickly. Food-wise, the mantra here is 'keep it simple', with the sourcing of ingredients afforded paramount importance. Portions are large and cooking, hearty, with dishes like baked fillet of pork wrapped in bacon, breast of chicken with lentils or whole baked sea bass with lime, ginger and chilli butter. Most people have a main dish and share a side and a dessert, but the smaller tapas plates are also very popular. The pub has a rustic feel, with scrubbed wooden floors and worn wooden tables and the rear terrace is a great spot in warmer weather.

Closing times
Closed Sunday dinner and bank holidays
booking essential at dinner

Prices
Meals: a la carte £ 22/28

Typical Dishes
Tasting board
Rump of lamb with fondant potato
Raspberry & vanilla custard tart with lemon curd ice cream

Southeast of city centre off A 3062. On-street parking.

4 The Albion Public House and Dining Rooms

Boyces Ave,
Clifton Village, Bristol, BS8 4AA
Tel.: (0117)9733522 – Fax: (0117)9739768
e-mail: info@thealbionclifton.co.uk
Website: www.thealbionclifton.co.uk

Otter Bright, Butcombe Bitter, St Austell Tribute, Sharp's Doom Bar

Tucked away down a cobbled street in a fashionable neighbourhood quarter, the trendy 17C Albion is exactly as a pub should be – fun, friendly and casual – with an equal split of drinkers and those out for a relaxed meal. The benches outside on the terrace make a pleasant spot to take in the comings and goings of the area, as well as providing the setting for the regular Sunday BBQ. Cooking is highly seasonal and the unfussy British menu changes twice a day as new produce arrives. Everything is homemade, from the rustic bread and nibbles such as goose ham and pickled damsons, to the tasty main courses such as cod with linguine or rib of Aberdeen Angus with oxtail for two. Booking is imperative, as drinkers multiply throughout the evening.

Closing times
Closed 25 December, 1 January, Sunday dinner and Monday
booking essential

Prices
Meals: £ 30 (dinner) and a la carte £ 24/39

In Clifton Village. Parking in Victoria Square or surrounding roads.

5 The Kensington Arms

35-37 Stanley Rd,
Bristol, B56 6NP

Tel.: (0117)9446444 – Fax: (0117)9248095
e-mail: info@thekensingtonarms.co.uk
Website: www.thekensingtonarms.co.uk

VISA MC AE

Morland Original Bitter, Ruddles County and Greene King IPA

The crest of the Royal Borough of Kensington and Chelsea swings on the board outside, proclaiming the motto 'quam bonum in unum habitare': what a good thing it is to dwell together in unity – and with this pub at the heart of the neighbourhood, what a good thing indeed. With its charming Victorian style, large wood-floored bar and impressive high-ceilinged dining room, you could be mistaken for thinking someone had simply picked up a London pub and dropped it down here. Menus change bi-monthly and have a strong British base, featuring maybe lamb kidneys on toast or venison suet pudding. Seasons play an important role, so you'll find hearty, nourishing dishes and proper homemade puddings in the colder months. Service is particularly warm.

Closing times
Closed 25 December and Sunday dinner

Prices
Meals: a la carte £ 20/30

In city centre.

6

Robin Hood's Retreat

197 Gloucester Rd,
Bristol, BS7 8BG
Tel.: (0117)9248639
e-mail: info@robinhoodsretreat.gmail.com
Website: www.robinhoodsretreat.co.uk

    AE

Sharp's Doom Bar, Skinner's Betty Stogs, Timothy Taylor Landlord

It's a fair trek from Sherwood Forest, so despite this pub's name, you're unlikely to catch a glimpse of the famous outlaw; although, with eight cask ales on constant rotation, if you stick around until last orders, the chances are you might spot some merry men. Drinkers are certainly welcome, but it's the food that's the focus here; British classics are reinterpreted with a nod to French techniques, the result being hearty, flavourful dishes. The large blackboard menus change daily, but might include dishes like ox cheeks with mash or fried halibut with homemade tartare sauce. This red-brick Victorian pub is situated in a busy part of the city, but a relaxed atmosphere reigns in its characterful bar and its spacious, rustic dining room.

Closing times
Closed 25 December
booking advisable at dinner

Prices
Meals: £ 20 (Sunday-Thursday lunch and early dinner) and a la carte £ 25/32

Typical Dishes
Crayfish with red cabbage & apple salad
West Country rib-eye steak & chips
Chocolate & honeycomb tart

In city centre. On-street parking or car park opposite.

Chew Magna

7 **Bear & Swan**

13 South Par,
Chew Magna, BS40 8SL
Tel.: (01275)331100 – Fax: (01275)331204
e-mail: bearandswan@fullers.co.uk
Website: www.bearandswan.co.uk

VISA MC AE

Fuller's London Pride, Butcombe Brewery, Bengal Lancer, HSB

This well-established village pub boasts a loyal local following and rustic charm aplenty. The delightful bar with its solid stone floor and inglenook fireplaces is the place to be for a good old pub classic; maybe a Somerset cheese ploughman's or sausages with bubble and squeak. For something more formal, head to the stone-walled dining room, where you'll find thick church candles on well-spaced, linen-laid tables. The chef is French, so it's no surprise to find some influences from his homeland among the dishes. Everything is fresh and homemade and there's always a good range to choose from; maybe curried parsnip and apple soup, followed by confit of duck or venison and mushroom pie – plus some interesting fish dishes on seafood Wednesdays.

Closing times
Closed Sunday dinner

Prices
Meals: a la carte £ 19/31

Typical Dishes
Chicken liver parfait
Seared scallops & polenta with roasted figs
Apricot and ginger crumble

8.25 mi south of Bristol via A 37 on B 3130. Parking.

8 Pony & Trap

Knowle Hill,
Newtown, Chew Magna, BS40 8TQ
Tel.: (01275)332627 – Fax: (01179)637730
e-mail: josh@theponyandtrap.co.uk
Website: www.theponyandtrap.co.uk

VISA

Butcombe, Courage Best ,Otter

With this whitewashed pub on their doorstep, the inhabitants of this tiny hamlet have plenty to smile about. The rear garden with its rolling countryside views is the place to be but the cosy stone-walled bar and oversized dining room windows make it just as welcoming whatever the weather. To say the food is local and seasonal is an understatement: the menu is written twice a day; meats are locally sourced and hung; fish comes from the nearby Chew Valley smokehouse; and eggs are collected from their own chickens out the back. The passionate chef keeps his cooking rooted firmly in the classical British vein, flavours are clean and clear, and the lamb 2 ways is establishing itself as a firm favourite. Service can sometimes be a little subdued.

Closing times
Closed Sunday dinner in winter and Monday
booking essential

Prices
Meals: a la carte £ 20/26

Typical Dishes
Cornish scallops & hodgepodge
Pork with celeriac purée
Rhubarb & ginger jelly

1.5 mi south of the village; follow signs for Bishop Stuttard. Parking.

9 **The Wheatsheaf**

Combe Hay,
BA2 7EG
Tel.: (01225)833504
e-mail: info@wheatsheafcombehay.com
Website: www.wheatsheafcombehay.com

VISA

Butcombe Ale

The Wheatsheaf began life as a farmhouse in 1576. Centuries and several seamless additions later, it boasts chic, über-modern styling typified by delightful pink flocked wallpaper and vivid artwork, and a relaxed atmosphere helped on its way by open fires, comfy low sofas and an abundance of books and magazines – not forgetting Milo and Brie, the pub's friendly resident spaniels. The flavourful, seasonal food is presented in a contemporary style – often on slate plates – and dishes might include homemade fish pie, game broth or slow-roasted belly pork with black pudding; with desserts such as chocolate fondant or almond and prune cake. Bedrooms follow the pub's lead, with a spacious, contemporary feel and an emphasis firmly on quality.

Closing times
Closed Sunday dinner and Monday except bank holidays when open for lunch

Prices
Meals: £ 26 (lunch Sunday) and a la carte £ 15/35

3 rooms: £ 140

4 mi south of Bath by A 367 and minor road south. Parking.

10 Wheelwrights Arms

Church Ln,
Monkton Combe, BA2 7HB
Tel.: (01225)722287 – Fax: (01225)722259
e-mail: bookings@wheelwrightsarms.co.uk
Website: www.wheelwrightsarms.co.uk

 **Butcombe Bitter and Sharp's Doom Bar**

If you're after a spot of peace and quiet, make a beeline for the sleepy village of Monkton Combe, where you can relax to the sound of birdsong in this charming 18C stone inn. A former carpenter's workshop, it's made up of two main buildings, both displaying attractive parquet floors, exposed stone walls and warming open fires. Menus offer a wide range of classical dishes from sandwiches and sharing plates to good value set lunches and tasty three course dinners. You might find blue cheese, almond and spinach tart, followed by sea bass with ratatouille or rabbit and pork braised in cider. Specials consist mainly of fish and, to finish, the treacle tart is always a good bet. Individually designed bedrooms are modern with rustic overtones.

Closing times
Open daily

Prices
Meals: £ 14 (weekday lunch) and a la carte £ 20/30

7 rooms: £ 85/145

Typical Dishes
Chicken liver parfait
Roast duck breast & mushroom ragout
Sticky toffee pudding & vanilla ice cream

 *2 mi southeast of Bath city centre by A 3062. Parking.*

11 The Bass and Lobster

Gorey Coast Rd,
Gorey, JE3 6EU
Tel.: (01534)859590 – Fax: (01534)858719
e-mail: mail@bassandlobster.com
Website: www.bassandlobster.com

  AE

 **No real ales offered**

A bright, modern pub set close to the sandy beach, with smartly laid wooden tables, a mock wooden floor, some banquette seating and a small decked terrace. Having lived and worked on the island for many years, the experienced owner has built up a network of local suppliers and uses these whenever possible. Fresh seafood and shellfish dominate the seasonal menu and dishes are simply cooked and immensely flavourful: try the roast fillet of local sea bass, the local Chancre crab linguini with prawns or some fantastic steely oysters. Wonderfully earthy Jersey Royals make a great side dish and the prices also bring a smile to one's face, with the lunch menu representing particularly good value. Smooth service comes from a friendly European team.

Closing times
Closed Monday-Tuesday in winter, Monday lunch and Sunday in summer

Prices
Meals: £ 13/17
and a la carte £ 24/37

 *On the coast road, just before the village. Parking by the sea wall.*

12 **The Swan Inn**

St Julian's Ave,
St Peter Port, GY1 1WA
Tel.: (01481)728969 – Fax: (01481)728969

Patois Guernsey Ale

From façade to food, this really is a 'proper' pub. The smart bottle-green Victorian exterior makes it easy to spot and its traditional styling is warm and welcoming; especially in winter when the cosy log burners are ablaze. It's owned by a gregarious French fellow – a former manager – and his enthusiasm can be felt right at the heart of the place. If you're after a generous serving of something satisfying try the homemade burgers, legendary club sandwich or popular fish pie. For a more sedate dining experience climb the stairs to a room akin to those aboard the Titanic. Here you'll find more ambitious dishes such as pork belly, lamb cutlets or seared fillet of sea bass – alongside some good value set menus that are offered early in the week.

Closing times
Closed 25 December and Sunday

Prices
Meals: a la carte £ 15/22

Typical Dishes
Home-cured salmon
Fish pie
Guernsey cheeses

In the centre of town. Parking on North Beach Pier (50yds).

13 **Coldstreamer**

Gulval,
TR18 3BB
Tel.: (01736)362072 – Fax: (01736)322072
e-mail: info@coldstreamer-penzance.co.uk
Website: www.coldstreamer-penzance.co.uk

VISA

Greene King Old Speckled Hen, Helford River and Legend

This handsome pub is set in the heart of Gulval and, like much of the village, was built by the Bolitho family. Following the death in service of Harry Bolitho it was given to the Coldstream Association, before being taken over by two local brothers. It's a spacious place, boasting a bright dining room and a large bar adorned with Coldstream Guards memorabilia. The concise, seasonal menu features fish from Newlyn, meat from Penzance and products from the village's now retired Smoker, and cooking is clean, generous and modern; lunch might offer salt cod fritters and dinner, more elaborate dishes like lamb rump with caramelised shallots. May sees an asparagus menu and the regular wine dinners prove popular. Bedrooms are fresh and well-appointed.

Closing times
Open daily

Prices
Meals: a la carte £ 18/26

3 rooms: £ 65/80

Typical Dishes
Pigeon breast salad
Megrim sole with beurre blanc
Rhubarb & apple parfait

1.2 mi northeast of Penzance off A30 in centre of village. Plenty of parking in the square.

14 **Pandora Inn**

Restronguet Creek,
Mylor Bridge, TR11 5ST
Tel.: (01326)372678
e-mail: info@pandorainn.com
Website: www.pandorainn.com

  MC

 **St Austell Tribute, Hicks Special Draught**

In a scenic spot and with its own pontoon, The Pandora Inn is unsurprisingly popular during the summer months, when folks arrive by boat and moor up outside – as well as by car, by bike and on shanks' pony – so the advice is: if you want a seat, you'd be best to arrive early. With its low ceilings and tables arranged around wood burning stoves, it's also a cosy place for a meal come winter. The seasonal menu makes the most of Cornish produce and beer comes from St Austell brewery. No 13C harbourside pub would be complete without a seafaring legend to go with it: The Pandora Inn was apparently thus named by a naval captain who was sent to Cornwall as a punishment after his ship, The Pandora, ran aground on the Great Barrier Reef.

Closing times
Closed 25 December
Prices
Meals: a la carte £ 20/32

Typical Dishes
Belly pork & Prawns
Fillet of halibut & citrus mash
Hot chocolate fondant

4 mi north of Falmouth by A 39, B 3292 and minor road east from Penryn. Parking.

England • South West • Cornwall

Perranuthnoe

15 **Victoria Inn**

Perranuthnoe,
TR20 9NP
Tel.: (01736)710309 – Fax: (01736)719284
e-mail: enquiries@victoriainn-penzance.co.uk
Website: www.victoriainn-penzance.co.uk

 **Sharp's Doom Bar, St Austell Tribute and Skinners Heligan Honey or Betty Stogs**

Simple but characterful, with a cosy, homely feel, this pink-washed inn sits in the heart of the village and appeals to drinkers and diners alike. Its owners are keen for it to remain a proper pub, so you'll see locals here for a beer alongside families who've hot-footed it in from the beach for lunch; sand between their toes. The short menu offers choices ranging from sandwiches and soups to wholesome pub classics like ham, free range eggs and real chips, as well as dishes like honey-roasted Cornish duck breast. A regularly changing blackboard menu offers seafood specials, and the chef-owner – a local boy returned home – is proud to showcase local produce. The rear terrace provides a pleasant suntrap. Simple bedrooms are nautically themed.

Closing times
Closed 1 week January, 25-26 December, 1 January, Sunday dinner and Monday in winter

Prices
Meals: a la carte £ 20/35
2 rooms: £ 45/70

 *3 mi east of Marazion, south of A 394. Parking.*

16 St Kew Inn

St Kew,
PL30 3HB
Tel.: (01208)841259
Website: www.stkewinn.co.uk

VISA

Wreckers, St Austell Brewery - Tinners, HSD, Tribute, Proper Job and two local ales

St Kew Inn was built in the 15C to serve the masons who constructed the magnificent next door church and boasts flag floors, stone walls and wooden beams. It sits in a quintessentially English location and its attractive front garden is as much of a draw as the pub itself, come the warmer weather. A massive electric umbrella means that sudden summer showers are not a problem, and there are heaters too, should it turn nippy. Cooking is fresh and tasty, with a wide range of appealing, good value dishes from which to choose; lunch means choices like Fowey mussels, Welsh rarebit, corned beef hash and a range of sandwiches, while dinner offers similar (minus the sandwiches), plus perhaps some grilled lemon sole or pan-fried lamb's liver.

Closing times
Closed 25 December
Prices
Meals: a la carte £ 20/32

Typical Dishes
House terrine with campagrain
Neck of lamb & pearl barley stew
Bramley apple & raisin crumble

3 mi northeast of Wadebridge by A 39 and minor road north. Parking.

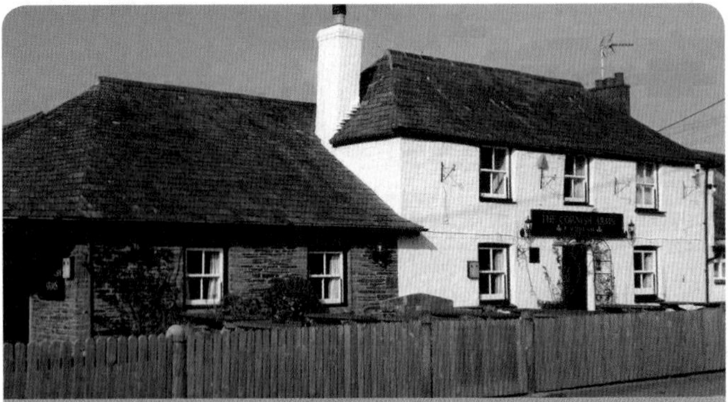

St Merryn

17 The Cornish Arms

Churchtown,
St Merryn, PL28 8ND
Tel.: (01841)520288
Website: www.rickstein.com

St Austell - Tinners, Tribute, Proper Job

When St Austell Brewery leased this pub to Rick Stein, the locals panicked at the thought of their beloved haunt being turned into a gastropub. They needn't have worried though as, despite the sympathetic refurbishment of the dining room and the addition of a smart terrace, it remains a proper pub, with a proper bar whose low beams, slate floors and pictures of regulars give it an undeniable dose of old world charm. The menu offers classic pub dishes such as ploughman's, ham, egg and chips, homemade curry or apple pie, with fish specials chalked up on boards. Cooking is sound and sensibly priced, but they don't take bookings, so arrive early on busy summer evenings. Every other Friday is open mic night, with local musicians to warm things up.

Closing times
Open daily

Prices
Meals: a la carte £ 16/30

West of Padstow on B 3276. Parking.

18 The Gurnard's Head

Treen,
Zennor, TR26 3DE
Tel.: (01736)796928
e-mail: enquiries@gurnardshead.co.uk
Website: www.gurnardshead.co.uk

 **Skinners Betty Stogs, St Austell Tribute, Tomos Watkins BItter**

Set in a remote location, surrounded by nothing but fields and livestock, The Gurnard's Head provides a warm welcome that sets you immediately at your ease. It's dog-friendly, with stone floors and shabby-chic décor, while blazing fires and brightly coloured walls help create a relaxed, cosy feel. The simple menu relies on regional produce, including some locally foraged ingredients. Dishes might include ham hock terrine with piccalilli, deep-fried Gurnard and chips, Provençal fish soup or a modern take on a classic cassoulet. Desserts are in the traditional vein, while the wine list includes a very interesting selection by the glass. Extremely comfy beds feature good quality linen and colourful throws. Breakfast is taken communally.

Closing times
Closed 4 days January and 24-25 December

Prices
Meals: a la carte £ 19/28

7 rooms: £ 60/90

Typical Dishes
White bean soup & soda bread
Pork belly with boulangère potatoes
Poached pear with chocolate mousse

 *6 mi west of St Ives by B 3306. Parking.*

Babbacombe

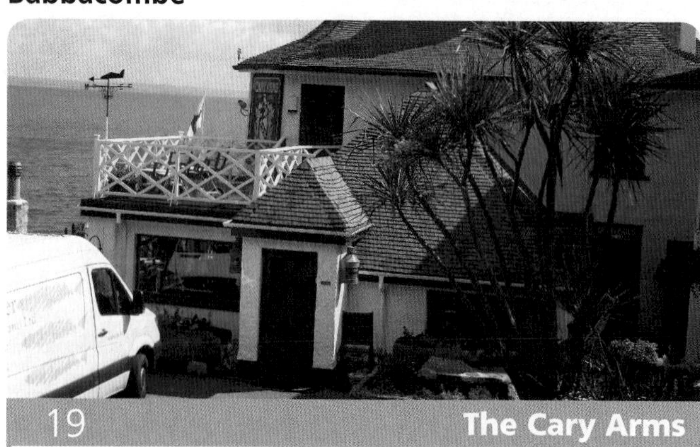

19 The Cary Arms

Babbacombe Beach,
Babbacombe, TQ1 3LX
Tel.: (01803)327110 – Fax: (01803)323221
e-mail: enquiries@caryarms.co.uk
Website: www.caryarms.co.uk

Otter Bitter, Otter Ale, Bays Bitter , Dartmoor Jail, Dartmoor Legend

Set in an idyllic spot on the English Riviera, The Cary Arms is built into the rocks, with terraces down to the shore and far-reaching views. Its boutique-chic, New England style bedrooms come with stunning bathrooms complete with roll-top baths. The stylish, ultra-comfy residents lounge continues the nautical theme, and there's even a spa room for treatments. If the rooms are all about luxury, the food, by contrast, is straightforward in style; we're talking reasonably priced pub dishes of simply cooked fish and meats. At the hub of the operation is its atmospheric stone and slate floored bar where you're served by chatty staff; in summer, there's also a wood burning pizza oven on the terrace, to make the most of that wonderful location.

Closing times
Open daily

Prices
Meals: a la carte £ 22/34
8 rooms: £ 100/250

Typical Dishes
Seared Brixham scallops
Devon steak & Otter ale pie
Warm treacle tart

Parking at adjacent beach car park.

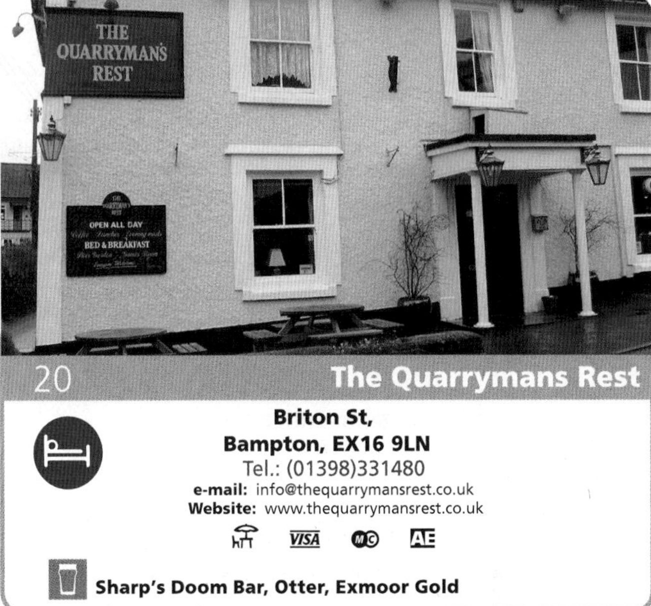

20 The Quarrymans Rest

Briton St,
Bampton, EX16 9LN
Tel.: (01398)331480
e-mail: info@thequarrymansrest.co.uk
Website: www.thequarrymansrest.co.uk

VISA AE

Sharp's Doom Bar, Otter, Exmoor Gold

With its relaxed, traditional open-fired bar, this 17C inn is still very much the village local. Its restaurant, with exposed brick and high-backed leather chairs is, by contrast, a more formal and intimate choice of dining room – but wherever you sit, the menu is the same. Chef-owner Paul prides himself on sourcing the best of local produce and dishes are substantial enough to render side orders redundant. Expect tried-and-tested classics, with the occasional Asian influence; perhaps salmon and crab fishcake, potted wild rabbit with pickles, homemade steak, ale and kidney pudding or braised shank of Devon lamb. The Sunday carvery is popular, staff are cheery and, if you're staying over, you'll find bedrooms clean, fresh and uncluttered.

Closing times
Closed Sunday dinner

Prices
Meals: a la carte £ 20/28
3 rooms: £ 45/85

6 mi north of Tiverton by A396 and B3190.

Branscombe

21 Masons Arms

Branscombe,
EX12 3DJ
Tel.: (01297)680300 – Fax: (01297)680500
e-mail: reception@masonsarms.co.uk
Website: www.masonsarms.co.uk

 **Branscombe Vale Brewery Branoc and Summa That, Gundog, Otter Bitter and Amber**

This charming 14C building with its characterful period features started life as a tiny cider-house, then became an inn and was later renamed due to frequent visits from the workers building Exeter Cathedral. Menus rely on local produce but influences are European, so for dessert you might find Italian-inspired hazelnut panna cotta, good old British sticky toffee pudding and French-influenced toffee and banana crème brûlée. The highlight of the bar menu is the local crab, landed on the beach just 10mins away; while in the restaurant one dish from every course has the main ingredient sourced from within ten miles and local meats can often be found cooking on a spit over the fire. Bedrooms, in the inn and cottages, boast antique furnishings.

Closing times
Open daily

Prices
Meals: £ 30 (dinner) and a la carte £ 21/31

21 rooms: £ 56/175

Between Seaton and Sidmouth; south of A 3052; in the village centre. Parking.

22 The Drewe Arms

Broadhembury,
EX14 3NF
Tel.: (01404)841267
e-mail: info@thedrewe.arms.com
Website: www.thedrewe.arms.com

 **Otter Bitter and several guest beers**

Set close to the church, in a beautiful cob and thatch village, The Drewe Arms is a quintessential English pub. Exposed beams and dark wood furnishings set the tone, and roaring open fires and flickering candlelight create a warm welcome. There's the choice of two characterful dining areas – each with its own menu, but both serving freshly prepared dishes crafted from quality, local produce. Light bites and pub classics such as ham hock or mussels Provençale are on offer in the bar, while the restaurant steps things up a gear, featuring more modern, international influences. You might find carpaccio of venison – followed by a complimentary sorbet – then seared fillet of halibut with wasabi mash or tarte tatin of sweet potato and fennel.

Closing times
Closed Monday
booking essential

Prices
Meals: a la carte £ 20/30

Typical Dishes
Carpaccio of beef with wasabi remoulade
Grilled wild sea bass
Chocolate marquise

 *5 mi northwest of Honiton by A 373. Parking in village square.*

23 **The Union Inn**

The Green,
Denbury, TQ12 6DQ
Tel.: (01803)812595
e-mail: theunioninn@aol.com
Website: www.theunioninndenbury.co.uk

Hunter's Denbury Dreamer, Jail Ale, Otter Bitter

Having worked away for many years, chef Robert Van'Halteren has finally returned to his local area – and to this characterful village pub overlooking the green. The main bar oozes character, boasting exposed brickwork, wooden beams and slate floors; not forgetting warming open fires and flickering candles. Regular newsletters keep the villagers informed about the up-coming folk, jazz and quiz nights, and trophies won by the local sports teams are on display. Menus feature tasty classics prepared in a fresh, modern manner: Wednesday is pie night, Fridays always offer a curry and at certain times there's a good value tasting menu available. Robert's time spent working with Marco Pierre White shows through in dishes such as trifle Wally Ladd.

Closing times
Open daily

Prices
Meals: £ 17 (Monday-Thursday dinner)
and a la carte £ 19/32

Typical Dishes
Home smoked duck breast
Confit pork belly
Clafoutis of raspberries

 *5 mi southwest of Newton Abbot by A 381.*

24 Fortescue Arms

East Allington,
TQ9 7RA
Tel.: (01548)521215
e-mail: info@fortescue-arms.co.uk
Website: www.fortescue-arms.co.uk

 **Butcombe Bitter, Dartmoor IPA**

Built over 200 years ago, this ivy-clad building was once part of the Fortescue family's Fallapit estate. It really is a place of contrasts: turn left and you're in a small beamed bar with a slate floor and wooden tables – where the regulars are supping on a locally brewed ales and listening to stories of the owner's lard sculpting and yodelling – turn right and you'll find yourself standing on carpet, among high-backed leather chairs. The menus match the rooms, so you'll discover a selection of pub classics and blackboard specials in the bar, and a concise à la carte featuring the odd Austrian dish (from the chef-owner's homeland) in the restaurant. Local fish and seafood feature highly. Bedrooms are too modest to recommend at present.

Closing times
Closed Monday lunch

Prices
Meals: a la carte £ 18/32

Typical Dishes
Smoked duck with fennel & grape salad
Pork fillet filled with ham & cheese
Apple strudel & crème patissière

 *4 mi northeast of Kingsbridge by B 3264, A 381 and minor road. Parking.*

Exton

25 **The Puffing Billy**

Station Rd,
Exton, EX3 0PR
Tel.: (01392)877888
e-mail: andrew@thepuffingbilly.co.uk
Website: www.thepuffingbilly.co.uk

VISA MC AE

Otter Bitter, Otter Ale and Exmoor Gold

Robert Louis Stevenson once said 'it is better to travel hopefully than to arrive' – but he hadn't been to the Puffing Billy. Set just round the corner from Exton station, this spacious pub is light, modern and boasts a distinct sense of style. The welcome really is first class but it's a popular place, so you might want to reserve your seats. Modern stools and tub chairs fill the bar, while the more formal dining room displays stylish banquettes and high-backed chairs. On your journey through the menu you'll discover something to suit every taste: comforting classics like steak and kidney pie; regionally inspired dishes such as local chicken with Devon cheese; and some more international influences, perhaps crab cakes in chilli and coriander.

Closing times
Closed 1 week in January

Prices
Meals: a la carte £ 20/30

Brown tourist sign off A376 to Exmouth, 3 mi. from junction 30 M5. Parking.

26 **The Hart Inn**

The Square,
Hartland, EX39 6BL
Tel.: (01237)441474
e-mail: bjornmoen@hotmail.com
Website: www.thehartinn.com

Sharp's Doom Bar, O-Hanlon's, Yellow Hammer, Otter Ale, Cotleigh, Sea Hawk

Boasting stonework dating back to the 14C, this is one of the oldest buildings in Hartland, and the huge beams, open fires and homely furnishings create a warm, friendly atmosphere. Formerly 'The New Inn', it's thought that the name was changed when the draymen kept going to the wrong address; its new title is believed to make reference to it being the 'heart' of the village, where the hunt used to meet. The chef is Norwegian so the regularly changing menu sees some Scandinavian influences, although the produce itself remains local and seasonal: meat and vegetables are supplied by nearby farms and fish is delivered from Appledore. Portions are generous and not for the faint-hearted; dishes could include roast spatchcock or braised Lundy lamb.

Closing times
Closed 25 December, Sunday dinner and Monday

Prices
Meals: a la carte £ 14/26

 *Between Bideford and Bude off A 39. Parking.*

27

The Holt

178 High St,
Honiton, EX14 1LA
Tel.: (01404)47707
e-mail: enquiries@theholt-honiton.com
Website: www.theholt-honiton.com

Otter Brewery - Ale, Bitter, Bright, Head, Amber

The McCaig family's mission statement is to provide a 'distinctive and sustainable taste of Devon' – and with one brother out front and one behind the scenes in the pub, and mum and dad brewing real ales just down the road, there seems to be no stopping them. Sourcing regional produce is a key part of their ethos, as is sustainability, so you'll find ingredients from small, local suppliers and eco-friendly menus printed on recycled hops and paper. Appealing menus change every 6 weeks, with tapas and light dishes on offer at lunchtime and a more substantial à la carte in the evening. Much of what you'll find on your plate is homemade – including the tasty sausages – and the curing and smoking of meats and fish takes place entirely on site.

Closing times
Closed 25-26 December, Sunday and Monday

Prices
Meals: a la carte £ 20/27

At lower end of High Street. Dowell Street car park (2 min walk).

28 **Bickley Mill Inn**

Stoneycombe,
Kingskerswell, TQ12 5LN
Tel.: (01803)873201
e-mail: info@bickleymill.co.uk
Website: www.bickleymill.co.uk

VISA MC AE

Otter Ale, Teignworthy, Bays

This modern-looking former flour mill is the last place you expect to find as you drive down winding country lanes and past a large quarry. You're greeted by a huge decked terrace, gardens built into rocky banks and a contemporary entranceway, and, despite the rustic furnishings, large open fireplaces and cosy bar, it feels decidedly modern inside, too. Menus take on a simple, traditional style and are keenly priced; you might find king prawn cocktail or devilled kidneys on toast, followed by shepherd's pie with cheddar and leek mash, or home-baked ham, free range eggs and chips – while the blackboard displays the latest fish, fresh from Brixham market. Individually designed bedrooms are bold and stylish; Owls and Eaves are two of the best.

Closing times
Closed 26-28 December and 1 January

Prices
Meals: £ 15 (lunch Monday-Saturday) and a la carte £ 17/21

12 rooms: £ 68/90

3 mi south of Newton Abbot by A380 and minor road east. Parking.

Knowstone

29 The Masons Arms

Knowstone,
EX36 4RY
Tel.: (01398)341231
e-mail: dodsonmasonsarms@aol.com
Website: www.masonsarmsdevon.co.uk

Inspectors' favourites

 **Cotleigh Tawny Bitter**

This pretty thatched inn is set in a secluded village in the beautiful foothills of Exmoor. It was built in the 13C by the masons who also constructed the village church, and exudes rural charm; its cosy beamed bar with inglenook fireplace often playing host to locals, their guns and their dogs. You'll find French and British classics on the menu, created using the finest of locally sourced produce. Dishes like Devon beef fillet and monkfish loin are sophisticated but never over-wrought; deliciously fresh and attractively presented, with pronounced, assured flavours. Dine beneath a celestial ceiling mural in the bright rear dining room, with delightful views out over the rolling hills towards Exmoor. Charming service complements the food.

Closing times
Closed first 2 weeks January, 1 week August, Sunday dinner and Monday
booking essential

Prices
Meals: £ 35 (Sunday lunch) and a la carte £ 34/45

7 mi southeast of South Molton by A 361; opposite the village church. Parking.

30 The Dartmoor Inn

Moorside,
Lydford, EX20 4AY
Tel.: (01822)820221 – Fax: (01822)820494
e-mail: info@dartmoorinn.co.uk
Website: www.dartmoorinn.com

VISA MC AE

Otter Ale, St Austell Tribute

Set on the fringes of the Dartmoor National Park, close to Lydford Gorge and the White Lady waterfall, the setting couldn't be more appealing; and this pub's shabby-chic, French farmhouse styling fits it perfectly. There's a cosy bar, a series of individually styled dining rooms, a lovely courtyard and a boutique selling homewares and accessories – as well as a selection of tasty, modern dishes that are a step above your usual pub fare. Choose from the set, easy dining or main à la carte menus, all displayed on a single page; the mixed grill of sea fish for two is a popular choice. Spacious bedrooms are named after the fabrics they feature. Breakfast includes unusual offerings such as herb-crusted goat's cheese with black pudding and bacon.

Closing times
Closed Sunday dinner and Monday lunch

Prices
Meals: £ 21 and a la carte £ 21/38

3 rooms: £ 85/125

Typical Dishes
Falmouth Bay scallops & artichoke purée
Devon Ruby beef fillet
Passion fruit tart

1 mi east on A 386. Parking.

Marldon

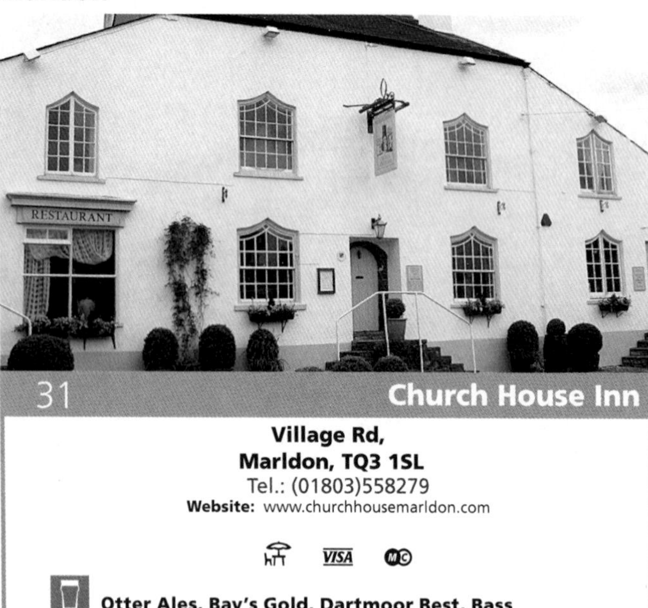

31 **Church House Inn**

Village Rd,
Marldon, TQ3 1SL
Tel.: (01803)558279
Website: www.churchhousemarldon.com

VISA

Otter Ales, Bay's Gold, Dartmoor Best, Bass

A charming inn of huge character, originally built in the 14C to provide accommodation for artisans constructing the nearby church, The Church House Inn was rebuilt in the 18C and still displays some of its original Georgian windows. Inside, it's fresh and simple; there are plenty of nooks and crannies in which to settle, and local art hangs on the walls. The menu leans towards the Mediterranean, but with some North African and Asian influences, so expect dishes like slow-cooked shoulder of lamb with Moroccan spiced sultanas or pan-fried king prawns in coriander, lime and ginger butter. Two special Italian main courses are available every Tuesday night and tasting evenings on every fourth Thursday feature cuisine from different countries.

Closing times
Open daily

Prices
Meals: a la carte £ 21/33

Between Torquay and Paignton off A 380. Parking.

32 **The White Horse Inn**

7 George St,
Moretonhampstead, TQ13 8PG
Tel.: (01647)440267 – Fax: (01647)440146
e-mail: info@whitehorsedevon.co.uk
Website: www.whitehorsedevon.co.uk

 **Legend, Jail Ale, Otter Ale**

It's hard to believe that this pub, set in the heart of rural Dartmoor, was semi-derelict when its owners took it on. While the locals gather in the bar to watch the sport, diners head for rustic, flag-floored rooms created from the converted stable and barn; or the sunny, Mediterranean-style courtyard. With an actor-turned-chef at the helm you might expect some melodrama in the kitchen; you won't get this, but you will get tasty, unfussy dishes with more than a hint of Italy; think homemade sliced focaccia or crab linguine, set alongside more traditional dishes like duck terrine or roast rare breed pork belly. Thin crust pizzas come straight from a custom-built oven, while desserts such as Eton mess finish your meal off with a flourish.

Closing times
Closed Sunday and lunch in winter and Monday

Prices
Meals: a la carte £ 19/30

 *In heart of village. Two car parks within 1min walk.*

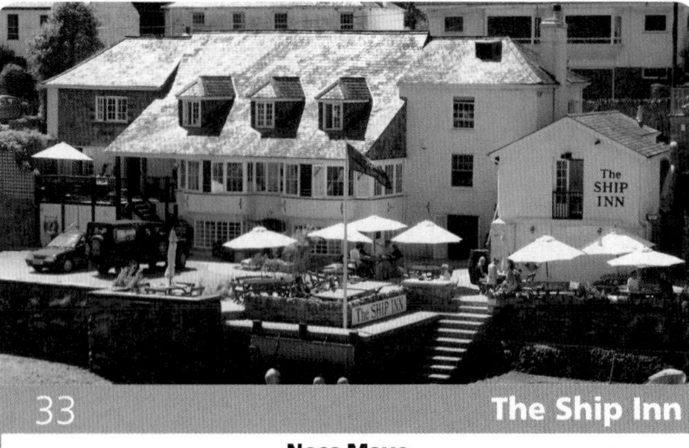

33

The Ship Inn

Noss Mayo,
PL8 1EW
Tel.: (01752)872387 – Fax: (01752)873294
e-mail: shipinn@nossmayo.com
Website: www.nossmayo.com

Jail Ale, St Austell Tribute, Proper Job, Palmers and Dartmoor

Wonderful waterside views are one of the main attractions of this fine pub, set in a peaceful spot on the south side of the Yealm Estuary. It's well run, large and very busy, with friendly staff who cope admirably under pressure. Its oldest part dates from the 18C and its characterful interior features wooden floors and open fires, while its collection of maritime memorabilia, including numerous old photographs, gives a tangible sense of seafaring history. The menu offers pub classics such as rib-eye steak, sausage and mash, ham or free range egg and chips. Desserts come from the tried-and-tested stable and might include lemon panna cotta or bread and butter pudding, while the wine list is well presented, with a good selection by the glass.

Closing times
Open daily
Prices
Meals: a la carte £ 21/32

Typical Dishes
Goat's cheese & roasted red pepper in filo pastry
Rump of lamb & fondant potato
Treacle tart & Chantilly cream

10.5 mi. southeast of Plymouth; signed off A 379; turn right into B 3186. Restricted parking, particularly at high tide.

34 **The Harris Arms**

Portgate,
EX20 4PZ
Tel.: (01566)783331 – Fax: (01566)783359
e-mail: info@theharrisarms.co.uk
Website: www.theharrisarms.co.uk

VISA

Bays Best, Sharp's Doom Bar and Otter Ales

With its simple black and white exterior, this is a place that you could easily drive past, but plenty of people already seem to know its secret. Pass through the classical bar-lounge and down the steep steps, and you'll find lovely views across the fields, along with a large decked terrace. The owners constantly flit to and fro but the atmosphere remains cheery and laid-back. Menus offer a concise selection of tried-and-tested dishes, supplemented by daily specials on the blackboard. Presentation is fresh and simple, and there's always plenty of flavour packed in. A well laid out, seasonally changing wine list really reflects the owners' experience in and passion for New Zealand and France; keep an eye out for the fundraising wine dinners.

Closing times
Closed 26 December, Sunday dinner and Monday

Prices
Meals: £ 17 (Sunday lunch) and a la carte £ 20/27

Typical Dishes
Braised pork cheek with sage sauce
Lamb shank & mint mash
Crème brûlée & raspberry sorbet

3 mi east of Launceston by A 388 and side road. Parking.

35 **Jack in the Green Inn**

London Rd,
Rockbeare, EX5 2EE
Tel.: (01404)822240 – Fax: (01404)823445
e-mail: info@jackinthegreen.uk.com
Website: www.jackinthegreen.uk.com

Otter Ale, Butcombe Bitter, Sharp's Doom Bar, Firefly Bitter

With its unassuming whitewashed exterior, this is a place that you could easily drive by – but if you did, you'd be missing out. Inside it's warm and welcoming, both in its décor and in the friendliness of the team. Weekend jazz sessions take place on the terrace during summer and the larger than life owner ensures the locals are kept in-the-know by sending out newsletters and recipe cards. They take a very serious approach towards the cooking here and have been supporting local producers for a long time. You'll find everything from pies and steaks to terrines and risottos, supplemented by daily specials – mostly fresh fish from the day boats. Refreshingly, bread, veg and water are all free of charge. Watch out for hot air balloons passing by.

Closing times
Closed 25 December-6 January

Prices
Meals: £ 25 and a la carte £ 26/40

Typical Dishes
Prawn cocktail
Steak & kidney pie
Dessert Plate

6.25 mi east of Exeter by A 30. Parking at the back.

36

The Tower Inn

Church Rd,
Slapton, TQ7 2PN
Tel.: (01548)580216
e-mail: towerinn@slapton.org
Website: www.thetowerinn.com

Butcombe Bitter, Otter Bitter, Otter Ale, St Austell Tribute

Leave your car in the car park as you enter the village and make the 10 minute walk up the hill: not only is it the easiest place to park but it's also a pleasant stroll. Built in 1347 as cottages for the workers building the next door chantry, the pub is now overlooked by the ruins of the former tower. It's a charming place, boasting dark red walls, polished tables and roaring fires, not forgetting fresh flowers and flickering candles. Menus differ from lunch to dinner and change every 3 months. It's pub food with an extra little twist; nothing gimmicky, just good cooking that adds something a little different, so your venison sausages might be served with sauerkraut and your fish and chips might come in vodka batter. Simple bedrooms await.

Closing times
Closed Monday in winter
Prices
Meals: a la carte £ 20/30
3 rooms: £ 65/85

Typical Dishes
Oven-baked Salcombe crab dumplings
Mini game pie & Exmoor venison loin
Platter of local cheeses & relish

6 mi southwest of Dartmouth by A 379; signed between Dartmouth and Kingsbridge. Parking with exceptionally narrow access.

37 **The Royal Oak**

Station Rd,
South Brent, TQ10 9BE
Tel.: (01364)72133 – Fax: (01364)73575
e-mail: info@oakonline.net
Website: www.oakonline.net

VISA

Dartmoor Jail, Legend and Teignworthy Reel ales

South Brent is not the prettiest of villages and most people pass it by when heading on to the coast, so The Royal Oak has its work cut out when it comes to pulling in more than the locals. The décor is clean and fresh yet somewhat traditional: a large bar leads through to a modern, roomy restaurant with an attractive courtyard, while the upstairs function room is used for everything from business meetings to judo sessions. At lunchtime there's a simple bar menu supplemented by a fish and a dish 'of the day'; while in the evening they offer more complex dishes such as seared pigeon breast or rump of lamb niçoise. The cheesecakes have become something of a speciality and the various events are always a hit. Bedrooms are modern and spacious.

Closing times
Closed 25 December dinner

Prices
Meals: a la carte £ 18/26

5 rooms: £ 60/90

Off A 38. Free parking in old railway station carpark.

38

The Kings Arms

Dartmouth Rd,
Strete, TQ6 0RW
Tel.: (01803)770377
e-mail: thekingsarms.strete@hotmail.com
Website: www.kingsarms-dartmouth.co.uk

 **Otter Ales, Adnams**

Behind its rather dour exterior hides a pub of consequence, serving the best, the wettest and the freshest seafood from Devon's sandy shores. The menu offers classical, honest-to-goodness dishes like herring roes on toast or fillet of turbot. There are oysters, mussels, lobster, crab, scallops and fish in abundance; all locally caught, simply cooked and very tasty. Non-seafood dishes might include confit of duck or steak and chips, with traditional desserts such as sticky toffee pudding. Like the food, the atmosphere is pleasingly down-to-earth. There is a snug bar and a raised dining room with pictures of seascapes on the walls; on a summer's day, head instead for the delightful rear garden which boasts fantastic views out over Start Bay.

Closing times
Open daily
Prices
Meals: a la carte £ 22/35

Typical Dishes
Seared scallops & Puy lentils
Roast loin of cod
Lavender brûlée & shortbread

 *4 mi southwest of Dartmouth by A 379. Parking.*

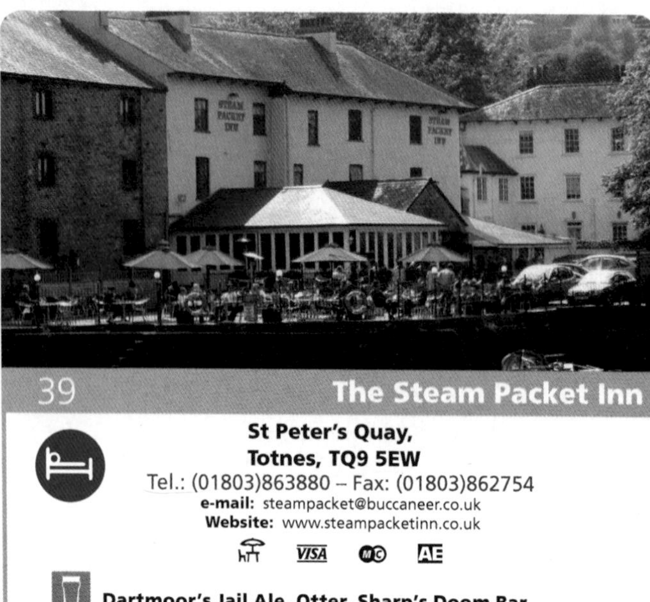

39 The Steam Packet Inn

St Peter's Quay,
Totnes, TQ9 5EW
Tel.: (01803)863880 – Fax: (01803)862754
e-mail: steampacket@buccaneer.co.uk
Website: www.steampacketinn.co.uk

VISA MC AE

Dartmoor's Jail Ale, Otter, Sharp's Doom Bar

Named after the postal ships that used to carry the mail, the Steam Packet Inn is situated in a fantastic location on the River Dart, just five minutes walk from the centre of town. With a vast terrace that catches the sun from dawn till dusk and a large conservatory looking out over the water, this is a great spot to relax and watch the comings and goings on the river – but plenty of other people know this too, so the pleasant serving team are often pushed to their limit. The eclectic, wide-ranging menu has something for everyone and ranges from classic lemon sole and West Country steak to kofta kebabs and even Thai dishes. Fresh fish from Looe is a speciality and a blackboard displays the latest catch. Elegant, contemporary bedrooms await.

Closing times
Open daily

Prices
Meals: a la carte £ 16/30
4 rooms: £ 60/80

Typical Dishes
Scallops with lardons
Pork belly with Colcannon
Vanilla crème brûlée with shortbread

At the bottom of the hill by the river. Parking.

40 **The Cow**

58 Station Rd,
Ashley Cross, Poole, BH14 8UD
Tel.: (01202)749569 – Fax: (01202)307493
e-mail: info@thecowpub.co.uk
Website: www.thecowpub.co.uk

 **Ringwood Best, Fuller's London Pride and guest ale Purbeck IPA**

Pubs next to railway stations are not normally celebrated for their cooking but this bovine beauty bucks the trend. What used to be a local dive has been transformed into a very pleasant stop-off point for a drink or a meal before travelling – as well as a destination in its own right. The lunch menu offers a mix of pub favourites and bistro classics; perhaps bubble and squeak or steak and ale pie. The evening menu – available only in the bistro – steps things up a gear with dishes such as pigeon ballotine or sea bass, while the bar area with its sofas, cow canvases and flat screen TV is principally for drinkers. Anyone wanting an evening meal here must make do with the dish chalked on the board; perhaps shepherd's pie or Thai green curry.

Closing times
Closed Sunday dinner

Prices
Meals: a la carte £ 22/32

Typical Dishes
Duck rillette & kohlrabi remoulade
Roasted rump of lamb & red cabbage
Dark chocolate truffle torte

At Parkstone Station. Parking.

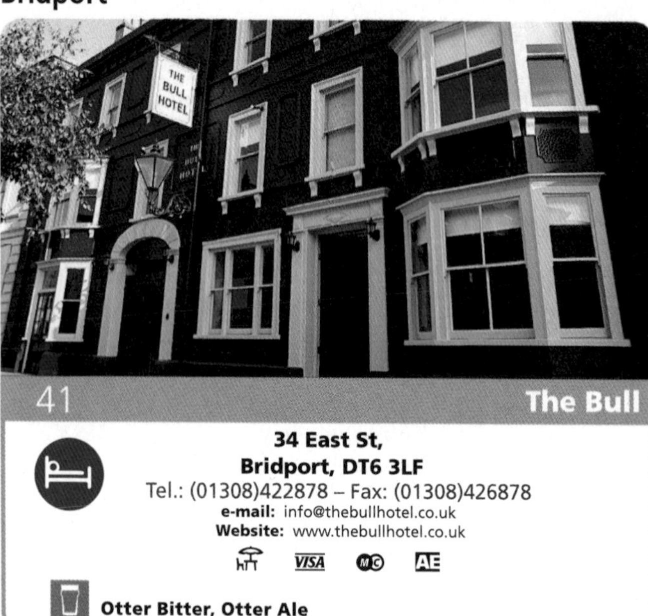

41 **The Bull**

34 East St,
Bridport, DT6 3LF
Tel.: (01308)422878 – Fax: (01308)426878
e-mail: info@thebullhotel.co.uk
Website: www.thebullhotel.co.uk

VISA MC AE

Otter Bitter, Otter Ale

From the moment you set foot in this Grade II listed building and are greeted by a vast contemporary portrait, you realise it's no ordinary place. A former regency style coaching inn, it has undergone a massive transformation, which has left an eclectic mix of period features and chic, contemporary décor – a touch of grandeur amongst the bustling streets of this busy market town. The ground floor is surprisingly compact, featuring a small bar overlooking a courtyard and a simple, fairly informal dining room, where you'll find a mix of classic English and Mediterranean brasserie dishes – crafted from local meats and fresh fish from Lyme Bay. The modern designer bedrooms are equally as appealing; residents' areas include a luxurious ballroom.

Closing times
Open daily

Prices
Meals: a la carte £ 18/38

14 rooms: £ 70/190

Typical Dishes
Lobster & Emmental soufflé
Roast rump of lamb with roasted beetroot
Hot chocolate fondant

In town centre on South side of main street. Parking.

42 **The Stapleton Arms**

Church Hill,
Buckhorn Weston, SP8 5HS
Tel.: (01963)370396
e-mail: relax@thestapletonarms.com
Website: www.thestapletonarms.com

Butcombe Bitter, Moor Brewery Revival , Cheddar Ales Potholer

Sister to The Queen's Arms in Corton Denham, The Stapleton Arms lies on the fringes of Blackmore Vale and makes an ideal base for exploring the region. Menus are modern British with Mediterranean influences, so you might find rosemary crusted rack of lamb or red and yellow chicory risotto; and if you book ahead, you can even arrange to carve your own Sunday roast at the table. The majority of ingredients are sourced from within 25 miles and local, seasonal produce is delivered daily from the markets and the farm next door. The pub itself is modern and stylish, and the individually designed bedrooms with their Egyptian linen and smart bathrooms follow suit. You can keep your packing light as they kindly provide maps, wellies and picnics.

Closing times
Open daily

Prices
Meals: a la carte £ 18/27

4 rooms: £ 72/120

Typical Dishes
Lyme Bay scallops with pancetta & black pudding
Pork belly with rhubarb compote
Gooey chocolate pudding with pistachio ice cream

7 mi west of Shaftesbury by A30 and minor road north. Parking.

43 **The New Inn**

14 Long St,
Cerne Abbas, DT2 7JF
Tel.: (01300)341274
e-mail: newinncernabbas@gmx.com
Website: www.newinncerneabbas.com

 **Palmers Copper Ale, IPA and Dorset Gold**

The picture postcard village of Cerne Abbas is overlooked by the famous Chalk Giant – and this 16C former coaching inn is another impressively sized and rather ancient village landmark. Its décor is traditional, with exposed beams and dark wood tables; there are old maps, prints and lithographs and a fine collection of hanging water jugs. The food follows suit, with traditional dishes like fishcakes, steak pie or pork belly; lunch includes soups and sandwiches, while things step up a gear at dinner. This is good pub grub with no unnecessary fuss – just freshly prepared, well-cooked, locally sourced produce. A pleasant decked area leads out to the pub's vast back garden with its delightful apple trees. Bedrooms are modest but set to improve.

Closing times
Closed Sunday dinner
November-March

Prices
Meals: a la carte £ 18/30

Typical Dishes
Lyme Bay scallops
Slow-roast pork belly
Custard tart with apple fritters

 *In the centre of the village. On street parking.*

44

The Acorn Inn

28 Fore St,
Evershot, DT2 0JW
Tel.: (01935)83228 – Fax: (01935)83707
e-mail: stay@acorn-inn.co.uk
Website: www.acorn-inn.co.uk

 **Otter, Doom Bar**

Situated in a quintessentially English picture postcard village, this characterful coaching inn's claim to fame is that it featured in Thomas Hardy's 'Tess of the d'Urbervilles'. Stone walls, oak panelling and flag floors feature throughout and a vast array of pictures and memorabilia adorn every available surface. The lunchtime menu displays a selection of British pub classics, with dinner welcoming in some more sophisticated choices – dishes such as stuffed quail or parmesan, tarragon and truffle oil soufflé, followed by saddle of rabbit or fillet of English beef with seared scallops. Complete your 'Hardy' experience by staying in one of the individually designed English country bedrooms, named after characters or places from his book.

Closing times
Open daily

Prices
Meals: £ 23 (lunch)
and a la carte £ 23/30

10 rooms: £ 70/135

 *9 mi south of Yeovil by A 37; in Holywell turn west. Parking.*

45 **The Museum Inn**

Farnham,
DT11 8DE
Tel.: (01725)516261 – Fax: (01725)516988
e-mail: enquiries@museuminn.co.uk
Website: www.museuminn.co.uk

Inspectors' favourites

VISA

Ringwood's Best, Timothy Taylor Landlord, Spitfire

Set in the heart of a picture postcard village, this part-thatched 17C country inn was built by the founding father of modern archaeology – General August Lane Fox Pitt Rivers – to provide refreshment and accommodation for visitors to his nearby museum. It retains many original features, including flagstone floors and an inglenook fireplace, and the walls are adorned with hunting artefacts. For dining there's the bar, two adjoining rooms, a conservatory and the 'Shed', a smart, linen-laid room that opens at weekends. The menu offers British classics alongside dishes of a more Mediterranean nature, and cooking is seasonal, unfussy and focused on quality local ingredients. Bedrooms range from small and cottagey to spacious with a four-poster.

Closing times
Closed 25 December

Prices
Meals: a la carte £ 30/44

8 rooms: £ 110/165

Typical Dishes

Portland crab tortellini

Creedy Carver duck breast & sausage with fondant potato

Apple tarte Tatin

7.5 mi northeast of Blandford Forum by A 354. Parking.

46 The Talbot

Blanford Rd,
Iwerne Minster, DT11 8QN
Tel.: (01747)811269
e-mail: enquiries@the-talbot.com
Website: www.the-talbot.com

Badger First Gold and other regularly changing guest ales

Until the late 19C the Bower family were the Lords of the Manor here and the large Talbot hound that guards this mock-Elizabethan building is thought to make reference to their family crest. The inn retains a satisfyingly unfussy, pub-like feel, with its lounge bar, simply laid dining room and an aptly named 'Village Bar' – where you'll find the locals play pool or darts. Cooking is hearty and generous, and local produce is a must. Sausages are made by the village butcher, beef and lamb are supplied by the local Estate and the Ploughman's features local cheeses. Menus change near-daily and might include starters of Gloucester Old Spot and pistachio terrine, followed by slow-roasted shoulder of lamb. Bedrooms are comfy and well-appointed.

Closing times
Open daily

Prices
Meals: a la carte £ 18/28
5 rooms: £ 60/105

Typical Dishes
Ceviche of black bream
Pork tenderloin & coconut risotto
Assiette of chocolate

6 mi south of Shaftesbury by A 350. Parking.

47 **The European Inn**

Piddletrenthide,
DT2 7QT
Tel.: (01300)348308
e-mail: petalguru@hotmail.co.uk
Website: www.european-inn.co.uk

  VISA 

Palmers Copper, Dorset Gold, St Austell Proper Job

Thus named to honour the European involvement in the Crimean war, in which the first landlord purportedly fought, this relaxing little inn is a gem of a place and the locals seem to love it. The new owners made complete career changes in order to run it: he used to work at an airport, while she had a stint as an air hostess before becoming a florist. They may not yet have much experience but have had the good sense to employ a talented local chef, whose cooking is simple but skilled. A concise menu offers unfussy dishes such as rabbit and ham hock terrine or lemon sole and chips, with Dorset produce well-used, including fish from the south coast day boats. Bedrooms are stylish with feature walls; those at the back offer countryside views.

Closing times
Closed Monday
booking advisable at dinner

Prices
Meals: a la carte £ 20/29
3 rooms: £ 75/100

Typical Dishes
Pigeon breast salad & black pudding
Fillet of bass with Cornish new potatoes
Set vanilla cream & rhubarb compote

North of Dorchester on B 3143 between White Lackington and Piddlehinton. Parking.

48 The Anchor

West St,
Shapwick, DT11 9LB
Tel.: (01258)857269 – Fax: (01258)858840
e-mail: anchorshapwick@btconnect.com
Website: www.anchorshapwick.co.uk

 **Ringwood Best, Palmers Gold, Keystone Large One, 49ER**

Set in a tiny hamlet in the heart of rural Dorset, this red-brick pub has the clean, cosy feel of a real local. Its traditionally furnished rooms boast flag floors, open fires and hunting prints; the friendly staff take time to chat and the requisite row of regulars reassuringly prop up the bar. The chef believes in keeping things simple and brings his own boldly flavoured fusion style to modern British cooking. Menus are written daily and feature game from local estates, fish from the south coast day boats and vegetables from local producers. Expect dishes a little different from the pub norm; perhaps venison carpaccio, Parma ham with honey baked figs or beer battered skate cheeks; plus tasty local cheeses and some good old fashioned puds.

Closing times
Closed Sunday dinner

Prices
Meals: a la carte £ 16/35

Typical Dishes
Grilled fillet of herring with ginger and carrots
Marinated goat chops
Melon and mint salad with Moscow Mule granita

 *7.5 mi southeast of Blandford Forum by B 3082. Parking.*

Wimborne St Giles

49 **The Bull Inn**

Coach Rd,
Wimborne St Giles, BH21 5NF
Tel.: (01725)517300
e-mail: bullwsg@btconnect.com
Website: www.bullwsg.com

 **Hall & Woodhouse Brewery - Sussex, Tangle Foot and Badger**

Down narrow country roads by the Earl of Shaftsbury's estate, you'll come across this smart, modern, olive green pub. Inside neutrally hued walls are covered in countryside prints and there's a mix of older-style furniture. All tables are set for dining, although a new sofa-furnished lounge for drinkers – who are partial to a real ale or two from the local brewery – is on its way. Dogs are as welcome as their owners and service is helpful and friendly. Menus change daily and sometimes even between services, with produce sourced from their farm and within the county's borders. This is not your usual pub fare: refined dishes use interesting ingredients and unusual cuts, so you might find quince tart or veal tongue. Bedrooms are smart and stylish.

Closing times
Open daily
Prices
Meals: a la carte £ 17/28
5 rooms: £ 45/120

From the village, take first right after crossing the river Allen. Parking.

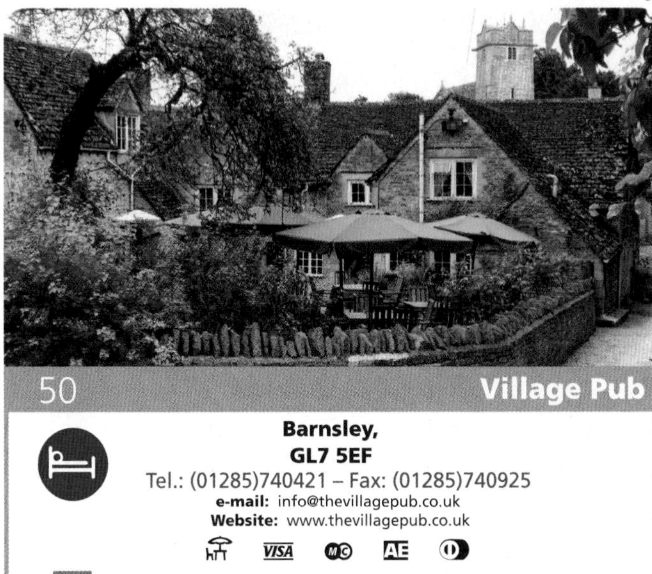

50 Village Pub

Barnsley,
GL7 5EF
Tel.: (01285)740421 – Fax: (01285)740925
e-mail: info@thevillagepub.co.uk
Website: www.thevillagepub.co.uk

VISA MC AE

Hook Norton Best Bitter, Butcombe IPA

One of the trailblazers of the gastro-revolution, The Village Pub ran out of steam somewhat in the late noughties but, now under the expert guidance of Calcot Manor, is once again on the up. With an interior straight out of any country homes magazine, it's got that cosy, open-fired village pub vibe down to a tee. The daily changing menu exudes modern appeal; nibbles like sea trout blinis are an irresistible teaser, there are starters like homemade country terrine, mains like braised lamb hotpot and comforting desserts such as treacle tart or rice pudding. Meat comes from within a 30 mile radius, with charcuterie often from Highgrove and vegetables from partner Barnsley House up the road. Individually styled bedrooms; Six has a four-poster.

Closing times
Open daily

Prices
Meals: a la carte £ 22/31
6 rooms: £ 90/160

Typical Dishes
Mussels with cider & wild garlic cream
Roast Great Farm chicken & sautéed potatoes
Warm treacle tart

4 mi northeast of Cirencester on B 4425. Parking.

51 **Horse & Groom**

Bourton-on-the-Hill,
GL56 9AQ
Tel.: (01386)700413 – Fax: (01386)700413
e-mail: greenstocks@horseandgroom.info
Website: www.horseandgroom.info

Inspectors' favourites

Goff's Jouster, Wye Valley Bitter, Purity's Ubu and Mad Goose, North Cotswold's Brewery's Shagweaver

Situated in a remote Cotswold village on the side of a hill it's not surprising that this Georgian stone pub attracts mainly diners, as, unless you live here, it's a long way to go for a drink. The relaxed atmosphere makes it popular with all ages and the friendly, well-paced service stands the test of even the busiest hour. Original beams, pine flooring and exposed stone feature throughout, while an attractive marble-topped counter steals focus in the bar. Here, two blackboards compete for attention: the first, a growing list of names of those waiting for a table and the second, an appealing list of British classics and more ambitious dishes. Cooking is unfussy and generous, and local produce features highly. Stylish, modern bedrooms await.

Closing times
Closed Sunday dinner except at bank holidays
booking essential

Prices
Meals: a la carte £ 20/35
5 rooms: £ 80/160

Typical Dishes
Warm salad of goat's cheese with puy lentils and chorizo
Home-cured Dexter salt beef
Granny G's Toffee meringue

1 mi west of Moreton in the Marsh by A 44. Parking.

52 The Gumstool Inn

Calcot,
GL8 8YJ
Tel.: (01666)890391 – Fax: (01666)890394
e-mail: reception@calcotmanor.co.uk
Website: www.calcotmanor.co.uk

Inspectors' favourites

Sharps Own, Butcombe Gold and Butcombe Original

Set in the grounds of Calcot Manor Hotel, on a 700 year old Estate, this converted farm out-building is now a highly attractive country pub. With wood-panelled walls, flag flooring and modern furnishings, it successfully combines classic country style with contemporary chic. It's warm and cosy in winter, bright and airy in the spring and the paved terrace is ideal in summer. The wide-ranging monthly menu is seasonal, rustic and hearty, but also accommodates for lighter appetites by offering some scaled-down main courses; while the extensive daily specials provide some interesting choices. Service is polite and friendly but make sure you give back what you get, as in the past miscreants were placed on the local gumstool and ducked in the pond.

Closing times
Open daily
booking essential

Prices
Meals: a la carte £ 25/33

Typical Dishes
Chicken liver parfait
Seared scallop salad & avocado
Classic crème brûlée

3.5 mi west of Tetbury on A 4135, in grounds of Calcot Manor Hotel. Parking.

53 Eight Bells Inn

Church St,
Chipping Campden, GL55 6JG
Tel.: (01386)840371
e-mail: neilhargreaves@bellinn.fsnet.co.uk
Website: www.eightbellsinn.co.uk

VISA

Hook Norton Best, Goff's Jouster, Purity UBU

If you're following the Cotswold Way Walk, this 14C pub, close to the historic high street of this old wool merchant's town, is well worth a visit. It originally accommodated the stonemasons working on St James's church, and later stored the eight bells from the church tower. Rebuilt in the 17C using the original stone and timbers, it has retained a good old community feel, welcoming drinkers and diners alike. The four neighbouring counties are represented behind the bar in their ale selection and they even offer scrumpy and perry on tap. Cooking is traditionally British – pies are the real thing, puddings are gloriously homemade and specials are just that, so arrive early if you want the full choice. Bedrooms combine character with mod cons.

Closing times
Closed 25 December

Prices
Meals: £ 17 (weekdays) and a la carte £ 25/32

7 rooms: £ 65/125

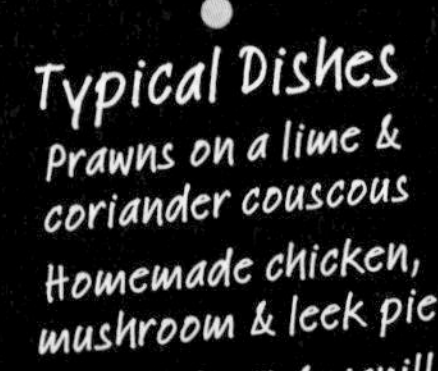

In centre of town. Unlimited parking on road.

54 The Green Dragon Inn

Cockleford,
GL53 9NW
Tel.: (01242)870271 – Fax: (01242)870171
e-mail: green-dragon@buccaneer.co.uk
Website: www.green-dragon-inn.co.uk

This characterful stone pub can be found nestled in a peaceful country lane that borders the grounds of the Cowley Manor hotel. The surrounding area is serious walking territory, so at lunchtime you'll find plenty of ramblers tucking into hearty burgers or sausages – alongside others sampling some of the more unusual dishes, such as deep fried pheasant and chestnut samosas or baked sea bass in a banana leaf. Huge open fireplaces are a focal point in two of the rooms and what better way to start the day than breakfast by a roaring fire? Keep an eye out for the carved mice that hide among the woodwork – the hallmark of Robert 'Mouseman' Thompson. Bedrooms are simple and modern; the St George suite is the best and boasts a super king-size bed.

Closing times
Open daily
booking essential

Prices
Meals: a la carte £ 25/35
9 rooms: £ 70/95

Typical Dishes
Fig, watermelon & feta cheese salad
Slow-cooked rump of lamb & spring vegetables
Homemade vanilla cheesecake

5 mi south of Cheltenham by A 435. Parking.

Ebrington

55 The Ebrington Arms

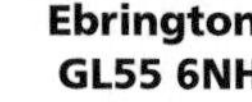

Ebrington,
GL55 6NH
Tel.: (01386)593223
e-mail: reservations@theebringtonarms.co.uk
Website: www.theebringtonarms.co.uk

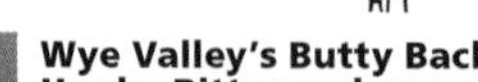

Wye Valley's Butty Bach, Uley Bitter, Stroud Organic, Hooky Bitter and one guest ale

This 17C inn snuggles into a charming chocolate box village in the glorious Cotswold countryside; its beamed, flag-floored bar with blazing log fire providing the hub from which locals and visitors come and go, while owners Claire and Jim oversee proceedings with humour and grace. The smart, stylish dining room, with its gilt-framed mirrors, provides an intimate atmosphere for a meal; there are monthly food nights – and fish and chips to take away. Tasty, robust, traditional dishes are cooked using local ingredients and up-to-date techniques; perhaps lamb leg steak or beef, Guinness and horseradish pie – with homemade desserts like passion fruit and orange tart to follow. Comfortable bedrooms with countryside views; room 3 has a four-poster.

Closing times
Open daily

Prices
Meals: a la carte £ 25/30
3 rooms: £ 90/110

Typical Dishes
Layered game terrine
Rump of Cotswold lamb with dauphinoise potatoes
Balsamic, lavender and almond crème brûlée with tuile biscuits

2 mi east of Chipping Campden by B 4035. Parking.

56 The Butchers Arms

Lime St,
Eldersfield, GL19 4NX
Tel.: (01452)840381
Website: www.thebutchersarms.net

  MC

 **Wye Valley Butty Bach and Dorothy Goodbody, St Austell Tribute, Timothy Taylor Landlord**

Apart from the modern sign swinging outside, this pub remains as traditional as ever. Two small rooms display original beams, part-oak flooring and a wood burning stove, while dried hops hang from the bar and memorabilia adorns the walls. A few of the small wooden tables are left for the local drinkers, while the rest are set for around 20 or so diners. With only one person in the kitchen the menu is understandably quite concise but it changes regularly – sometimes even from service to service – and despite the lack of man-power, everything from the bread to the ice cream is homemade. Cooking sees refined pub dishes alongside a few more unusual items such as Bath Chaps (pig's cheeks); while vegetables arrive courtesy of a local villager.

Closing times
Closed one week early January, one week late August, Sunday dinner, Monday, and Tuesday lunch

booking essential

Prices
Meals: a la carte £ 30/37

Typical Dishes
Pan-fried scallops with chorizo
Aged rib of Hereford beef
Marmalade pudding

 *South of M50 between Junctions 1 and 2. Parking.*

Lower Oddington

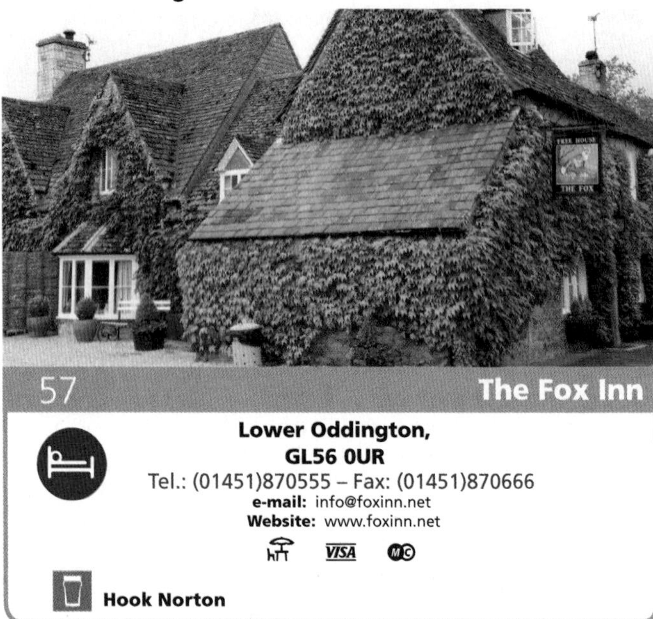

57 The Fox Inn

Lower Oddington,
GL56 0UR
Tel.: (01451)870555 – Fax: (01451)870666
e-mail: info@foxinn.net
Website: www.foxinn.net

VISA MC

Hook Norton

Set in a peaceful Cotswold village, this charming 16C creeper-clad inn boasts exposed beams, flagged floors and open fires. When the sun's out, the pretty garden is the place to be and, as the night draws in, the covered terrace makes the perfect retreat. It's just as appealing in the winter too, with plenty of cosy corners to snuggle into in the candlelit bar or characterful Red Room. Cooking hits just the right note – hearty, with a satisfyingly unpretentious style – and the produce is reassuringly local, with many ingredients sourced from local markets, and game from nearby Adlestrop. Steak and kidney pie is a favourite at lunch and the homemade puddings are a hit whatever the time of day. Uniquely designed bedrooms display lovely antiques.

Closing times
Closed 25 December
booking essential

Prices
Meals: a la carte £ 20/35
3 rooms: £ 75/95

Typical Dishes
Spinach & parmesan risotto
Sirloin steak
Sticky toffee pudding

3 mi east of Stow-on-the-Wold by A 436. Parking.

58 **The Wheatsheaf Inn**

West End,
Northleach, GL50 3EZ
Tel.: (01451)860244
e-mail: info@cotswoldswheatsheaf.com
Website: www.cotswoldswheatsheaf.com

St Austell's Tribute, Hook Norton and Purity

The pretty Cotswold town in which this characterful 17C former coaching inn sits was once famous for its thriving wool trade, and there are many reminders of the town's interesting history including its 12C church and busy market square. There's still plenty going on today: the owners will book guests a day's local fishing or shooting, or organise tickets to events such as the Cheltenham festivals; they also host their own events such as a monthly book club and occasional jazz evenings. Dine in either the stone-floored, open-fired bar or one of two dining areas. The daily changing menus feature flavourful pub classics like steak frites or ham hock terrine and local staff provide friendly service. Bedrooms aren't currently recommendable.

Closing times
Open daily

Prices
Meals: £ 13 (lunch)
and a la carte £ 13/45

In centre of town. Ample parking.

Paxford

59 Churchill Arms

Plaxford,
GL55 6XH
Tel.: (01386)594000 – Fax: (01386)594005
e-mail: info@thechurchillarms.com
Website: www.thechurchillarms.com

VISA

Three local ales

Despite a troubled past few years, this traditional Cotswold stone inn is on the up. Set in a picture postcard location, it boasts views over pretty stone houses, the nearby church and rolling open fields; as well as a charming interior with exposed beams, stone floors and a large wood burning stove. The enclosed rear garden is popular in summer, especially on a Thursday night, when you'll find the locals playing the old Oxfordshire game 'Aunt Sally'. Cooking displays a real mix of influences, ranging from unfussy pub classics on the blackboard to more restaurant-style dishes on the à la carte; finished off with tasty nursery puddings. Bedrooms are cosy with good country views but be aware that silence doesn't reign until the pub doors close.

Closing times
Open daily

Prices
Meals: a la carte £ 20/35

4 rooms: £ 55/90

3 mi east of Chipping Campden by B 4035. On street parking.

60 **The Bell**

Sapperton,
GL7 6LE
Tel.: (01285)760298 – Fax: (01285)760761
Website: www.foodatthebell.co.uk

 **Uley Old Spot, Otter Bitter, Bath Ales Gem**

On a warm summer's day head for this pretty village, where, set above the road, you can relax amongst the neatly-lawned gardens and paved terraces of this charming pub. Exposed stone and wood beams feature throughout and colourful modern art adorns the walls. The wide-ranging daily menu displays an array of British dishes with the odd Mediterranean touch; lunch offers several dishes in a choice of sizes and dinner boasts some more substantial offerings. Specials consist mainly of seafood and evolve constantly throughout the day. Cooking is refined yet rustic and a glance at the back of the menu assures you of the local or regional origins of the produce used. Completing the package is an interesting wine list and friendly, well-paced service.

Closing times
Closed 25 December

Prices
Meals: a la carte £ 26/33

Typical Dishes
Hand-pressed terrine of game
Rack of lamb with aubergine & smoked paprika
Pear frangipane

 *5 mi west of Cirencester by A419. Parking.*

61 The Swan

Southrop,
GL7 3NU
Tel.: (01367)850205 – Fax: (01367)850517
e-mail: info@theswanatsouthrop.co.uk
Website: www.theswanatsouthrop.co.uk

Inspectors' favourites

Hooky, Swan Bitter and Tribute

Run by an experienced couple, this swan is a very smart and well-heeled bird; a splendid creeper-clad inn, in the picture perfect village of Southrop. There are some restaurant-style dishes on the menu, but these are combined with classic pub staples; so expect choices such as chicken liver and foie gras parfait or roast haunch of venison to be found alongside steak, kidney and mushroom pie and Lancashire hot pot. The other main influence on the chef's cooking is his mother's Italian roots, hence the bruschetta, ribollita and other Mediterranean delights on the menu – and the fresh foccacia delivered to the tables as you arrive. Modern art graces the walls, flowers brighten the tables and there's a happy mix of visitors and locals.

Closing times
Closed 25 December and Sunday dinner

Prices
Meals: £ 16 and a la carte £ 25/30

Typical Dishes

Skillet roast foie gras with duck egg and brioche
Chump of Southrop Lamb with flageolet beans and bacon
Apple, almond and red berry crumble

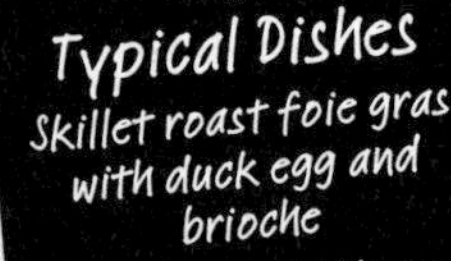

3 mi northwest of Lechlade on Eastleach rd. Parking around the village.

62 **The Trouble House**

Cirencester Rd,
Tetbury, GL8 8SG
Tel.: (01666)502206
e-mail: contact@troublehousetetbury.co.uk
Website: www.troublehousetetbury.co.uk

VISA

Wadworth 6X and Henrys IPA

The 'trouble' in the pub's name refers to rumours of old hauntings but no ghosts have been seen here for a while; well apart from Liam, the chef, who turned up in the kitchen again four years after leaving. The busy roadside setting isn't ideal and the exterior may not seem all that appealing but it's worth stopping off here for the warm welcome and tasty food. The interior has a shabby, homely style and there's a characterful, ultra-low beam in the bar; a place where the owners hope to encourage more of the locals to come and drink. Dishes range from sardines on toast to more ambitious offerings like rib of beef roasted in hay for two; and the Salcombe crab gratin and duck fat chips are favourites. The daily specials usually feature fish.

Closing times
Closed Sunday dinner and Monday

Prices
Meals: a la carte £ 22/32

2 mi northeast on A 433. Parking.

Upper Oddington

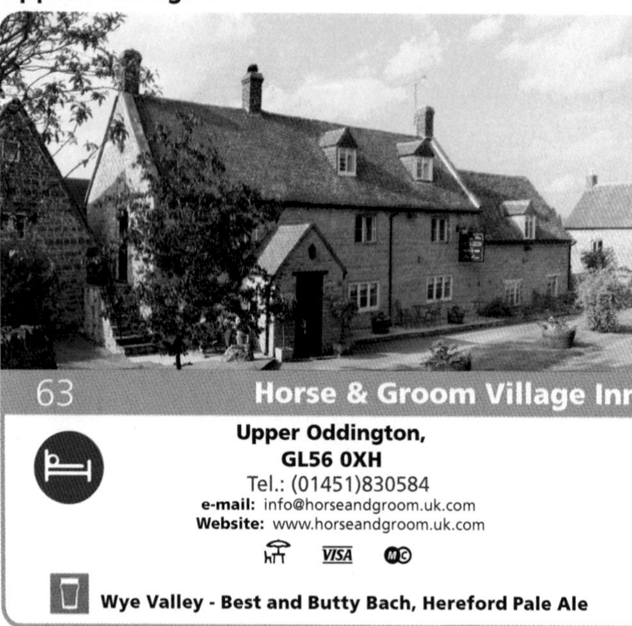

63 **Horse & Groom Village Inn**

Upper Oddington,
GL56 0XH
Tel.: (01451)830584
e-mail: info@horseandgroom.uk.com
Website: www.horseandgroom.uk.com

VISA

Wye Valley - Best and Butty Bach, Hereford Pale Ale

Not far from the delightful market town of Stow-on-the-Wold, you'll come across Upper Oddington; designated as an Area of Outstanding Natural Beauty. At its heart stands this part-16C mellow-stone inn, where sunshine floods in through the windows of the lovely central bar and on colder days, a log fire crackles. Flip over the menu and you'll discover that everything here is seasonal, local and ethically sourced, with consideration given to sustainability and organic farming methods. Meat and game are farm and estate sourced, cheese is locally produced and you might even see villagers popping in to swap their home-grown veg for a pint or two. Cosy bedrooms come with a serious breakfast that includes local eggs and Gloucester Old Spot sausages.

Closing times
Open daily

Prices
Meals: a la carte £ 20/30

7 rooms: £ 79/110

Typical Dishes

Smoked bacon & black pudding warm salad

Tuscan style braised Old Spot pork belly

Regional cheese with fig, hazelnut salami & water biscuits

2 mi east of Stow-on-the-Wold by A 436. Parking.

64 **The Queens Arms**

Corton Denham,
DT9 4LR
Tel.: (01963)223017
e-mail: relax@thequeensarms.com
Website: www.thequeensarms.com

   AE

Moor Revival, Highgate Dark Mild and regularly changing guest ales including Adnams Extra

This charming 18C stone pub is set in an attractive area but it's the enthusiastic owner's uncompromising ethos that really drives this place forwards. The regulars, both drinkers and diners, are his top priority, so he does his best to offer top quality produce at realistic prices – from fresh fruit juices and local whiskies to seasonal meats and veg. The menus, which are printed on brown paper, change daily. Lunch focuses mainly one or two courses, maybe slow-cooked autumn fruits with black pudding or a Somerset ploughman's of ham, cheddar and a pork pie; while the evening menu presents a more formal three course selection, with the likes of braised lamb shank or a plate of game for two. Bedrooms are charming, well-appointed and good value.

Closing times
Open daily
booking advisable
Prices
Meals: a la carte £ 20/28
5 rooms: £ 70/130

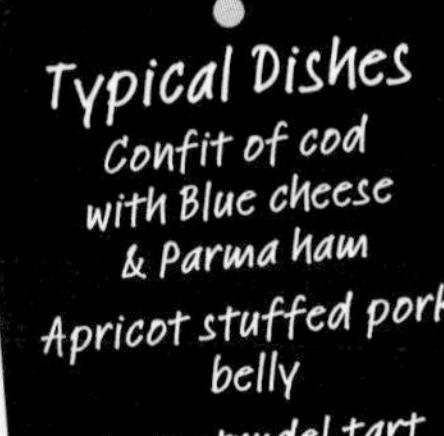

3 mi north of Sherborne by B 3145 and minor road west. Parking.

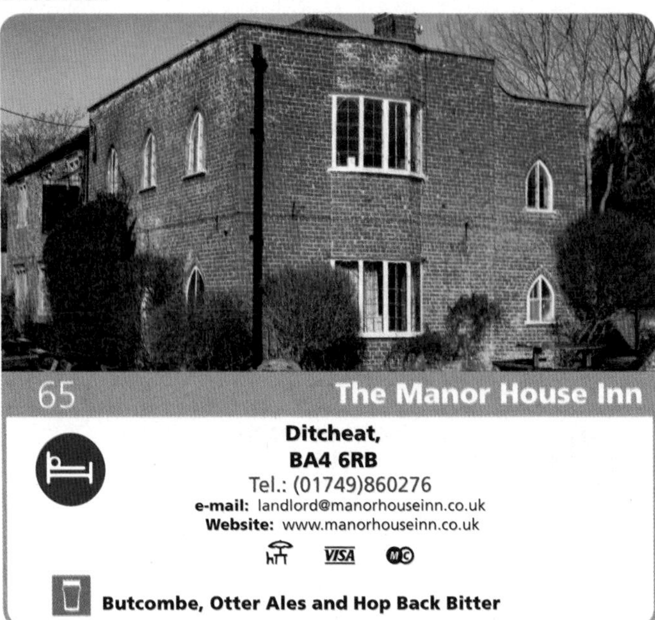

65 **The Manor House Inn**

Ditcheat,
BA4 6RB
Tel.: (01749)860276
e-mail: landlord@manorhouseinn.co.uk
Website: www.manorhouseinn.co.uk

VISA

Butcombe, Otter Ales and Hop Back Bitter

Originally owned by Lord of the Manor Edmund Dawe, this 17C coaching inn on the Somerset Levels boasts exposed stone walls, polished flag floors and roaring log fires. Champion racehorse trainer Paul Nicholls comes from the village and the Bath & West showground is just down the road, so it's no surprise that racing is at the heart of this pub – and you'll often find the locals in the old skittle alley watching the meets. There are no light bites on offer here, just good meaty (and veggie) dishes to get your teeth into. Using locally grown or reared produce, cooking is traditional and honest with international touches; Sunday lunch in particular provides good value and variety. Cosy, well-equipped bedrooms are housed in the former stables.

Closing times
Closed Sunday dinner

Prices
Meals: a la carte £ 23/36

3 rooms: £ 55/85

Typical Dishes
Tempura king prawns
Lamb rump & minted potatoes
Selection of Barbers cheeses

4 mi south of Shepton Mallet by A 37 and minor road left. Parking.

66

Woods

4 Banks Sq,
Dulverton, TA22 9BU
Tel.: (01398)324007 – Fax: (01398)323366
Website: www.woodsdulverton.co.uk

 **St Austell, Exmoor, Cottage and Otters**

Owned by a highly regarded local publican, this former bakery can't quite decide whether it wants to be a pub or a restaurant. It doesn't really matter though because as soon as you walk through the door you know you're in for a treat: the décor is charming, a great deal of the furniture has been made by the owner himself and the walls are lined with culinary-themed paintings. Local, traceable produce is important and as such, most meat comes from the owner's farm. Cooking offers classical dishes with a French slant – light bites and a few more substantial plates at lunch, with dishes stepping it up a gear at dinner. Once a year the town turns into a mini Marseille, as the chef brings French ingredients together in a culinary celebration.

Closing times
Open daily

Prices
Meals: a la carte £ 25/30

Typical Dishes

Onion, potato & thyme soup with smoked duck

Corn-fed chicken leg confit

Granny Smith apple tarte Tatin

 *13 mi north of Tiverton by A 396 and B 3222. 3 car parks and on-street parking.*

75 **Lord Poulett Arms**

High St,
Hinton St George, TA17 8SE
Tel.: (01460)73149
e-mail: reservations@lordpoulettarms.com
Website: www.lordpoulettarms.com

VISA

Branscombe Branoc, Otter Ale

The Lord Poulett offers everything you could possibly want from a pub. A picture perfect, lavender-framed terrace overlooks a boules pitch to a wild, untamed secret garden, while inside lovely old tables and squashy armchairs are set in a detailed country interior filled with hops and glowing candles. The kitchen creates an interesting seasonal menu with its roots planted firmly in the Med. Lunchtime sees a selection of gourmet sandwiches and lighter dishes, while in the evening the menu expands: there's always a 'West Bay catch of the day' and an extra mature local steak with tasty triple-cooked chips. These are followed by locally made ice creams, tempting desserts and West Country cheeses. Smart, stylish bedrooms boast feature baths.

Closing times
Closed 25-26 December and 1 January

Prices
Meals: a la carte £ 22/32

4 rooms: £ 65/95

Typical Dishes
Jerusalem soup
Sticky lamb with apricot & chickpea tajine
Apple & blackcurrant crumble

1 mi northwest of Crewkerne by minor road. Parking.

67 **The Devonshire Arms**

Long Sutton,
TA10 9LP
Tel.: (01458)241271 – Fax: (01458)241037
e-mail: mail@devonshirearms.com
Website: www.thedevonshirearms.com

 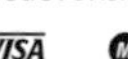 

Moor Revival, Moor Merlins Magic, Bath Ales Spa

This spacious Grade II listed hunting lodge is set right on the village green and boasts a contemporary interior, with a relaxing, open-plan bar and more formal dining room. The chef is Russian and his menu appealingly eclectic, with plenty of fish and locally sourced meats. It has a French bias but includes influences from all over Europe, so expect to see words like bresaola, brûlée, clafoutis and chorizo as you whet your appetite with nibbles like fresh olives or pistachios. Main dishes could include local chicken livers, pollock with pan-fried squid or veal burger with hand-cut chips, while dessert might mean homemade ice cream or dark chocolate fondant. The extremely comfortable bedrooms boast excellent quality bed linen and toiletries.

Closing times
Closed 25-26 December and 1 January

Prices
Meals: a la carte £ 22/29

9 rooms: £ 70/130

Typical Dishes

Chargrilled scallops with black pudding

Slow-cooked rare breed of beef

Ginger sticky toffee with Grand Marnier caramel sauce

4 mi east of Langport by A372. Parking.

68 The Pilgrims at Lovington

Lovington,
BA7 7PT
Tel.: (01963)240597
e-mail: jools@thepilgrimsatlovington.co.uk
Website: www.thepilgrimsatlovington.co.uk

VISA

Cottage Brewery Champflower

It's set at a main junction, and at first sight is hardly inspiring, but step inside The Pilgrims and it's a different matter entirely. It's pristine and personally run, and whether you sit in amongst the owners' cookbook collection in the bar side of the pub or in the bright, fresh restaurant, the décor is delightful and a relaxed atmosphere reigns. Their motto is 'the pub that thinks it's a restaurant,' and the homemade bread, the Spanish bar nibbles, the interesting wine list and the cider which comes from down the road all prove their point, as does the appealing menu of British and Mediterranean dishes created using quality produce from local suppliers. Contemporary, comfortable bedrooms, luxurious bathrooms and substantial breakfasts.

Closing times
Closed Sunday dinner, Monday and Tuesday lunch

Prices
Meals: a la carte £ 22/35
5 rooms: £ 80/120

4 mi southwest of Castle Cary by B 3153. Parking.

69 **The Vobster Inn**

Lower Vobster,
BA3 5RJ
Tel.: (01373)812920 – Fax: (01373)812247
e-mail: davila@btinternet.com
Website: www.vobsterinn.co.uk

Butcombe Bitter, Butcombe Blonde

Its owners' propensity to produce good food, coupled with their enthusiastic, hands-on approach has made the Vobster Inn a real destination pub, and though they may have put themselves on the map, they haven't forgotten the locals, so you are as welcome to snuggle up on a sofa for a drink, a bowl of chips and a chat as you are to enjoy a three course meal in the spacious restaurant. Mr and Mrs Davila hail from Galicia in North West Spain, so you might find paella or Spanish omelette alongside cottage pie or Ploughman's on the menu; Mediterranean ingredients and techniques are married with local produce – fish specials come courtesy of the catch at St Mawes - and the cooking has an honest, rustic edge to it. Three cosy, modern bedrooms.

Closing times
Closed Sunday dinner and Monday

Prices
Meals: a la carte £ 18/28

3 rooms: £ 60/95

Typical Dishes

Home-smoked duck breast

Fillet of bass, herb crushed potatoes

Bread & butter pudding with poached pear

6 mi northwest of Frome by A 362 towards Radstock; Vobster is signed after approx 5.5 mi. Parking.

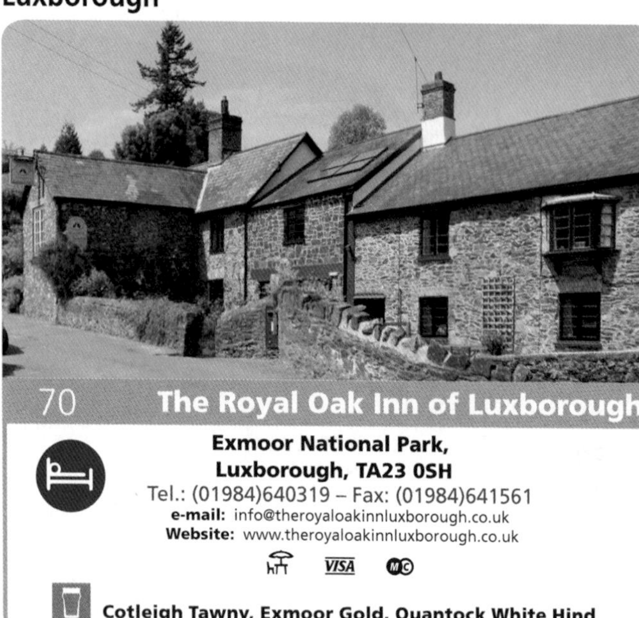

70 The Royal Oak Inn of Luxborough

Exmoor National Park,
Luxborough, TA23 0SH
Tel.: (01984)640319 – Fax: (01984)641561
e-mail: info@theroyaloakinnluxborough.co.uk
Website: www.theroyaloakinnluxborough.co.uk

VISA MC

Cotleigh Tawny, Exmoor Gold, Quantock White Hind

Set in a secluded wooded valley between the Brendon and Croydon Hills, the beautiful landscapes of Luxborough are a well kept secret. Passing through this peaceful countryside is the Coleridge Way, a walk that follows the routes that the romantic poet took when drawing inspiration for his works. The Exmoor Park authorities are understandably reluctant to put up signs, so it can be tricky finding this red sandstone pub, but it's definitely worth the search. The seasonal menu offers substantial dishes of classically prepared, boldly flavoured foods and despite an international edge to the cooking, focuses on quality, local ingredients, including Exmoor meat and Cornish seafood. Bedrooms are compact but charming; one has its own terrace.

Closing times
Closed 25 December

Prices
Meals: a la carte £ 16/32

11 rooms: £ 65/100

Off A 39 east of Minehead (signed) or off B 3224 Exford to Taunton road. Parking.

71 Tarr Farm Inn

Tarr Steps,
TA22 9PY
Tel.: (01643)851507 – Fax: (01643)851111
e-mail: enquiries@tarrfarm.co.uk
Website: www.tarrfarm.co.uk

 **Exmoor Ale, Exmoor Gold**

At 55m in length and with 17 spans, Tarr Steps is one of Britain's finest clapper bridges. It dates back to around 1000 BC and, according to local legend, was built by the devil in order to win a bet. Here, in the idyllic Exmoor countryside, you'll find Tarr Farm Inn, a true destination pub, run by a highly regarded team who can't do enough for you. There's seating for every occasion, so you can have afternoon tea outside, lunch by the bar and dinner in the restaurant. Lunch ranges from sandwiches to a hearty three courses, while the evening menu displays some more ambitious choices such as Cornish sea bass with cockles and clams. Bedrooms are elegant, luxurious and provide every conceivable extra; and breakfast is definitely not to be missed.

Closing times
Closed 1-12 February

Prices
Meals: £ 15/20
and a la carte £ 22/28

9 rooms: £ 75/150

Typical Dishes

Smoked organic salmon

Stuffed saddle of West Country lamb

Dark chocolate marquise with hazelnut ice cream

Signed off B 3223 Dulverton to Exford road. Parking.

Tintinhull

72 **The Crown and Victoria Inn**

14 Farm St,
Tintinhull, BA22 8PZ
Tel.: (01935)823341 – Fax: (01935)825786
e-mail: info@thecrownandvictoria.co.uk
Website: www.thecrownandvictoria.co.uk

Butcombe - Doom Bar, Potholer, Yeovil - Cotleigh, Dartmoor and Cottage ales

This solid stone pub resembles a private house and in a former life, was the local school. It's located next to award winning National Trust gardens but manages to put on a good show itself, with an attractive weeping willow and mature trees on display in its spacious grounds. The owners are very keen and, since they previously ran a training company, only the best team will do – names of staff members and visitor numbers are even listed on the blackboards alongside their suppliers. Mark has a real interest in all things culinary and ensures the ingredients that they source are local, organic and ethically produced. Cooking has an honest, classical base and everything is fresh, tasty and largely homemade. Bedrooms are cosy and welcoming.

Closing times
Closed Sunday dinner

Prices
Meals: a la carte £ 20/30
5 rooms: £ 75/95

Typical Dishes
Black pudding with foie gras
Duck with Madeira sauce
Rhubarb galette & panna cotta ice cream

5 mi northwest of Yeovil by A 37. Parking.

73 The Rising Sun Inn

West Bagborough,
TA4 3EF
Tel.: (01823)432575
e-mail: jon@risingsuninn.info
Website: www.risingsuninn.info

 **Exmoor Ale, Butcombe, Proper Job**

Having previously survived a fire that raged through the surrounding hillside, the future of this inn was once again in the hands of the gods when it went into receivership. Its prospects were secured, however, when white knights appeared in the form of Jon and Christine Brinkman, an ambitious, experienced couple with no fear of hard work and dedication; who, in just a few months, turned the place around. On the menu you'll find a good balance of traditional and modern dishes, each one crafted from local ingredients and presented with an obvious element of care. A seamless mix of wood and slate creates a warm, intimate atmosphere and you rest assured that with this couple at the helm, the Sun will continue to rise more brightly every day.

Closing times
Closed Sunday dinner and Monday from September until April

Prices
Meals: a la carte £ 20/30

Typical Dishes
Scallops with garlic & cheddar crust
Belly pork & cider sauce
Sticky toffee pudding

10.5 mi northwest of Taunton off A 358. Parking in the road.

Winsford

74 **The Royal Oak Inn**

Exmoor National Park,
Winsford, TA24 7JE
Tel.: (01643)851455
e-mail: enquiries@royaloakexmoor.co.uk
Website: www.royaloakexmoor.co.uk

   AE

Exmoor Ale, Exmoor Gold, Exmoor Stag

Close to where the Winn Brook ford flows over a winding country lane in Exmoor National Park you'll find the picturesque village of Winsford and the equally delightful Royal Oak. A thatched 12C building full of rustic charm, it was a farmhouse and dairy before finding its calling as a country pub. In tune with its surroundings, the cooking uses local, seasonal produce and everything from the bread to the ice cream is homemade. Dishes are predominantly British and arrive exactly as described. Open to residents during the week (upon request) and to visitors at weekends, the adjacent restaurant steps things up a gear at dinner. Smart bedrooms offer four-poster, queen or king size beds and come with homemade biscuits and jet powered showers.

Closing times
Open daily

Prices
Meals: £ 25 (dinner) and a la carte £ 18/28

8 rooms: £ 70/150

Typical Dishes
Devilled kidneys
Braised lamb suet pudding
Wild berry Eton mess

5 mi north of Dulverton by B 3223; opposite the village green. Parking.

76 **The Royal Oak**

Cues Ln,
Bishopstone, SN6 8PP
Tel.: (01793)790481
e-mail: royaloak@helenbrowningorganics.co.uk
Website: www.royaloakbishopstone.co.uk

 **Arkell's Real Ales, Donnington**

At the rurally set Royal Oak, where the décor is rustic and open fires create a relaxing feel, they assert that 'great food starts off with good farming' and they're not wrong. Of course, it helps that the nearby organic farm which supplies it is owned by Helen Browning, who also owns the pub. The menu changes twice daily, according to which ingredients are fresh, local and in season; these might include berries or nettles foraged from the local hedgerows; veal, pork or beef from the farm, and vegetables provided by local growers in exchange for dinner vouchers. Less local are ingredients like cannelloni beans and unfiltered extra virgin olive oil; these come from the Abruzzo region of Italy, courtesy of the chef, who has a house there.

Closing times
Open daily

Prices
Meals: a la carte £ 22/32

Typical Dishes
Crab & tomato tart
Organic pork tenderloin & mash
Chocolate soup

 *6 mi east by A 4312 off A 420. Parking.*

77 **The Northey**

Bath Rd,
Box, SN13 8AE
Tel.: (01225)742333 – Fax: (01225)742333
e-mail: office@ohhcompany.co.uk
Website: www.ohhcompany.co.uk

Wadworth 6X and seasonally changing guest ales

Having passed from one generation of Warburtons to the next, this traditional-looking coaching inn is a real family affair. It's a sizeable place, with an open-plan interior and fairly modern styling: the bar boasting low level seating and vivid artwork; the large rear dining room, heavy wooden furniture and a more formal feel. The chef has extensive experience cooking in pubs countrywide, so you can rest assured that the appealing monthly menus are as good as they sound, if not better. Dishes are unfussy, seasonal and British, and everything is made on the premises, including the bread. There are always some tasty local steaks to be found and, with seafood arriving fresh from Cornwall, fish dishes – particularly the mussels – are a strength.

Closing times
Open daily

Prices
Meals: £ 16 (lunch) and a la carte £ 24/32

 *4.75 mi from Bath on A 4. Parking.*

78 **The Ship Inn**

Burcombe Ln,
Burcombe, SP2 0EJ
Tel.: (01722)743182
e-mail: theshipburcombe@mail.com
Website: www.theshipburcombe.co.uk

Wadworth 6X, Ringwood Best and Butcombe Bitter

If you find yourself anywhere near the delightful village of Burcombe on a sunny summer's day, be sure to make your way to this charming 17C pub. Its riverside garden is just the place to linger over a leisurely lunch, with only the wind in the trees and the quack of the local ducks to disturb the silence. If you arrived too late to nab a table, then head inside; with its open fire, low oak beams and chunky wood furniture, the pub itself is an equally enchanting place to dine. The seasonal menu offers honest portions of traditional dishes; perhaps pan-fried pigeon breast, homemade fishcakes, pot-roasted lamb shank or smoked fish kedgeree. Lunch bites offer a lighter alternative and the twice-daily changing specials board adds interest.

Closing times
Open daily
Prices
Meals: a la carte £ 23/31

Typical Dishes
Beer-battered herring roe
Pork belly & sage mash
Lemon & ginger crunch

5.25 mi west of Salisbury by A 36 off A 30. Parking.

79 **The Red Lion**

74 High St,
Cricklade, SN6 6DD
Tel.: (01793)750776
e-mail: info@redlioncricklade.co.uk

Wadworth 6X, Moles Best, Bath Spa

Just off the Thames path, you'll find this immensely charming 17C inn. With a cosy, low-beamed interior crammed full of bric-a-brac, it looks like a proper pub; and pleasingly, it adopts a good old English attitude too. The bar serves 4 regular and 5 guest ales, as well as 30 speciality bottled beers, which can be sampled while tucking into a pub classic, dog at feet. Next door is a small but airy stone-walled dining room boasting a beautiful carved slab. Here you'll find classical dishes such as oysters, venison stew and treacle tart, with beer recommendations for every dish. Produce is fresh and extremely local – and if you're down a pound or two, they'll accept some home-grown fruit or veg as payment. Comfy bedrooms are in the old stables.

Closing times
Closed Monday
booking essential

Prices
Meals: £ 15/20
and a la carte £ 18/31

5 rooms: £ 75

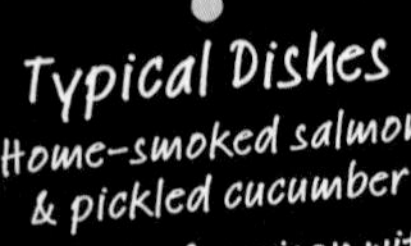

Typical Dishes
Home-smoked salmon & pickled cucumber
Haunch of venison with garlic mash
Treacle tart & clotted cream

6 mi northwest by A419. On street parking.

80 Bath Arms

Clay St,
Crockerton, BA12 8AJ
Tel.: (01985)212262 – Fax: (01985)218670
e-mail: batharms@aol.com
Website: www.batharmscrockerton.co.uk

VISA MC

Porter's Ale, Crockerton Classic, Cornish Coaster

The Bath Arms offers a warm welcome, open fires and plenty of country appeal, with a wealth of outdoor space. It is situated on the Longleat Estate and is run by local boy Dean Carr – originally from Warminster – who returned from his culinary experiences in the Big Smoke to put some love back into this community pub. Dishes such as roast scallops with carrot and spicy sultanas or fillet of halibut with asparagus, green beans and pancetta bring a touch of modernity to the menu. The favourites – like the popular fishcakes or the sticky beef – as well as the grills and the snacks keep it practical, while traditional desserts like bread and butter pudding or mixed berry pavlova round things off nicely. Ultra-spacious, contemporary bedrooms.

Closing times
Open daily

Prices
Meals: a la carte £ 17/26
2 rooms: £ 80/95

Typical Dishes
Roast scallops with minted carrots
Sticky beef & red cabbage
Lemon curd cheesecake

2 mi south of Warminster by A 350 on Shear Water rd. Parking.

81 **The Potting Shed**

The Street,
Crudwell, SN16 9EW
Tel.: (01666)577833
e-mail: bookings@thepottingshedpub.com
Website: www.thepottingshedpub.com

Timothy Taylor's Landlord, Bath Ales Gem, Butcombe Best

Despite its contemporary name and décor, The Potting Shed is very much a proper pub, where locals gather for a pint and a chat. Situated opposite its sister establishment, the Rectory Hotel, it consists of five spacious, light-filled rooms, with open fires and a relaxing feel. The pub's large gardens provide it with an abundance of fresh, seasonal herbs and vegetables – and the horticultural theme continues inside, with trowel door knobs, wheelbarrow lights and fork and spade bar pump handles. Monthly changing menus offer fresh, satisfying dishes like local trout, wild rabbit fettuccine and apple and blackberry crumble. Lollipops on the bar ensure that the kids are kept happy, while dog biscuits do the same for your four-legged friends.

Closing times
Open daily

Prices
Meals: a la carte £ 24/29

Typical Dishes
Cockle & mussel chowder with tempura fritters
Daube of beef & wild mushrooms
Sticky toffee pudding

4 mi north of Malmesbury by A 429. Parking.

82 Forester Inn

Lower St,
Donhead St Andrew, SP7 9EE
Tel.: (01747)828038
Website: www.theforesterdonheadstandrews.co.uk

VISA MC AE D

Butcombe, Otter and Butts ales

Set down narrow lanes in a delightful Wiltshire village, this 13C thatched pub has a gloriously rustic feel. Exposed stone walls feature throughout and vast open fires ensure that it's always cosy. There's a lovely bar crammed with cookery books and two main dining areas – one in a cleverly added extension that's perfectly in keeping. A fine French butcher's block houses the menus, which display a strong seafood base: the constantly changing fish selection originates from the Brixham day boats and there's a daily 3 course menu dedicated to seafood. The owner is passionate about Spain so you'll find plenty of charcuterie and tapas-based dishes in the bar. Puddings are truly warming and the homemade gin and tonic sorbet is well worth a try.

Closing times
Closed Sunday dinner

Prices
Meals: £ 18 and a la carte £ 20/30

Typical Dishes
Crab soup
Fritto misto of Cornish fish
Apple tarte Tatin

5 mi east of Shaftesbury by A 30. Parking.

East Chisenbury

83 **Red Lion Freehouse**

East Chisenbury,
SN9 6AQ
Tel.: (01980)671124 – Fax: (01980)671136
e-mail: enquiries@redlionfreehouse.com
Website: www.redlionfreehouse.com

VISA

No real ales offered

Enthusiastically run, cosy, and proudly impervious to the modern trend for designer pubs, the Red Lion is a charming thatched property with a pretty little garden, set in a tiny hamlet on the edge of Salisbury Plain. Seven simple wooden tables are set around the bar, a wood burner crouches in the inglenook and exposed beams lend a reassuringly solid air. Dishes are pleasingly down-to-earth – yet precisely composed and packed with flavour. There's a great value lunch menu, a roast on Sundays and a daily changing, seasonal à la carte whose dishes might include ox cheek croquettes, wild boar terrine, coq au vin or roast partridge. The resident Springer Spaniel often welcomes you with a wag or six of his tail and service is equally convivial.

Closing times
Closed 2 weeks January, Sunday dinner and Monday
booking advisable

Prices
Meals: £ 15 (weekday lunch) and a la carte £ 25/35

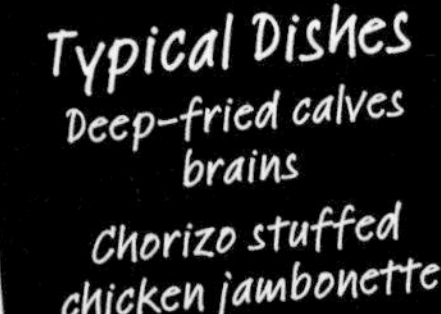

Typical Dishes
Deep-fried calves brains
Chorizo stuffed chicken jambonette
Yoghurt tapioca & roasted pineapple

The Village is between Pewsey and Amesbury off the A345. Parking.

84 The Angel Inn

High St,
Heytesbury, BA12 0ED
Tel.: (01985)840330
e-mail: admin@angelheytesbury.co.uk
Website: www.theangelheytesbury.co.uk

6X, Moorland and Greene King IPA

This pretty looking pub has a typically English feel, its spacious bar home to wood fires and comfy sofas and its beamed dining room packed with locals discussing the shoot and the beer, dogs by their sides. Two further dining areas have a more formal feel; exposed brickwork and open fires adding an air of rusticity. Menus change as and when, depending on what produce is freshly available; maybe a rich homemade cauliflower soup or a salmon and cod fishcake to start, followed by a four-bone rack of lamb or pork tenderloin with cider gravy. Steaks are a speciality, the Camembert for two to share is fast becoming a favourite, and simple pub classics include the ever popular ham, egg and chunky chips. Bedrooms are not currently recommendable.

Closing times
Closed Sunday dinner

Prices
Meals: a la carte £ 16/30

4 mi southeast of Warminster on A36. Parking.

85 **The Lamb Inn**

High St,
Hindon, SP3 6DP
Tel.: (01747)820573 – Fax: (01747)820605
e-mail: info@lambathindon.co.uk
Website: www.lambathindon.co.uk

VISA MC AE

Young's Ordinary, St Austell Tribute

The Lamb is all you'd expect from a 13C inn in the middle of a busy market town; a cosy, characterful collection of bars and dining rooms featuring heavy beams, flag floors, inglenook fireplaces and antique furniture. There's a Scottish theme throughout, so expect a plethora of plaid and tartan to go with the deep red walls and the impressive selection of malt whisky. Extensive menus continue where the décor leaves off, with dishes like pickled Orkney herrings, Macsween haggis and oak-smoked salmon. These sit alongside local dishes like 21-day matured Stourhead farm beef, Wiltshire rarebit and the famous Boisdale burger plus there are a few Mediterranean specials like moules marinière or risotto. Smart bedrooms; some with four-posters.

Closing times
Open daily

Prices
Meals: a la carte £ 19/29

19 rooms: £ 50/115

Typical Dishes
Dunkeld oak smoked salmon
Pork shoulder with spiced apple relish
Citrus posset

12 mi west of Wilton by A 30 on B 3089. Parking.

86 The Tollgate Inn

Ham Grn,
Holt, BA14 6PX
Tel.: (01225)782326 – Fax: (01225)782805
e-mail: alison@tollgateholt.co.uk
Website: www.tollgateholt.co.uk

   MC

Sharp's Doom Bar, Moles of Melksham, Tunnel Vision and Three Castles of Pewsey

The Tollgate Inn dates back to the 16C and is very much part of the local community. The comfy seats in its delightfully cosy fire-lit bar are made for curling up in – so don't be surprised to find that one of the pub's cats has beaten you to it. Eat in the more traditional downstairs dining room or upstairs in the former chapel; come summer, the pleasant garden is the only place to be. The daily changing menu focuses on local produce and could include steamed Cornish mussels, confit of duck leg or the ever popular beef Wellington. Puddings might be of the rice or sticky toffee varieties, there's plenty of homemade ice cream; and chutneys and jams are for sale on the bar. Four comfortable bedrooms are named after the aforementioned felines.

Closing times
Closed 25 December, 1 January, Sunday dinner and Monday
booking essential

Prices
Meals: £ 15/20
and a la carte £ 20/30
4 rooms: £ 50/100

Midway between Bradford-on-Avon and Melksham on B 3107. Parking.

87 The Bath Arms

Longleat,
Horningsham, BA12 7LY
Tel.: (01985)844308 – Fax: (01985)845187
e-mail: enquiries@batharms.co.uk
Website: www.batharms.co.uk

Inspectors' favourites

Horningsham Pride, Spotted Pig Bitter and fortnightly changing guest ale including Golden Apostle

This pub is found within the Longleat estate and boasts a rustic, dog-friendly bar with an open fireplace, a grand main dining room and a delightful terrace, witness to some impressive sunsets. Appealing menus offer everything from light dishes, salads and sandwiches through to main courses like stuffed saddle of rabbit or braised shoulder of lamb. The sharing plate is popular and the fishcakes are a veritable institution. Much of the produce comes from the estate – game, specialist cheeses and even flavoured organic vodkas – they rear pigs and even have their own vegetable garden. Staff clearly enjoy their work and are willing to go the extra mile for their customers. Quirky, individually themed bedrooms offer good levels of comfort.

Closing times
Open daily
Prices
Meals: £ 15/30
15 rooms: £ 85/150

Typical Dishes
Smoked mackerel with orange jelly
Horningsham chicken & wild garlic
Rhubarb jelly & custard

3 mi southwest of Warminster by A 362 and minor road. Parking.

88 **The Somerset Arms**

Church St,
Maiden Bradley, BA12 7HW
Tel.: (01985)844207
e-mail: lisa@thesomersetarms.co.uk
Website: www.thesomersetarms.co.uk

  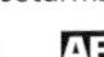 AE

 **Wadworth 6X and Henry's Original IPA**

Henry the Great Dane provides a larger-than-life greeting and, once ensconced in the open-fired lounge, with its quirky bookshelf wallpaper, mirrors and retro light shades, you'll find the chatty local staff just as hospitable. Dishes on the oft-changing menu might include smoked salmon mousse, confit duck or roasted monkfish. Steaks are a speciality and cooking is hearty, rustic and full of flavour. Wherever possible, produce comes from within a 30 mile radius; eggs come courtesy of their own hens, and some of the vegetables and herbs are grown in the garden. Events like quiz evenings, steak nights and artisan markets pull in the regulars, while visitors will appreciate the contemporary bedrooms, one of which features a free-standing bath.

Closing times
Closed Sunday dinner and Monday; restricted opening in January

Prices
Meals: a la carte £ 16/35

5 rooms: £ 80/120

 *5 mi south of Frome by A 361 and on B 3092. Parking.*

England • South West • Wiltshire

89 The Old Spotted Cow

The Street,
Marston Meysey, SN6 6LQ
Tel.: (01285)810264 – Fax: (01285)810899
e-mail: anna@theoldspottedcow.co.uk
Website: www.theoldspottedcow.co.uk

  AE

 **Mole Trap, Butcombe, White Horse**

With its sheep and chickens, and looking for all the world like somebody's private farmhouse, this pub sits firmly in the country dining league. Once neglected but now lovingly restored, it is enthusiastically run by Anna Langley and provides a proper pub for locals with plenty of real ales to accompany the honest, rustic, seasonal cooking. Dishes range from pub classics like devilled whitebait to the more unusual roasted Pollock and chorizo or spicy grilled pork belly; a good combination of British sustenance and worldly spices that find their influences in Anna's grandmother's Lancastrian recipes and her own upbringing in Kenya. Popular events include Sunday roasts, barbecues and monthly spice nights. One comfortable, contemporary bedroom.

Closing times
Closed Monday except bank holidays

Prices
Meals: a la carte £ 18/25

1 room: £ 70/90

 *Between Fairford and Cricklade. Parking.*

90 The Wheatsheaf at Oaksey

Wheatsheaf Ln,
Oaksey, SN16 9TB
Tel.: (01666)577348
e-mail: info@thewheatsheafatoaksey.co.uk
Website: www.thewheatsheafatoaksey.co.uk

Sharp's Doom Bar, Butcombe Bitter, Goffs' Jouster

The Wheatsheaf is very much a community pub, patronised by locals – the chef-owner and his son even cook lunch for the village school twice a week. With its vast open fireplace, low leather sofas and selection of magazines, the bar is the best place to sit. The rear dining room is the more modern alternative and the fuchsia pink snug is perfect for smaller parties. The blackboard menu changes according to what's fresh in; dishes might include shepherd's pie, or Gloucester Old Spot sausage and mash, with mature local steaks and salmon smoked in-house. The experienced chef spent several years working in Thailand, so expect to see the occasional Asian dish too. There are lighter offerings at lunchtime and appealing nursery puddings.

Closing times
Closed Sunday dinner and Monday

Prices
Meals: a la carte £ 20/35

Typical Dishes
Smoked salmon salad
Longhorn beef & ox tongue pudding
Hazelnut cream

5.5 mi north of Malmesbury; signed from A 429. Parking.

Ramsbury

91 **The Bell**

The Square,
Ramsbury, SN8 2PE
Tel.: (01672)520230 – Fax: (01672)520832
e-mail: jeremy@thebellramsbury.com
Website: www.thebellramsbury.com

 **Ramsbury Brewery: Bell Bitter, Ramsbury Gold**

This Victorian pub takes up a prominent position within the village of Ramsbury and since being spruced up by its new owners in 2007, has gone from strength to strength. Head past the bar, around the odd dog or two and you'll find yourself amongst plump, cosy sofas, where you can sit and study the constantly evolving menus. The à la carte offers classic pub dishes with the odd modern touch and a section dedicated solely to tempting, locally sourced steaks; there's also a slightly simpler set menu for those working to a budget. The atmospheric bar is the perfect place to dine, but if you prefer things a little quieter head for the pleasant restaurant. Couple good food with charming, honest service and the Bell definitely strikes the right note.

Closing times
Closed 25 December, dinner Sunday and bank holiday

Prices
Meals: £ 15/20
and a la carte £ 22/30

4 mi northwest of Hungerford by B 4192 and minor road west. Parking.

92 The George & Dragon

High St,
Rowde, SN10 2PN
Tel.: (01380)723053
e-mail: thegandd@tiscali.co.uk
Website: www.thegeorgeanddragonrowde.co.uk

Butcombe, Fuller's London Pride and Sharp's Doom Bar

This 16C coaching inn has a rustic feel throughout, its cosy inner boasting solid stone floors, wooden beams and open fires. There's a strong emphasis on seafood, with fish delivered daily from Cornwall to ensure it arrives on your plate in tip-top condition. That the menu is written anew each day also speaks volumes about the pub's take on food; seafood dishes could be a plate of fishy hors d'oeuvres, pan-fried cod with bacon or a whole grilled lemon sole; more meaty choices might include rack of lamb or roast fillet of beef. Some dishes come in two sizes and can be taken as either a starter or a main course. There is also a good value set three course menu. Old-world charm meets modern facilities in the individually designed bedrooms.

Closing times
Closed Sunday dinner
booking essential

Prices
Meals: £ 18 (lunch)
and a la carte £ 25/40

3 rooms: £ 55/75

2 mi northwest of Devizes by A 361 on A 342. Parking.

93 **The Beckford Arms**

Fonthill Gifford,
Tisbury, SP3 6PX
Tel.: (01747)870385
e-mail: info@beckfordarms.com
Website: www.beckfordarms.com

Keystone Large One, Butcombe and Milestone Lion's Pride

Set next to the 10,000 acre Fonthill Estate, this sizeable pub fits perfectly with the area, arranging fishing and shooting trips, offering picnic hampers and even providing a dog bath. Once here, you may find it hard to tear yourself away; there's a large garden with hammocks, a petanque pitch and a truly delightful terrace; as well as a cosy bar and a dining room with polished tables. In the former, if you're lucky, a chicken or suckling pig will be turning on the spit above the fire and bacon will be smoking in the chimney. The à la carte offers classical, country-led dishes, weekdays, afternoon tea and Saturdays, brunch. Enjoy them in front of a big screen movie on Sundays, then retire to a small but pleasant, modern designer bedroom.

Closing times
Open daily
booking advisable

Prices
Meals: a la carte £ 19/28
8 rooms: £ 70/90

Typical Dishes
Duck hearts on toast
Chargrilled onglet & mash
Hot chocolate pudding with pistachio ice cream

6 mi northeast of Shaftesbury by A 350 and Greenwich Rd.
Parking

94 **King John Inn**

Tollard Royal,
SP5 5PS
Tel.: (01725)516207 – Fax: (01725)553019
e-mail: info@kingjohninn.co.uk
Website: www.kingjohninn.co.uk

 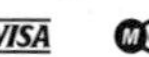

 **Ringwood's Best, Sixpenny Brewery and Timothy Taylor Landlord**

The owner's interior design background helped take this red-brick Victorian pub from derelict to delicious; now it's all open-plan and open fires, with quarry tiled floors, scrubbed wooden tables and beautiful black and white hunting photos. The daily changing, classically based menu offers unfussy dishes like Welsh rarebit, pigeon breast wrapped in bacon or twice-baked cheese soufflé; local produce is prevalent, with game a speciality in season. Service ranges from friendly to forgetful – although Bumble Bee the Border Terrier evens the balance, attentive to regulars and visitors alike. Stylish, comfortable bedrooms blend antique furniture with modern facilities like flat screens; there's freshly baked bread for sale and a wine shop too.

Closing times
Open daily

Prices
Meals: a la carte £ 20/40
8 rooms: £ 100/150

5 mi southeast on B 3081. Parking.

95 **The Bridge Inn**

Upper Woodford,
SP4 6NU
Tel.: (01722)782323
e-mail: enquiries@thebridgewoodford.co.uk
Website: www.thebridgewoodford.co.uk

Summer Lightning, Wadworths 6X, Ringwood Best

Situated in the Woodford Valley, a few miles south of Stonehenge, the aptly named Bridge Inn stands on the banks of the Avon overlooking the river crossing; its garden, with picnic tables from which to watch the swans and ducks, an al fresco diner's delight. The pub is modern, with a light, airy feel. Its relaxed atmosphere means that locals with dogs rub shoulders with diners and you can peek through the glass windows to see the chefs hard at work in the kitchen. Lunch sees a light bites menu of interesting sandwiches, while the à la carte offers dishes such as fishcakes, pot-roasted lamb shank or the popular pork belly. This is the sister pub to The Ship Inn at Burcombe; get your hands on a loyalty card and you can reap the benefits of both.

Closing times
Closed Sunday dinner
January-February

Prices
Meals: a la carte £ 23/31

Typical Dishes
Scallops with pea purée & black pudding
Asparagus, spinach, courgette & parmesan torte
Hot chocolate fondant

North of Salisbury off A 360; follow signs for The Woodfords. Parking.

96 **The Angel Inn**

Upton Scudamore,
BA12 0AG
Tel.: (01985)213225 – Fax: (01985)218182
e-mail: mail@theangelinn.co.uk
Website: www.theangelinn.co.uk

VISA

Wadworth 6X, Butcombe and one local guest beer

It may be the dependable village local, but things have moved on at The Angel Inn. True, it looks the same from the outside, but inside it's been flipped back-to-front and the bar's been moved from the upper to the lower level. There's no need to panic though – the large dining room still has a pleasant, cottage-like feel, while the lovely garden and terrace are as appealing as ever, providing a wonderful suntrap. Menus are fairly formal and not your typical pub grub; you might find home-cured gravadlax, roasted venison steak or salt-cured duck breast, with plenty of specials – usually fish – on the board. Lunch offers a good value set menu and puddings are of the good old-fashioned variety. Individually themed bedrooms are cosy and well-kept.

Closing times
Open daily

Prices
Meals: a la carte £ 15/30
10 rooms: £ 80/85

Typical Dishes

Terrine of duck confit with brioche

Fillet of beef with foie gras butter

Blueberry cheesecake

Village signed off A 350 to the north of Warminster. Parking.

The names Gas Street Basin, Custard Factory and Mailbox may not win any awards for exoticism, but these are the cutting edge quarters fuelling the rise of modern day Birmingham, at the heart of a region evolving from its grimy factory gate image. Even the Ironbridge Gorge, the cradle of the Industrial Revolution, is better known these days as a fascinatingly picturesque tourist attraction. The old urban landscapes dot a region of delightful unspoilt countryside with extensive areas of open moorland and hills, where stands Middle Earth, in the shape of Shropshire's iconic Wrekin hill, true inspiration of Tolkien. Shakespeare Country abounds in pretty villages, such as Henley-in-Arden, Shipston-on-Stour and Alcester, where redbrick, half-timbered and Georgian buildings capture the eye. Taste buds are catered for courtesy of a host of local specialities, not least fruits from the Vale of Evesham and mouth-watering meats from the hills near the renowned gastro town of Ludlow.

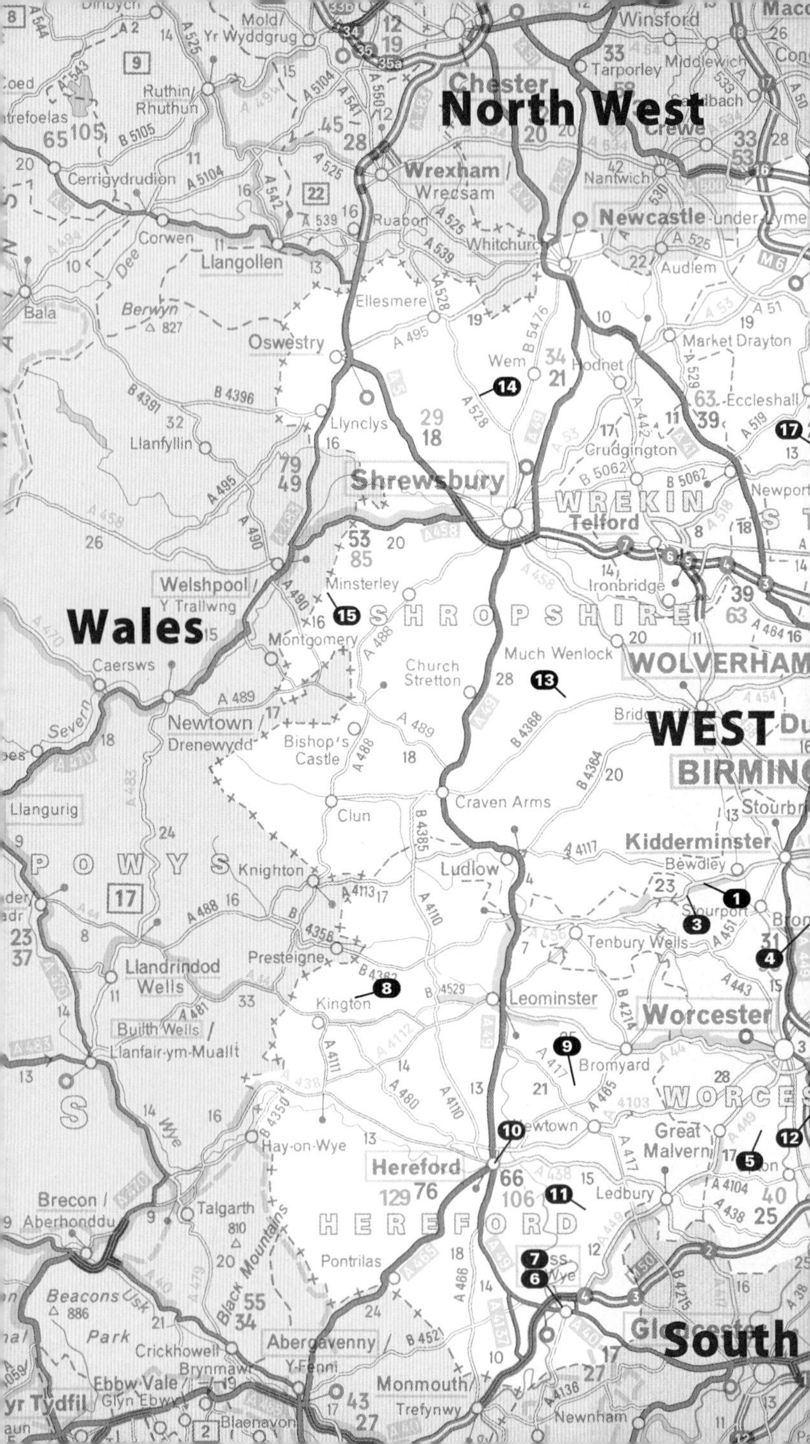
North West
Wales
WEST
South
Mold/
Yr Wyddgrug
Winsford
Tarporley
Middlewich
Chester
Ruthin/
Rhuthun
Crewe
Nantwich
Cerrigydrudion
Wrexham /
Wrecsam
Ruabon
Corwen
Llangollen
Whitchurch
Newcastle-under-Lyme
Audlem
Bala
Berwyn
Ellesmere
Market Drayton
Oswestry
Wem
Hodnet
Eccleshall
Llynclys
Llanfyllin
Crudgington
Shrewsbury
WREKIN
Telford
Newport
Welshpool /
Y Trallwng
Minsterley
Ironbridge
SHROPSHIRE
Montgomery
Much Wenlock
WOLVERHAM
Caersws
Church
Stretton
Newtown /
Drenewydd
Severn
Bishop's
Castle
BIRMING
Clun
Craven Arms
Llangurig
Stourbr
Kidderminster
POWYS
Knighton
Ludlow
Bewdley
Stourport
Tenbury Wells
Presteigne
Llandrindod
Wells
Kington
Leominster
Worcester
Builth Wells /
Llanfair-ym-Muallt
Bromyard
WORCES
Hay-on-Wye
Great
Malvern
Hereford
Brecon /
Aberhonddu
Talgarth
Ledbury
HEREFORD
Pontrilas
Black Mountains
Beacons
Park
Crickhowell
Brynmawr
Abergavenny /
Y-Fenni
Ebbw Vale /
Glyn Ebwy
Monmouth/
Trefynwy
Blaenavon
Newnham

East Midlands
MIDLANDS
West
South East
Baslow
Chesterfield
Bakewell
Chatsworth House
Park
Clay Cross
Hardwick Hall
Tuxford
Ollerton
Little Moreton Hall
Kidsgrove
Leek
Matlock
Alfreton
Mansfield
Newark-on-Trent
Sutton-in-Ashfield
DERBY
Ripley
Heanor
Southwell
Ashbourne
Belper
Hucknall
STOKE-ON-TRENT
Ilkeston
NOTTINGHAM
Stone
Uttoxeter
Derby
Bingham
West Bridgford
Sudbury
Long Eaton
Stafford
Abbots Bromley
Burton-upon-Trent
Rempstone
Rugeley
Swadlincote
Loughborough
Cannock
Ashby de la Zouche
Brownhills
Lichfield
Coalville
LEICESTER
Walsall
Tamworth
Sutton Coldfield
Atherstone
Hinckley
Oadby
Uppingham
Nuneaton
Market Harborough
Bedworth
Lutterworth
Halesowen
Solihull
COVENTRY
Husbands Bosworth
Rugby
Rothwell
Kenilworth
NORTHAM
WARWICK
Redditch
Henley
Royal Leamington Spa
Wellingborough
Droitwich
Warwick
Alcester
Southam
Daventry
Stratford-upon-Avon
Ettington
Pershore
Evesham
Towcester
Chipping Campden
Shipston-on-Stour
Banbury
Broadway
Wolverton
Moreton
Brackley
Milton Keynes
Tewkesbury
Winchcombe
Chipping Norton
Buckingham
Bletchley
Stow-on-the-Wold
Chelte
OXFORD
Bicester
BUCKINGHAM
Northleach
Woodstock
Burford
Blenheim Palace
Kidlington

1 **The Royal Forester**

Callow Hill,
DY14 9XW
Tel.: (01299)266286
e-mail: contact@royalforesterinn.co.uk
Website: www.royalforesterinn.co.uk

VISA MC AE

Timothy Taylor Landlord, Hobson's 'Best Bitter', Wye Valley 'HPA '

Dating back to 1411, The Royal Forester, in the Wyre Forest, is reputedly one of the oldest pubs in Worcestershire and, despite its modern feel, retains a rustic richness of character typified by the dining room's exposed stone walls. Cooking is flavourful, simple in style and reasonably priced, although side dishes can push the bill up. The informative, bi-monthly menu explains what's in season, with produce often supplied by regulars in exchange for dinner credits; perhaps some local venison, or honey from local beekeepers. The atmosphere is easy-going and those of a musical bent will be pleased to hear the tinkle of the grand piano in the bright bar. Food-themed bedrooms are fresh and modern; Aubergine, Pear and Cherry are the largest.

Closing times
Open daily

Prices
Meals: £ 13 and a la carte £ 20/36

7 rooms: £ 55/79

Typical Dishes

Pan-seared scallops with spiced cauliflower and curried lentils

Roast loin of venison with potato terrine and quince purée

Vanilla crème brûlée with Madeleine

3 mi southwest of Bewdley Parking.

2 Bell & Cross

Holy Cross,
Clent, DY9 9QL
Tel.: (01562)730319 – Fax: (01562)731733
Website: www.bellandcrossclent.co.uk

 **Kinver Edge, Enville Ale, Timothy Taylor Landlord**

Set down a maze of narrow lanes the Bell & Cross stands at what the locals call 'the old crossroads'. Colourful window boxes greet you at the front and round the back there's a spacious, well-kept lawn boasting lovely country views. The inside is made up of a series of rooms: the bar with its red leather banquettes and listed counter is particularly characterful. Football mementoes adorn the hall, harking back to the time when the owner cooked for the England football squad – but it's unlikely that they were given as much choice on their menus: there's sarnies, light bites and pub classics, with more substantial dishes being added at dinner; not forgetting a set menu and some blackboard specials too. Influences range from Asia to the Med.

Closing times
Closed 25 December, 26 December dinner and 31 December-1 January dinner

Prices
Meals: £ 17 (weekday lunch and Monday-Thursday dinner) and a la carte £ 18/27

Typical Dishes
White onion & Irish apple cider soup
Slow-cooked shoulder of Cornish lamb
Coconut ice pavlova

 *Between Stourbridge and Bromsgrove off northbound A 491; the pub is on the left hand side in Holy Cross. Parking.*

3

The Colliers Arms

Tenbury Rd,
Clows Top, DY14 9HA
Tel.: (01299)832242
e-mail: thecolliersarms@aol.com
Website: www.colliersarms.com

  MC

 **Hobson's Best Bitter, Bewdley Old School, Wye Valley Butty Bach, Three Tuns Cleric's Cure**

The owners may be young but they've settled in nicely and are running the place well. Keeping the locals happy is their main priority, so you'll find a pool table in the cosy bar area and regular quiz and theme nights taking place throughout the year. To the rear, a lovely terrace provides the perfect suntrap and, beyond this, you'll find the hens and vegetable garden that supply the pub. Cooking is unfussy but flavoursome, with a classical base – and dishes are usually brought to the table by the owners themselves. They bake their own bread and tasty homemade cookies, and nearly all produce comes from within 10 miles. Smaller suppliers are favoured and you'll often find them in the pub, personally sampling the dishes they contributed to.

Closing times
Closed Sunday dinner

Prices
Meals: £ 15 (dinner Monday-Thursday) and a la carte £ 15/20

Typical Dishes
Chicken, black pudding & tarragon terrine
King prawn & lobster bisque risotto
Banana tarte Tatin

 *9 mi west of Kidderminster by A 456. Parking.*

4 **The Chequers**

Kidderminster Rd,
Cutnall Green, WR9 0PJ
Tel.: (01299)851292 – Fax: (01299)851744
Website: www.chequerscutnallgreen.co.uk

Wye Valley HPA, Timothy Taylor Landlord and Sadler's Stumbling Badger

If football's your thing, then make for the 'Players Lounge' of this lightly washed roadside pub and sit among photos of the old England team while indulging in a spot of lunch – which may well have been cooked up by the former team chef. Despite the fact that rich burgundy colours and modern furnishings have been introduced, exposed beams and original quarry-tiled floors maintain a cosy, traditional feel throughout the place; while the shelves above the bar counter display a collection of timeless food items such as Colman's mustard and HP and Worcestershire Sauces. Menus are Asian-led but also offer a good selection of light bites and pub classics – while some more adventurous fish and offal-based specials are chalked up on the board.

Closing times
Closed 25 December, dinner 26 December and 1 January

Prices
Meals: a la carte £ 18/27

3 mi north of Droitwich Spa on A 442. Parking.

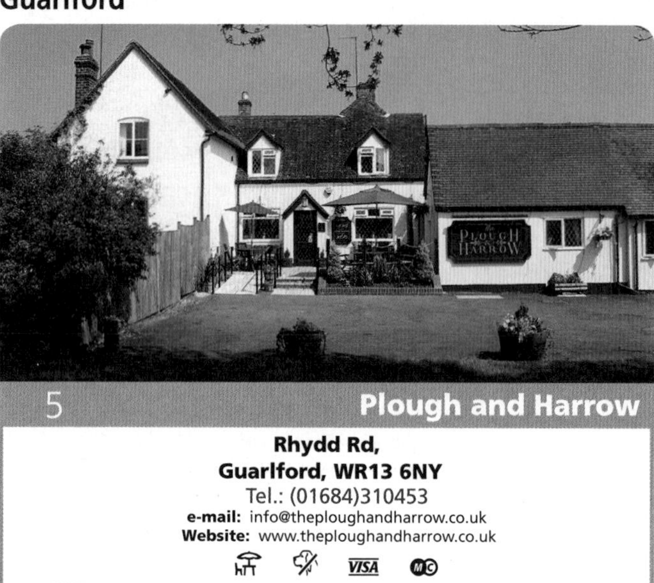

5 Plough and Harrow

Rhydd Rd,
Guarlford, WR13 6NY
Tel.: (01684)310453
e-mail: info@theploughandharrow.co.uk
Website: www.theploughandharrow.co.uk

VISA

Wadworth IPA and 6X

This white and yellow-washed pub may be off the beaten track but that doesn't stop the owners and their team from putting their hearts and souls into the place. There's a snug feel throughout, from the traditional dark wood bar with its blazing log fire to the more formal dining area in the old timbered skittle alley. Outside, a huge garden and field provide plenty of fruit and veg, which Michael cooks and Juliet brings to the table. Seasonality is key here, with menus often changing daily and local and ethical considerations playing their part. Lunch sees a light menu served throughout, with many dishes available in two sizes, while dinner offers a shorter à la carte (served only in the dining room) and simpler bar snacks during the week.

Closing times
Closed 25 December, 1 January, Sunday dinner and Monday

Prices
Meals: a la carte £ 20/30

Typical Dishes
Kipper pâté & toast
Shepherd's pie
Banana Eton mess

2 mi east of Great Malvern by B 4211. Parking.

6 The Lough Pool at Sellack

Sellack,
Ross-on-Wye, HR9 6LX
Tel.: (01989)730236 – Fax: (01981)570322
e-mail: david@loughpool.co.uk
Website: www.loughpool.co.uk

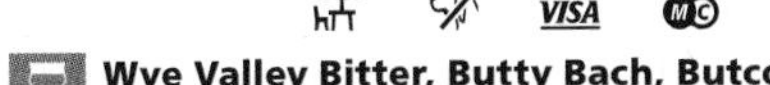

Wye Valley Bitter, Butty Bach, Butcombe Bitter, Sharp's Doom Bar and Adnams

This characterful black and white pub takes its name from the lake just across the road; legend has it that the former cottage became a pub in 1867 under the law passed by Duke of Wellington, whereby anyone who paid two guineas could turn their home into a public house. Inside it's still very traditional, with wooden beams, open fires and garlands of hops. Seasonally changing menus offer dishes with a mixture of British, Mediterranean and Asian influences; perhaps pork rillette or carpaccio of Herefordshire beef to start, followed by fillet of lemon sole or ravioli of root vegetables. In sourcing their ingredients, the pub fully supports local producers; a fact made obvious by the entire page devoted to crediting them on the menu.

Closing times
Closed 25 December, Easter, Sunday dinner and Monday except Bank Holidays

Prices
Meals: £ 16 (Sunday lunch) and a la carte £ 20/28

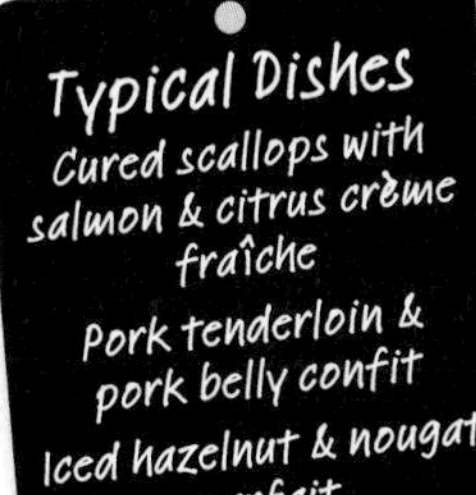

3.25 mi northwest of Ross-on-Wye; turn right off A 49 (Hereford) and follow signs for Hoarwithy. Parking.

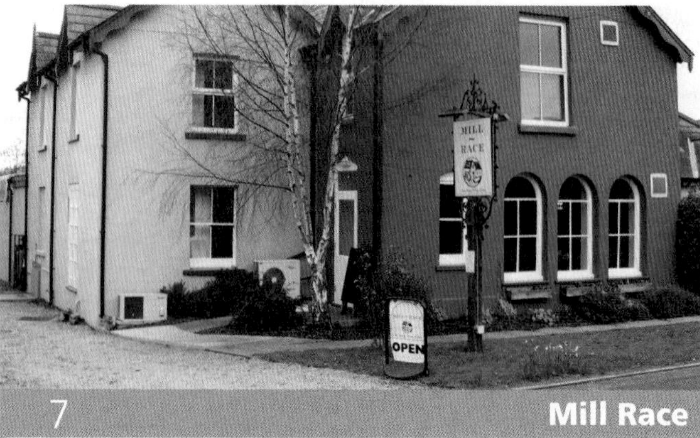

7 Mill Race

Walford,
Ross-on-Wye, HR9 5QS
Tel.: (01989)562891
e-mail: enquiries@millrace.info
Website: www.millrace.info

 **Wye Valley Ales and guest ales from Malvern Brewery and Wickwar Brewery**

This isn't the kind of place you expect to find in a small country village – but the locals aren't complaining. It looks nothing like a pub, either outside or in; save for the bar counter that is. You enter via a Gothic-style door and pass a board pinpointing their local suppliers. Straight ahead, the chefs are hard at work in the semi open-plan kitchen; follow it round and you'll find a community notice board and leaflets for nearby attractions. It really is the village local, so you'll find regulars standing around the bar and families out for the night in the darker, slate-floored areas. Cooking is fairly simple and lets the ingredients speak for themselves. The small team flit about, coping well when it's busy – which it usually is.

Closing times
Open daily

Prices
Meals: a la carte £ 18/30

 *4 mi south of Ross-on-Wye by B 4234. Parking.*

12 **The Inn at Stonehall**

Stonehall Common,
WR5 3QG
Tel.: (01905)820462
e-mail: info@theinnatstonehall.com
Website: www.theinnatstonehall.com

VISA

Malvern Brewery's Black Pear

Just 2 miles from the M5 lies the peaceful little hamlet of Stonehall Common and, at its heart, this smart, modern dining pub surrounded by a large garden and orchard. Offering lovely views over Evesham Vale towards Bredon Hill, it started life as 'The Fruiterers Arms', providing refreshment for the local fruit pickers, who harvested the now rare Worcestershire black pear – the inn being one of the few places to still have fruiting trees. At the front there's a comfy lounge where they serve light bites and beers from local artisan brewers; to the rear, an airy dining room that looks out over the terrace. Menus are simple and concise, featuring well-prepared, flavoursome dishes that follow the seasons, with desserts something of a speciality.

Closing times
Closed first week January, Sunday dinner and Monday

Prices
Meals: £ 15 (lunch) and a la carte £ 25/27

5.75 mi southeast of Worcester by A 38 and Norton rd. Parking.

8 **The Stagg Inn**

Titley,
HR5 3RL
Tel.: (01544)230221 – Fax: (01544)231390
e-mail: reservations@thestagg.co.uk
Website: www.thestagg.co.uk

Hobson's Best and Town Crier, Ludlow Best and Gold, Wye Valley Butty Bach

Situated at the meeting point of two former drovers roads, this characterful part-medieval, part-Victorian pub was once called 'The Balance', as it marked the point where farmers would stop to weight their wool. Inside, it's delightfully cosy – one room was once a butcher's shop and another still displays an old bread oven. Cooking is fittingly straightforward, relying on classically based recipes, careful preparation and top quality produce; they even raise their own pigs, ducks and geese, so you'll find homemade sausages, duck eggs and preserves for sale too. Menus are short, simple and to the point, while the dishes themselves are truly satisfying. Bedrooms in the pub are snug but can be noisy; opt for one in the nearby former vicarage.

Closing times

Closed 2 weeks between January and February, first 2 weeks in November, 25-26 December, 1 January, Sunday dinner and Monday

booking essential

Prices

Meals: a la carte £ 25/34

6 rooms: £ 70/130

Typical Dishes

Scallops on parsnip purée

Fillet of Herefordshire beef

3 crème brûlées

3.5 mi northeast of Kington on B 4355. Parking.

9 Three Crowns Inn

Bleak Acre,
Ullingswick, HR1 3JQ
Tel.: (01432)820279 – Fax: (08700)515338
e-mail: info@threecrownsinn.com
Website: www.threecrownsinn.com

 **Wye Valley, Butty Bach, Hobson's Best Bitter**

This part-timbered, red-brick inn boasts a rustic country interior with slate floors, warming open fires and hops hanging from the ceiling; as well as pretty flowery curtains hung at tiny windows and a collection of cookery books and food guides scattered around. Menus are concise, offering three choices per course Monday to Saturday lunchtime and four, daily changing choices per course in the evening. Dishes feature simple, classical combinations and you'll often see influences from the chef's North Eastern roots showing through, as well as some tasty fresh fish – a passion born from time spent working in Padstow with Rick Stein. Prices are unusually set per course. Upstairs, the spacious, modern bedroom boasts a huge free-standing bath.

Closing times
Closed 25-26 December and Monday

Prices
Meals: £ 15/27
1 room: £ 95

 *1.25 mi east of village on unsigned country lane. Parking.*

10 **The Wellington**

Wellington,
HR4 8AT
Tel.: (01432)830367
e-mail: info@wellingtonpub.co.uk
Website: www.wellingtonpub.co.uk

Hobson's Best, Wye Valley HPA and Butty Bach and one regularly changing guest ale

Who hasn't idly commented, whilst eating out, that they reckon they could do better? Rare is the person who actually does something about it, however. One exception is the chef-owner of The Wellington, who, before his monumental career change, used to work in PR. He's now at the helm of this bright and airy neighbourhood pub, where locals gather fireside in the spacious bar and all-comers enjoy flavourful dishes in the more formal conservatory dining room. Simple pub classics like fish and chips are chalked on a blackboard in the bar, while the daily changing à la carte offers choices like rabbit ravioli or slow roasted belly of Gloucester Old Spot pork, with desserts such as warm chocolate fondant pudding or rhubarb crème brûlée.

Closing times
Closed 25-26 December, Sunday dinner and Monday lunch

Prices
Meals: a la carte £ 24/30

5 mi north by A 49. In village centre. Parking.

11 **The Butchers Arms**

Woolhope,
HR1 4RF
Tel.: (01432)860281
e-mail: food@butchersarmswoolhope.co.uk
Website: www.butchersarmswoolhope.co.uk

 **Wye Valley Butty Bach, Hobsons Best Bitter, Three Tuns 1642**

Hidden away deep in the countryside, this half-timbered 16C inn boasts a characterful interior with open fires, wattle walls and beams slung so low you're forced to duck. Saws and pitchforks hang from the walls, while the pretty garden, with its babbling brook and weeping willow, offers delightful views over farmland. Chef-owner Stephen Bull was one of the pioneers of modern British cooking; expect the daily changing menu to offer simple sounding, classically based dishes like Goodrich Middle White sausages, mash and onion gravy or his speciality twice-baked soufflé – meticulously executed and full of flavour. A focus on regional produce means that lamb comes from over the road, fruit and veg from nearby farms and herbs from their own garden.

Closing times
Closed Sunday dinner and Monday except bank holidays

Prices
Meals: a la carte £ 19/29

 *9 mi north of Ross-on-Wye by A 449 and B 4224. Parking.*

England • West Midlands • Hereford and Worcester

13 The Feathers at Brockton

Brockton, Much Wenlock,
TF13 6JR
Tel.: (01746)785202
e-mail: feathersatbrockton@googlemail.com
Website: www.feathersatbrockton.co.uk

  MC

 **Hobson's Best, Woods Parish Ale**

This rustic 16C pub is situated on the edge of the village, in an area popular with walkers. Take your pick from four dining areas: all are snug with warm, homely décor, open fires and lots of stripped wood, exposed beams and thick stone walls. It's a personally run place and the atmosphere is relaxing and unpretentious, with the focus firmly on the food. Having learnt his trade in the Big Smoke, chef-owner Paul returned to Shropshire to open The Feathers back in 2004 – and his tasty cooking has been attracting customers ever since. Mainly traditional in style, with some Mediterranean influences, dishes make use of local produce and might include corn-fed chicken breast, shoulder of lamb or steak and ale pie. Comfortable, stylish bedrooms.

Closing times
Closed Monday and lunch Tuesday

Prices
Meals: £ 18 and a la carte £ 20/40

4 rooms: £ 50/75

Typical Dishes
Garlic king prawns
Slow-cooked lamb shoulder & leeks
Vanilla panna cotta & summer berries

 *5 mi southwest of Much Wenlock on B 4378. Parking.*

14 The Burlton Inn

Burlton,
SY4 5TB
Tel.: (01939)270284
e-mail: enquiries@burltoninn.com
Website: www.burltoninn.com

    AE

 **Robinson's Unicorn, Hartleys Cumbria Way and Dragon's Fire**

Set on a busy road in a small village between Ellesmere and Shrewsbury, this traditional 18C whitewashed inn welcomes you with a colourful flower display. Since the current owners took over it has undergone a transformation – most notably a terrace, fountain and landscaped garden have been added. It's a characterful place with exposed beams, tiled floors, scrubbed pine tables and some soft seating by a wood burning stove. To one side there's a dining area but you can eat throughout; although it can get busy in the bar with local drinkers, especially on a Friday. The straightforward lunch menu offers snacks and pub classics, while in the evening some more adventurous dishes appear too. Neat, wood-furnished bedrooms boast spacious bathrooms.

Closing times
Closed 25 December and Sunday dinner

Prices
Meals: a la carte £ 18/32
6 rooms: £ 85

 *8 mi north of Shrewsbury on A 528. Parking.*

15 **The Sun Inn**

Marton,
SY21 8JP
Tel.: (01938)561211
e-mail: suninnmarton@googlemail.com
Website: www.suninn.org.uk

  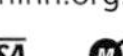 MC

 **Hobson's Best, Six Bells, Monty's Brewery and regularly changing guest ales**

A welcoming country pub on the English-Welsh border, The Sun Inn is a family affair, with father and son in the kitchen and their respective spouses looking after the customers out front. On one side of the counter is a cosy bar with a wood burning stove; here choices like fish and chips, steak and ale pie and homemade faggots are chalked up on a blackboard. On the other side is a brightly painted restaurant, with chunky pine tables. Here they offer a concise, regularly changing à la carte menu of classic dishes like salmon and prawn mousse, roast loin of local venison or slow-roast belly pork, supplemented by fresh fish boards in the summer. Darts, dominoes and regular events including themed food evenings and quiz nights bring in the locals.

Closing times
Closed Sunday dinner and Monday except bank holidays, and lunch Tuesday

Prices
Meals: a la carte £ 20/30

Typical Dishes
Tea-smoked chicken
Slow roast belly pork
Blueberry cheesecake

 *8.5 mi southeast of Welshpool on B 4386. Parking.*

16 The George

Alstonefield,
DE6 2FX
Tel.: (01335)310205
e-mail: emily@thegeorgeatalstonefield.com
Website: www.thegeorgeatalstonefield.com

Marston's Pedigree, Burton, Brakspear's Oxford Gold, Jennings Cumberland and Ringwood's Boondoggle

The moment you walk in The George, feel the warmth from the roaring fires and start to soak up the cosy, relaxed atmosphere, you just know that it's going to be good. A traditional pub set on the village green, it's simply furnished, with stone floors, scrubbed wooden tables and pictures of locals on the walls. The bubbly manager – the third generation of her family to have owned the pub – brings a woman's touch to the place, with the latest fashion mags for flicking through and candles and fresh flowers on every table. Like the décor, the food is simple but well done. The menus change daily according to the produce available; the team use local suppliers where possible and also grow some of their own vegetables in the garden.

Closing times
Closed 25 December

Prices
Meals: a la carte £ 19/39

7.5 mi north of Ashbourne by A 515. Parking.

Ranton

17 **Hand and Cleaver**

Butt Ln,
Ranton, ST18 9JZ
Tel.: (01785)822367
e-mail: cathy@handandcleaver.co.uk
Website: www.handandcleaver.co.uk

VISA MC AE

Cottage Brewing Company, Banks's and Salopian's Shropshire Gold

The Goltons had a good thing going with their first pub venture: the only problem was that once they'd got it running like clockwork, it was no longer a challenge; so they upped and left for a new one – enter the Hand and Cleaver. They had a battle on their hands from the start but that seems to be the way they like it and their determination is starting to paying off. It's a huge place, with a pleasant garden, a spacious lounge and a dining room with booths. The menu offers extensive choice, from tasty nibbles such as deep-fried cauliflower to classical dishes like stuffed lamb's heart or slow-braised rolled pork belly. Dishes are carefully crafted, arrive exactly as described and are truly satisfying. All wines are available by the glass.

Closing times
Closed Monday

Prices
Meals: a la carte £ 20/30

Typical Dishes
Pressed gammon & herb terrine
Fillet of Staffordshire beef, truffle jus
Malva pudding

5 mi west of Stafford by minor roads. Frankwell car park opposite.

18 The Baraset Barn

1 Pimlico Ln,
Alveston, CV37 7RJ
Tel.: (01789)295510
e-mail: barasetbarn@lovelypubs.co.uk
Website: www.barasetbarn.co.uk

Purity UBU

Set just outside the small village of Alveston, this red-brick pub started life over 200 years ago as a simple barn. It still displays original flagstone floors, exposed brickwork and wooden beams, but contemporary furnishings show it's come a long way from its roots. If the sun's out, there's plenty of room on the large decked terrace but there's lots of choice inside too. Start with a drink in the atmospheric lounge among shimmering fabrics and brushed velvet, before picking a spot in the airy conservatory or characterful main dining room. Good-sized menus offer something for everyone, ranging from sharing plates and 28-day aged Herefordshire beef, to daily fish specials and spit-roast of the day; maybe chicken, duck or even suckling pig.

Closing times
Closed Sunday dinner

Prices
Meals: £ 15 (Monday-Friday and early dinner) and a la carte £ 20/30

2 mi east of Stratford- upon- Avon on B 4086. Parking.

19 The Fox & Goose Inn

Front St,
Armscote, CV37 8DD
Tel.: (01608)682293 – Fax: (01608)682293
e-mail: mail@foxandgoosecountryinnarmscote.co.uk
Website: www.foxandgoosearmscote.co.uk

Hook Norton Bitter, Fullers London Pride, Marston's Pedigree and two weekly changing guest ales

This creeper-clad, red-brick inn is situated at the centre of a small village and boasts a pleasant little garden and decked terrace to the rear. Having started life as two cottages, it's equally compact inside, consisting of a locals' snug and an open-plan bar/restaurant with a cosy log burner at its centre. Menus are concise, offering straightforward, classically based dishes, which are supplemented by an extensive selection of daily blackboard specials. Cooking is flavoursome and uses good ingredients; in summer you might find whitebait and scallops, and in winter, comforting stews and casseroles. Quirky, individually styled bedrooms boast bold colour-themes, which are centred around Cluedo characters; claw-foot baths add an extra touch.

Closing times
Open daily

Prices
Meals: a la carte £ 15/50
4 rooms: £ 45/110

Typical Dishes
Rock oysters
Drunken duck marinated in juniper & vegetables
Sticky toffee pudding

2.5 mi north of Shipston-on-Stour by A 3400. Parking.

20 The King's Head

21 Bearley Rd,
Aston Cantlow, B95 6HY
Tel.: (01789)488242 – Fax: (01789)488137
e-mail: info@thekh.co.uk
Website: www.thekh.co.uk

 **Greene King Abbot, Purity Gold, Brew XI**

Set close to the Cotswolds, the picturesque village of Aston Cantlow is home to the 13C Norman church where, in 1557, Shakespeare's parents were married – and this ivy-clad, black and white inn is thought to have provided the setting for their wedding breakfast. Inside, the bar is everything you'd expect, with low beamed ceilings, flagged floors and an open log fire. Seasonal menus feature traditional dishes, with local meats and fish to the fore; choose from pub classics like pie of the week or more comprehensive dishes such as ballotine of chicken or seared fillet of sea bass. Regular duck suppers celebrate the pub's past, when during wartime rationing the landlord was unusually allowed to serve duck – as he reared his own out the back.

Closing times
Closed 25 December

Prices
Meals: £ 15 and a la carte £ 22/30

 *3 mi south of Henley-in-Arden off B 4089. Parking.*

21 The Chequers Inn

91 Banbury Rd,
Ettington, CV37 7SR
Tel.: (01789)740387
e-mail: hello@the-chequers-ettington.co.uk
Website: www.the-chequers-ettington.co.uk

 **Tetleys' Cask, Hooky Gold and JW Lees Bitter**

The signs outside scream country gastropub but to assume so would be off the mark; with its chandeliers, brushed velvet furniture and round-backed Regency chairs, this place is anything but formulaic. The bar is a popular spot with villagers, no doubt pleased with the large selection of beers as well as their local's transformation from run down boozer to smart, contemporary inn. Tasty dishes like grilled sea bass fillet with red lentil & coconut puree show the kitchen's ability to cleverly combine flavours; but be aware that dishes come exactly as described on the menu, so a side dish is generally required. Local ingredients are well used, from the Stratford sourced meat to the mustard from Tewkesbury. Friendly service completes the package.

Closing times
Closed Sunday dinner and Monday

Prices
Meals: a la carte £ 20/27

 *5.5 mi southeast of Stratford-upon-Avon by A 422. Parking.*

22 The Fox & Hounds Inn

Great Wolford,
CV36 5NQ
Tel.: (01608)674220
e-mail: info@thefoxandhoundsinn.com
Website: www.thefoxandhoundsinn.com

Hook Norton, Purity Ubu, Bass, Wye Valley and Cottage Brewing Co

This pub lies at the heart of a small village which, in turn, is nestled in the rolling Cotswold Hills. Built in 1540 from local stone, it's a traditional English country inn – small, cosy and characterful – with flagged floors, a large inglenook fireplace and hops hanging from low beamed ceilings. With the owner out front and her son in the kitchen, it's very much a family affair. Menus are chalked up on the board daily and feature largely rustic pub fare, alongside a few more modern, globally-influenced dishes. The chef is passionate about local produce, sourcing Chastleton beef, venison from Todenham and game from nearby shoots; while the bread, bacon and sausages are all made on-site. Simple, pine-furnished bedrooms offer country views.

Closing times
Closed 6-20 January for meals, Sunday dinner and Monday

Prices
Meals: a la carte £ 26/40
3 rooms: £ 50/80

Typical Dishes
Dexter beef Bresaola
Roe deer & cabbage
Rhubarb & ginger crumble

4 mi northeast of Moreton-in-Marsh by A 44. Parking.

23 The Halford Bridge

Fosse Way,
Halford, CV36 5BN
Tel.: (01789)740636 – Fax: (01789)748159
e-mail: su@thehalfordbridge.co.uk
Website: www.thehalfordbridge.co.uk

 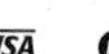 

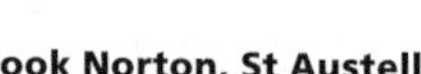

Hook Norton, St Austell's Tribute

This imposing stone building set on the Fosse Way dates from 1567, its wide central archway a reminder of its former life as a stop off point for coach and horses travelling the famous Roman road. Head right for the atmospheric bar and lounge with its ornately carved furniture, or left for the dining room; on sunny days, cross the cobbles to the enclosed courtyard. Classic combinations are given a personal twist on the seasonally changing menu, so your steak might come with stilton stuffed vine tomatoes or duck breast might be served on a mushroom and lentil ragout. Service from local staff is everything it should be: enthusiastic, chatty and well organised. Nuttily named bedrooms vary greatly in shape and size; most have wooden beams.

Closing times
Closed Sunday dinner

Prices
Meals: £ 14 (Monday-Thursday) and a la carte £ 21/28

10 rooms: £ 70/85

9 mi north of Moreton in Marsh by A 429. Parking.

24 The Howard Arms

Lower Green,
Ilmington, CV36 4LT
Tel.: (01608)682226 – Fax: (01608)682874
e-mail: info@howardarms.com
Website: www.howardarms.com

Old Hooky Hook Norton, Purity Brewing Co, Warwickshire Beer Company

This 400 year old Cotswold stone inn, set on a peaceful village green, is the very essence on an English country pub. Bright flower displays welcome you at the front, and round the back there's a small garden and terrace. Inside, you'll find the expected stone-faced walls, exposed beams, flagged floors and a huge inglenook fireplace, and a mix of chairs, pews and benches; there's also a raised-level dining room with a large dresser and fully laid dark wood tables. Blackboards are dotted about the place, displaying hearty dishes that are mainly British-based; you might find braised beef and ale pie or calves liver and bacon. Featuring antique furniture, the original bedrooms are warm and cosy; those in the extension are more contemporary.

Closing times
Open daily
Prices
Meals: a la carte £ 15/25
8 rooms: £ 90/145

Typical Dishes
Twice-baked Red Leicester cheese soufflé
Grilled lemon sole & garlic prawns
Chocolate mousse in a puff pastry case

4 mi northwest of Shipston-on-Stour, in the centre of the village. Parking.

25 **The Boot Inn**

Old Warwick Rd,
Lapworth, B94 6JU
Tel.: (01564)782464
e-mail: bootinn@hotmail.com
Website: www.lovelypubs.co.uk

London Pride, Old Speckled Hen, UBU

Whether you're hastening down the M40 or pottering along on a narrow boat, it's worth stopping off at this large, buzzy red-brick pub. Set close to the junction of the Grand Union and Stratford-upon-Avon canals, it draws in a mixed crowd – from the young to the old, businesspeople to pleasure seekers – and you may well wonder where they all come from. With its traditional quarry-floored bar, modern first floor restaurant and large terrace complete with barbeque, it's deservedly popular, so booking is a must. Dishes vary greatly, from bar snacks and burgers through to sharing plates and more sophisticated fish specials. The crispy oriental duck and the bubble and squeak are mainstays, as is the scallop dish, which changes slightly every day.

Closing times
Open daily
booking essential

Prices
Meals: a la carte £ 20/26

2 mi southeast of Hockley Heath on B 4439; on the left hand side just before the village. Parking.

26 **The Red Lion**

Long Compton,
CV36 5JS
Tel.: (01608)684221 – Fax: (01608)684968
e-mail: info@redlion-longcompton.co.uk
Website: www.redlion-longcompton.co.uk

Adnams Broadside, Hook Norton Hooky Gold, Hooky Bitter and Bass

With its flag floors and log fires, this 18C former coaching inn has the character of a country pub, and its stylish interior boasts a warm, modern feel. The seasonal menu offers classic pub dishes like homemade steak and Hook Norton pie, pan-fried calves liver or fish and chips, with old favourites like rhubarb crumble or warm chocolate fudge cake for dessert. These are tasty, home-cooked dishes from the tried-and-tested school of cooking – so if you're after something a little more adventurous, try the daily specials board instead. Staff are pleasant and smartly attired; Cocoa, the chocolate Labrador, also gives a warm welcome. Bedrooms may be slightly on the small side, but are stylish and contemporary, with a good level of facilities.

Closing times
Open daily

Prices
Meals: £ 15 (lunch and early dinner) and a la carte £ 23/35

5 rooms: £ 55/100

5 mi north of Chipping Norton by A 3400. Parking.

England • West Midlands • Warwickshire

Preston Bagot

27 **The Crabmill**

Claverdon,
Preston Bagot, B95 5EE
Tel.: (01926)843342
e-mail: thecrabmill@lovelypubs.co.uk
Website: www.thecrabmill.co.uk

 **Greene King Abbot Ale, IPA, Purity UBU, Tetleys**

This characterful timbered pub is the ideal place to kick-back and relax, whether you sit in the lawned garden, on the peaceful terrace or inside the pub itself. It's made up of various beamed snugs and lounges, which display a mix of traditional old wood furniture and contemporary leather chairs set at black wood tables. You can eat anywhere but if you're tucked away in a corner and it's busy – which it usually is – you may need to flag down one of the team to place your order. The good-sized à la carte offers modern Mediterranean-influenced dishes, with some lighter bites available until the early evening. Start with a tasty sharing plate and move onto one of the interesting main courses, maybe ostrich fillet wrapped in Serrano ham.

Closing times
Closed Sunday dinner
booking essential

Prices
Meals: a la carte £ 25/30

Typical Dishes
Beetroot & vodka cured salmon
Ostrich fillet & dauphinoise potatoes
Red wine poached pear with cinnamon mascarpone

 *1 mi east of Henley-in-Arden on A 4189. Parking.*

28

The Bell Inn

The Green,
Tanworth-in-Arden, B94 5AL
Tel.: (01564)742212
e-mail: thebell@realcoolbars.com
Website: www.thebellattanworthinarden.co.uk

   AE

Timothy Taylor Landlord and several rotating guest ales

Standing in the centre of an affluent village, next to a charming 13C church, The Bell Inn is a place of real contrasts. It's whitewashed exterior may appear traditional but inside, original beams and old wood floors are juxtaposed with bold décor and contemporary furnishings. Most of the pub is laid out with dark wood polished dining tables but there are a few comfy seats left around the bar for drinkers; in one corner there's a small shop and a counter acting as the village post office, which the bar staff also man. Cooking is surprisingly classical and most dishes are rooted in the traditional pub vein – fish is a particular strength and the theme nights and wine tasting evenings go down a storm. Bedrooms continue the stylish, modern theme.

Closing times
Open daily

Prices
Meals: a la carte £ 19/26

9 rooms: £ 41/122

4.5 mi northwest of Henley-in-Arden by A 3400 and Tanworth Road; close to church. Parking.

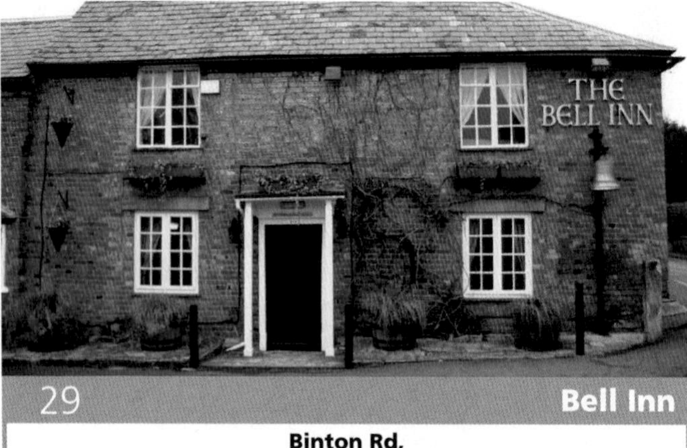

29 Bell Inn

Binton Rd,
Welford-on-Avon, CV37 8EB
Tel.: (01789)750353 – Fax: (01789)750893
e-mail: info@thebellwelford.co.uk
Website: www.thebellwelford.co.uk

  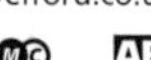 AE

Purity Gold & UBU, Hooky Bitter, Hobsons, Flowers Original (OB) and Well's Bombardier

Standing deep in the Warwickshire countryside and dating back over 300 years, this red-brick inn, with its attractive terrace, boasts its fair share of history – as Shakespeare is said to have met with fellow writers Drayton and Johnson here, shortly before his death. Inside, you'll find various snugs boasting wooden beams, flagstone floors and open fireplaces, as well as a glass-roofed dining room. Taking advantage of local produce, extensive menus display a real mix of dishes, which include at least three vegetarian options. You'll find traditional offerings, maybe beef and tomato casserole, alongside more adventurous dishes, like lemon sole stuffed with brie. Tuesdays see 'Fish and Chip Suppers' and Fridays offer a 'Taste of India' menu.

Closing times
Open daily

Prices
Meals: £ 16 (lunch)
and a la carte £ 20/27

4 mi west of Stratford-upon-Avon by B 439 and a lefthand turn south. Parking.

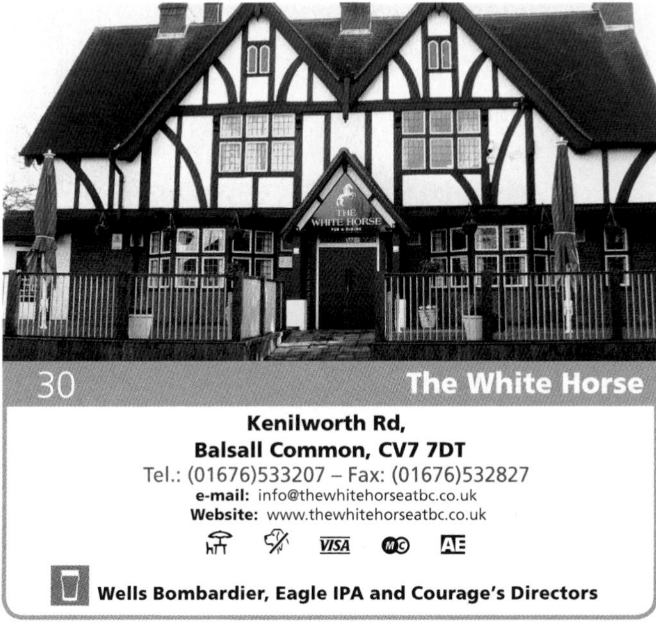

30 The White Horse

Kenilworth Rd,
Balsall Common, CV7 7DT
Tel.: (01676)533207 – Fax: (01676)532827
e-mail: info@thewhitehorseatbc.co.uk
Website: www.thewhitehorseatbc.co.uk

VISA MC AE

Wells Bombardier, Eagle IPA and Courage's Directors

It may be the village local, but this striking timbered building is far from your typical rustic country pub, having brought with it a touch of glamour from the town. It's a large place, with a decked terrace to the front and a sizeable paved dining area to the rear. Inside, you'll find a spacious modern lounge boasting low-backed leather chairs and an equally stylish L-shaped dining area that provides light relief from the bustle of the bar. Menus are easy-to-read and stick mainly to British pub classics, with dishes such as prawn cocktail or garlic field mushrooms, followed by spit-roast chicken or 21-day aged Hereford steaks. Some more Mediterranean influences can often be found in the way of rustic breads, charcuterie boards and risottos.

Closing times
Open daily

Prices
Meals: £ 13 (lunch)
and a la carte £ 22/28

5 mi northwest of Kenilworth by A 452. Parking.

Chadwick End

31 **The Orange Tree**

Warwick Rd,
Chadwick End, B93 0BN
Tel.: (01564)785364 – Fax: (01564)782988
e-mail: theorangetree@lovelypubs.co.uk
Website: www.lovelypubs.co.uk

 **Greene King IPA, Fullers London Pride and Purity Brewing UBU**

Set in a small but affluent village, The Orange Tree is a sizeable place – even without the neat lawned gardens and spacious terrace. Characterful country dining it is not – it's smart, contemporary and can get a tad on the loud side. The large bar is set over various levels, some with characterful wooden beams, all with comfy modern seating; and there's a dining room with chunky wood tables, low-backed chairs and leather banquettes. The same, wide-ranging menu is served throughout and offers something for everyone. You'll find several dishes in a choice of size, as well as salads, sharing plates, pizzas, pastas and grills: the free range spit-roast chicken with a choice of sauces is something of a speciality. Service is polite and friendly.

Closing times
Closed 25 December and Sunday dinner
booking essential

Prices
Meals: £ 15 (weekdays) and a la carte £ 15/28

 *On A 4141 midway between Solihull and Warwick. Parking.*

England's biggest county has a lot of room for the spectacular; it encapsulates the idea of desolate beauty. The bracing winds of the Dales whistle through glorious meadows and deep, winding valleys, while the vast moors are fringed with picturesque country towns like Thirsk, Helmsley and Pickering. Further south the charming Wolds roll towards the sea, enhanced by such Georgian gems as Beverley and Howden. Popular history sits easily here: York continues to enchant with its ancient walls and Gothic Minster, but, owing to its Brontë links, visitors descend on the cobbled street village of Haworth with as much enthusiasm. Steam railways criss-cross the region's bluff contours, while drivers get a more streamlined thrill on the Humber Bridge. Yorkshire's food and drink emporiums range from quaintly traditional landmarks like the country tearoom and fish and chip shops proudly proclaiming to be the best in England, to warm and characterful pubs serving heart-warming local specialities.

North East
North West
YORKSHIRE
DURHAM
NORTH YORKSHIRE
LANCASHIRE
CHESHIRE
NORTH PENNINES
Yorkshire Dales National Park
Peak District National Park
Penrith
Appleby
Ullswater
Patterdale
Shap
Orton
Tebay
Ambleside
Windermere
Kendal
Sedbergh
Whernside
Kirkby Lonsdale
Ingleton
Clapham
Settle
Lancaster
Middleton-in-Teesdale
Bishop Auckland
Brough
Barnard Castle
Bowes
Kirkby Stephen
Darlington
Stockton-on-Tees
Newton Aycliffe
Sedgefield
Eaglescliffe
Scotch Corner
Richmond
Reeth
Swale
Hawes
Leyburn
Bedale
Northallerton
Thirsk
Ripon
Pateley Bridge
Fountains Abbey
Boroughbridge
Knaresborough
Wharfe
Threshfield
Ure
Long Preston
Gisburn
Skipton
Ilkley
Otley
Harewood
Wetherby
Clitheroe
Ribble
Colne
Keighley
Bingley
Nelson
Padiham
Burnley
Blackburn
Accrington
BRADFORD
LEEDS
Halifax
Brighouse
Todmorden
Rawtenstall
Rochdale
Bury
Darwen
Chorley
Bolton
Wigan
Oldham
Huddersfield
Holmfirth
Dewsbury
Wakefield
Garforth
Castleford
Barnsley
MANCHESTER
Leigh
Ashton-under-Lyne
Glossop
Stocksbridge
Conisbrough
Rotherham
SHEFFIELD
Altrincham
Hyde
Stockport
High Peak
Castleton
Widnes
Knutsford
Wilmslow
Whaley Bridge
Chapel-en-le-Frith
Northwich
Dronfield
Staveley
Macclesfield
Buxton
Baslow
Chesterfield
Winsford
Middlewich
Congleton
Bakewell
Chatsworth House
Tarporley
Sandbach
Little Moreton Hall
Clay
Hardwick

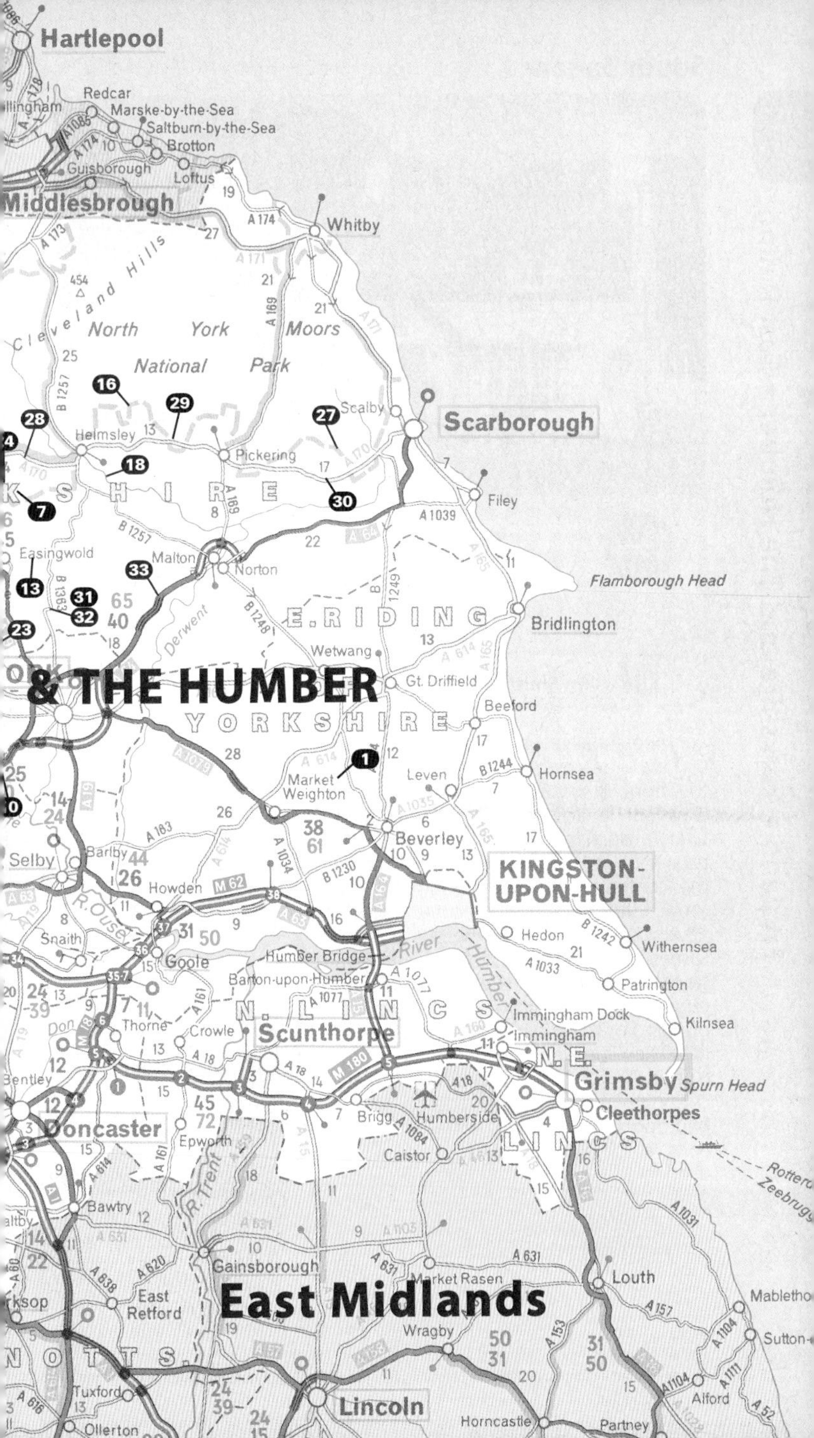

Hartlepool
Redcar
Marske-by-the-Sea
Saltburn-by-the-Sea
Brotton
Guisborough
Loftus
Middlesbrough
Whitby
Cleveland Hills
North York Moors
National Park
Scalby
Scarborough
Helmsley
Pickering
Filey
Easingwold
Malton
Norton
Flamborough Head
E. RIDING
Bridlington
Wetwang
Gt. Driffield
& THE HUMBER
YORKSHIRE
Beeford
Market Weighton
Leven
Hornsea
Beverley
Selby
Barlby
Howden
KINGSTON-UPON-HULL
Snaith
Goole
Humber Bridge
Hedon
Withernsea
Barton-upon-Humber
River Humber
Patrington
Immingham Dock
Immingham
Kilnsea
Thorne
Crowle
Scunthorpe
N. LINCS
N. E. LINCS
Grimsby
Spurn Head
Cleethorpes
Bentley
Doncaster
Epworth
Brigg
Humberside
Caistor
Rotterdam
Zeebrugge
Bawtry
R. Trent
Gainsborough
Market Rasen
Louth
East Retford
East Midlands
Wragby
NOTTS
Tuxford
Lincoln
Ollerton
Horncastle
Partney
Alford
Mablethorpe
Sutton-on-Sea
R. Ouse
Derwent
Don

South Dalton

1 **The Pipe and Glass Inn**

West End,
South Dalton, HU17 7PN
Tel.: (01430)810246
e-mail: email@pipeandglass.co.uk
Website: www.pipeandglass.co.uk

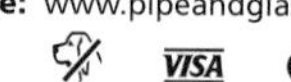

John Smith, Black Sheep, Wold Top and Old Mill Brewery

Very personally run by its experienced owners – he cooks, while she looks after the front of house – the 17C Pipe and Glass Inn is a deservedly popular place. Grab a drink and a seat beside the log burner or just head straight for a table in the contemporary dining room to enjoy food that's carefully executed, big on flavour and comes in generous portions. Dishes are made with local, seasonal and traceable produce wherever possible, and might include venison and juniper suet pudding or roast loin of red deer; desserts like The Pipe and Glass chocolate plate (subtitled 'Five reasons to love chocolate') continue the decadent theme. Luxury bedrooms are equipped with all mod cons and come with their own patios overlooking the estate woodland.

Closing times
Closed 2 weeks January, Sunday dinner and Monday except bank holidays

Prices
Meals: a la carte £ 21/40

2 rooms: £ 150

5 mi northwest of Beverley by A 164, B 1248 and side road west. Parking.

2 Crab and Lobster

Dishforth Rd,
Asenby, YO7 3QL
Tel.: (01845)577286 – Fax: (01845)577109
e-mail: anything@crabandlobster.co.uk
Website: www.crabandlobster.co.uk

Golden Pippin Ale, Theakston Best Bitter, Copper Dragon

From the moment you set eyes on this pub, you'll realise it's no ordinary place. Old advertisements and lobster pots hang from the walls, thatched crabs and lobsters sit on the roof – and even the umbrellas are thatched. Inside it's just as quirky, with charming exposed beams hung with knick-knacks aplenty and all kinds of characterful memorabilia strewn over every surface. The menu, unsurprisingly, features plenty of seafood, with the likes of fish soup, fishcakes, fish pie, shellfish and lobster; alongside traditional British favourites such as cheese soufflé, pork cheek confit and crusted loin of lamb. Split between an 18C Georgian Manor and log cabins, stylish bedrooms are themed around world-famous hotels; some boast private hot tubs.

Closing times
Open daily

Prices
Meals: £ 18 (lunch)
and a la carte £ 17/30

Typical Dishes
Yorkshire game terrine
Swordfish loin with curried king prawns
"Crabs" sticky date pudding

4 mi southwest of Thirsk by B 1448 and A 168. Parking.

Aysgarth

3 George and Dragon Inn

Aysgarth,
DL8 3AD
Tel.: (01969)663358 – Fax: (01969)633773
e-mail: ganddinn@hotmail.com
Website: www.ganddinn.com

Black Sheep Bitter, John Smith Cask, Yorkshire Dales Brewery, George & Dragon and one guest ale

Set in the heart of prime walking country, close to the breathtaking waterfalls of the River Ure, this 17C coaching inn makes the perfect base for exploring Wensleydale. This is a proper pub in all senses of the word: there's not a plasma screen in sight and if you've made yourself comfy in the laid-back bar, you're welcome to settle in for the night. The large restaurant winds its way around the front of the building, first taking on a French brasserie style and then ending up in a Victorian themed room; there's also a patio with great views of Pen Hill. Unfussy pub classics include plenty of local meats, game and old-fashioned puddings and there's a good value early evening menu. Bedrooms are comfy and well-priced; some boast whirlpool baths.

Closing times
Closed 2 weeks in January

Prices
Meals: £ 13/16
and a la carte £ 15/30

7 rooms: £ 40/100

7 mi west of Leyburn by A 684. Parking.

4 The Malt Shovel

Main St,
Brearton, HG3 3BX
Tel.: (01423)862929 – Fax: (01423)862929
e-mail: bleikers@themaltshovelbrearton.co.uk
Website: www.themaltshovelbrearton.co.uk

   VISA

 **Black Sheep, Timothy Taylor Landlord and one guest ale**

The Bleiker family are best known for their successful smokehouse but Jürg, the founder, has left his sons-in-law in charge and moved on to combine his family's two greatest loves – food and music. The Malt Shovel is a rather quirky, shabby-chic pub boasting a panelled, fire-lit bar, an opera-themed 'Red Room', an elegant 'Green Room' and a conservatory. There's a small kiln outside the kitchen and whatever meat, game or fish is in season will be smoking away. Dishes are largely classical with continental flavours, so will feature the likes of moules frites or Wiener schnitzel, with some smaller tapas-style plates available at lunch. On Sundays they host jazz sessions and from time to time son D'arcy and wife Anna give the odd opera recital.

Closing times
Closed Monday, Tuesday and Sunday dinner

Prices
Meals: a la carte £ 27/42

Typical Dishes
'Taste from the smoke Kiln'
Trio of beef
Sticky toffee pudding

 *4 mi west of Ripley by B 6165 and Brearton road. Parking.*

Broughton

5 **The Bull**

Broughton,
BD23 3AE
Tel.: (01756)792065 – Fax: (01756)792065
e-mail: enquiries@ribblevalleyinns.com
Website: www.thebullatbroughton.co.uk

Hetton Pale Ale, Timothy Taylor Landlord

The Bull is a member of Ribble Valley Inns – but don't expect some sort of faceless corporate brand – this is the bourgeoning pub company set up by Nigel Haworth and Craig Bancroft, co-proprietors of Lancashire's celebrated Northcote. They have led the way in promoting the specialities of their region and The Bull is no different. Expect real ales, local meats and cheeses, as well as traditional British dishes, rediscovered classics and the sort of puddings that make you feel patriotic. The Bull is an appropriate moniker as this pub is big and solid looking. It's at the side of Broughton Hall and inside is made up of assorted snugs and spaces, with beams, stone floors and log fires. It's cosy in winter and charming on a summer's day.

Closing times
Closed 25 December

Prices
Meals: a la carte £ 17/28

Typical Dishes
Charles Ashbridge treacle-baked rare breed rib
Herdwick mutton pudding
Bread & butter pudding

3 mi west of Skipton on A 59. In the grounds of Broughton Hall Country Park Estate. Parking.

Burnsall,
BD23 6BU
Tel.: (01756)720204 – Fax: (01756)720292
e-mail: redlion@daelnet.co.uk
Website: www.redlion.co.uk

VISA MC AE

Timothy Taylor, Theakston, Copper Dragon

This appealing stone inn sits at the heart of a small rural community on the banks of the River Wharfe. It has a warm yet worn feel, which isn't all that surprising when you learn that it has cellars dating back to the 12C and a wood-panelled bar from its 16C ferryman's inn days. There's plenty of choice when it comes to where to sit – the cosy bar with its copper-topped counter, the laid-back lounge or the more formally dressed dining room. The choice of food is similarly wide, with a bar menu of pub favourites; an à la carte featuring local lamb in spring, East Coast fish in summer and game in winter; and a blackboard of daily specials. Bedrooms are traditional with modern overtones; those in the nearby manor house are more contemporary.

Closing times
Open daily
Prices
Meals: £ 31 (dinner)
and a la carte £ 23/34
25 rooms: £ 65/153

7 mi north of Bolton Abbey by B 6160. Parking.

Byland Abbey

7 **The Abbey Inn**

Byland Abbey,
YO61 4BD
Tel.: (01347)868204 – Fax: (01347)868678
e-mail: info.appletreeinn@virgin.net
Website: www.theappletree.org

VISA

Black Sheep, Timothy Taylor

Set in a stunning location across from the ruins of the Byland Abbey, with views over the surrounding countryside, this historic inn is open all day; serving breakfast, morning coffee and afternoon tea as well as lunch and dinner to the area's many visitors. A wine shop offers plenty to interest oenophiles, including some lesser known labels, while the three rustic dining areas – Abbey Cider, Brown Brothers and Louis Roederer – continue the theme. The concise menu offers dishes such as blue cheese soufflé, pan-fried hake or stuffed chicken breast, as well as pub favourites like sausage and mash or beef and cask ale hotpot pie, and desserts like banana panna cotta. Spacious, high quality bedrooms boast luxurious bathrooms to match.

Closing times
Closed Tuesday
booking essential

Prices
Meals: £ 16 (lunch)
and a la carte £ 16/32

3 rooms: £ 100/200

6 mi southwest of Helmsley by A 170 and minor road south; opposite the ruins of Byland Abbey. Parking.

8 **Carlton Bore**

Carlton Husthwaite,
YO7 2BW
Tel.: (01845)501265
e-mail: chefhessel@aol.com
Website: www.carltonbore.co.uk

 **Black Sheep, Hambleton Bitter**

Four stuffed boars on the wall named Gordon, Delia, Jamie and Rick show that the owners of this characterful stone inn have a sense of humour. There's nothing funny about the food though: the appealing menu offers plenty of pub favourites, with starters/light bites such as game meatballs or devilled lambs kidneys on toast and main courses like slow-cooked pork belly, braised lamb shank or steak and ale pie. Portions are huge and dishes well-priced; Monday steak nights are particularly good value. Warm and welcoming, this 17C inn has three brightly decorated rooms; the middle room has comfy cushions and tables laid up for dining, while the room next to the bar is more suited to drinkers – and diners who like to be in the thick of the action.

Closing times
Open daily

Prices
Meals: a la carte £ 19/23

Typical Dishes
Bore benedict
Steamed game suet pudding
White chocolate and toasted marshmallow cheesecake

 *5 mi southeast of Thirsk off A 19. Parking.*

Carthorpe

9 Fox and Hounds

Carthorpe,
DL8 2LG
Tel.: (01845)567433 – Fax: (01845)567155
e-mail: helenjt36@btinternet.com
Website: www.foxandhoundscarthorpe.co.uk

Black Sheep Bitter, Worthington's

If you like a bit of history with your lunch, then this ivy-clad stone pub could be the place for you. Photos, curios and old farming equipment cover every surface, and there's an old water pump and anvil on display – the pub having started life several centuries ago as the village smithy. For the last 26 years, the Fitzgerald/Taylor family have been in charge and you'll find present owners Helen and Vincent hard at work in the kitchen, preparing a huge array of tasty dishes crafted from well sourced local produce: fish from Hartlepool, meat from the butcher in Bedale, flour grown and milled in Yorkshire, and products from the nearby dairy. For those who just can't choose, organic flour, honey, and homemade jams and chutneys are for sale.

Closing times
Closed first week January, 25-26 December and Monday

Prices
Meals: £ 17 (Tuesday-Thursday) and a la carte £ 20/34

Typical Dishes
Grilled pear & Parma ham
Steak & kidney pie with shortcrust pastry
Steamed suet sponge & custard

9 mi north of Ripon by minor road via Wath and Kirklington. Parking.

10

Ye Old Sun Inn

Main St,
Colton, LS24 8EP
Tel.: (01904)744261
e-mail: kelly.mccarthy@btconnect.com
Website: www.yeoldsuninn.co.uk

Timothy Taylor Landlord, Black Sheep Bitter, Moorhouse's "Ye Old Sun Inn" and Bradfield Brewery

The demise of many a local post office has highlighted their importance in the local community, but Ye Old Sun Inn is a good example of how significant a role the pub plays in local life. This family-run pub does it all: from selling homemade produce from their small deli to holding cookery demonstrations. They are also great ambassadors for local suppliers, several of whom are name-checked on the menu. The open fires and rustic feel make this a very popular place with the local community, although race days at the Knavesmire bring a regular invasion of interlopers. The menus change monthly and are as seasonal as ever. Those not from these parts can take advantage of the three very smart bedrooms in the recently acquired house next door.

Closing times
Closed Monday lunch

Prices
Meals: £ 18 (lunch)
and a la carte £ 25/35

3 rooms: £ 75/120

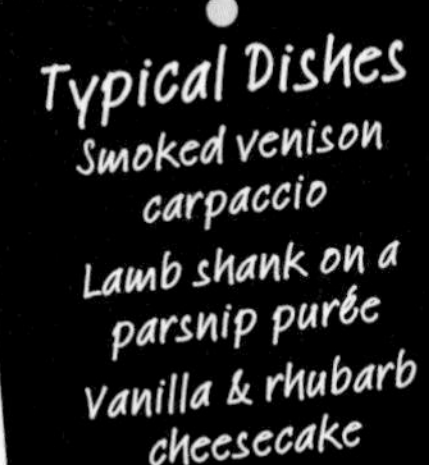

3 mi northeast of Tadcaster by A 659 and A 64. Parking.

11 **The Tiger Inn**

Coneythorpe,
HG5 0RY
Tel.: (01423)863632
Website: www.tiger-inn.co.uk

VISA

Black Sheep Bitter and Timothy Taylor Landlord

With a name like that you might be expecting something rather exotic, but this is a simple-looking pub, with just the odd picture or cuddly toy giving a nod to the eponymous feline; the inn's moniker apparently comes from local tales about a travelling circus, which purportedly kept its animals here in the late 1800s. These days, The Tiger Inn is a family-owned and popular place, with polite, friendly service and a bustling atmosphere, particularly in the front bar. Cooking is hearty and substantial, with classic pub dishes like fish and chips, Yorkshire hotpot, roast saddle of rabbit or the locally renowned steak and ale pie. The monthly changing menu is supplemented by fish specials – and there are gourmet sandwiches available at lunchtime.

Closing times
Open daily
booking advisable

Prices
Meals: £ 19 and a la carte £ 19/23

Typical Dishes
Homemade monkfish "scampi"
Lamb shoulder Irish stew
Frangipane & griottine cherry tart

5 mi northeast of Knaresborough by A 59 and minor road north. Parking.

12 **Wyvill Arms**

Constable Burton,
DL8 5LH
Tel.: (01677)450581
e-mail: info@thewyvillarms.co.uk
Website: www.thewyvillarms.co.uk

VISA

John Smith, Theakstons, Black Sheep

As you approach this ivy-clad stone pub you might recognise the large Elizabethan stately home immediately in front it; that's if you're a fan of the 2006 film Wind in the Willows. To the rear you'll find pleasant gardens and a small sitting area; while inside classical décor and rustically themed furnishings provide a warm, intimate feel. For dining, there's the choice of a small open-fired bar, a stone-floored area with banquettes and a more formal room with high-backed chairs. There's plenty of choice on the menu too, which features local, traceable produce in carefully prepared, classical dishes. You'll find tasty mature steaks, daily fish specials and Nigel's Yorkshire puddings are a must on Sundays. Bedrooms are simple but well-kept.

Closing times
Open daily

Prices
Meals: a la carte £ 20/35

3 rooms: £ 60/75

3.5 mi east of Leyburn on A 684. Parking.

Crayke

13 **The Durham Ox**

Westway,
Crayke, YO61 4TE
Tel.: (01347)821506 – Fax: (01347)823326
e-mail: enquiries@thedurhamox.com
Website: www.thedurhamox.com

Black Sheep, Timothy Taylor Landlord, Theakston's

Set in a sleepy little hamlet, next to Crayke Castle, the 300 year old Durham Ox is a bustling, family-run pub which boasts pleasant views over the vale of York and up to the medieval church. You'll receive a warm welcome whether you sit in the carved wood-panelled bar with its vast inglenook fireplace or more formal beamed dining room; but when the weather's right, head straight for the rear courtyard, as this is definitely the place to be. The regularly changing menu features plenty of fresh seafood, local meats and Crayke game; as well as tasty chicken from the rotisserie. Set in converted farm cottages, the cosy bedrooms display original brickwork and quarry tiling; some are suites, some are set over two floors and some have jacuzzis.

Closing times
Open daily
booking essential

Prices
Meals: a la carte £ 27/37
5 rooms: £ 80/150

2 mi east of Easingwold on Helmsley rd. Parking.

14 The Travellers Rest

Dalton,
DL11 7HU
Tel.: (01833)621225
e-mail: annebabsa@aol.com

 **No cask ale offered**

A community needs a pub. And the more remote the village it serves, the more important the pub. At The Travellers Rest, Anne greets her customers warmly and seems to know everyone by name; there is often a regular or three to be found in the bar – and the take away fish and chips night goes down a storm. If eating in, choose from the bar or one of two dining rooms; the first has quirky bookshelf wallpaper, while the second is more formal, with linen-clad tables. The menu is chalked up on blackboards and offers plenty of fresh, homemade dishes including the likes of fishcakes or Thai green curry as well as pub favourites like steak and chips. The homemade terrines are worth seeking out – while the duck with orange sauce remains a classic.

Closing times
Closed 25-26 December, 1 January, dinner Sunday and Monday
dinner only and Sunday lunch

Prices
Meals: a la carte £ 18/30

 *7.5 mi northwest of Scotch Corner by A 66. Parking.*

15 The Blue Lion

East Witton,
DL8 4SN
Tel.: (01969)624273 – Fax: (01969)624189
e-mail: enquiries@thebluelion.co.uk
Website: www.thebluelion.co.uk

 **Theakston's Black Sheep Bitter, Black Sheep Riggwelter**

Set in a delightful village, this former coaching inn boasts a truly rustic interior, pleasingly untouched by the minimalist makeover brigade. Dine in the flag-floored bar or in the high-ceilinged, wood-floored dining room; either way you'll sit at a polished wooden table in the glow of candlelight and enjoy unfussy, hearty cooking made from local produce. The menu is chalked up above the fire in the bar and dishes might include homemade pork pie, cassoulet of duck leg or roast wild venison. The wine list is of particular note and offers bottles at a wide range of prices. Bedrooms in the main house are furnished with antiques, including a four-poster in Room 3, while the rooms in the converted stable are more contemporary in style.

Closing times
Closed 25 December
booking essential

Prices
Meals: a la carte £ 22/43
15 rooms: £ 68/140

 *3 mi southeast of Leyburn on A 6108. Parking.*

16 **The Plough Inn**

Main St,
Fadmoor, YO62 7HY
Tel.: (01751)431515 – Fax: (01751)432492
e-mail: enquiries@theploughfadmoor.co.uk
Website: www.theploughfadmoor.co.uk

Black Sheep Best Bitter, Gt Newsome Brewery Sleck Dust

Set in a delightful location by the village green, the 18C Plough Inn sits on the edge of the North York Moors, midway between Pickering and Helmsley. Get here early to bag the snug with its open fire, or pick from various cosy rooms and hidey holes, including the formal half-panelled dining room, or one of the outside picnic tables. Like the décor, the cooking is traditional in style, with freshly prepared dishes such as sausage and mash or steak and mushroom suet pudding, as well as classic desserts such as crème brûlée or treacle tart. Produce is sourced locally where possible, and the two course special menu is a steal. If you like camping, then this is the inn for you: dine in the pub, and your pitch in the site behind it comes free.

Closing times
Closed 25 December, Sunday dinner, Monday except bank holidays and Tuesday

Prices
Meals: a la carte £ 16/25

2.25 mi northwest of Kirbymoorside. Parking.

Ferrensby

17 **The General Tarleton Inn**

Boroughbridge Rd,
Ferrensby, HG5 0PZ
Tel.: (01423)340284 – Fax: (01423)340288
e-mail: gti@generaltarleton.co.uk
Website: www.generaltarleton.co.uk

  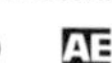

 **Black Sheep Bitter, Timothy Taylor Landlord**

With four spacious dining rooms, an airy glass-roofed courtyard and al fresco dining in both the garden and on the lovely decked terrace, you're spoilt for choice at this 18C coaching inn. One of the forerunners of today's gastropubs, it still helps to lead the way for others; its menu featuring a strong seasonal base, with traceability and local supplier relationships at its core. Tasty, warming dishes include old favourites such as steak and ale pie, as well as more ambitious offerings like seafood in a pastry bag – their speciality – followed by char-grilled haunch of venison or Goosnargh duckling in gingerbread sauce; finished off with maybe panna cotta and green apple sorbet. Individually styled bedrooms are luxurious and very comfy.

Closing times
Open daily

Prices
Meals: £ 15 (lunch) and a la carte £ 25/33

13 rooms: £ 75/150

 3 mi north of Knaresborough by A 6055. Parking.

18 **The Star Inn**

High St,
Harome, YO62 5JE
Tel.: (01439)770397 – Fax: (01439)772833
e-mail: jpern@thestarinnatharome.co.uk
Website: www.thestaratharome.co.uk

    MC

Leeds Brewery, Wold Brewery and Cropton ales

It already boasted a cosy bar and a rustic dining area but this charming 14C pub is now also the proud owner of a chic, modern dining room complete with chef's table; not forgetting a smart new garden designed by Jo Campbell, which provides many of the herbs and veg that appear on your plate. Cooking is firmly rooted in tradition but shows evidence of modern techniques, the result being typical pub dishes but with a more sophisticated edge. The ingredients used are the best available: wild mushrooms from just outside, free range poultry, milk-fed piglets and local Whitby fish – if you fancy seeing for yourself, book a place on their 'Chef for the Day' course. Comfy bedrooms can be found nearby in Cross House Lodge, which is also owned by them.

Closing times
Closed Monday lunch and Sunday dinner
booking essential

Prices
Meals: a la carte £ 25/45

2.75 mi southeast of Helmsley by A 170. Parking.

19 **Angel Inn**

Hetton, Skipton,
BD23 6LT
Tel.: (01756)730263 – Fax: (01756)730363
e-mail: info@angelhetton.co.uk
Website: www.angelhetton.co.uk

VISA MC AE

Timothy Taylor Landlord, Hetton Pale Ale, Black Sheep

Don't be fooled by the relatively remote setting – you have to book ahead to get a table in the bar and even then it can be a bit of a scrum. It's jammed with character and charm but the long serving staff all ably anticipate their customers' needs. There is also a more formal dining room available. The flexible menu uses plenty of local bounty; there is something for everyone, at sensible prices and the cooking is eminently satisfying. Wine is a huge draw here – and the cave is well worth a visit. You'll find the luxuriously appointed bedrooms in a converted stone farm building. There is many a chef and restaurateur around the country who owe their success to the formative years they spent at this iconic 18C Yorkshire institution.

Closing times
Closed 10 days in January, 25 December, dinner 26 and 31 December
booking essential

Prices
Meals: a la carte £ 22/30

20 The Charles Bathurst Inn

Langthwaite,
DL11 6EN
Tel.: (01748)884567 – Fax: (01748)884599
e-mail: info@cbinn.co.uk
Website: www.cbinn.co.uk

Timothy Taylor Landlord, Theakston Best Bitter, Black Sheep Best Bitter & Riggwelter

This characterful 18C hostelry is named after a local land and lead mine owner, and former resident. Sitting on the edge of the Pennine way, high in the hills of Arkengarthdale, it boasts commanding views over the surrounding countryside and is so remotely set, that the only sound you'll hear is the 'clink' of quoits being thrown by the locals. Inside you're greeted by open fires, various timbered snugs and a charming dining room hung with old monochrome photos and sepia lithographs. Unusually inscribed on a mirror, the daily menu offers refined yet hearty classical British dishes, with the likes of asparagus and Wensleydale tart, followed by local meats; maybe fillet of beef on oxtail terrine. Bedrooms are spacious and extremely comfy.

Closing times
Closed 25 December

Prices
Meals: a la carte £ 23/34
19 rooms: £ 105/120

Typical Dishes
Butternut squash & parmesan risotto
Sirloin steak with chips & creamed leeks
Sticky toffee pudding with ice cream

3.25 mi northwest of Reeth on Langthwaite rd. Parking.

21 The Sandpiper Inn

Market Pl,
Leyburn, DL8 5AT
Tel.: (01969)622206 – Fax: (01969)625367
e-mail: hsandpiper99@aol.com
Website: www.sandpiperinn.co.uk

VISA MC

Black Sheep, Copper Dragon Brewery, Dent Brewery

A friendly Yorkshire welcome is extended to the Dale walkers who come to refuel at this stone built part 16C pub, situated just off the main square.Visitors can rest their blistered feet by the fire in the split-level, beamed bar, or plump for a seat in the more characterful dining room. A small enclosed terrace out the back provides a third alternative for when it's sunny, but you'll have to come inside to read the blackboard menus, found hanging on the walls amidst the general clutter of decorative pictures, books and ornaments. Subtle, refined cooking offers a modern take on the classics, so expect dishes like ham hock terrine and piccalilli, pressed Dales lamb or slow-cooked Wensleydale beef. Two homely bedrooms are on the first floor.

Closing times
Closed Monday and restricted opening on Tuesday in winter

Prices
Meals: a la carte £ 22/34

2 rooms: £ 65/80

Typical Dishes

Terrine of venison & rabbit with spiced apple chutney

Roasted halibut with chips & mushy peas

Iced whisky parfait & poached Yorkshire rhubarb

In town centre. Limited parking available in the Market Place.

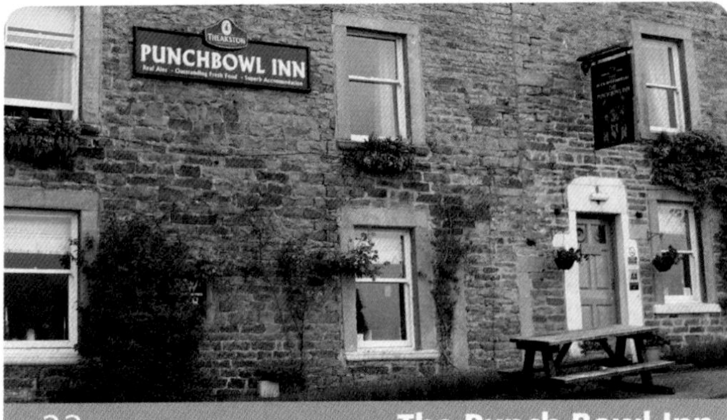

22 The Punch Bowl Inn

Low Row,
DL11 6PF
Tel.: (01748)886233 – Fax: (01748)886945
e-mail: info@pbinn.co.uk
Website: www.pbinn.co.uk

VISA

Theakston's Best Bitter, Black Sheep Best Bitter & Riggwelter, Timothy Taylor Landlord

A traditional 17C stone-built inn whose rustic exterior is a complete contrast to its modernised, shabby-chic style interior, with its open fires and scrubbed wooden tables. It's a popular stop off point for walkers, who refuel on classic dishes like duck liver parfait, braised local lamb shank or beef and red wine casserole; but don't go looking for a paper menu, since dishes are listed on mirrors above the fireplace. There's a selection of filled ciabatta at lunchtime, tasty desserts such as spiced apple tart and custard and bi-monthly steak nights which prove popular with the villagers. Supremely comfortable bedrooms are decorated in a fresh, modern style; all of them have views over Swaledale, while the superior rooms are more spacious.

Closing times
Closed 25 December

Prices
Meals: a la carte £ 18/25

11 rooms: £ 98/120

Typical Dishes
Smoked & cured fish platter
Supreme of chicken with glazed shallots & broccoli
Yorkshire parkin with apple compote

In the middle of hamlet. Parking.

Newton-on-Ouse

23 **The Dawnay Arms**

Newton-on-Ouse,
YO30 2BR
Tel.: (01347)848345
e-mail: dine@thedawnayatnewton.co.uk
Website: www.thedawnayatnewton.co.uk

Timothy Taylor Landlord, Tetleys, Hambleton Brewery

This capacious 18C inn boasts a handsome rustic style, thoroughly in tune with its rural surroundings. It's got the low beamed ceilings and the roaring fires. It's got the walls filled with countryside art and the solid stone floors. It's got the locally-crafted chunky wood tables. All that, and a stuffed armadillo too. A native Yorkshireman cooks up tasty, good value dishes in the kitchen, with everything fresh, homemade and seasonal; the lunch menu offers sandwiches and pub classics like shepherd's pie alongside fish stew or slow roast rump of lamb, while the dinner menu might tempt you with confit pork belly or ballotine of chicken. The more formal rear dining room looks out over the terrace and gardens and down to the River Ouse.

Closing times
Open daily

Prices
Meals: £ 13 and a la carte £ 16/28

8 mi northwest of York by A 19 and minor road west. Parking.

24 The Black Swan

Oldstead,
YO61 4BL
Tel.: (01347)868387
e-mail: enquiries@blackswanoldstead.co.uk
Website: www.blackswanoldstead.co.uk

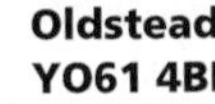

Black Sheep Best Bitter, Copper Dragon Best Bitter and Peroni

The Black Swan is a proper village pub and a real family affair. The Banks have lived and farmed in Oldstead for generations – and still do – and also own a lovely guesthouse just down the road. The pub is stone-built and has a characterful beamed, flag-floored bar with welcoming open fires, where you'll find top-rate bar meals such as beef casserole. Head to the upstairs dining room for more ambitious dishes like duck terrine with foie gras, followed by herb-crusted fillet of wild turbot. Cooking is modern and highly skilled but remains satisfyingly unpretentious, and they are particularly proud of the sourcing of their meats. Antique-furnished bedrooms boast modern fabrics, luxurious bathrooms and patios overlooking the surrounding farmland.

Closing times
Closed lunch Monday-Wednesday

Prices
Meals: a la carte £ 25/40

4 rooms: £ 125/180

Typical Dishes
Salmon ravioli & lobster bisque
Sirloin of Aberdeen Angus beef with crushed potatoes & parsnips
Apple Bakewell tart & confit rhubarb

7.5 mi southwest of Helmsley by A 170 and minor road via Byland Abbey. Parking.

Osmotherley

25 **The Golden Lion**

6 West End,
Osmotherley, DL6 3AA
Tel.: (01609)883526
e-mail: goldenlionosmotherley@yahoo.co.uk
Website: www.goldenlionosmotherley.co.uk

Timothy Taylor Best, York Brewery Ales

The Golden Lion has probably done more to invigorate walkers than sunshine and a following wind. Found in the historic village of Osmotherley, it represents the starting line for those about to set off on the Lyke Wake walk or at least those contemplating the walk. There's nothing fancy about this place and that's the beauty of it – just a rustic, warm interior with open fires, great beers and staff who make you feel instantly at ease. The food also fits neatly into these surroundings. There's a bit of French, a little Italian with some pasta dishes but, above all, food that satisfies, whether that's a piece of roasted halibut or a local mature steak accompanied by a pint in front of the fire. The three bedrooms are quite modern in style.

Closing times
Closed 25 December, lunch Monday and Tuesday

Prices
Meals: a la carte £ 20/24
3 rooms: £ 80/90

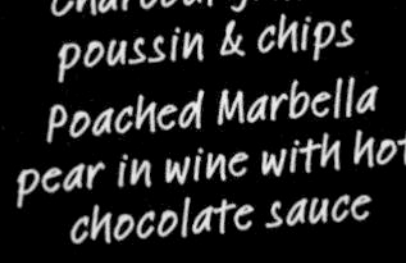

Typical Dishes
Smoked haddock risotto
Charcoal grilled poussin & chips
Poached Marbella pear in wine with hot chocolate sauce

6 mi northeast of Northallerton by A 684. Parking in the village.

26 The Crown Inn

Roecliffe,
YO51 9LY
Tel.: (01423)322300 – Fax: (01423)322033
e-mail: info@crowninnroecliffe.com
Website: www.crowninnroecliffe.com

 **Theakston's, Sharp's Doom Bar, Nellie Dean, Swing Low, Black Sheep, Caledonian IPA**

Delightfully set by the village green, this smart 16C inn displays a stylish country interior with stone floors, exposed beams and open fireplaces. Out the front there's a small terrace and inside, the choice of three different rooms – one decorated in red, one in green, and the last, housing the bar counter. The good-sized menus are chalked up the board as well as being printed out and display a nice balance of meat and fish. Dishes like the crab soup, tempura prawns, fish pie and belly pork are mainstays and the dedicated 'meat free' menu ensures that vegetarians are well-catered for. A carefully chosen wine list provides the perfect accompaniment. Smart new bedrooms boast antique-style furnishings, feature beds and free-standing baths.

Closing times
Closed Sunday dinner

Prices
Meals: £ 20 (dinner)
and a la carte £ 19/26

4 rooms: £ 100/130

Typical Dishes
Local pork belly with sweet soy & ginger
Dales lamb shank dauphinoise
Trio of Wakefield rhubarb

 *1 mi west of Boroughbridge by minor road. Parking.*

Sawdon

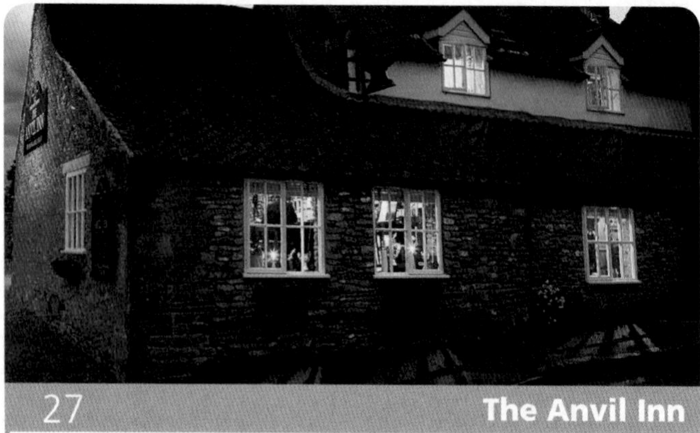

27 **The Anvil Inn**

Main St, Sawdon,
Scarborough, YO13 9DY
Tel.: (01723)859896
e-mail: info@theanvilinnsawdon.co.uk
Website: www.theanvilinnsawdon.co.uk

 MC

 **Copper Dragon Best Bitter, Wold Top, Daleside**

As its name suggests, this charming inn was formerly a smithy, and much of the associated paraphernalia remains, including bellows, an open forge and the original anvil. In marked contrast, but blending in seamlessly, is the boldly coloured, contemporary sitting room. Cooking is classical in essence, with the odd international influence, so expect crispy duck and pancakes alongside Shetland mussels or slow-roasted daube of beef. Local chef Mark prides himself on the use of locally sourced produce; eggs come from the pub's own hens and the local Stillington pork is a firm favourite. There are only seven tables in the intimate restaurant, so be sure to book ahead; particularly for Sunday lunch, which has become something of an institution.

Closing times
Closed 25-26 December, 1 January and Monday

Prices
Meals: a la carte £ 18/28

Typical Dishes
Red wine & oxtail risotto with parmesan wafer
Fillet of halibut with saffron & brown shrimp risotto
Spanish orange cake & homemade almond ice cream

12 mi southwest of Scarborough by A 170 to Brompton and minor road north. Parking.

28 **The Hare Inn**

Scawton,
YO7 2HG
Tel.: (01845)597769
e-mail: info@thehareinn.co.uk
Website: www.thehareinn.co.uk

 **Black Sheep Bitter, Timothy Taylor Landlord**

The appeal of many a pub lies in its far-flung setting and The Hare's location couldn't be more remote – it nestles in the depths of the North Yorkshire Moors, close to Rievaulx Abbey and Sutton Bank, which, as many gliders know, is where you'll find some of the country's best views. But The Hare is more than just a hideaway – it's also got plenty of character, with parts of the pub dating back to the 13C. For some, it even resembles a smart scout hut and would certainly win a badge for hospitality. The food is equally pleasing and local, whether that's the local asparagus, whole roast sea bass, sweet new season lamb or 'proper' puddings like lemon posset. It gets pretty jam packed at weekends so a little patience is sometimes required.

Closing times
Closed Sunday dinner and Monday

Prices
Meals: a la carte £ 30/40

 *Between Thirsk and Helmsley off north side of A 170. Parking.*

Sinnington

29 **Fox and Hounds**

Main St,
Sinnington, YO62 6SQ
Tel.: (01751)431577 – Fax: (01751)432791
e-mail: fox.houndsinn@btconnect.com
Website: www.thefoxandhoundsinn.co.uk

VISA MC

Copper Dragon Best Bitter, Black Sheep Special

It's easy to see why this handsome stone pub, dating from the 18C, is something of a local institution: it has charm, is run smoothly and offers something for everyone. It's divided into a number of areas; if you want to chat to the good burghers of Sinnington sit in the bar but there's also a dining room at the back. The menu is all about flexibility, with virtually all the starters available in larger sizes for main courses. Local specialities include the Bleikers smoked salmon, the scallops with black pudding or the Swaledale 'Old Peculiar' cheese soufflé. There is something comforting about the main courses, such as slow-cooked shoulder of lamb or fish pie. If staying overnight, then book ahead as the bedrooms get snapped up quickly.

Closing times
Closed 25-26 December

Prices
Meals: a la carte £ 21/32

10 rooms: £ 59/110

Typical Dishes

Twice-baked Yorkshire blue cheese soufflé

Trio of guinea fowl

Treacle tart with orange anglaise & ginger ice cream

Just off A 170 between Pickering and Kirkbymoorside. Parking.

30

Coachman Inn

Pickering Rd west,
Snainton, YO13 9PL
Tel.: (01723)859231 – Fax: (01723)850008
e-mail: info@coachmaninn.co.uk
Website: www.coachmaninn.co.uk

 **Wold Top Bitter and Wold Gold**

This Grade II listed inn dates back to 1776 and was the last staging post before Scarborough for the coaches taking the York mail. It boasts a well-tended garden to the rear and a charming interior: there's a rustic bar displaying quarry tiles and chunky wood furniture and a spacious linen-clad dining room which runs the length of the building, finishing in a small garden room at the end. The place is run with some formality – menus are presented in smart folders and cooking is very much in the classical vein, although with a modern, refined style of presentation. Produce is seasonal and of good quality but prices remain fair. Lunch offers simpler pub favourites and the concise wine list is well thought out. Bedrooms are smart and spacious.

Closing times
Open daily
Prices
Meals: a la carte £ 15/30
3 rooms: £ 70/85

Typical Dishes
Wild mushroom & quails egg salad with pea panna cotta
Pork fillet & violet potatoes
Pineapple tarte Tatin

 *0.5 mi west by A 170 on B 1258. Parking.*

Sutton-on-the-Forest

31 **The Blackwell Ox Inn**

Huby Rd,
Sutton-on-the-Forest, YO61 1DT
Tel.: (01347)810328 – Fax: (01347)812738
e-mail: enquiries@blackwelloxinn.co.uk
Website: www.blackwelloxinn.co.uk

   VISA

Timothy Taylor Landlord, Black Sheep Bitter, John Smith's Cask

A smart, contemporary inn with a homely bar/lounge and a more formal, linen-clad dining room. There are snacks chalked on a board plus a daily changing à la carte menu; starters like foie gras on toasted brioche may feature but these sit alongside more down-to-earth dishes like pan-fired pigeon breast, or creamy garlic wild mushrooms on toast. Main courses could include local rib-eye steak with chips or half a roast chicken and desserts range from bread and butter pudding to cherry and boozy prune clafoutis. Bedrooms are spacious and stylish, with excellent modern bathrooms. Some feature four-poster beds and Room 2 has a roll-top bath in the room; such a high standard finish makes sense when you know that the inn is owned by a local builder.

Closing times
Closed 25 December, 1 January and Sunday dinner

Prices
Meals: £ 14 and a la carte £ 15/30

7 rooms: £ 65/110

Typical Dishes
Scallops with caramelised cauliflower & truffle-infused spinach
Venison rack & fondant potatoes
Chocolate & walnut brownie with toasted marshmallows

8 mi north of York by B 1363. Parking.

32 Rose & Crown

Main St,
Sutton-on-the-Forest, YO61 1DP
Tel.: (01347)811333 – Fax: (01347)811333
e-mail: mail@rosecrown.co.uk
Website: www.rosecrown.co.uk

VISA MC AE

Inspectors' favourites

Black Sheep Best, York Brewery Yorkshire Terrier

The small, cosy front bar creates a welcoming and intimate atmosphere and the dining room and conservatory add to the overall charm. There is a bewildering array of menus available, from 'early bird' to 'light bites', from the à la carte to a list of 'classics' – but don't be frightened off as you'll almost certainly find something that appeals – to your appetite and your pocket – whether that's the sirloin of Yorkshire beef, pork cutlet with black pudding, ham hock terrine or just a Caesar salad. Local cheeses go into the potato cakes; the piccalilli is homemade and the haddock uses a local York beer for its batter. Perhaps the pub's best feature is the enclosed rear garden which comes with a super terrace and an impressively sized gazebo.

Closing times
Closed Sunday dinner and Monday
booking essential

Prices
Meals: £ 20 and a la carte £ 22/28

On B 1363 north of York. Parking.

Whitwell-on-the-Hill

33 **The Stone Trough Inn**

Kirkham Abbey,
Whitwell-on-the-Hill, YO60 7JS
Tel.: (01653)618713
e-mail: info@stonetroughinn.co.uk
Website: www.stonetroughinn.co.uk

Timothy Taylor Landlord, Tetley's, Black Sheep and two weekly changing local guest ales

Set in the Howardian Hills, overlooking the River Derwent and the ruins of Kirkham Abbey, this attractive stone pub is named after what was thought to be a stone trough outside its door – but was later revealed to be the base of a 10C cross erected by a French knight. It's a building of real size, with various beamed rooms and charming snugs scattered about, a large press still in situ and open fires aplenty; not forgetting a games room and terrace. Cooking is straightforward and filling, with a strong classical base and menus display a mix of local and cosmopolitan dishes; you might find honey-glazed ham hock or rabbit pie, followed by Eton Mess or treacle tart. Produce is local, seasonal and home-grown. Specials are chalked on the board daily.

Closing times
Open daily

Prices
Meals: a la carte £ 20

5 mi southwest of Malton off A 64; follow signs for Kirkham Priory. Parking.

34 The Milestone

84 Green Ln,
Sheffield, S3 8SE
Tel.: (0114)2728327
e-mail: bookings@the-milestone.co.uk
Website: www.the-milestone.co.uk

Bradfield, Acorn, Kelham Island and Wentworth Breweries

That the owners of The Milestone can boast their own herd of free range pigs speaks volumes about their approach to food: passionate about organic, locally sourced produce, they consider the quality of their ingredients to be the key to their success and don't believe in buying in things like bread, pasta and puddings, since they can make them in-house. Some of the hearty dishes on the 'gastro' menu – like the lamb burger, and the beef bourguignon – have become classics, but the emphasis here is on evolution and seasonality, so what's on offer changes frequently. While downstairs is spacious, with understated décor, simple wood tables and banquettes, the beamed first floor room provides a more formal dining space, with a menu to match.

Closing times
Open daily
Prices
Meals: £ 20/30

Between A 61 and River Don. Parking in Green Lane and Ball Street.

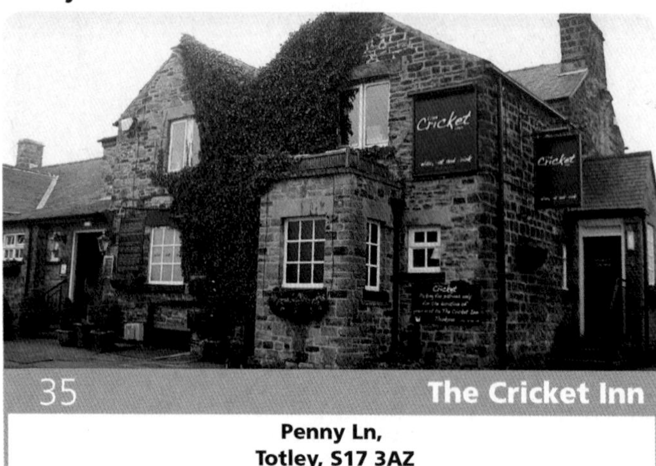

35 **The Cricket Inn**

Penny Ln,
Totley, S17 3AZ
Tel.: (0114)2365256
Website: www.relaxeatanddrink.co.uk

 **Thornbridge Brewery - Lord Marples, Ashford, Jaipur**

Hidden away in a delightful spot in the valley, next to the cricket ground, this is a proper pub in every sense of the word. Three rooms boast open fires and rustic wood floors; the walls are filled with cricketing paraphernalia, while the scrubbed tables are home to bottles of Sheffield's spicy Henderson's Relish. Food comes in big, hearty portions, not for the faint-hearted, and there's something for everyone, from sandwiches and snacks like home-roasted pork scratchings, to things like cheese on toast or homemade fishcakes, as well as dishes such as steak and ale pie or slow-braised shoulder shank of lamb. 'Cricket Inn boards' come in ploughman's and fisherman's varieties, there's a little person's menu and some nice nursery style puddings.

Closing times
Open daily
Prices
Meals: £ 15 and a la carte £ 18/25

6 mi southwest of Sheffield by A 61, A 621 and Hillfoot Rd. Parking.

36 **Shibden Mill Inn**

Shibden Mill Fold,
Halifax, HX3 7UL
Tel.: (01422)365840 – Fax: (01422)362971
e-mail: simonheaton@shibdenmillinn.com
Website: www.shibdenmillinn.com

VISA AE

Theakston XB, Moorhouse's Shibden Bitter, Black Sheep Bitter, Twaithes Original and Copper Dragon's Golden Pippin

Set in the valley, overlooking a stream, this whitewashed inn started life as an early 14C corn mill, was later used for spinning and, in 1890, was sold to a brewing company. Today, you'll find a charming open-fired bar full of nooks, crannies and locals, and a rustic upstairs restaurant with recently exposed original oak beams. Menus offer plenty of choice, with dishes ranging from the traditional – maybe home cured corned beef hash, roast rib-eye or treacle tart – to the more modern, such as crab trifle with lemon cocktail, scallops with bacon crème caramel or butternut squash fondant. For something a little different, come to a gourmet dinner evening or experimental guinea pig night. Individually appointed bedrooms are comfy and cosy.

Closing times
Open daily
Prices
Meals: a la carte £ 16/40
11 rooms: £ 72/111

Typical Dishes
Crab & coriander croquettes
Duo of Yorkshire lamb
Twice-baked Belgian chocolate brownie

Northeast : 2.25 mi by A 58 and Kell Lane (turning left at Stump Cross public house) on Blake Hill Rd. Parking.

Hepworth

37 **The Butchers Arms**

38 Towngate,
Hepworth, HD9 1TE
Tel.: (01484)682361
e-mail: info@thebutchersarms.co.uk
Website: www.thebutchersarms.co.uk

VISA

 **Black Sheep and Timothy Taylor Landlord**

Set on the fringes of a sleepy hamlet this stone-built inn really is hidden away but with its rustic bar, smart dining room and a choice of delightful terraces, it's well worth searching out. A vibrant sign outside proudly announces the owner's philosophy – 'The Butchers Arms, A great place to meat' – and the skilled cooking offers suitably robust, country style dishes. The bewildering array of menus ranges from your usual daily blackboard and à la carte selections to more interesting Yorkshire tapas choices and even a water menu. All produce comes from within a strict 75 mile radius but most originates from closer to home; be it trugs of gooseberries left on the doorstep by the neighbours, game shot just down the road or homemade chutneys.

Closing times
Closed 2 weeks in January
booking essential

Prices
Meals: £ 15 (lunch)
and a la carte £ 15/42

Typical Dishes
English salad plate
Round green farm venison loin & cottage pie
Elderflower jelly

7 mi southeast of Huddersfield by A 616, New Mill Rd, and Butts Lane. Parking.

38 **Olive Branch**

Manchester Rd,
Marsden, HD7 6LU
Tel.: (01484)844487
e-mail: eat@olivebranch.uk.com
Website: www.olivebranch.uk.com

VISA

Greenfield Ales Delph Donkey

Set on a busy main road, this stone-built drovers' inn houses many small and characterful rooms, each adorned with food-themed pictures, sepia photos, old menus and more. Most tables are set for dining and there's a chatty, bustling atmosphere, while for warmer weather, a decked terrace and secluded garden are hidden round the back. The large menu displays an even split between meat and seafood, ranging from pigeon and venison to sea bass and monkfish; with daily specials displayed on large yellow post-it notes around the bar. Taking on a traditional style, cooking is robust, straightforward and uses local produce wherever possible. Service is friendly, if sometimes lacking a little in direction. Bedrooms are modern, comfy and very unique.

Closing times
Dinner only and Sunday lunch

Prices
Meals: £ 19 and a la carte £ 26/46

3 rooms: £ 73/105

1 mi northeast on A 62. Parking.

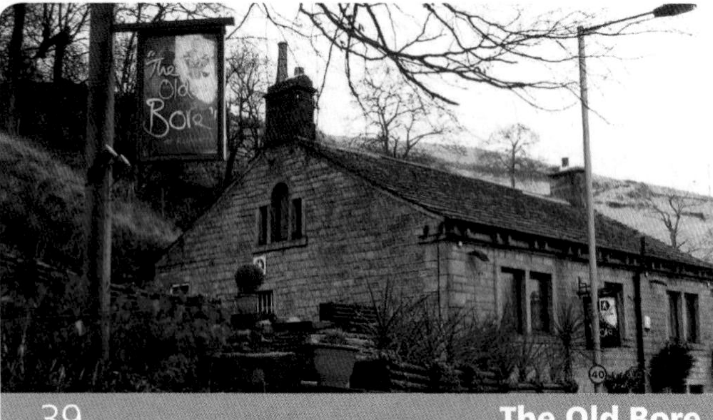

39 **The Old Bore**

Oldham Rd,
Rishworth, HX6 4QU
Tel.: (01422)822291
e-mail: chefhessel@aol.com
Website: www.oldbore.co.uk

Timothy Taylor Landlord, Black Sheep and Golden Bore

Hidden away in a charming landscape dotted with reservoirs and traversed by pleasant walks, this 19C stone coaching inn makes the ideal stop off point for anything from a refreshing northern ale to a full 3 course dinner. It's a cosy, characterful place bursting with knick-knacks and memorabilia, from quirky hunting scene wallpaper and stag antler chandeliers to framed food-related articles and pewter tankards. Service is smooth and welcoming, and matched by appealingly robust cooking. Produce is seasonal and local game is usually a feature; you might find braised beef brisket or game suet pudding on offer, along with options such as Coquilles St Jacques with wild mushroom sauce on Fish Fridays. Theme nights and jazz evenings are common.

Closing times
Open daily

Prices
Meals: a la carte £ 24/30

Typical Dishes
Crispy lamb breast strips
Creamy seafood thermidor pie
Strawberry mille-feuille

 *6 mi southwest of Halifax by A 58 and A 672. Parking.*

40 The Millbank

Mill Bank,
Sowerby Bridge, HX6 3DY
Tel.: (01422)825588
e-mail: eat@themillbank.com
Website: www.themillbank.com

 **Timothy Taylor Landlord and Tetley's**

Set on a steep hill in a remote Yorkshire village, The Millbank isn't the kind of place you discover just by driving past, so the fact that it's popular is a sure sign they're doing something right. Its elevated position means that it boasts commanding views over the Ryburn Valley and whatever the weather you can be sure to find a pleasing outlook. The extensive à la carte offers a diverse range of dishes, from fish and chips to rabbit and chorizo meatballs, with the French onion tart being a particular favourite. There's plenty of choice when it comes to drinks too, with real ales, bottled beers from around the globe and an excellent wine list. Always keeping their loyal locals in mind, they hold regular events such as 'Pie and Pea' night.

Closing times
Closed 1 January and Monday
booking essential

Prices
Meals: £ 16 (lunch and Fri-Sat early dinner) and a la carte £ 22/32

2.25 mi southwest by A 58. Parking on the road in front of the pub.

41 **Woodman Inn**

Thunder Bridge,
HD8 0PX
Tel.: (01484)605778 – Fax: (01484)604110
e-mail: thewoodman@connectfree.co.uk
Website: www.woodman-inn.co.uk

Ossett Brewery, Timothy Taylor Best and Landlord, Black Sheep Best Bitter and one weekly changing guest ale

If you're following one of the many footpaths that pass by the Southern Pennines, be sure to seek out this peaceful wooded valley and the small hamlet of Thunder Bridge. Here you'll find this traditional 19C Yorkshire-stone inn, with its wood-faced bar – complete with convivial locals – leather furnished lounge and more formal linen-laid restaurant which opens in the evening. Service is polite and efficient wherever you sit: the restaurant is great for special occasions but the bar is more atmospheric. Extensive menus change with the seasons and have a distinct British bias. Lunch sees hearty classics served in generous portions, while dinner takes on a more ambitious approach. Simple, well-kept bedrooms are located in old weavers' cottages.

Closing times
Closed dinner 25 December

Prices
Meals: £ 16/19

12 rooms: £ 48/60

Typical Dishes
King scallops with cauliflower tempura
Pork belly & wild boar sausage with mash
Sticky toffee pudding

5.75 mi southeast of Huddersfield by A 629; after Kirkburton follow signs to Thunder Bridge. Parking.

42 The Fox and Hounds

Hall Park Rd,
Walton, LS23 7DQ
Tel.: (01937)842192
e-mail: basil@thefoxandhoundswalton.com
Website: www.thefoxandhoundswalton.com

Timothy Taylor Landlord, Black Sheep

Tucked away in the centre of a sleepy little West Yorkshire village, this characterful stone pub has two rooms set for dining, plus a cosy snug (home to Basil, the stuffed fox), which also has tables set aside for drinkers. Pleasant country décor takes in low beamed ceilings and countryside prints; the table mats are adorned with hunting cartoons and a fish tank on the bar provides a relaxing diversion as you sup your pint. The menu tends towards classic British dishes, with more adventurous offerings available on the specials board. Cooking is hearty and robust and makes good use of local produce; the wide choice further extended by an early evening menu of pub favourites. The atmosphere is friendly and service is chatty and knowledgeable.

Closing times
Open daily
booking essential

Prices
Meals: £ 18 (lunch)
and a la carte £ 20/40

3 mi east of Wetherby by minor road; between A 659 and B 1224. Parking.

Scotland may be small, but its variety is immense. The vivacity of Glasgow can seem a thousand miles from the vast peatland wilderness of Caithness and Sutherland's Flow Country; the arty vibe of Georgian Edinburgh a world away from the remote and tranquil Ardnamurchan peninsula. And how many people link Scotland to its beaches? But wide golden sands trim the Atlantic at South Harris, and the coastline of the Highlands boasts empty islands and turquoise waters. Meantime, Fife's coast draws golf fans to St Andrews and the more secretive delights of the East Neuk, an area of fishing villages and stone harbours. Wherever you travel, the scent of a dramatic history prevails in the shape of castles, cathedrals and rugged lochside monuments to the heroes of old. Food and drink embraces the traditional, too, typified by Aberdeen's famous Malt Whisky Trail. And what better than Highland game, fresh fish from the Tweed or haggis, neeps and tatties to complement a grand Scottish hike…

Lewis
Stornoway
St. Kilda
Tarbert
North Uist
Lochmaddy
South Uist
Lochboisdale
Barra
Castlebay
Uig
Dunvegan
Portree
Skye
Kyle of Lochalsh
Rhum
Mallaig
Coll
Tiree
Tobermory
Mull
Craignure
Fionnphort
Oban
Colonsay
Islay
Port Askaig
Jura
Port Ellen
Lochgilphead
Kintyre
Campbeltown
Arran
Brodick
Rothesay
Lochinver
Ullapool
Tongue
Lairg
Brora
Dornoch
Dingwall
Nairn
Inverness
Loch Ness
Aviemore
Newtonmore
Grantown
Braemar
Fort William
Ben Nevis
SCOTLAND
Crianlarich
Crieff
Perth
Stirling
Kinross
Falkirk
Dumbarton
Greenock
GLASGOW
Ardrossan
Hamilton
Kilmarnock
Ayr
EDINBURGH
Lanark
Peebles
Moffat
Hawick
Dumfries
Cairnryan
Stranraer
Kirkcudbright
Carlisle
Workington
Whitehaven
Keswick
North West
Windermere
Man
Peel
Ramsey
Malin Head
Buncrana
Giant's Causeway
Letterkenny
Portrush
Londonderry/Derry
Coleraine
Ballycastle
Antrim Glens
Donegal
Strabane
Northern Ireland
Ballymena
Larne
Bundoran
Omagh
Enniskillen
Sligo
Lisburn
BELFAST
Bangor
Armagh
Boyle
Monaghan
Newry
Newcastle
Dundalk
Ireland
Dunnet
Loch Linnhe
Firth of Lorn
Loch Fyne
Firth of Clyde
Solway Firth
Cairngorm Mountains
Sea of the Hebrides
4
5
7
8
9
10
11
12
13
14
15
16
17
18
19

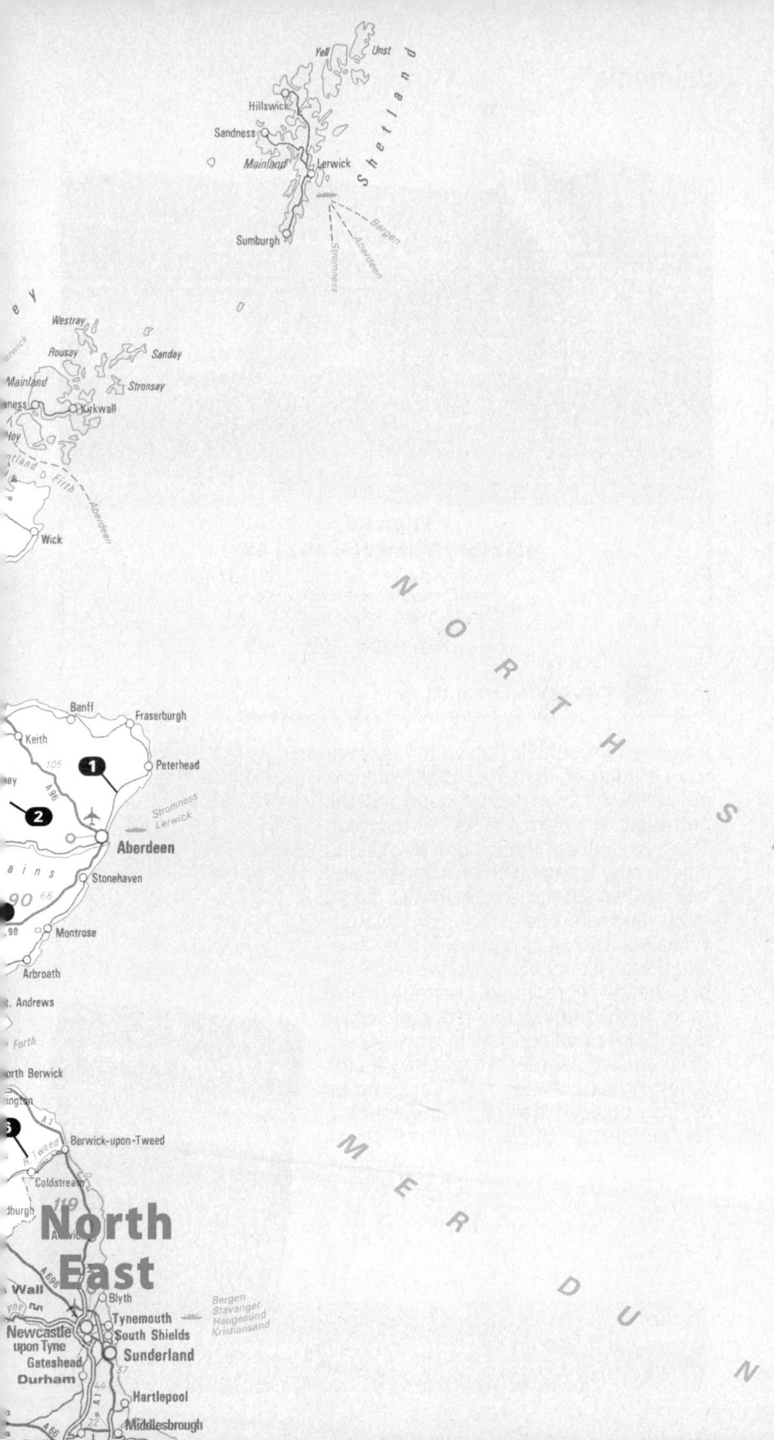

Yell
Unst
Shetland
Hillswick
Sandness
Mainland
Lerwick
Bergen
Aberdeen
Stromness
Sumburgh
Westray
Rousay
Sanday
Mainland
Stronsay
Kirkwall
Hoy
Firth
Aberdeen
Wick
NORTH SEA
MER DU NORD
Banff
Fraserburgh
Keith
Peterhead
Stromness
Lerwick
Aberdeen
Stonehaven
Montrose
Arbroath
Forth
Berwick-upon-Tweed
Coldstream
North East
Wall
Blyth
Tynemouth
Bergen
Stavanger
Haugesund
Kristiansand
Newcastle upon Tyne
South Shields
Gateshead
Sunderland
Durham
Hartlepool
Middlesbrough

Balmedie

1 Cock and Bull

Ellon Rd,
Blairton, Balmedie, AB23 8XY
Tel.: (01358)743249 – Fax: (01358)742466
e-mail: info@thecockandbull.co.uk
Website: www.thecockandbull.co.uk

VISA MC AE

Caledonian 80 Shilling

A quirky, atmospheric pub with a sense of fun befitting of its name; check out the mural on the men's toilet door and the profusion of knick-knacks throughout. There's a choice of three rooms in which to dine: a cosy lounge with an open fire and low leather sofas, a more formal dining room and an open, airy conservatory. Wherever you sit, the menu's the same, and there's plenty of choice. We're talking big, hearty portions of honest, manly food, with nothing too fancy or fiddly: think black pudding, slow roast pork belly or chargrilled Aberdeenshire steak. There's a freshly made burger every day – maybe venison or beef; they are rightly famous for their fish and chips and prices are the right side of reasonable, particularly at lunchtime.

Closing times
Open daily

Prices
Meals: £ 22 (Sunday) and a la carte £ 22/30

Typical Dishes
Ingrams pork rillette
Butter roasted halibut with pancetta cream
Poached rhubarb tarte Tatin

6 mi north of Aberdeen by A 90. Parking.

2 **The Glenkindie Arms**

Glenkindie,
AB33 8SX
Tel.: (01975)641288
e-mail: iansimpson1873@live.co.uk
Website: www.theglenkindiearms.co.uk

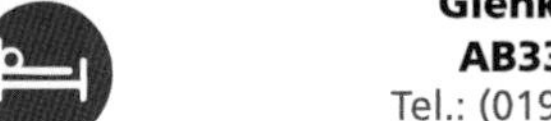

Inveralmond, Deeside and Cairngorm breweries

The Glenkindie Arms is a rustic Highland inn, set in a remote location in the middle of prime hunting and fishing territory; and at 400 years old, it has plenty of charm. The large bar with its roaring open fire, tartan carpets and huge collection of malt whiskies honours its Scottish roots and provides good views out across the surrounding countryside. The daily changing menu is chalked up the blackboard and offers four choices per course; you might find cullen skink or Peterhead mackerel, followed by lamb's liver, rabbit or mature steak. Dishes make the most of what's in season and available locally (including wild mushrooms that grow just outside the door), and are straightforward, well-cooked and tasty. Simple bedrooms complete the picture.

Closing times
Closed November-April, Monday and Tuesday
booking essential

Prices
Meals: a la carte £ 20/25
3 rooms: £ 35/70

10 mi northeast of Ballater, by A 93, B 9119, and A 97. Parking.

Memus

3 **Drovers**

Memus,
DD8 3TY
Tel.: (01307)860322
e-mail: info@the-drovers.com
Website: www.the-drovers.com

 **Greene King IPA, Inveralmond Breweries Ossian**

Set in a lovely location on the fringes of a peaceful hamlet, this remote Highland inn was once a crofter's cottage. You'll probably need your sat nav to find it, but when you do, you'll be rewarded with 360° countryside views. The snug bar reminds you that you're in prime cattle country – its sage coloured walls filled with highland cow prints, mounted cow heads and a superb collection of highland cow horns, as well as a welcoming open fire – but there's also a more formal dining room if that's what you're after. Dishes are hearty and warming, with plenty of comfort food on offer, such as braised pork belly, mashed potato and liver; the weekly changing four-choice set menu providing the best value. Cheery local service helps to set the tone.

Closing times
Open daily

Prices
Meals: a la carte £ 24/38

Typical Dishes
Asparagus with duck egg & crispy pancetta
Roe deer loin & truffle mash
Tayberry tart & rhubarb sorbet

4 mi north of Kirriemuir by B 955 and minor road east. Parking.

4 **The Oyster Inn**

Connel,
PA37 1PJ
Tel.: (01631)710666 – Fax: (01631)710042
e-mail: stay@oysterinn.co.uk
Website: www.oysterinn.co.uk

VISA MC AE

Deuchar's IPA, Arran Blonde

With views over the Falls of Lora and across to the mountains, this brightly coloured inn is steeped in history. The 18C Ferryman's Bar got its name from serving nearby ferry passengers, although it was better known as the Glue Pot because people used to get 'stuck' waiting for the return boat. It boasts stone walls, log fires and a pleasant rear terrace – as well as a pool table, a dartboard and a menu of pub classics. The smarter pine-furnished restaurant is adorned with lobster pots and nautical memorabilia and offers a regularly changing seafood menu and lovely views of the sun setting over the bay. Bedrooms boast pine furniture, colourful prints and contemporary throws; budget bunk rooms are available. Touch a glue pot to bring you luck.

Closing times
Closed 26 December

Prices
Meals: a la carte £ 15/55
11 rooms: £ 55/125

Typical Dishes
Haggis tricolour
Grilled langoustines
Sticky toffee pudding

5 mi north of Oban by A 85. Parking.

Scotland • Argyll and Bute

5 **Tayvallich Inn**

Tayvallich,
PA31 8PL
Tel.: (01546)870282
e-mail: info@tayvallichinn.co.uk
Website: www.tayvallichinn.co.uk

VISA MC AE

Fyne Ales

The Tayvallich Inn's sign shows the silhouette of a lobster, which gives a clue as to what this pub is all about: the chef knows a thing or two about seafood and you can expect to see plenty of locally caught, seasonal fish and shellfish including langoustines, mussels, lobster and lemon sole, as well as scallops by the bucket load. The menu also offers classic pub dishes like steak and chips and a popular curry of the day; the owners worked on local fish farms before taking over the reins here and make the most of their extensive local connections to source the best produce possible. Dine in the bar, in the more formal dining area or out on the decked terrace, with its rustic style bench seating and picturesque views out over the bay.

Closing times
Closed Monday November-March

Prices
Meals: a la carte £ 16/26

12 mi west of Lochgilphead by A 816, B 841 and B 8025; on west shore of Loch Sween. Parking.

6

The Wheatsheaf

Main St,
Swinton, TD11 3JJ
Tel.: (01890)860257 – Fax: (01890)860688
e-mail: reception@wheatsheaf-swinton.co.uk
Website: www.wheatsheaf-swinton.co.uk

 **Deuchars IPA**

Set in the heart of the village overlooking the green, this substantial stone inn is far from your typical pub. Inside there are numerous sofa-filled rooms and two small dining areas – one boasting linen-laid tables and leather chairs; the other an attractive pine ceiling and matching furniture. The hands-on owners are extremely passionate about food but drinkers are equally as welcome. The lunchtime menu displays pub classics, while the concise evening à la carte is slightly more adventurous, offering maybe smoked duck with poached pear, followed by loin of venison. Well-presented plates feature flavoursome local produce, with seafood from Eyemouth and meat from the surrounding border farms. Bedrooms are spacious, cosy and well-equipped.

Closing times
Closed lunch
Monday-Tuesday

Prices
Meals: £ 32 (dinner)
and a la carte £ 19/35

10 rooms: £ 75/138

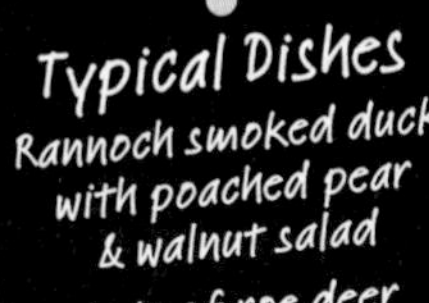

 *In the centre of the village. Plenty of parking on the road.*

7 **The Sorn Inn**

35 Main St,
Sorn, KA5 6HU
Tel.: (01290)551305 – Fax: (01290)553470
e-mail: craig@sorninn.com
Website: www.sorninn.com

Inspectors' favourites

VISA MC

Texas Ale, Peter's Well

It may not look much from outside but this simple whitewashed inn proves you should never judge a book by its cover. It's very much a family affair, with the father checking you in to one of the neat bedrooms and the son preparing your meals. The first clues as to the quality of the food are the framed menus in reception and the presence of the chefs' Holy Bible 'Larousse' on the shelf. Move through to the snug bar and you'll be presented with a choice of robust dishes including homemade pastas, fresh fish and some great quality steaks, which are cooked to perfection. For more refined cooking, head for the dining room, where'll you find carefully and knowledgeably executed dishes with a Mediterranean edge, such as chump of lamb with cous cous.

Closing times
Closed 2 weeks January and Monday

Prices
Meals: £ 19/24
and a la carte £ 19/29
4 rooms: £ 40/70

2 mi east of Catrine by B 713. Parking.

8 The Kings Wark

36 The Shore,
Leith, EH6 6QU
Tel.: (0131)5549260
e-mail: thekingswark@gmail.com
Website: www.kingswark.com

Deuchar's IPA, Caley 80/-, Bitter & Twisted, Schiehallion

Often described as a 'silver thread in a ribbon of green', the Water of Leith flows from the Pentland Hills to Leith Harbour where, on the quayside, you'll find this brightly coloured pub. Built in 1434 as a royal armoury and store for King James I's wine and provisions, it later found use as a naval yard and a royal palace. It's a proper old-fashioned place and hugely characterful inside, with scrubbed floorboards, exposed beams, stone walls and heavily embossed wallpaper. The hand-written bar menu lists hearty, rustic dishes including the likes of stews and roast meats, as well as some Mediterranean flavours. For something more substantial, head for the restaurant, where you'll find an ambitious main menu and tasty blackboard specials.

Closing times
Closed 25-26 December

Prices
Meals: a la carte £ 13/30

Typical Dishes
Smoked cod kedgeree
Borders roe deer & braised venison neck with pearl barley
Honey & saffron tart

Off the south side of Bernard Street, A 199. Parking across the street on the shore.

9 The Ship on the Shore

24-26 The Shore,
Leith, EH6 6QN
Tel.: (0131)5550409
e-mail: seafood@theshipontheshore.co.uk
Website: www.theshipontheshore.co.uk

 **No real ales offered**

With its neat blue façade inset with ship's navigation lights and modelled on the Royal Yacht Britannia, this period building on the quayside looks ready to set sail. Inside, the walls are papered with European maritime charts; scrubbed wooden floors mimic a ship's deck; and it's filled with nautical bric à brac. Regulars prop up the bar and a friendly service team buzz around, creating a relaxed, informal atmosphere. The kitchen follows a philosophy of 'sustainable Scottish seafood served simply with style', and 99% of the menu is just this. Popular classics are a mainstay, while fresh daily specials are featured on numerous blackboards; you'll find everything from Cullen Skink to whole roast sea bass, and the odd meat dish on offer too.

Closing times
Open daily

Prices
Meals: £ 15 and a la carte £ 30/45

Typical Dishes
Cullen skink
Fruits de mer for two
Cheesecake

 *On east side of river. On-street parking.*

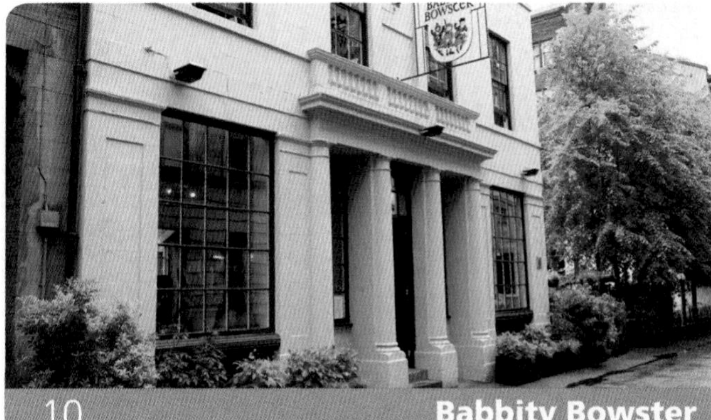

10 Babbity Bowster

16-18 Blackfriars St,
Glasgow, G1 1PE
Tel.: (0141)5525055 – Fax: (0141)5527774
e-mail: babbity@btinternet.com

Deuchar's IPA, Kelburn Misty Law, Bitter & Twisted, Peter's Well

If you're wondering about the name, 'babbity' means to 'bob', a 'bowster' is the wheelshaft of a watermill and the 'babbity bowster' is an old country dance which used to be performed at Scottish balls. Located on the edge of the Merchant City, this double-fronted Georgian building has become part of tradition itself, and one glance at the fiercely Scottish décor and regional memorabilia tells you why. The cheery owner always goes the extra mile; although it's hard not to be satisfied when there's such a fine selection of local ales and whiskies around. Cooking is firmly rooted in tradition, with straightforward, seasonal Scottish favourites including cullen skink, neeps and tatties. For more elaborate dishes, head to the upstairs restaurant.

Closing times
Closed 25 December and 1 January

Prices
Meals: a la carte £ 15/21

 *In city centre north of the Central railway station.*

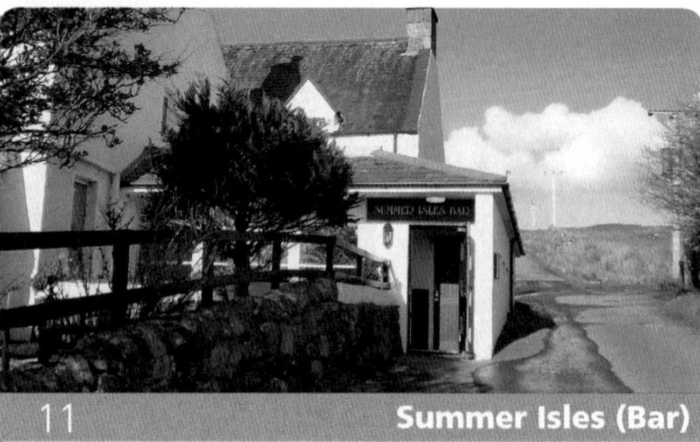

11 Summer Isles (Bar)

Achiltibuie,
IV26 2YG
Tel.: (01854)622282 – Fax: (01854)622251
e-mail: info@summerisleshotel.com
Website: www.summerisleshotel.com

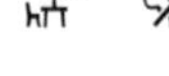

An Teallach, Beinn Dearg, Crofters' Pale Ale

Set to the side of the Summer Isles Hotel, this was originally an old crofters' bar and dates back to the mid-19C. Still popular with the locals today, it boasts two snug rooms filled with black ash tables, a large lawned area with bench seating and a small two-table terrace affording glorious views over the Summer Isles themselves. Daily changing menus have a strong seafood base but there are plenty of other Scottish-sourced ingredients on offer too, with dishes such as fresh pea soup, chicken breast stuffed with skirlie or local Aberdeen Angus steak. The star of the show, however, has to be the plump, tasty langoustines; which are best enjoyed with a chilled glass of Sauvignon Blanc. Comfy bedrooms are available in the adjoining hotel.

Closing times
April-October
Prices
Meals: a la carte £ 20/30

Typical Dishes
Summer Isles fish soup scented with orange, Pernod and tarragon
Seafood platter
Steamed apricot & Amaretto pudding

15 mi northwest of Ullapool by A 835 and minor road west from Drumrunie. Parking.

12 **Applecross Inn**

Shore St,
Applecross, IV54 8LR
Tel.: (01520)744262 – Fax: (01520)744400
e-mail: applecrossinn@btconnect.com
Website: www.applecross.uk.com

Red Cuillin, Young Pretender, Hebridean Gold

Set between the mountains of the mainland and the Isle of Skye, the Applecross Peninsula provides a tranquil haven from the world outside. It seems miraculous that this charming Highland inn can get so busy, as access to the tiny fishing village is either via a 24 mile coastal track or steep zigzagging mountain pass; albeit accompanied by panoramic views over the Kintail Mountains and Outer Hebrides. Menus offer local, seasonal produce, and with stunning views over the water to the distant hills of Skye, you might even be able to see where many of the ingredients come from. Fresh seafood arrives regularly from Applecross Bay and venison from the nearby estate. Smart, comfy bedrooms are set in old fishermen's cottages and boast sea views.

Closing times
Closed 25 December and 1 January
booking essential

Prices
Meals: a la carte £ 25/40
7 rooms: £ 50/100

Typical Dishes
Haggis flambé in Drambuie
Applecross Bay prawns & salad
Raspberry cranachan

From Kishorn via Belach nam Bo (Alpine Pass) or round by Shieldaig and along the coast. Parking.

13 **Cawdor Tavern**

The Lane,
Cawdor, IV12 5XP
Tel.: (01667)404777 – Fax: (01667)454584
e-mail: enquiries@cawdortavern.co.uk
Website: www.cawdortavern.co.uk

   AE

 **Orkney Dark Island, Red McGregor, Three Sisters**

Macbeth may have died several centuries before it was built, but the next door castle is well-known for its role in Shakespeare's tragedy, and this smart whitewashed pub was once its joiners' workshop. It's an immensely charming place and is very passionately run by the owner – who, having purchased both the Orkney and Atlas breweries, isn't short of an award winning ale or two. Exposed beams and wooden-panelling abound and it's hard to choose between the lovely open-fired bar, characterful lounge and traditional restaurant. The wide-ranging, classical menu offers a good selection of frequently changing dishes; you might find trio of Scottish black pudding, haggis and white pudding, followed by Highland venison with bramble and juniper jus.

Closing times
Closed 2 weeks January, 25 December and 1 January
booking essential

Prices
Meals: a la carte £ 16/26

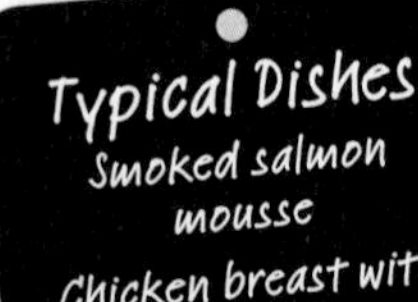

 *5 mi south of Nairn by B 9090. Parking.*

14 Kylesku (Bar)

Kylesku,
IV27 4HW
Tel.: (01971)502231
e-mail: info@kyleskuhotel.co.uk
Website: www.kyleskuhotel.co.uk

VISA

No draught beers offered

Breathtaking views of Loch Glendhu and the spectacular surrounding scenery make this inn an essential stop-off point if you're ever in the area. Friendly staff welcome guests and there's a cosy, homely atmosphere in the spacious, fire-lit bar. Sup on local ale while you trade tales with walkers and cyclists, before settling down to eat seafood so local it practically swam in the door. Langoustines and fish come from the jetty in front of the bar and mussels are rope grown 200 yards away. Classic dishes might include salmon fishcakes or a fish pie, a satisfying bowl of soup or a platter of mature local cheeses, while if you're after something a little more meaty, try a mature local steak. Eight comfortable bedrooms upstairs in the hotel.

Closing times
March - October

Prices
Meals: £ 29 (dinner)
and a la carte £ 20/31

Typical Dishes
Loch Glendhu langoustine bisque
Spaghetti marinara with salmon
Blueberry & vanilla panna cotta

32 mi north of Ullapool by A 835, A 837 and A 894. On street parking.

Lewiston

15 **Loch Ness Inn**

Lewiston,
IV63 6UW
Tel.: (01456)450991
e-mail: info@staylochness.co.uk
Website: www.staylochness.co.uk

Cairngorm Trade Winds, Red Cuillin and several weekly changing guest ales

Aside from the name, there's nothing inside to suggest a link with the mythical monster, or even Scotland for that matter; making this an honest local pub rather than just a tartan-clad tourist attraction. You'd never guess that it had once stood derelict, especially when you're rubbing shoulders with the locals in the buzzing bar or relaxing on the wood-furnished terrace. The dining area consists of two spacious rooms featuring exposed stone walls, black slate floors and new timbered beams; where at lunchtime you'll find a small blackboard menu of pub classics, and at dinner, more restaurant-style dishes such as risotto or confit of duck. Named after local lochs and glens, the individually styled bedrooms have a pleasant, country feel.

Closing times
Open daily
Prices
Meals: a la carte £ 17/30
12 rooms: £ 57/99

Typical Dishes
West Coast mussels
Loin of Torridon venison & sweet potatoes
Homemade fresh berry cheesecake

14 mi southwest of Inverness by A 82. Parking.

16 **Plockton Hotel**

41 Harbour St,
Plockton, IV52 8TN
Tel.: (01599)544274 – Fax: (01599)544475
e-mail: info@plocktonhotel.co.uk
Website: www.plocktonhotel.co.uk

 **Plockton Bay, Arran Blonde, Clansman, Hebridean Gold**

Set on the waterfront overlooking Loch Carron, this building started life as two small cottages before being transformed into an inn. Boasting an unusual black exterior, it stands out among the other whitewashed buildings in this small National Trust village; and not just on appearance. Owned by the Pearson family for over 20 years, it has a friendly, welcoming feel. The bar is the centre of activity but there's a small terrace and restaurant if you fancy something quieter. Their speciality is seafood but you'll also find Highland meats and plenty of locally grown Scottish produce, in dishes like casserole of venison, seafood bake or Plockton smokies. Bedrooms are split between the pub and an annexe; those to the front boast great bay views.

Closing times
Open daily
Prices
Meals: a la carte £ 15/35
15 rooms: £ 55/120

 *5 mi north of Kyle of Lochalsh. Parking 50 yards away in village car park.*

Scotland • Highland

Waternish

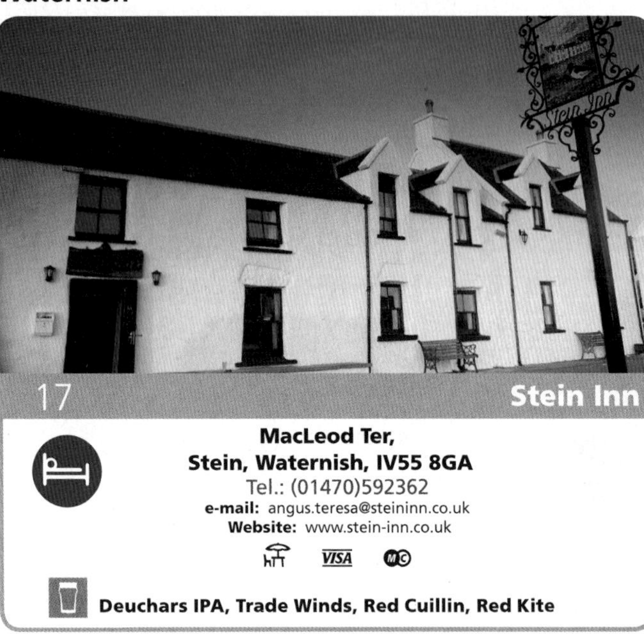

17 **Stein Inn**

MacLeod Ter,
Stein, Waternish, IV55 8GA
Tel.: (01470)592362
e-mail: angus.teresa@steininn.co.uk
Website: www.stein-inn.co.uk

VISA

Deuchars IPA, Trade Winds, Red Cuillin, Red Kite

Set towards the northwest end of the island, on the Waternish Peninsula, this whitewashed building dates back to 1790 and beyond, and is the oldest inn on Skye. Large black lettering on the side wall states its purpose; to the rear there are picnic benches for the warmer months; and inside, a characterful wood-panelled bar and stone-walled lounge with an open fire form the heart of the pub. At lunchtime you'll find the likes of fresh crab sandwiches, ploughman's with Scottish cheeses and maybe even a haggis toastie; while dinner is more substantial and might include Skye scallops, local venison or Scottish salmon. Bedrooms are simple and well-kept, and with no TVs, you're free to watch the comings and goings of picturesque Loch Bay instead.

Closing times
Open daily

Prices
Meals: a la carte £ 15/40

5 rooms: £ 40/100

Typical Dishes

Pan fried scallops in butter

Battered haddock

Homemade fruit crumble

22 mi west of Portree by A 87, A 850 and B 886; on the shore of Loch Bay. Parking.

18 The Anglers Inn

Main Rd,
Guildtown, PH2 6BS
Tel.: (01821)640329
e-mail: info@theanglersinn.co.uk
Website: www.theanglersinn.co.uk

VISA MC AE

Inspectors' favourites

Inveralmond

This whitewashed pub is situated in a tiny hamlet in the heart of Perthshire – not far from Scone Palace, where the Scottish Kings were crowned – and boasts lovely distant mountain views. It may not look much from the outside (it could be any of a hundred Scottish country inns) but this pub is different: in fact, it's hardly a pub at all, as drinkers must stay in the bar area and it's diners-only in the more formal, laminate-floored room. The good value menu displays a classical base and some fairly ambitious dishes such as smoked fish three ways or roast chicken breast with aubergine Parmigiano; ingredients are fresh and well prepared, and cooking is careful. Bedrooms are clean and simple, with freezers available to hunters and fishermen.

Closing times
Closed Monday

Prices
Meals: £ 15 (lunch)
and a la carte £ 21/31

5 rooms: £ 50/100

Typical Dishes
Anglers fish cakes
Roast venison with red cabbage & wild mushrooms
Crème brûlée

7 mi north of Perth by A 93. Parking.

19

The Strathardle Inn

Kirkmichael,
PH10 7NS
Tel.: (01250)881224 – Fax: (08717)145736
e-mail: strathardleinn@btconnect.com
Website: www.strathardleinn.co.uk

 **Thrappledouser and Pentland IPA**

As you leave the village of Kirkmichael, heading south towards Blairgowrie on the A924, you pass by this 18C drover's inn, opposite the river. Stop off instead and experience the warm welcome extended by the owners; they hail from Yorkshire originally but are now deeply rooted in this beautiful part of Scotland – a fact that reveals itself in their judicious use of seasonal produce from the surrounding countryside. Cooking is robust and technically sound, with a Scottish twist. The concise lunch menu offers pub favourites like fish and chips, while dinner might feature local venison, smoked salmon or sirloin steak highlander and can be taken in either the bar or the dining room, both of which boast open fires. Bedrooms are simple and modern.

Closing times
Closed Monday lunch and Tuesday-Friday lunch November-March

Prices
Meals: a la carte £ 18/30
8 rooms: £ 40/80

Typical Dishes
Shetland crab cakes
Medallions of wild local venison
Peach Melba crème brûlée

Between Pitlochry and Blairgowrie on A 924. Parking.

It's nearly six hundred years since Owen Glyndawr escaped the clutches of the English to become a national hero, and in all that time the Welsh passion for unity has bound the country together like a scarlet-shirted scrum. It may be only 170 miles from north to south, but Wales contains great swathes of beauty, such as the dark and craggy heights of Snowdonia's ninety mountain peaks, the rolling sandstone bluffs of the Brecon Beacons, and Pembrokeshire's tantalising golden beaches. Bottle-nosed dolphins love it here too, arriving each summer at New Quay in Cardigan Bay. Highlights abound: formidable Harlech Castle dominates its coast, and Bala Lake has a railway that steams along its gentle shores. Hay-on-Wye's four pubs and eighteen bookshops turn perceptions on their head, and Welsh cuisine is causing a surprise or two as well: the country teems with great raw ingredients now employed to their utmost potential, from the humblest cockle to the slenderest slice of succulent lamb.

North West
West Midlands
WALES
LIVERPOOL
BAILE ÁTHA CLIATH
Southport
Liverpool Bay
Belfast
Dublin
Douglas (I. of Man)
Liverpool
Holyhead / Caergybi
Holy Island
Isle of Anglesey
ANGLESEY
Amlwch
Llanerchymedd
Llangefni
Rhosneigr
Beaumaris
Menai Bridge
Newborough
Bangor
Caernarfon
Caernarfon Bay
Great Ormes Head
Llandudno
Conwy
Colwyn Bay / Bae Colwyn
Rhyl
Prestatyn
Abergele
Penmaenmawr
Llanfairfechan
Bethesda
Carnedd Llewelyn
Llanberis
Capel Curig
Llanrwst
Betws-y-Coed
Snowdon
Snowdonia
Beddgelert
Blaenau Ffestiniog
Ffestiniog
Penrhyndeudraeth
Porthmadog
Criccieth
Pwllheli
Abersoch
Aberdaron
Nefyn
Lleyn Peninsula
Harlech
GWYNEDD
National Park
Barmouth
Dolgellau
Cader Idris
Tywyn
Aberdovey
Machynlleth
Mallwyd
Bala
Pentrefoelas
Cerrigydrudion
Corwen
Llangollen
Berwyn
Oswestry
Denbigh / Dinbych
St. Asaph
Ruthin / Rhuthun
Mold / Yr Wyddgrug
Flint / Fflint
Holywell
Mostyn
Queensferry
Wrexham / Wrecsam
Ruabon
Chester
Birkenhead
Wallasey
Hoylake
Bootle
Formby
Ainsdale
Ormskirk
Skelmersdale
Wigan
St. Helens
Warrington
Widnes
Runcorn
Frodsham
Ellesmere Port
Bebington
Chorley
Bolton
Bury
Darwen
Leyland
Leigh
Altrincham
Northwich
Winsford
Middlewich
Tarporley
Sandbach
Crewe
Nantwich
Newcastle-under-Lyme
Audlem
Whitchurch
Ellesmere
Wem
Market Drayton
Hodnet
Eccleshall
Newport
Shrewsbury
Llynclys
Llanfyllin
Welshpool / Y Trallwng
Caersws
Newtown / Drenewydd
Montgomery
Bishop's
Minsterley
Stretton
Telford
Ironbridge
Bridgnorth
WREKIN
SHROPSHIRE
WOLVERHAMPTON
Grudgington

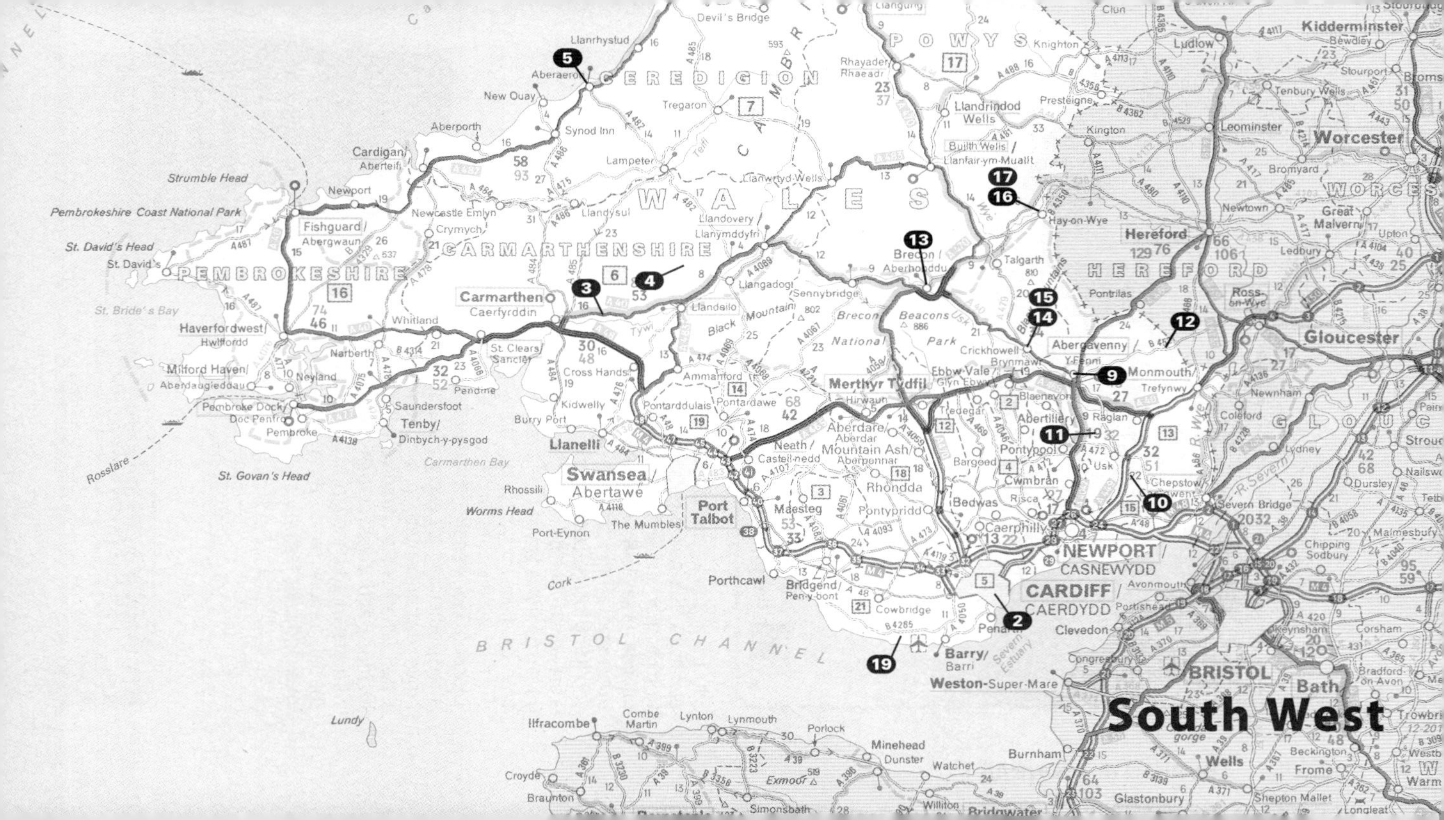

South West
BRISTOL
Bath
Wells
Weston-Super-Mare
Clevedon
CARDIFF / CAERDYDD
NEWPORT / CASNEWYDD
Chepstow
Monmouth / Trefynwy
Abergavenny / Y-Fenni
Merthyr Tydfil
Swansea / Abertawe
Port Talbot
Llanelli
Carmarthen / Caerfyrddin
Tenby / Dinbych-y-pysgod
Pembroke
Pembroke Dock / Doc Penfro
Milford Haven / Aberdaugleddau
Haverfordwest / Hwlffordd
St. David's
Fishguard / Abergwaun
Cardigan / Aberteifi
Aberaeron
Hereford
Gloucester
Worcester
Kidderminster
Ludlow
Leominster
Brecon / Aberhonddu
Hay-on-Wye
Builth Wells / Llanfair-ym-Muallt
Llandrindod Wells
Rhayader / Rhaeadr
Llandovery / Llanymddyfri
Llandeilo
Lampeter
Tregaron
Devil's Bridge
W A L E S
POWYS
CEREDIGION
CARMARTHENSHIRE
PEMBROKESHIRE
HEREFORD
Brecon Beacons National Park
Black Mountain
Pembrokeshire Coast National Park
BRISTOL CHANNEL
Carmarthen Bay
St. Bride's Bay
Strumble Head
St. David's Head
St. Govan's Head
Worms Head
Lundy
Ilfracombe
Lynton
Lynmouth
Minehead
Exmoor
Glastonbury
Frome
Rosslare
Cork

1 **The White Eagle**

Rhoscolyn,
LL65 2NJ
Tel.: (01407)860267
e-mail: white.eagle@timpson.com
Website: www.white-eagle.co.uk

 **Cobblers, Weetwood Eastgate Ale, Reverend James**

Set in a small coastal hamlet on the peninsula, this pub boasts great sea views from its spacious decked terrace. From the outside it may look more like a restaurant but swing a right through the door and you'll find locals playing on slot machines in a cosy open-fired bar. It's rightly popular, so you might have to wait for a table; fill your time by glancing over the display of the owners' business history – they also own Timpson Shoe Repairs. The monthly menu offers something for everyone and dishes arrive well-presented, in a contemporary style; whether it's traditional battered haddock and chips or pan-fried salmon with prawn and chorizo butter. Daily fish specials, regular pie or sausage weeks and weekend beer festivals also feature.

Closing times
Open daily

Prices
Meals: a la carte £ 20/37

5 mi south of Holyhead by B 4545 and minor road south. Parking.

2

The New Conway

53 Conway Rd,
Cardiff, CF11 9NW
Tel.: (029)20224373
Website: www.theconway.co.uk

VISA MC AE D

 **Greene King IPA, Otley, Vale of Glamorgan, Newmans**

Set in a residential area just north of the city and very much a place for local drinkers, The New Conway offers everything from a pint and a bowl of chips whilst you watch the rugby, through to a three course meal and a bottle of wine from the well-priced list. A makeover has given the pub a light, modern feel, with comfy sofas by the fire and shelves crammed with books and board games. Although prone to the odd over-elaboration, their approach to food is, in the main, pleasingly simple: using fresh, seasonal and local produce to create tasty pub classics like steak and chips, toad in the hole or apple and raisin crumble. Having chosen from the daily changing blackboard menu, place your order at the bar; service is friendly and efficient.

Closing times
Closed 25 December

Prices
Meals: a la carte £ 24/35

Typical Dishes
Creamed goat's cheese & evaporated Guinness
Welsh lamb with liquorice & prune purée
Welsh cakes with white chocolate & Earl Grey mousse

 *Parking in neighbouring roads.*

3 **Y Polyn**

Nantgaredig, Carmarthen,
SA32 7LH
Tel.: (01267)290000
e-mail: ypolyn@hotmail.com
Website: www.ypolynrestaurant.co.uk

VISA

Otley 01 and Otley Boss

Collectively, the owners here have a wealth of experience, gleaned from their various backgrounds, and you can be sure that they know what they're doing. Set in a great corner location, next to a stream and with views across the surrounding fields, this pub attracts diners from far and wide. Contemporary colours lead the way in the dining room but it also manages to maintain some of its original rustic style – yet despite the casual attire of the servers, most guests still dress to the nines. Cooking is in the classical vein but has a modern edge and, as you would expect, is hearty, tasty and uses local produce wherever possible. The simpler lunch selection is priced accordingly, while in the evening, the choice expands under a set menu.

Closing times
Closed 25-26 December, Sunday dinner and Monday

Prices
Meals: £ 15/30
and a la carte £ 20/35

Typical Dishes
Middle White pork rillettes & rhubarb chutney
Duck shepherd's pie
Local yoghurt & cream panna cotta with honey roast plums

5 mi east of Carmarthen on A 40; from Nantgaredig 1 mi south by B 4310 on B 4300. Parking.

4 **The Angel**

Salem, Llandeilo,
SA197LY
Tel.: (01558)823394
e-mail: rodpeterson@btconnect.com
Website: www.angelsalem.co.uk

   VISA MC

 **Brains Reverend James and regularly-changing guest ales**

The Angel Inn's inviting bar lounge offers comfy sofas and open fires, while a meal in its Edwardian style dining room comes with linen-laid tables. The flavourful cooking falls mostly into the traditional category, with dishes such as pressed ham hock and roast fillet of Welsh beef. Words like sushi, wasabi, spaghetti and tiramisu also crop up on the menu, and there are some unusual combinations, too, in dishes such as the salmon with Welsh rarebit, poached egg and asparagus. Whilst the dinner menu comes at a set cost, dishes on the shorter lunch menu are individually priced. The blackboard displays simpler pub classics like lamb's liver and bacon; there's homemade fudge served with your coffee and homemade chutneys come with the cheese.

Closing times
Closed Sunday dinner, Monday and Tuesday

Prices
Meals: a la carte £ 25/30

Typical Dishes
Smoked haddock cake
Fricassée of chicken with mushrooms & tarragon
Apple custard crème brûlée

 *3 mi north of Llandeilo by A 40 off Pen-y-bane road. Parking.*

Aberaeron

5 Harbourmaster

Quay Par,
Aberaeron, SA46 0BA
Tel.: (01545)570755
e-mail: info@harbour-master.com
Website: www.harbour-master.com

HM Best Bitter and Cwrw Glasglyn

With its vibrant blue exterior, you'll spot this place a mile off; not that the owners need worry about being noticed, as their reputation for good food and hospitality goes before them. As the name suggests, it once belonged to the harbourmaster, and, as such, offers lovely views across the water. Inside, there's a modern bar-lounge with an oval pewter-topped counter and open-plan kitchen, as well as a more traditional wood-panelled dining room – make a play for 'cwtch', a table offering excellent harbour views. Choose between bar snacks, a set price lunch or a more substantial evening à la carte with daily specials. Split between the house and nearby cottage, bedrooms are comfy and brightly decorated; some boast oversized windows or terraces.

Closing times
Closed 25 December

Prices
Meals: a la carte £ 19/38

13 rooms: £ 60/250

In town centre overlooking the harbour. Parking on the harbour road.

7 Pen-y-Bryn

Pen-y-Bryn Rd,
Upper Colwyn Bay, Colwyn Bay, LL29 6DD
Tel.: (01492)533360
e-mail: pen.y.bryn@brunningandprice.co.uk
Website: www.penybryn-colwynbay.co.uk

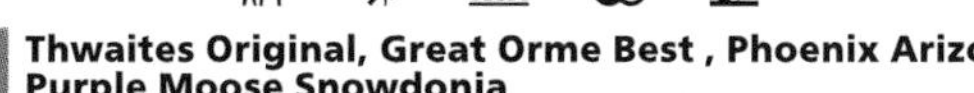

Thwaites Original, Great Orme Best , Phoenix Arizona, Purple Moose Snowdonia

You might need your sat nav, as even when you've located the right residential street, you could easily pass Pen-y-Bryn by. Looking more like a medical centre than a place to dine, it boasts impressive panoramic views over Colwyn Bay, especially from the garden and terrace. The spacious, open-plan interior is crammed full of pictures, bookcases and pottery, yet despite these and the oak floors, old furniture and open fires, it has a modern, laid-back feel. The extensive daily menu offers plenty of choice, ranging from a classical ploughman's to more adventurous pheasant-based dishes; while during 'Beer and Bangers' weeks 12 varieties of sausage and over 20 beers are also offered. Large tables make it ideal for families or groups of friends.

Closing times
Closed 25 December

Prices
Meals: a la carte £ 20/30

Typical Dishes
Salmon & smoked haddock fish cakes
Braised shoulder of Welsh lamb
Belgian waffle & butterscotch sauce

1 mi southwest of Colwyn Bay by B 5113. Parking.

Tyn-y-Groes

6 **The Groes Inn**

Tyn-y-Groes,
LL32 8TN
Tel.: (01492)650545 – Fax: (01492)650855
e-mail: reception@groesinn.com
Website: www.groesinn.com

VISA MC AE D

Great Orme Brewery and Groes Ale

Located in the foothills of Snowdonia, with the estuary in front and the mountains behind, the setting couldn't be more beautiful. Flowers greet you at the door and the characterful beamed interior is filled with pictures, copperware and china; all bathed in flickering firelight. If you're after nooks and crannies, there are several small rooms encircling the comfy bar, as well as an airy conservatory and an intimate dining room. The bar menu features local Welsh and British dishes in neatly presented, generous portions, while at dinner the restaurant steps things up a gear. Specials feature fish from the nearby waters, lamb reared on the salt marshes and game from local estates. Bedrooms have lovely views; some boast balconies or terraces.

Closing times
Closed 25 December

Prices
Meals: a la carte £ 23/40
14 rooms: £ 85/125

Typical Dishes
Creamy smoked haddock & Parmesan
Pan-fried lamb's liver & mustard mash
Apple & cinnamon crumble

3 mi south of Conwy on B 5106. Parking.

8 Glasfryn

Raikes Ln,
Sychdyn, Mold, CH7 6LR
Tel.: (01352)750500 – Fax: (01352)751923
e-mail: glasfryn@brunningandprice.co.uk
Website: www.glasfryn-mold.co.uk

  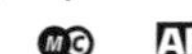

Snowdonia Ale, Timothy Taylor Landlord, Flowers Original, Hawkshead Bitter, Deuchars IPA, Hobsons' Twisted Spire

An early example of Arts and Crafts architecture, this glazed red-brick building was intended to be a judges' residence for the nearby courts but, never used, was turned into a farmhouse, before later falling into disrepair. It's a sizeable place, able to cater for a few hundred at every sitting, with some tables seating up to 20 at a time. Order at the large central bar and watch your order whizz past in the vacuum tube system on its way to the kitchen. Menus offer plenty of choice, from pub classics such as fish and chips to culinary classics such as plaice Véronique, with some lighter dishes alongside. Portions are generous, prices are sensible and service is surprisingly swift. The garden and terrace boast nice views over the town below.

Closing times
Closed 25 December

Prices
Meals: a la carte £ 21/30

Typical Dishes
Crab & shrimp cocktail
Beef & onion pie with chips & peas
Fig pudding with cinnamon custard

1 mi north by A 5119 on Civic Centre rd. Parking.

9 The Hardwick

Old Raglan Rd,
Abergavenny, NP7 9AA
Tel.: (01873)854220
e-mail: info@thehardwick.co.uk
Website: www.thehardwick.co.uk

VISA

Rhymney Brewery and several guest ales including Breconshire Brewery, Otley and Tudor

To pass by this pub would be a culinary crime but with its unassuming whitewashed exterior, could be all too easily done. Since winning BBC2's 'Great British Menu', chef Stephen Terry has become somewhat of a local celebrity, but he takes it in his stride and is often found chatting away to the locals. His philosophy is one of simplicity, and local produce is of paramount importance – so much so, that he's regularly on the farm rather than the phone when placing orders. Menus are lengthy and feature both British and Mediterranean influences, with dishes ranging from Welsh rarebit and salt beef hash to cured meat antipasti boards and gnocchi with Italian artichokes. It's deservedly popular, so booking is essential. Bedrooms are due to open late 2010.

Closing times
Open daily
booking essential

Prices
Meals: £ 24 (lunch)
and a la carte £ 27/40

8 rooms: £ 120

Typical Dishes
Hot local pork terrine
Plaice & butter beans with kale & chicken cream
Poached pear with chocolate mousse & rice pudding

2 mi southeast by A 40 and B 4598. Parking.

10 Raglan Arms

Llandenny, Usk,
NP15 1DL
Tel.: (01291)690800 – Fax: (01291)690155
e-mail: raglanarms@aol.com
Website: www.raglanarms.com

 **Wye Valley Butty Bach and Breconshire Brewery**

With fireside leather sofas, simply laid scrubbed pine tables and vases filled with fresh flowers, The Raglan Arms offers a wholesome cosiness; dining happens mostly in the front of the room, while drinkers tend to congregate in the conservatory at the back. Menus change slightly at each service and are short and to the point. The kitchen is clearly serious about food, using local produce wherever possible and employing a range of cooking styles. Dishes could include home cured bresaola, imam bayildi with mint and crème fraîche or goujons of lemon sole, while dessert might mean a panna cotta or some homemade ice cream and sorbets. There is always a sandwich available at lunch, and main courses offer particularly good value for money.

Closing times
Closed Sunday dinner and Monday

Prices
Meals: £ 22 (Sunday lunch) and a la carte £ 19/35

Typical Dishes
Rosemary & garlic risotto with Italian sausage
Cod fillet with chorizo & butter beans
Trio of chocolate

4.25 mi northeast of Usk by A 472 off B 4235. Parking.

Nant-y-Derry

11 The Foxhunter

Nant-y-Derry, Abergavenny, NP7 9DD
Tel.: (01873)881101
Website: www.thefoxhunter.com

VISA 

 **Bath Ales and Wye Valley Brewery**

Thanks to owner Matt Tebbutt's skill in the kitchen – and his TV appearances – this former station master's house is a popular destination for gastronomes. Inside, the feel is fresh and bright, with food prints on the walls, flagstone floors and wood burning stoves. The simply laid tables are set out in rather regimented rows in the main dining room; sit instead by the fireside in the cosy central space. The short menus change at each service and feature dishes which range in style from classic British to fusion; perhaps Longhorn sirloin, mozzarella and beef tomato, or sashimi of tuna with warm pepperonata salad. Portions are large and hearty and come served with tasty homemade bread; the wine list is impressive, with plenty of range in price.

Closing times
Closed Sunday dinner and Monday

Prices
Meals: £ 24 and a la carte £ 28/35

Typical Dishes
Brecon venison terrine, toasted brioche & fig chutney
Middle White pork loin with red cabbage & pear
Potted figs & clotted cream

 *6.5 mi south of Abergavenny by A 4042 and minor road. Parking.*

12 The Bell at Skenfrith

Skenfrith,
NP7 8UH
Tel.: (01600)750235 – Fax: (01600)750525
e-mail: enquiries@skenfrith.co.uk
Website: www.skenfrith.co.uk

Inspectors' favourites

Wye Valley Bitter, HPA and several guest ales including Kingstone Bitter and Mayfield Brewery

The Bell offers uncomplicated warmth: a seat in a comfy sofa by the inglenook, candles and meadow flowers on the tables and friendly, unobtrusive service. The weekly changing menu features classics styled in a modern manner: dishes might include Wye Valley smoked salmon, a vegetable risotto, or a carpaccio of Brecon beef. Cooking is clean and fresh and lets the ingredients speak for themselves; the local suppliers of the produce invariably credited on the menu. The fruits of the vine are also taken seriously here; there is a large selection of wines by the glass and an impressive choice of champagnes. Bedrooms are understated in their elegance, with super-comfy beds, fluffy towels and personalised toiletries. Heckham Peckham is the best.

Closing times
Closed last week January, first week February and Tuesday November-Easter
booking essential

Prices
Meals: £ 24 (Sunday lunch) and a la carte £ 20/35
11 rooms: £ 75/220

Typical Dishes
Confit salmon fillet & baby leeks
Brecon beef fillet with steak & kidney pudding
Toffee soufflé & caramelised banana

11 mi west of Ross-on-Wye by A 49 on B 4521. Parking.

13 **The Felin Fach Griffin**

Felin Fach,
Brecon, LD3 0UB
Tel.: (01874)620111
e-mail: enquiries@felinfachgriffin.co.uk
Website: www.felinfachgriffin.co.uk

Inspectors' favourites

VISA

Wye Valley Bitter, Breconshire Brewery Golden Valley, Otley Brewery 01 and Tomos Watkin OSB

A terracotta-coloured former farmhouse set in picturesque countryside, this pub is rather unique, in that you'll find visitors aged from 1-100 and from all walks of life – which creates an almost bohemian atmosphere. Bright paintwork, colourful art and the scattering of magazines about the place provide a very 'lived in' feel and the atmosphere is extremely laid-back. The young staff interact well but, just as importantly, have a good knowledge of what they're serving. Starters like local goat's curd with black olive purée or brawn with apricot chutney are followed by Welsh Cobb coq au vin or red mullet with salt cod brandade – and are a cut above your usual pub grub. If you've eaten yourself to a stand still, super-comfy bedrooms await.

Closing times
Closed 24-25 December

Prices
Meals: £ 19/27
and a la carte £ 22/35

7 rooms: £ 75/120

4.75 mi northeast of Brecon by B 4602 off A 470. Parking.

14 The Bear

High St,
Crickhowell, NP8 1BW
Tel.: (01873)810408 – Fax: (01873)811696
e-mail: bearhotel@aol.com
Website: www.bearhotel.co.uk

VISA MC AE

 **Bass, Reverend James, Rumney, Ansells**

The well-maintained Bear stands proudly on the main street of this small town, its hanging baskets creating a riot of colour. Step through the front door into its hugely characterful lounge bar, with its shiny brass and open fireplaces, and you can well believe that it has been here since 1432. Diners can sit here or in the more formal restaurant; the latter may be more romantic but the former is undoubtedly the more appealing. The menu offers tasty, tried-and-tested dishes such as prawn cocktail, Welsh rarebit, fish and chips or lasagne. The 'specials' add interest and a young cheery team provide swift and assured service, even when busy. Bedrooms are available in the hotel: the most characterful feature beams, four-posters and fireplaces.

Closing times
Closed 25 December

Prices
Meals: a la carte £ 20/30

Typical Dishes
Shredded duck salad with chilli dressing
Welsh braised lamb shank
Crème brûlée

 *In the town centre. Parking.*

15 Nantyffin Cider Mill Inn

Brecon Rd,
Crickhowell, NP8 1SG
Tel.: (01873)810775
e-mail: info@cidermill.co.uk
Website: www.cidermill.co.uk

 **Reverend James, Rhymney Best**

Situated just across from the River Usk, this converted 16C cider mill flies the flag for Welsh produce, with short, simple menus which feature predominantly Mediterranean influences. The à la carte focuses on meat dishes, whith choices like rack of local spring lamb or Madgett's Farm free range duck breast, while the sprecials menu is structured around the best seasonal fish and shellfish, with some hearty game in winter. Most people dine in the homely bar, with its wood burning stoves, while the spacious barn – home to the original cider press – has a completely different feel, with clothed tables, wicker chairs and skylights. Real ales, and of course cider, are available on tap, while the short wine list offers plenty for under £30.

Closing times
Closed 25-26 December, Monday except bank holidays and Sunday dinner from October-March

Prices
Meals: a la carte £ 20/28

Typical Dishes
Home-smoked duck salad
Lemon sole with parsley sauce
Chocolate marquise with orange segments

 *1.5 mi west of Crickhowell on A 40. Parking.*

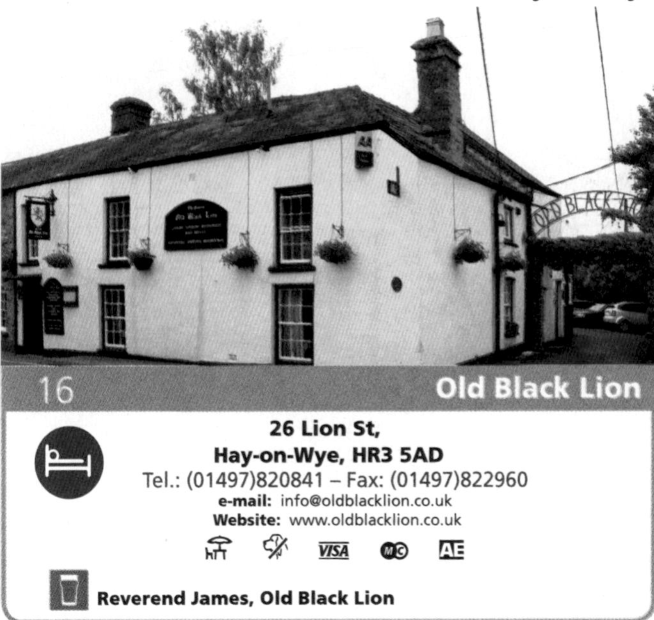

16

Old Black Lion

26 Lion St,
Hay-on-Wye, HR3 5AD
Tel.: (01497)820841 – Fax: (01497)822960
e-mail: info@oldblacklion.co.uk
Website: www.oldblacklion.co.uk

VISA AE

Reverend James, Old Black Lion

This part-13C pub stands on the site of the old gates in this ancient market town and would once have provided refuge for travellers passing from Ireland to England. Although its visitors have now changed – here for the antique shops and annual literary festival – the pub has not. Inside you'll find low beams, scrubbed wooden tables and plenty of old world charm, albeit among more modern, brightly coloured walls. The food here is tasty, honest and arrives in hearty portions, and menus offer a seemingly endless list of dishes – with even more favourites chalked up on the board – maybe duck on parsnip purée or herb crusted lamb. Bedrooms in the main building display antique furnishings; those opposite boast rich colours and modern bathrooms.

Closing times
Closed 24-26 December

Prices
Meals: a la carte £ 22/31

10 rooms: £ 35/115

In the town centre. Parking.

17 **Three Tuns**

4 Broad St,
Hay-on-Wye, HR3 5DB
Tel.: (01497)821855 – Fax: (01497)821955
e-mail: info@three-tuns.com
Website: www.three-tuns.com

 **Wye Valley, Butty Bach, Three Tuns**

After being devastated by fire in 2005, the future of this Grade II listed pub – thought to be the oldest surviving building in Hay-on-Wye – was left hanging in the balance. Thankfully though, two dedicated locals picked up the pieces, managing to save many original features including cruck truss beams, a period dog-leg staircase and large inglenook fireplace. Downstairs, the bar leads through to cosy sofas set beneath a big glass roof and then on to the terrace; find a seat, study the hearty, classical menu and make for the bar to order. The deep-fried cod in local Wye Valley Butty Bach beer-batter is a favourite but if you'd rather have it crab-crusted, head upstairs, where you'll discover friendly table service and a more formal atmosphere.

Closing times
Closed Monday, Tuesday and Sunday dinner

Prices
Meals: a la carte £ 22/28

Typical Dishes
Smoked salmon roulade & wild rocket potato salad
Pot roasted beef with roast potatoes
White chocolate & raspberry brûlée

 *In town centre.*

18 The Talkhouse

Pontdolgoch, Newtown,
SY17 5JE
Tel.: (01686)688919
e-mail: info@talkhouse.co.uk
Website: www.talkhouse.co.uk

VISA

Montys Mojo, Montys Moonshine

Run by an experienced husband and wife team, The Talkhouse has the look and feel of a small house. There's a comfy lounge with old photos of the village on the wall, and a cosy bar with seats around the fire for the drinkers. The colourful rear garden, with its gazebo and terrace, is the owners' pride and joy and the best tables in the house are those in the back room which overlook it. Cooking has a very masculine feel, with hearty portions and bold flavours; the menu is chalked up on a blackboard and changes daily. Dishes might include Welsh lamb rump or pan-fried fish; desserts are read out at the end and might include cheesecake or sticky toffee pudding. Bedrooms have antique pine furniture and colourful furnishings; Myfanwy is the best.

Closing times
Closed Sunday dinner and Monday
booking essential

Prices
Meals: a la carte £ 22/32
3 rooms: £ 70/125

1.5 mi. northwest of Caersws on A 470. Parking.

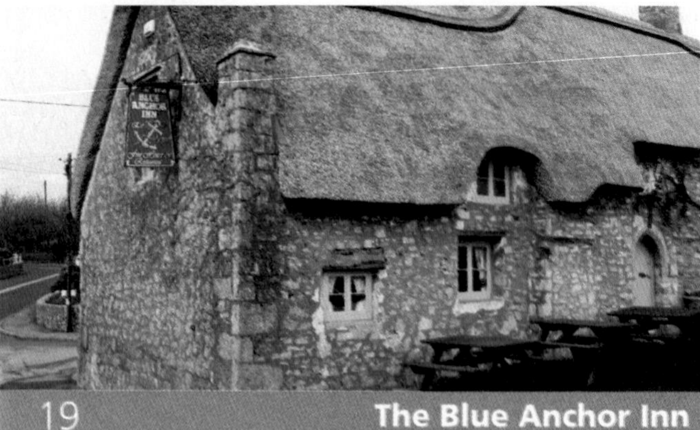

19 The Blue Anchor Inn

East Aberthaw,
CF62 3DD
Tel.: (01446)750329
e-mail: colemanjeremyj@googlemail.com
Website: www.blueanchoraberthaw.com

Wadworth 6X, Brains Bitter, Wye Valley IPA, Theakston Old Peculiar and Tomos Watkins OSB

The name of this pub dates back to 1380, when East Aberthaw was a bustling trading port and the ships that moored in the bay would leave with their anchors covered in a distinctive blue mud. Inside the stone walls and thatched roof of this medieval pub you'll find low beamed ceilings, exposed brick walls, and nooks and crannies aplenty. You enter into a slate-floored drinkers bar and dimly lit dining area but the real surprise is the vast upstairs restaurant which is open for dinner and Sunday lunch. Cooking is traditional and wholesome with straightforward presentation and flavoursome combinations. At lunch you'll find simple dishes such as grilled gammon or beef stew, and in the evening, more interesting offerings like pan-seared wood pigeon.

Closing times
Closed Sunday dinner
Prices
Meals: a la carte £ 15/26

Typical Dishes
Pan-seared wood pigeon
Pan-fried fillet of sewin
Panna cotta & poached rhubarb

Turn at the cement factory and follow the road for approximately 1 mile. Parking opposite the pub.

20 Pant-yr-Ochain

Old Wrexham Rd,
Gresford, LL12 8TY
Tel.: (01978)853525
e-mail: pant.yr.ochain@brunningandprice.co.uk
Website: www.pantyrochain-gresford.co.uk

 **Flowers IPA, Timothy Taylor Landlord, Weetwood Cheshire Cat, Phoenix Arizona**

This is neither a typical rustic inn nor a 21C dining pub – but a classical country manor house in disguise. With Tudor wattle and daub walls backing a 16C inglenook fireplace, it's steeped in history. Outside, mature gardens and well manicured lawns stretch down to a small lake; and on a warm summer's day, lunch on the terrace or lawn is hard to beat. In rainier weather, follow the polished quarry tile floors to a large central bar and choose one of the numerous rooms surrounding it; some with ancient beams and exposed brick walls, all with nooks and crannies aplenty. The daily changing menu offers hearty, wholesome dishes, ranging from pub classics to more interesting offerings like hake with crab butter; but beware – it's over 12s only here.

Closing times
Open daily

Prices
Meals: a la carte £ 20/35

Typical Dishes
Pork, apricot & pistachio terrine
Pork belly & black pudding with boulangère potatoes
Sticky toffee pudding

 *3.5 mi northeast of Wrexham by A 483 on B 5445; then 1 mi south of Gresford. Parking.*

21 The Hand at Llanarmon

Llanarmon Dyffryn Ceiriog,
LL20 7LD
Tel.: (01691)600666 – Fax: (01691)600262
e-mail: reception@thehandhotel.co.uk
Website: www.thehandhotel.co.uk

Weetwoods' Eastgate and Cheshire Cat, Stonehouse Station Bitter, Brains Reverend James

Set at the crossroads of two old drovers' roads, The Hand has been providing hospitality for several centuries and its current owners are continuing the tradition with flair, providing a warm welcome and hearty meals to travellers through this lush valley. Rustic charm abounds in the form of stone walls, open fires and ancient beams; there' s a cosy bar, a spacious dining room, a pool room and quite a collection of taxidermy. The daily changing menu offers loads of choice, with plenty of wholesome pub classics like steak and kidney pie or slow braised lamb shank. Portions are generous and cooking is fresh and flavoursome. Cosy bedrooms have hill views and recently modernised bathrooms – plus a decanter of sherry for a late night tipple.

Closing times
Open daily

Prices
Meals: a la carte £ 18/32

13 rooms: £ 50/125

Typical Dishes

Local game terrine with dark fruit chutney

Ceiriog Valley lamb shoulder

Lemon tart & vanilla ice cream

 *At the head of Ceiriog Valley northwest of Oswestry. Parking.*

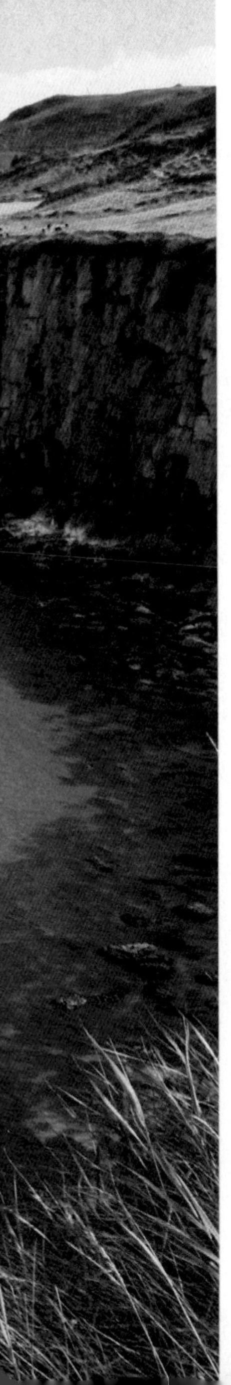

The presiding image of Northern Ireland for outsiders is buzzing Belfast, lying defiantly between mountain and coast. Its City Hall and Queen's University retain the power to impress, and it was within its mighty shipyards that the Titanic first saw the light of day. But the rest of the Six Counties demands attention, too. The forty thousand stone columns of the Giant's Causeway step out into the Irish Sea, part of a grand coastline, though Antrim can also boast nine scenic inland glens. County Down's rolling hills culminate in the alluring slopes of Slieve Donard in the magical Mourne Mountains, while Armagh's Orchard County is a riot of pink in springtime. Fermanagh's glassy, silent lakelands are a tranquil attraction, rivalled for their serenity by the heather-clad Sperrin Mountains, towering over Tyrone and Derry. On top of all this is the cultural lure of boisterous oyster festivals and authentic horse fairs, while farmers' markets are now prominent all across the province.

Hebrides
Coll
Tiree
Tobermory
Loch Linnhe
Mull
Craignure
Fionnphort
Oban
Colonsay
Scotland
Lochgilphead
Loch Fyne
Islay
Port Askaig
Jura
Rothesay
Port Ellen
Malin Head
Kintyre
Brodick
Campbeltown
Giant's Causeway
Arran
Firth of Clyde
Buncrana
Lough Foyle
Portrush
Letterkenny
Londonderry/Derry
Coleraine
Ballycastle
Antrim Glens
North Channel
138
Donegal
NORTHERN IRELAND
A5
A6
A77
Cairnryan
Bundoran
Omagh
48
Larne
Stranraer
N15
Loughs
Lough Neagh
N16
IRELAND
Enniskillen
Lisburn
Bangor
Sligo
73
BELFAST
N4
A4
M1
53
Armagh
Erne
N2
1
2
3
4
5
Boyle
Monaghan
Newry
A1
53
Man
Newcastle
Peel
Cavan
154
Dundalk
Longford
Ardee
Lough Ree
215
36
Ireland
Drogheda
IRISH
Athlone
Mullingar
Navan
Kinnegad
91
R. Boyne
M1
N2
N6
214
55
IRL
Tullamore
M4
DUBLIN
Naas
Birr
M7
N7
Dún Laoghaire
Anglesey
193
Portlaoise
Roscrea
Bray
N7
Glendalough
Holyhead
A55
173
926
Wicklow
Carlow
158
N8
248
Caernarfon
Kilkenny
R. Suir
Arklow
Snowdon
Wales
Cashel
R. Barrow
N9
N11
140
Clonmel
179
Caher
New Ross
Enniscorthy

1 The Pheasant

410 Upper Ballynahinch Rd,
Annahilt, BT26 6NR
Tel.: (028)92638056 – Fax: (028)92638026
e-mail: info@thepheasantrestaurant.co.uk
Website: www.thepheasantrestaurant.co.uk

VISA AE

No real ales offered

Set in the heart of County Down, this sizeable yellow-washed inn has a typically Irish feel; right through from the old Guinness posters to the warm welcome and laid-back atmosphere. It has a Gothic style, featuring stained glass, hunting murals and ornaments aplenty; the traditional open-fired bar being the place to sit when it's cold and the patio providing the ideal spot in warmer months. Cooking uses seasonal produce, with local seafood the speciality in summer and game from the nearby estate in winter – and children are well catered for too, with a dedicated selection of freshly prepared dishes; not forgetting toys and climbing frames. It's a popular place, so if you're in a group it could be worth booking the snug or Gamekeepers Loft.

Closing times
Closed 25-26 December

Prices
Meals: £ 20 (lunch) £24 (dinner) and a la carte £ 20/35

1 mi north of Annahilt on Lisburn rd. Parking.

2 **Coyle's**

44 High St,
Bangor, BT20 5AZ
Tel.: (028)91270362 – Fax: (028)91270362
e-mail: coylesbar@ymail.com
Website: www.coylesbistro.co.uk

VISA

Strangford Lough Ales

If you're after a quiet drink and a good meal then this black painted, typically Irish pub is the place to come: there are no rowdy groups or noisy sports fans, just families and friends catching up and couples out for dinners à deux. There's the choice of laid-back bistro with small bar area or smarter first floor restaurant – each with a different menu, but both highlighting a selection of low fat dishes. In the bar you'll find the likes of macaroni cheese, fishcakes or steak, as well as more international flavours such as chilli and ginger chicken. While the bistro menu steps things up a gear with offerings such as smoked salmon and blini gâteau, followed by scallops with spinach risotto or red pepper crusted pork with gnocchi Romana.

Closing times
Closed 25 December

Prices
Meals: a la carte £ 22/25

Typical Dishes
Strangford Lough mussels
Asian style pork belly
Chocolate & chestnut truffle cake

In the town centre. Pay and display parking 2 min walk.

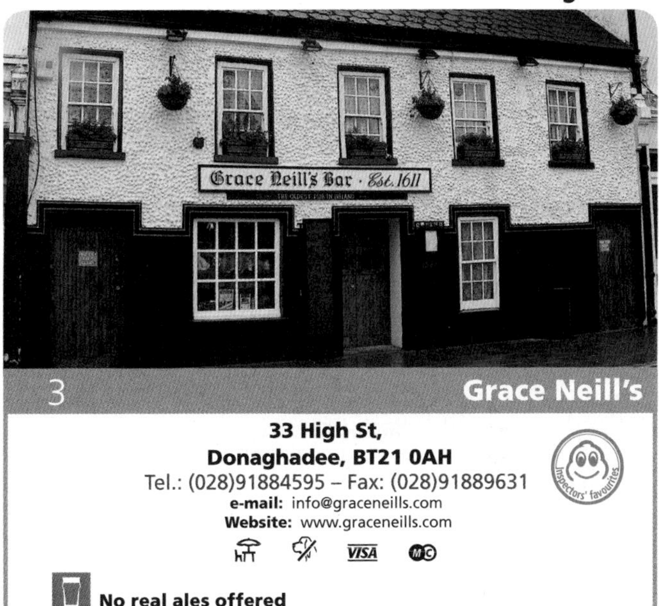

3 Grace Neill's

33 High St,
Donaghadee, BT21 0AH
Tel.: (028)91884595 – Fax: (028)91889631
e-mail: info@graceneills.com
Website: www.graceneills.com

Inspectors' favourites

VISA

No real ales offered

Having first opened as The King's Arms in 1611, the oldest pub in Ireland is still going strong. Renamed in the 1900s after a former landlady who would greet every visitor with a kiss, it boasts characterful beamed snugs crammed full of antique bottles and old pictures; and is the place where smugglers once gathered to plot and scheme. The extensive menu is satisfyingly classical; you might find Portavogie prawn cocktail or Strangford Lough mussels, followed by homemade burgers or local beef and Guinness pie – supplemented by a list of daily seafood specials. For those tight on time, lunch also presents the option of an 'express' menu. Live music is a feature at the weekends and a guitar and tin whistle can always be found behind the bar.

Closing times
Open daily

Prices
Meals: a la carte £ 13/30

Typical Dishes

Lightly curried monkfish & celeriac chips

Homemade fish pie

Chocolate, orange and Guinness brownie with vanilla ice cream

In town centre. Parking.

Donaghadee

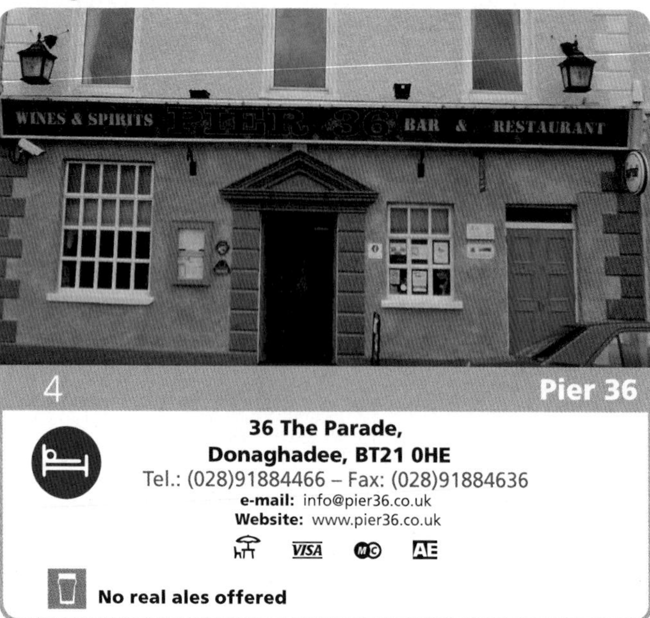

4 Pier 36

36 The Parade,
Donaghadee, BT21 0HE
Tel.: (028)91884466 – Fax: (028)91884636
e-mail: info@pier36.co.uk
Website: www.pier36.co.uk

VISA MC AE

No real ales offered

Set opposite the lighthouse, on the waterfront of a picturesque harbour, you couldn't pick a better spot for this family-run pub. The hospitality here is second to none; the owners having thought of every last detail, right through to reading glasses for those who have forgotten theirs. It's a spacious place, with a traditional open-fired bar, a contemporary dining room and always plenty going on, including Jazz Wednesdays, Motown Fridays and regular steak/seafood nights. Extensive menus range from the traditional to the modern and offer plenty of fresh local seafood, as well as good value 'Light Lunches' and 'Tea Time Tasters'; you'll find as many as 12 desserts and some tempting weekend breakfasts. Simple, comfy bedrooms boast sea views.

Closing times
Closed 25 December

Prices
Meals: £ 20 (Sunday lunch) and a la carte £ 20/35

7 rooms: £ 50/90

On the harbour front. Parking in the street and at the rear.

5 The Plough Inn

3 The Square,
Hillsborough, BT26 6AG
Tel.: (028)92682985 – Fax: (028)92682472
e-mail: patbaldwin@hotmail.co.uk
Website: www.bar-retro.com

 **Hilden Real Ale selection**

From its lush forest and glistening 40 acre lake to its impressive 17C castle and steep streets lined with antique shops, picturesque Hillsborough has plenty to offer, including the locally acclaimed Plough Inn. Having been trading since 1752, it's extremely well-established in the local community – but it's not your usual type of pub. Inside it's almost three establishments in one: the regulars and older folk can be found dining on pub classics in the dark wood bar or on seafood and steak in the similarly styled dining room, while the younger crowds gather upstairs in the stylish bistro, which offers a modern, international menu. Families usually settle next door in the all day café-cum-weekend nightclub and there are plenty of terraces too.

Closing times
Open daily

Prices
Meals: £ 17/25
and a la carte £ 20/35

Typical Dishes
Seared scallops with mango salsa
Venison and beef duo
Forced rhubarb brûlée

 *At the top of the hill in the square. Parking.*

It's reckoned that Ireland offers forty luminous shades of green, and of course an even more famous shade of black liquid refreshment. But it's not all wondrous hills and down-home pubs. The country does other visitor-friendly phenomena just as idyllically: witness the limestone-layered Burren, cut-through by meandering streams, lakes and labyrinthine caves; or the fabulous Cliffs of Moher, unchanged for millennia, looming for mile after mile over the wild Atlantic waves. The cities burst with life: Dublin is now one of Europe's coolest capitals, and free-spirited Cork enjoys a rich cultural heritage. Kilkenny mixes a renowned medieval flavour with a taste for excellent pubs; Galway, one of Ireland's prettiest cities, is enhanced by an easy, boho vibe. Best of all, perhaps, is to sit along the quayside of a fishing village in the esteemed company of a bowl of steaming fresh mussels or gleaming oysters and the taste of a distinctive micro-brewery beer (well, makes a change from stout...).

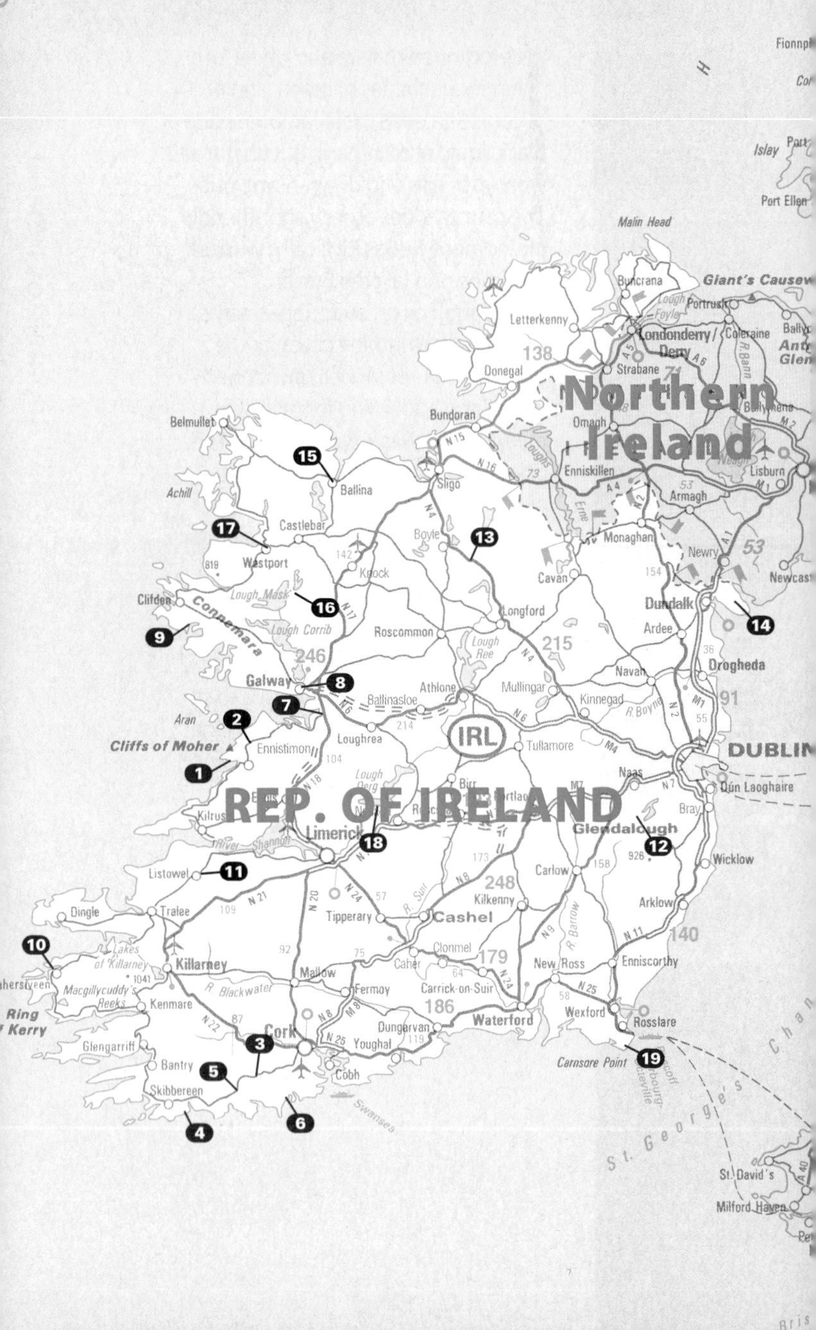

Northern Ireland
REP. OF IRELAND
IRL
DUBLIN
Malin Head
Giant's Causeway
Buncrana
Lough Foyle
Portrush
Letterkenny
Londonderry / Derry
Coleraine
Strabane
Donegal
Omagh
Bundoran
Belmullet
Enniskillen
Lisburn
Armagh
Sligo
Ballina
Achill
Castlebar
Boyle
Monaghan
Newry
Westport
Knock
Cavan
Clifden
Lough Mask
Connemara
Lough Corrib
Dundalk
Longford
Roscommon
Lough Ree
Ardee
Drogheda
Galway
Navan
Athlone
Mullingar
Kinnegad
Ballinasloe
Aran
Cliffs of Moher
Ennistimon
Loughrea
Tullamore
Lough Derg
Birr
Naas
Dún Laoghaire
Bray
Kilrush
Limerick
River Shannon
Glendalough
Listowel
Carlow
Wicklow
Kilkenny
Dingle
Tralee
Tipperary
Cashel
Arklow
Lakes of Killarney
Killarney
Mallow
Caher
Clonmel
New Ross
Enniscorthy
Macgillycuddy's Reeks
Kenmare
R. Blackwater
Fermoy
Carrick-on-Suir
Ring of Kerry
Cork
Dungarvan
Waterford
Wexford
Rosslare
Glengarriff
Youghal
Bantry
Cobh
Carnsore Point
Skibbereen
Swansea
St. George's Channel
St. David's
Milford Haven
Islay
Port Ellen
Fionnphort
Tiree

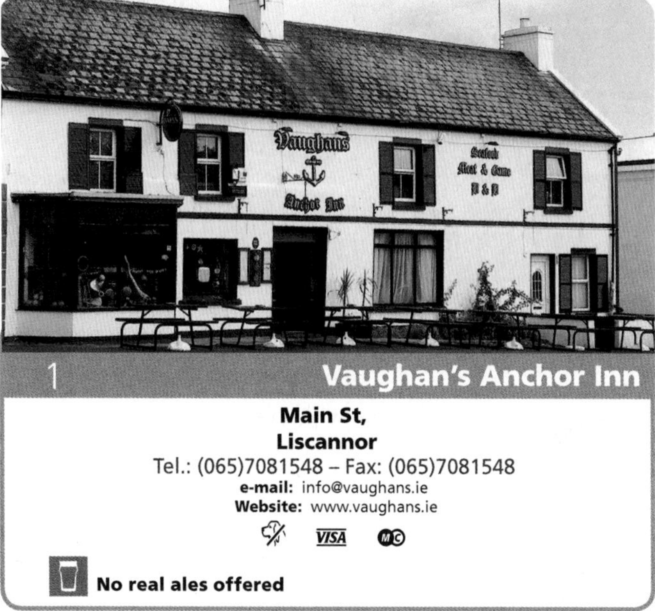

1 Vaughan's Anchor Inn

Main St,
Liscannor
Tel.: (065)7081548 – Fax: (065)7081548
e-mail: info@vaughans.ie
Website: www.vaughans.ie

VISA MC

No real ales offered

There aren't many pubs where you can sit and sip a pint of the black stuff, have a natter over a seafood platter and then pick up your groceries. One such place is to be found in the picturesque fishing village of Liscannor, along the rugged road to the much-visited Cliffs of Moher. A proper, family-run pub, it has built up a fine reputation over the last three decades, and chef Denis' seafood-based menus are a big part of the reason why. Eat at simple wooden tables in the cosy, old-style bar or in the newer but equally informal restaurant; typical pub favourites are on offer at lunch, with more adventurous, elaborate meals - from oysters and lobster to duck and foie gras - served in the evening. There are plans to refurbish the bedrooms.

Closing times
Closed 24-25 December

Prices
Meals: a la carte € 25/40

Typical Dishes
Crab & seaweed risotto
Sea scallops, crayfish & pork belly
Tasting of Guinness desserts

2 km from Lahinch by coast road, on main route to Cliffs of Moher. Parking.

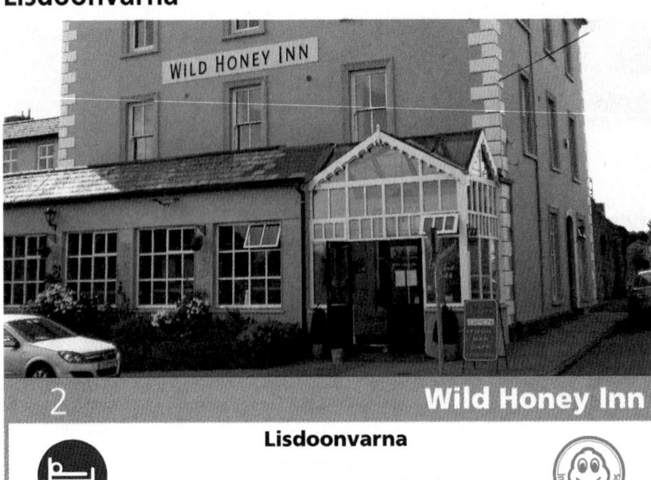

2 Wild Honey Inn

Lisdoonvarna

Tel.: (065)7074300 – Fax: (065)7074490
e-mail: info@wildhoneyinn.com
Website: www.wildhoneyinn.com

Inspectors' favourites

 **Smithwick's**

With the Cliffs of Moher and the limestone landscape of The Burren on the doorstep, this characterful inn makes a great base for exploring County Clare; but it's also a great place to discover some tasty cuisine. The chef-owner has plenty of experience and with his wife and daughter out front, is well supported. There's a sizeable bar with turf fire, a linen-laid dining room used mainly for parties and a peaceful residents' lounge for those staying in one of the comfy, simply furnished bedrooms. Lunch consists of soups, salads and sandwiches, while dinner offers a wider selection of classics, but the specials are where the chef's skill really comes into its own – they may sound simple but the results are truly satisfying and great value. Bookings not accepted.

Closing times
Closed January-12th February and restricted opening November, December, late February and March

Prices
Meals: a la carte € 24/38

14 rooms: € 55/90

On the edge of the town on the Ennistimon rd. On street parking.

3 Poacher's Inn

Clonakilty Rd,
Bandon
Tel.: (023)8841159
e-mail: poachersinn@gmail.com
Website: www.poachersinnbandon.com

VISA MC

Inspectors' favourites

Smithwicks

It's not big, brash or colourful, but that doesn't mean the Poacher's Inn is lacking in a good old Irish pub atmosphere; in fact, if you're looking for the locals, this is probably where you'll find them. Inside, it's almost two operations in one. The ground floor is the more 'pubby' of the two: the front room displaying framed maps and local prints on wood-panelled walls, and the cosy snug, simple stool seating and low-level tables. Here you can choose from a light snack menu – the steak sandwich on homemade bread being a particular favourite. The more formal upstairs restaurant opens at the end of the week, offering a hearty, classical menu of locally caught fish and seafood, with Kinsale sole, monkfish and scallops all featuring highly.

Closing times
Closed 25 December

Prices
Meals: a la carte € 18/36

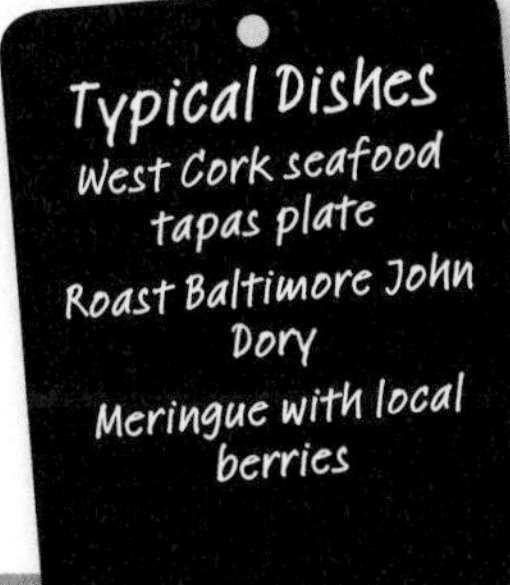

2 km southwest on N 71. Parking.

Castletownshend

4 **Mary Ann's**

Main St,
Castletownshend
Tel.: (028)36146
e-mail: maryanns@eircom.net
Website: www.westcorkweek.com/maryanns/

 **No real ales offered**

You've little chance of missing this boldly painted pub or, for that matter, its larger than life owner. It's set in the heart of a sleepy village, up a steep, narrow street and the walk is sure to help you work up an appetite. If not, then while away some time in The Warren, the pub's art gallery, where the owner proudly displays his collection of modern Irish art. After this, head for the rustic bar, linen-laid restaurant, or if the weather's right, the garden, where an enclosed dining area boasting gingham tablecloths and a mature fruiting vine provides the perfect suntrap. Menus are all-encompassing and offer plenty of choice; seafood is usually a feature and there's often several authentic Asian dishes courtesy of the Malaysian chefs.

Closing times
Closed 24-26 December, 3 weeks in January and Monday and lunch Tuesday October-April

Prices
Meals: € 28 (dinner) and a la carte € 23/45

 *Between Rosscarbery and Skibbereen south of N 71. Parking in the main street.*

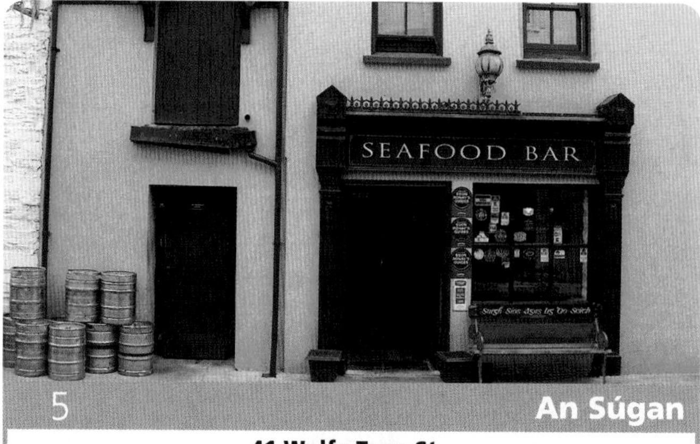

5

An Súgan

41 Wolfe Tone St,
Clonakilty
Tel.: (023)8833719 – Fax: (023)8833825
e-mail: ansugan4@eircom.net
Website: www.ansugan.com

  MC

 **No real ales offered**

Offering charm aplenty and a real sense of history, this salmon-pink pub with its traditional shop front, is everything you could ask for. Run by a capable family team, it has established itself as something of a local institution, but along with the regulars you'll also find plenty of visitors. The logo – depicting a fish, a lobster and several shellfish – provides a good idea of what to expect, with menus based around the daily arrival of fresh, local seafood. The all day selection offers light dishes such as seafood salad or salmon and potato cakes, while more substantial evening offerings might include coquille of seafood or salmon in filo pastry. Specials might involve stuffed crab claws or black sole; less fishy plates are available too.

Closing times
Closed 25-26 December and Good Friday

Prices
Meals: € 30 (dinner)
and a la carte € 30/40

Typical Dishes
Gubeen cheese, smoked salmon & Castletownbere crab
Súgan seafood basket
West Cork strawberry trifle

 *East of town centre. Parking in the street.*

6 **Bulman**

Summercove, Kinsale

Tel.: (021)4772131
e-mail: toddies@eircom.net
Website: www.thebulman.com

VISA MC AE

 **No real ales offered**

Named after the Bulman Buoy, this pub has a great location, affording views of Kinsale and the bay. Its décor is fittingly maritime themed, with an impressive theodolite and a ceiling bedecked with dolphins, anchors and buoys. Scrubbed tables and open fires give a rustic feel; pictures from yesteryear fill the walls, while the stacks of cookery books attest to the owners' foodie credentials. Fresh, local seafood is the star of the daily changing menu; choose between simply cooked dishes like seafood chowder, fresh mussels or grilled hake fillet. Lunch is served in the cosy bar and dinner in the more formal first floor restaurant. The bar is also host to regular live music, when locals and visitors alike can be found enjoying the craic.

Closing times
Closed 25 December, Monday and Good Friday

Prices
Meals: a la carte € 22/29

Typical Dishes
Seafood chowder
Grilled half local lobster
Rhubarb & raspberry crème brûlée

 *By the waterfront.*

8 Sheridan's on the Docks

3 Dock St (1st floor),
Galway
Tel.: (091)564905
Website: www.sheridansonthedocks.com

 **No real ales offered**

This unassuming grey-stone pub belongs to Galway's famous cheesemongers, Sheridan's, which gives an indication of their enthusiasm for all things food related. The ground floor houses the lively, 'pubby' part of the establishment, where culinary offerings are limited to boards of cheese and charcuterie, soups and stews; but head upstairs for a contrast of candlelit proportions, with a menu of passionately prepared, modern Irish dishes, like wild brill with pork belly or local cockles and lettuce heart. The word 'seasonal' is frequently bandied around, yet here they mean it: produce is locally sourced, often to the point of having been foraged by the chef, so expect to find anything from wild mushrooms to herbs like woodruff on the menu.

Closing times
Closed Sunday and Monday
booking advisable for dinner

Prices
Meals: a la carte € 40

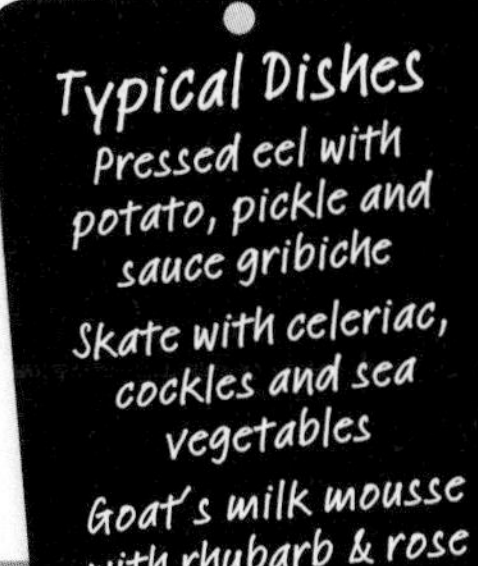

 *Parking meters on the dockside.*

Kilcolgan

7 **Moran's Oyster Cottage**

The Weir,
Kilcolgan
Tel.: (091)796113 – Fax: (091)796503
e-mail: moranstheweir@eircom.net
Website: www.moransoystercottage.com

VISA MC AE

Smithwicks

The name says it all: it's been run by seven generations of Morans; it's speciality is oysters; and with whitewashed walls and lovely golden thatch, it's every bit a country cottage. Set in a tiny hamlet down winding country lanes, you'd never find it unless you knew it was there – and on a summer's day it'll soon become apparent that plenty of people do. The latest Moran to take the helm, Michael, continues to follow the family's philosophy of straightforward cooking and good hospitality. The menu barely changes – but then why change something that works so well? Throughout the year you'll find tasty prawns, mussels, crab, smoked salmon and lobster, and daily baked brown bread. September is native oyster season, so is the best time to visit.

Closing times
Open daily
Prices
Meals: a la carte € 34/64

5 min from the village of Clarinbridge. Parking in road.

9 **O'Dowds**

Roundstone

Tel.: (095)35809
e-mail: odowds@indigo.ie
Website: www.odowdsbar.com

 **Smithwicks**

The O'Dowd family have been dispensing gastronomic delights at this eye-catching blue-hued pub for over one hundred years. Sit in either the cosy, fire-lit bar or the more spacious, wood-panelled dining room to enjoy fresh, simply cooked seafood. Tender, sweet crab arrives straight from the shore, teamed with a glorious garlic butter to make the perfect meal; while the likes of brill, turbot and plaice are given the respect they deserve – simply lightly dusted with flour and then shallow fried. If you're coming for dinner, be sure to book ahead, and if lunch is your thing, then arrive early, otherwise you may find yourself watching enviously from the quayside as others tuck into home-baked soda rolls and steaming bowls of seafood chowder.

Closing times
Closed 25 December and Good Friday
booking advisable

Prices
Meals: a la carte € 20/35

On R 341 13 km from Clifden. Parking outside and on the quayside.

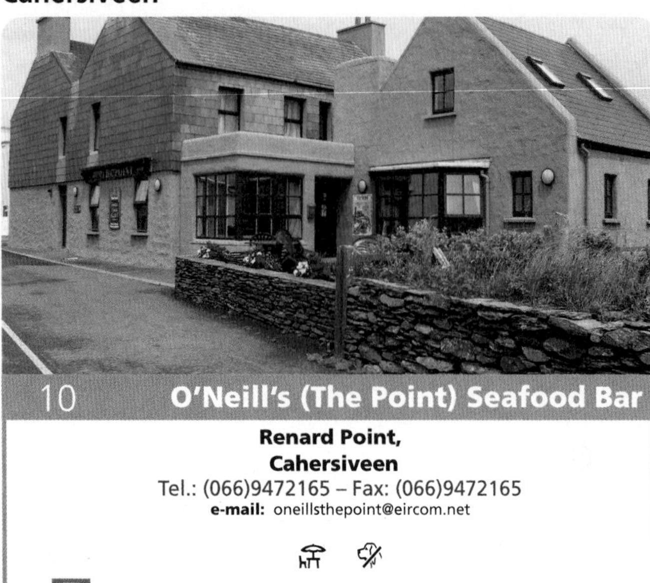

10 O'Neill's (The Point) Seafood Bar

Renard Point,
Cahersiveen
Tel.: (066)9472165 – Fax: (066)9472165
e-mail: oneillsthepoint@eircom.net

No real ales offered

This striking blue pub has been run by the O'Neill family for over 150 years and, satisfyingly, several different generations are still involved. Standing beside the Valentia Island car ferry terminal, right by the slipway, visitors come and go in waves, as the ferries arrive and depart. The interior has a pleasantly dated feel, with family photographs adorning the walls, alongside various items of seafaring memorabilia. The menu has a strong seafood base, cooking is traditionally Irish and the portions are generous. Salmon comes from the adjacent smokehouse and local fishermen bring their day's catch – which might include squid, monkfish or lobster – to the door. Unusually, they don't take credit cards and don't serve chips or puddings.

Closing times
Closed November-February

Prices
Meals: a la carte € 28/38

Typical Dishes
Hot crab claws with chilli
Pan-fried hake in garlic
Irish Coffee

West of Cahersiveen: follow the signs for the ferry. Parking.

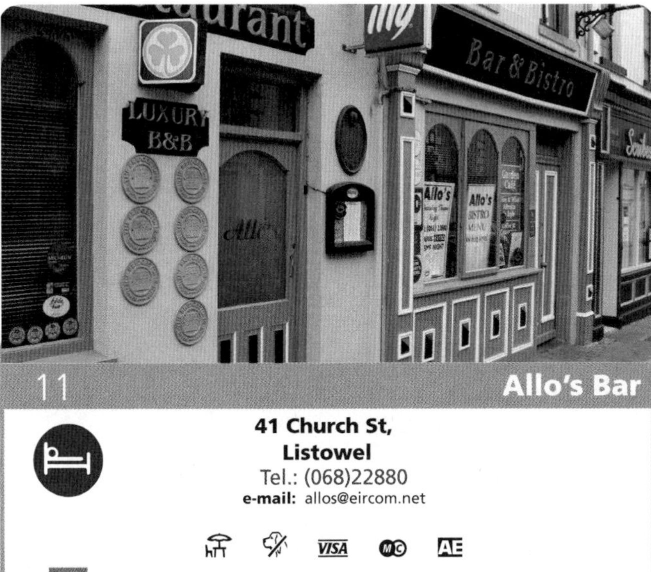

11 Allo's Bar

41 Church St,
Listowel
Tel.: (068)22880
e-mail: allos@eircom.net

VISA MC AE

No real ales offered but a large selection of Irish whiskies

Home to the writers Keane and MacMahon, this lively market town is often described as the literary capital of Ireland, and whether you're a wannabe food critic or an aspiring author, you'll do well to head for this brightly painted bar. It's a true rustic Irish pub, a little lacking in exterior upkeep maybe, but laid-back, and full of charm and character. The walls are packed with old photos, tobacco and whiskey advertisements, and jugs dangle from the ceiling. Drinkers gather in the main bar while diners tuck into good old rustic home cooking in the room next door. The pork belly and steak have established themselves as favourites and puddings are hard to resist. Upstairs, each bedroom has its own floor and boasts a four-poster or sleigh bed.

Closing times
Closed 1 January, Sunday, Monday and bank holidays
booking essential

Prices
Meals: a la carte € 25/50
3 rooms: € 60/100

In the town centre, off north corner of the Square. Parking in front on street and at rear.

12 **Ballymore Inn**

Ballymore Eustace

Tel.: (045)864585 – Fax: (045)864747
e-mail: theballymoreinn@eircom.net
Website: www.ballymoreinn.com

VISA MC AE

 **No real ales offered**

Set in a small village close to the Aga Khan's stud, this pub's claim to fame is that Clint Eastwood and Larry Hagman have popped in on their way to the races. To the rear, a large bar screens sporting events and hosts live music, while to the front there's a spacious dining area with red leather banquettes, mosaic flooring and a Parisian brasserie feel. Lunchtime sees salads, homemade pizzas, stir fries and risottos, with some more substantial dishes appearing at dinner. The owner is keen to promote small artisan producers, so you'll find organic veg, meat from quality assured farms and farmhouse cheeses. Portions are generous but you won't want to miss the tasty bread or homemade tarts and pastries. Pleasant staff always go the extra mile.

Closing times
Open daily

Prices
Meals: € 22/35
and a la carte € 35/42

Typical Dishes
Ardsallagh goat's cheese & pomegranate
Duncannon scallops
Homemade meringue & chestnut purée

 *9 km south of Naas by R 411. Parking.*

13 **The Oarsman**

Bridge St,
Carrick-on-Shannon
Tel.: (071)9621733 – Fax: (071)9621734
e-mail: info@theoarsman.com
Website: www.theoarsman.com

   MC

Galway Hooker Pale Ale, Hooker Brewery summer Ale

With the River Shannon just 50m away and always a boatman or two inside, this pub's name is perfectly apt. Its double-fronted windows are filled with pottery, county flags and old artefacts, while a plethora of objects adorn the walls and an array of fishing tackle is displayed above the bar. This is a traditional pub through and through, family-owned, with rough wooden floors, old beams and stone-faced walls – and, unsurprisingly, frequented by the locals, especially at lunch. Snacks are available in the afternoon and there's a fairly substantial bar menu in the evening, while later in the week the comfy upstairs area offers dishes such as confit of Thornhill Farm duck or trio of Kettyle lamb. Cooking is simple and produce, laudably local.

Closing times
Closed Sunday and Monday

Prices
Meals: € 30/35
and a la carte € 20/40

In the town centre. On-street meters and parking at rear of pub.

14 **Fitzpatricks**

Rockmarshall,
Jenkinstown
Tel.: (042)9376193 – Fax: (042)9376274
e-mail: danny@fitzpatricks-restaurant.ie
Website: www.fitzpatricks-restaurant.com

VISA MC

McArdles

On the coast road to the peninsula, at the foot of the Cooley Mountains, you'll find this classical whitewashed pub overlooking Dundalk Bay. To call it characterful would be an understatement: this is a place where you can take in the whole of the Irish experience. The car park and gardens are filled with colourful flowers set in old bicycles, boots and even a bed; while inside there's a beautiful bar with brass rails and memorabilia aplenty, including a fascinating collection of old chamber pots and Victorian toiletries. The extensive menu features hearty, flavoursome portions of traditional dishes, with local seafood and steaks something of a speciality. More adventurous offerings can be found in the restaurant, which opens later in the week.

Closing times
Closed 24-27 December, September-May and Good Friday

Prices
Meals: € 25 (dinner) and a la carte € 50/60

Typical Dishes
Scallop & crab lasagne
Slow-braised beef ribs
Griottine cherry crème brûlée

9 km northeast of Dundalk following N 52 on R 173. Parking.

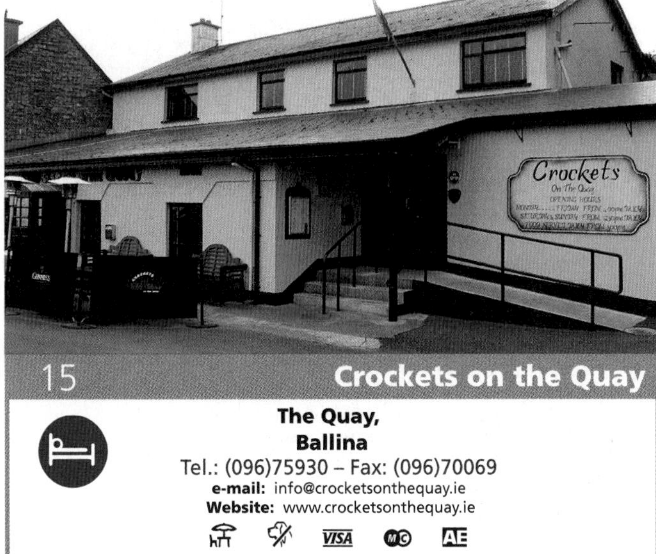

15 Crockets on the Quay

The Quay,
Ballina
Tel.: (096)75930 – Fax: (096)70069
e-mail: info@crocketsonthequay.ie
Website: www.crocketsonthequay.ie

VISA AE

No real ales offered

This pub's vibrant orange exterior is matched on the inside by a lively atmosphere where there's always something going on, be it a poker night, traditional Irish music session or trivia quiz; and sports fans aren't forgotten either, with TVs in almost every corner, as well as two plasma screens and a pool table in the garden. The place itself is rather dimly lit, but the light fittings that are located above each worn table really put the spotlight where it matters – on the food. They don't serve lunch here but there's a popular early evening menu, which is followed by a larger selection of generously proportioned dishes and local Irish steaks. Bedrooms are modest, affordable and well-kept; those above the restaurant are the most peaceful.

Closing times
Closed 25 December, lunch Monday-Friday and Good Friday

Prices
Meals: € 20 (Sunday lunch) and a la carte € 25/50

8 rooms: € 40/70

On the northeast edge of town by N 59 besides the River Moy. Parking.

Ballinrobe

16 **JJ Gannons**

Main St,
Ballinrobe
Tel.: (094)9541008 – Fax: (094)9520018
e-mail: info@jjgannons.com
Website: www.jjgannons.com

VISA

No real ales offered

The eponymous Gannon family have welcomed guests to this pub for more than 75 years; it's now run by the third generation, who offer as cheery a reception as their predecessors. The building dates from 1838, but its interior is modern in style. There's an atmospheric front bar, a dimly lit chill-out area and a smart, spacious restaurant, which provides extra space when the bar gets too busy. Cooking is satisfying and reassuringly familiar. Traditional dishes might include local beef or slow-roasted shoulder of local lamb; fish features as a special and desserts might include warm apple pie or traditional bread and butter pudding. Weekly themed evenings are popular; stay overnight afterwards in one of the spacious, comfortable bedrooms.

Closing times
Closed 25 December and Good Friday

Prices
Meals: € 25 (dinner) and a la carte € 25/40

10 rooms: € 65/150

In the centre of town on the one-way system. Parking.

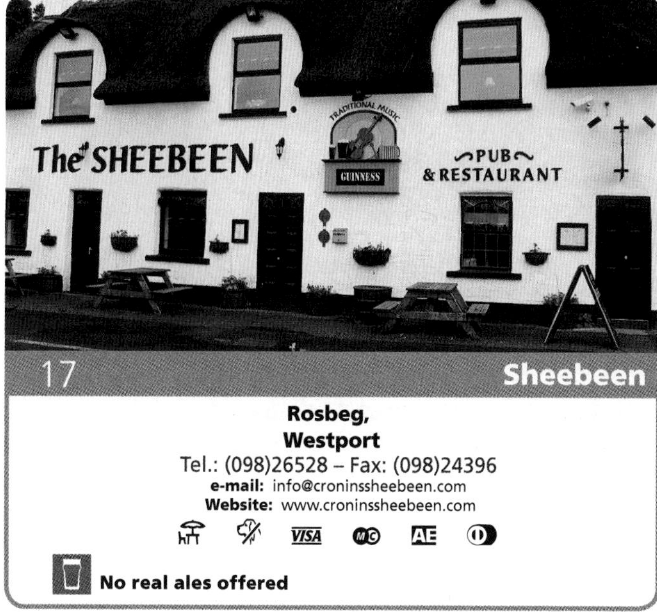

17 **Sheebeen**

Rosbeg,
Westport
Tel.: (098)26528 – Fax: (098)24396
e-mail: info@croninssheebeen.com
Website: www.croninssheebeen.com

VISA

No real ales offered

This attractive whitewashed, thatched pub is situated to the west of town, looking out over Clew Bay and in the shadow of famed mountain, Croagh Patrick. According to legend, this was where St. Patrick fasted for 40 days and 40 nights before banishing all the snakes from Ireland. Fasting not your thing? Cooking here is fresh and simple – everything is homemade, including the bread – with the more interesting dishes to be found among the large selection of daily specials. Try the local fish and seafood, which is accurately prepared and full of flavour – perhaps cod terrine, lobster, sea trout or John Dory. Live music nights take place every Friday and Saturday; but during the week, don't be surprised to hear Peggy Lee blasting out instead.

Closing times
Closed lunch weekdays November-mid March

Prices
Meals: a la carte € 25/40

West of the town beyond Westport Quay. Parking.

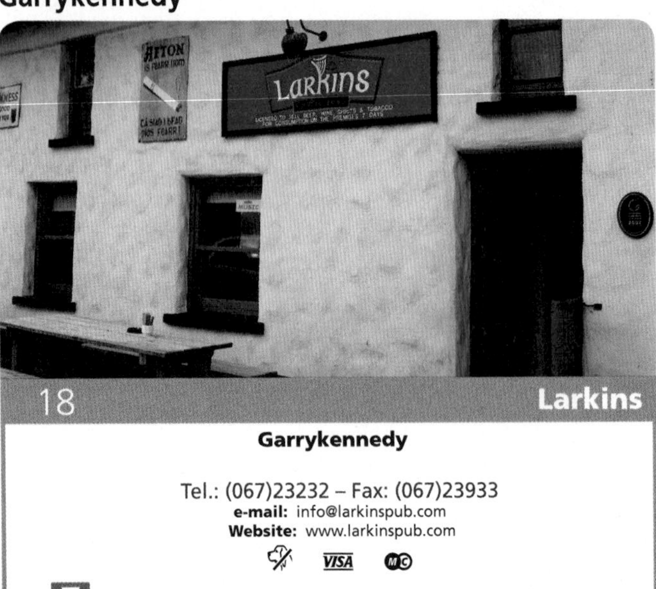

18 Larkins

Garrykennedy

Tel.: (067)23232 – Fax: (067)23933
e-mail: info@larkinspub.com
Website: www.larkinspub.com

VISA MC

No real ales offered

Set in a charming location on the shores of Lough Derg, this thatched, whitewashed pub dates back around 300 years and is popular with the sailing set, particularly in the summer. As traditional inside as out, it boasts old flag and timber floors, a long wooden bar and original open fireplaces; and plays host to regular Irish folk music sessions and traditional Irish dancing groups. Throughout the day, the bar menu offers straightforward, unfussy dishes such as seafood chowder, homemade burgers or steak. In the evening, however, things step up a gear, with the likes of honey-roast duckling, herb-crusted fillet of cod or pan-fried lamb cutlets. Having come from farming backgrounds, the owners are passionate about sourcing local Irish produce.

Closing times
Closed 25 December, Good Friday and Monday-Friday lunch (November-April)

Prices
Meals: a la carte € 30/36

9 km west of Nenagh by R 494 and minor road north.
Free public car park opposite.

19 The Lobster Pot

Ballyfane, Carne

Tel.: (053)9131110 – Fax: (053)9131401

If you're on your way to the ferry crossing at Rosslare or returning from a stroll along the nearby beach, this bold green pub is definitely worth calling in at. Every nook and cranny of the spotless interior is chock full of nautical memorabilia, and as soon as you see the staff in their smart waistcoats, you know that they take things seriously here. Extensive menus feature tasty, home-style cooking, with a simple selection of light bites at lunch and a dinner menu exclusively for adults – as children must leave by 5pm. There are a few steaks and grills on offer, but, as the name suggests, it's mostly seafood, with oysters and lobster the house specialities. Be sure to arrive early though, as this place is Carne's not-so-well-kept secret.

Closing times
Closed January-mid February, 25-26 December, Good Friday and Monday except bank holidays

Prices
Meals: a la carte € 35/55

South of Rosslare Harbour. Parking.

Index of towns

M

N

O

P

R

S

T

Index of pubs & inns

K

L

M

N

O

P

Q

R

S

T

U – V

W

Y

eating
out in
pubs

Michelin Maps & Guides

Michelin Maps & Guides
Hannay House,
39 Clarendon Rd
Watford WD17 1JA
Tel: (01923) 205247
Fax: (01923) 205241
www.ViaMichelin.com
eatingoutinpubs-gbirl@
uk.michelin.com

Manufacture française des pneumatiques Michelin

Société en commandite par actions
au capital de 304 000 000 EUR.
Place des Carmes-Déchaux
63 Clermont-Ferrand (France)
R.C.S. Clermont-Fd B 855 200 507

Dépôt légal Septembre 2010
Printed in France 07-10

Typesetting:

NORD COMPO, Villeneuve-d'Ascq (France)
Printing and binding:
CANALE, Turin (Italy)

Photography

Project manager: Alain Leprince
Agence ACSI – A Chacun Son Image
242, bd. Voltaire– 75011 Paris

Location Photographs:

Jérôme Berquez, Frédéric Chales, Ludivine Boizard, Jean-Louis Chauveau/ACSI

Thanks to:

The Hinds Head,
Bray

P12: Ariy/Fotolia.com
P22: Full moon /Fotolia.com
P24: C. Labonne/Michelin
P56: D. Hughes /Fotolia.com
P115: D. Harding /Fotolia.com
P116: C. Eymenier/Michelin
P188: Robert /Fotolia.com
P200: K. Eaves /Fotolia.com
P232: D. Hughes /Fotolia.com
P342: C. Jones/Fotolia.com
P442: D. Hughes /Fotolia.com
P477: Steheap/Fotolia.com
P478: S. Smith/Fotolia.com
P524: O. Forir/Michelin
P547: D. Hughes/Fotolia.com
P548: L. Green/Fotolia.com
P573: H. Hudson/Fotolia.com
P574: O. Forir/Michelin
P582: O. Forir/Michelin

YOUR OPINION MATTERS!

To help us constantly improve this guide, please fill in this questionnaire and return to:

Eating out in Pubs 2011
Michelin Maps & Guides,
Hannay House, 39 Clarendon Road,
Watford, WD17 1JA, UK

First name: ....
Surname: ....
Address: ....
Profession: ....

< 25 years old	☐	25-34 years old	☐
35-50 years old	☐	> 50 years	☐

1. How often do you use the Internet to look for information on pubs?

Never ☐
Occasionally (once a month) ☐
Regularly (once a week) ☐
Very frequently (more than once a week) ☐

2. Have you ever bought Michelin guides?

☐ Yes ☐ No

3. If yes, which one(s)?

Eating out in Pubs ☐
The Michelin Guide Great Britain & Ireland ☐
The Green Guide (please specify titles) ☐

....

Other (please specify titles) ☐

....

4. If you have previously bought Eating out in Pubs, what made you purchase this new one?

....

....

5. If you buy the Michelin Guide Great Britain & Ireland, how often do you buy it?

Every year ☐
Every 2 years ☐
Every 3 years ☐
Every 4 years or more ☐

ABOUT EATING OUT IN PUBS :

6. Did you buy this guide:

For holidays? ☐
For a weekend/short break? ☐
For business purposes? ☐
As a gift? ☐
For everyday use ☐

7. **How do you rate the different elements of this guide?**

NB: **1. Very Poor** **2. Poor** **3. Average** **4. Good** **5. Very Good**

	1	2	3	4	5
Selection of pubs	☐	☐	☐	☐	☐
Number of pubs in London	☐	☐	☐	☐	☐
Geographical spread of pubs	☐	☐	☐	☐	☐
Menu Prices	☐	☐	☐	☐	☐
Practical information (services, menus)	☐	☐	☐	☐	☐
Photos	☐	☐	☐	☐	☐
Description of the pubs	☐	☐	☐	☐	☐
Cover	☐	☐	☐	☐	☐
The format & size of the guide	☐	☐	☐	☐	☐
Guide Price	☐	☐	☐	☐	☐

8. **How easily could you find the information you were looking for ?**

....

....

9. **Please rate the guide out of 20 ..../20**

10. **Which aspects could we improve?**

....

....

....

....

....

....

11. **Was there a pub you particularly liked or a choice you didn't agree with? Perhaps you have a favourite address of your own that you would like to tell us about? Please send us your remarks and suggestions.**

....

....

....

....

....

....

....

....

....

....

Manufacture Francaise des Pneumatiques Michelin
46 avenue de Breteuil
75324 Paris Cedex 07
France